P9-DZY-131

Contested Values

Democracy and Diversity
in American Culture

Contested Values

Democracy and Diversity in American Culture

Michael Kammen

Cornell University

St. Martin's Press

New York

Editor: Louise H. Waller
Managing editor: Patricia Mansfield-Phelan
Associate project editor: Nicholas Webb
Production supervisor: Alan Fischer
Art director: Sheree Goodman
Text design: Rod Hernandez
Cover design: Sheree Goodman

Library of Congress Catalog Card Number: 92-62719
Copyright © 1995 by St. Martin's Press, Inc.
All rights reserved. No part of this book may be reproduced, stored in a retrieval system, or transmitted by any form or by any means, electronic, mechanical, photocopying, recording, or otherwise, except as may be expressly permitted by the applicable copyright statutes or in writing by the Publisher.
Manufactured in the United States of America.
9 8 7 6 5
f e d c b a

For information, write:
St. Martin's Press, Inc.
175 Fifth Avenue
New York, NY 10010

ISBN: 0-312-09085-4

Acknowledgments

Every Hour Is Lunch Hour at the Dreadnought Club by Joseph Keppler, Jr. Pen and ink, crayon, and graphite on textured paper, 14⅜ × 22⅜ inches. *Puck,* v. 69, no. 1787, May 31, 1911, pp. 7–8. Courtesy of the Huntington Library.

It is a violation of the law to reproduce the selections in this volume by any means whatsoever without the written permission of the copyright holder.

To my students
at Cornell University
1965–1995

I speak of fiercely contested things, practical in the extreme, that tortured the souls of the founders. . . . I say, unless a people conserve this yeast, it will not raise much bread.

William Carlos Williams
In the American Grain (1925)

Preface

Many instructors, like myself, coming from and working in different yet closely connected disciplines, teach courses concerning American culture from the late nineteenth century to the very recent past. Student interest in the numerous transformations that have occurred over that period is quite strong—indeed, it is intense and enthusiastic. For that reason—and others—I have edited *Contested Values*.

The major changes in American history—and the debates concerning them—are reasonably well documented and described in scholarly literature, textbooks, and in the varied classroom presentations we make to our students. Much less accessible, however, especially to undergraduates, are the intensely felt contests that occurred between those individuals who sought change and those who resisted it, between those moved by nostalgia and those activated by reliable memory, between those who regarded change as inevitable and beneficial and those who regarded change as inevitable yet problematic.

For these transformations of values to be both comprehensible and meaningful, students need to know what participants said about changes, what disputes arose, how they were resolved, and the implications of these controversies. Above all, however, it is the reasoning—the logic or illogic—offered on behalf of conflicting visions of American life that our students ought to be familiar with. Such firsthand information helps students acquire a finer sense of history as process; further, exposure to primary sources should also enable them to respond in sensible ways to the cultural divisiveness that is such a significant and lively fact of life in our own time.

My point, then, is not the old cliché: the more things change, the more they remain the same. Rather, my point is that conflicting perspectives about social values and cultural norms have long been with us, but the *substance* of the debates has changed as American society—with its configurations of class, ethnicity, and power—has altered. Consequently, the more things do change, the more it truly matters what advocates with different motives have said about these changes, pro and con.

The only uncontested feature of *Contested Values* can be found in its genesis and gestation. I have enjoyed a wonderfully cordial relationship with the staff of St. Martin's college division, most notably with Louise Waller, the acquisitions editor in history who believed in the project and nourished it with shrewd suggestions and good-humored support throughout. I also thank Huntley McNair Funsten, who worked so diligently on matters ranging from permissions to preparation of copy for the compositor.

In the final stages of the book's development I appreciated the cheerful cooperation of associate editor Lynnette Blevins and editorial assistant Jennifer Marrone, and Nicholas Webb, my meticulous project editor. Joanne Daniels, editor-in-chief of the college division, made it possible for *Contested Values* to see the light of day. I hope that its reception turns out to vindicate her good faith.

I wish to thank the following individuals who reviewed *Contested Values* for St. Martin's Press: Robert H. Abzug, University of Texas at Austin; Paul Boyer, University of Wisconsin at Madison; Lewis A. Erenberg, Loyola University of Chicago; Thomas L. Haskell, Rice University; and Robert A. McCaughey, Barnard College.

Dr. David R. Brigham, versatile research associate at the Huntington Art Collections in San Marino, California, called to my attention the remarkable drawing by Joseph Keppler, "Every Hour Is Lunch Hour at the Dreadnought Club." It appeared in a fine exhibition that he planned for the Huntington's Virginia Steele Scott Gallery in 1993, "From Allegory to Activism: Changing Images of Women in American Illustration, 1890–1920."

Dina Evangelista of the history department at Cornell University prepared final copy of the introduction, headnotes, and bibliographical materials.

My Cornell students in American history, graduate as well as undergraduate, have provided uncommon intelligence, stimulation, and gratification through the years—more than enough to compensate for the occasional headache that a few might have caused. The teacher's life, like this book, is all about dialogue. My students have successfully managed to maintain their side of the educational dialogue. I can only hope that future students will be stimulated by the dialogues contained in *Contested Values*.

Above Cayuga's Waters   Michael Kammen

Contents

Introduction   1

1 **Looking Back: Differing Perceptions of the Civil War**   13
Jefferson Davis, *An Address on Behalf of the Southern Historical Society (1882)   15*
U. S. Grant, *Conclusion to Personal Memoirs (1886)   19*
Oliver Wendell Holmes, Jr., *The Soldier's Faith (1895)   22*
Suggestions for Further Reading   25

2 **Can Americans Reform Their Society and Economic System?**   27
Lester Frank Ward, *Psychic Factors of Civilization (1893)   29*
William Graham Sumner, *The Absurd Effort to Make the World Over (1894)   34*
Suggestions for Further Reading   41

3 **The Philanthropic Impulse: Helping People in a Democracy**   43
Andrew Carnegie, *The Gospel of Wealth (1889)   45*
Jane Addams, *Charitable Effort (1902)   50*
Suggestions for Further Reading   55

4 **What Role for the Negro in American Society?**   57
Booker T. Washington, *The Atlanta Exposition Address (1895)   59*
W. E. B. Du Bois, *Of Mr. Booker T. Washington and Others (1903)   63*
Suggestions for Further Reading   70

5 **Pacifism and Militarism: Is Peace Best Preserved through Military Preparedness?**   71
William James, *The Moral Equivalent of War (1910)   73*
Theodore Roosevelt, *Warlike Power—The Prerequisite for the Preservation of Social Values (1914)   80*
Suggestions for Further Reading   85

6 **Can Industrialization Be Efficient and Humane? The Conflict over Scientific Management**   87
Frederick W. Taylor, *The Principles of Scientific Management (1911)   89*
Final Report of the Commission on Industrial Relations . . . (1916)   96
Suggestions for Further Reading   113

7 **Americanization versus Cultural Pluralism**   115
Edward A. Ross, *American Blood and Immigrant Blood (1914)   117*

Horace M. Kallen, *Democracy versus the Melting Pot (1915)* 121
Suggestions for Further Reading 128

8 Birth Control: Nay and Yea   129
Mary Alden Hopkins, *Birth Control and Public Morals: An Interview
  with Anthony Comstock (1915)* 131
Charlotte Perkins Gilman, *Birth Control (1915)* 136
Suggestions for Further Reading 141

**9 The Scopes Trial: Evolution versus
Scriptural Christianity   143**
Clarence Darrow, *For the Defense (1925)* 145
William Jennings Bryan, *For the Prosecution (1925)* 152
Suggestions for Further Reading 161

10 Do Women Want National Prohibition?   163
Louise Gross, *Why Women Desire Repeal (1928)* 165
Mrs. Henry W. Peabody, *Women's Crusade against Repeal or
  Modification (1928)* 169
Suggestions for Further Reading 176

**11 The Quality of American Culture Compared
to Other Cultures: Two Views   177**
H. L. Mencken, *On Being an American (1922)* 179
Booth Tarkington, *America and Culture (1929)* 184
Suggestions for Further Reading 189

**12 Internationalism versus Isolationism:
Entering World War II   191**
Henry R. Luce, *The American Century (1941)* 193
Charles A. Lindbergh, *Lindbergh's Isolationist Speech (1941)* 200
Suggestions for Further Reading 204

13 The Experience of Jazz: Provenance and Performance   205
Richard Meryman, *Interview with Louis Armstrong (1966)* 207
Duke Ellington, *Music Is My Mistress (1973)* 211
Suggestions for Further Reading 217

**14 America on Film: Distorted Images and Dismal
Prospects?   219**
Ralph Ellison, *The Shadow and the Act (1949)* 221
Gilbert Seldes, *Myth and Movies (1950)* 226
Arthur L. Mayer, *Myths and Movies (1951)* 235
Suggestions for Further Reading 242

**15 The Supreme Court in a Democratic Polity:
Activism versus Restraint   243**
Felix Frankfurter, *Concurring Opinion in* Dennis et al. *v.* United
  States *(1951)* 245
Hugo Black, *Dissenting Opinion in* Dennis et al. *v.* United States
  (1951) 249
Suggestions for Further Reading 250

16 Environmentalism and Its Critics   251
Rachel Carson, *Silent Spring (1962) 253*
I. L. Baldwin, *Chemicals and Pests (1962) 258*
Time, *Pesticides: The Price for Progress (1962) 263*
Suggestions for Further Reading 267

**17 Blacks in America: Integration or Separatism?
Nonviolence or Militance?   269**
Martin Luther King, Jr., *Letter from Birmingham Jail (1963) 271*
Malcolm X, *The Autobiography of Malcolm X (1964) 281*
Suggestions for Further Reading 287

18 The Role of Journalists in Vietnam   289
Phillip Knightley, *A Feature Writer's Perspective (1984) 291*
Major General Winant Sidle, *An Army General's Perspective
(1984) 293*
David Halberstam, *A Reporter's Perspective (1984) 295*
Suggestions for Further Reading 297

19 Women and Work: Differences of Class and Race   299
Gloria Steinem, *The Importance of Work (1979) 301*
Gloria Steinem, *An Introductory Statement (1979) 305*
Mary E. Mebane, *An Open Letter to Gloria Steinem (1971) 309*
Margaret Sloan, *What We Should Be Doing, Sister (1971) 310*
Suggestions for Further Reading 312

A Note About the Author   313

Contested Values

Democracy and Diversity
in American Culture

INTRODUCTION

Contested values have always been quite visible in American culture. Examined historically, with appropriate attention to the most prominent issues, they richly enhance our understanding of the forces that have shaped our society, our politics, and our beliefs.

When conflicts occurred, of course, there often were more than just two prevalent views or positions. The United States contained, after all, a mixed and diverse people. Indeed, throughout our history multiple perspectives have been much more common than single-mindedness. For purposes of discussion, however, it is useful to look at significantly divisive situations where contrasting positions were articulated forcefully and each one was widely shared by contemporaries. That dualistic perspective informs and shapes the nineteen sets (or "chapters") of primary texts that comprise this collection.

Some of the dialogues that follow arose from directly confrontational spectacles where powerful personalities dramatized the clash of values. William Jennings Bryan versus Clarence Darrow (concerning evolution) at the Scopes trial in 1925, or Felix Frankfurter versus Hugo Black on the Supreme Court (concerning communism) in 1951 provide vivid examples.

Other dialogues were somewhat more sequential in the sense that someone staked a position in print and then someone else, equally opinionated, offered a prompt response within months. The dialogue between Edward A. Ross and Horace M. Kallen concerning Americanization (1914–15) supplies one illustration, and the dialogue between Gilbert Seldes and Arthur L. Mayer concerning the quality (or mediocrity) of Hollywood films (1950–51) provides another.

Some of the contrasts can be understood, at least in part, by differences of class or gender, religion, race, or ethnic origin. With equal frequency, however, we encounter contested values involving two white men of the same social class, or two black men (such as Martin Luther King, Jr., and Malcolm X, both the sons of preachers), or two white women of the same class disputing the need for national Prohibition.

In general, we are more likely to expect and notice intergenerational conflicts, or occasions where inherited dogma and lived experience are at odds, than we are to recognize situations where men and women with similar origins or allegiances come into conflict. When William Graham Sumner and Lester Frank Ward, both prominent social theorists in the late

1

Victorian era, disagree over the prospects for planned progress, we should pay close attention. The same is true when Booker T. Washington and W. E. B. Du Bois disagree about education and opportunities for African Americans. And the same is true when William James and Theodore Roosevelt differ about the relative merits of pacifism and military preparedness.

The primary purpose of these selections, however, is not for the reader to proclaim a winner or denigrate a loser. It is far more important that we learn to recognize the complexity of the past—and hence of the present—and that we observe how people experienced and responded to American culture in different ways. Critical inquiry helps us to acknowledge the contested character of human experience. Historical knowledge is thereby empowering because it illuminates the conflicts and inequities of influence that we encounter almost routinely.

In retrospect, there do seem to have been winners and losers in some, though not all, of these interchanges. More meaningful from an historical perspective, however, is the realization that a position that eventually "lost" remained dominant for quite a long time and, therefore, profoundly affected millions of lives.

We want to learn why a position that may now appear perverse or flawed seemed compelling once upon a time. Coming to grips with that question obliges us to think about the role of public opinion in human affairs and about why values change over time. In short, we learn to understand historically rather than to apply hindsight casually. Hindsight is certain to involve sitting in judgment, whereas an historical understanding is more likely to jog us toward empathetic insight and, if we are fortunate, perhaps even wisdom.

Although each chapter in this book provides a particular "contest" of values, quite a few persistent themes and attitudes recur throughout. It may be helpful here to notice some of the most prominent ones. Assessing the quality (or the potential) of American culture and society is a matter that surfaces in several ways, especially in the dialogues between Ross and Kallen, between H. L. Mencken and Booth Tarkington, between Henry R. Luce and Charles A. Lindbergh, between Seldes and Mayer, between Gloria Steinem and Mary Mebane. Those dialogues remind us that defining "Americanism" has been a national preoccupation for more than a century now, causing respected viewers even to speculate from time to time about the "meaning of America."

Other motifs resurface as well. "Survival of the fittest," a phrase drawn from popularized Darwinism, appears in the writing of Oliver Wendell Holmes, Andrew Carnegie, and Frederick Winslow Taylor, and not merely in the dialogue between Ward and Sumner, who were known as Reform Darwinists and Social Darwinists (that is, advocates of the views that men and women could, or could not, hope to alter or improve social conditions).

The belief that wealthy and socially advantaged people (an elite) know what is best for all, often called paternalism, appears in the writings of Sumner, Carnegie, Taylor, Ross, Mrs. Henry W. Peabody (the Prohibitionist), Luce, and Lindbergh. It even provides a certain tension within the essay by progressive reformer Jane Addams.

A concern with race and with "racial traits" is not confined to the dialogues between Washington and Du Bois, or between King and Malcolm X. It arises in the conflicts between Ross and Kallen over immigration, between Steinem and Mebane over work, and in a famous exchange not included here, between two distinguished writers: Norman Mailer and James Baldwin.[1]

How to maximize the economic and social benefits of industrialization—or conversely, how to minimize its adverse consequences—emerges in no fewer than four of the dialogues, particularly in the pieces written by Sumner, Carnegie, Washington, and Taylor. Readers will also find that "captain of industry" was a commonly used phrase, whereas "robber baron" doesn't appear.

Above all (and perhaps it is no surprise), democracy itself turns out to be the single most dominant theme in these dialogues. Ralph Ellison, the writer who contributes to Chapter 14, elucidates with compelling eloquence (in a separate essay) why democracy has been absolutely central to the history of public discourse in the United States.

> No matter how we choose to view ourselves in the abstract, in the world of work and politics Americans live in a constant state of debate and contention. And we do so no matter what kinds of narrative, oral or written, are made in the reconstruction of our common experience. American democracy is a most dramatic form of social organization, and in that drama each of us enacts his role by asserting his own and his group's values and traditions against those of his fellow citizens. Indeed, a battle-royal conflict of interests appears to be basic to our conception of freedom, and the drama of democracy proceeds through a warfare of words and symbolic actions by which we seek to advance our private interests while resolving our political differences. Since the Civil War this form of symbolic action has served as a moral substitute for armed warfare, and we have managed to restrain ourselves to a debate which we carry on in the not always justified faith that the outcome will serve the larger interests of democracy.[2]

Readers will note that in the Ward–Sumner debate (1893–94) Ward asserted that democracy at that time was "the weakest of all forms of government," yet had the potential to become the strongest. Sumner, on the other hand, derided democracy as a shallow cliché: "Everything connected with this domain of political thought is crusted over with false historical traditions, cheap philosophy, and undefined terms, but it is useless to try to criticize it. The whole drift of the world for five hundred years has been toward democracy."

Interpreting democracy became an issue between Washington and Du Bois, and it also became involved in the controversy over scientific management. In his retort to Edward A. Ross, Horace Kallen reminded readers that "democracy in operation" is based on the assumption that "there are human capacities which it is the function of the state to liberate and to protect in growth." William Jennings Bryan, however, invoked a different definition of democracy in defending the Tennessee law that made it a crime to teach evolution. The people's elected representatives had passed the law. "Has it come to a time," Bryan asked, "when the minority can take charge of a state like Tennessee and compel the majority to pay their teachers while they take religion out of the heart of the children of the parents who pay the teachers?" This question, in various forms, persists in lively fashion within many contemporary American communities.

H. L. Mencken, always the iconoclast, expressed his unabashed regret that ever since 1825 "*vox populi* has been the true voice of the nation." Two decades later, when Henry Luce promoted his nationalistic notion of an American century, he declared that it was foolish for people to worry about our "constitutional democracy" when worldwide revolutions presented a more serious concern. Ten years after that, in 1951, Justice Felix Frankfurter pleaded for judicial restraint on the grounds that "courts are not representative bodies. They are not designed to be a good reflex of a democratic society."

Meanwhile, even in discussing the kinds of films that Hollywood ought to produce, Gilbert Seldes insisted that movies should become a "genuinely democratic, instead of a mass-minority, entertainment; and in a democracy like ours, encouragement of individual interests and satisfaction of many various desires are the surest protection against . . . the ultimate emergence of the mass man."

Finally, looking at the three-way discussion of journalistic coverage of the war in Vietnam, readers will notice Phillip Knightley's admonition that "the first step that led to the uncovering of My Lai [a village massacre] was, as in so many stories, that most elementary act in the democratic process: an ordinary citizen writing to his congressman." David Halberstam recalls that he and his fellow journalists felt torn by the democratic ideal. "Were we going to be loyal first and foremost to the ideals of American democracy, or were we going to be loyal to—in the immortal words of so many American officials—'the team'?"

The varied ways of perceiving and invoking democratic values is, indeed, the single most engaging and persistent problem that we will explore in these dialogues.

Nonetheless, by way of background, we ought to recognize that contested values appeared well before the past century. We only need to recall the intense debate between Federalists and anti-Federalists over the proposed Constitution in 1787–88; or the famous controversy in the U. S. Senate between orators Daniel Webster and Robert Y. Hayne over states' rights (1830); or the Lincoln–Douglas debates in 1858 concerning the extension of slavery in newly opened territories.

For approximately a century, beginning in the 1770s, many of the most heated controversies in the United States involved, in one form or another, a tension between individualism and what we might call community orientation. Historically, the appropriate labels were liberalism and republicanism. Liberalism implied free enterprise, the pursuit of happiness in the private sector, and a noninterventionist role for government. Republicanism brought to mind civic responsibilities, public obligations, and communities knit together with an emphasis on virtue, mutual care, and modest life-styles.

By the later nineteenth century, when the sources in this book take up the story, that much-proclaimed American commitment to freedom of the individual along with the reality of social mobility came to be increasingly in tension with a desire for social order and organization. We can see that tension in the growing strength of the temperance movement—a serious effort to control alcohol abuse—and in the frequency with which temperance was mocked in minstrel shows, an immensely popular form of public entertainment.

The growing concern for social order was also manifest in the publication of etiquette manuals, guides to civility in a society that seemed excessively crude. Codes of behavior might help to regulate the urban middle and upper classes, but were likely to be contested, scorned, or ignored by immigrant newcomers and Americans on the go as part of the westward movement. The urgency of manifest destiny—national as well as personal—made matters of decorum seem less consequential in the trans-Appalachian and trans-Mississippi regions. The unbridled quest for prosperity took priority over propriety.

By the turn of the century, however, reformers and social theorists of all sorts had other ideas. Readers will find that Sumner and Taylor, Ross and Bryan, Peabody and Frankfurter each acknowledged, in his or her own way, that the progressive development of organized society necessitated some loss of liberty or reduced potential for individualism. As William Graham Sumner put it (in Chapter 2), the "advance of a new country" from simplicity to structure was "attended all the way along by stricter subordination and higher discipline. All organization implies restriction of liberty. The gain of power is won by narrowing individual range." Many people who lived through that profound cultural transformation nevertheless resented their diminished sense of freedom and opportunity. Social order had its costs, and the costs were publicly contested.[3]

Conflicts over values did not occur only between liberals and conservatives, modernizers and traditionalists, rationalists and evangelicals. Many of the most interesting disagreements took place *within* the women's movement, *within* the labor movement, and *within* individual families where children received conflicting signals concerning values from their parents. A few illustrations can make these generalizations more concrete.

During the 1890s and early years of the twentieth century, for example, a dispute arose among advocates of women's suffrage over whether or not a literacy test should be required for those who wished to vote. Elizabeth Cady Stanton feared the impact of ignorant immigrants on the quality of civic culture. It troubled her that "foreigners are our judges and jurors, our legislators and municipal officials, and decide all questions of interest to us." To many of her comrades, however, that exaggerated claim seemed to be no more than a strategic ploy to win the support of nativist males on behalf of middle-class white women. Harriot Stanton Blatch published in the *Woman's Journal* a letter to her mother insisting that it was wrong to connect literacy with political judgment: "Let me assure you the spirit of freedom is not a treasure hidden in America, but is everywhere throbbing in the heart of growing Democracy."

Similarly, the American Federation of Labor also supported the literacy test requirement in order to reduce the influx of non-Anglo-Saxon immigrants—competition that might work for lower wages. Tensions between skilled workers in the AFL and unskilled workers who eventually joined the CIO (Congress of Industrial Organizations) were connected to differences in class and ethnicity as well as training. These conflicts were especially manifest in the history of labor's struggle with management from the 1880s onward and weakened labor's "hand" in dealing with corporate capitalism.[4]

Two important figures in the history of American popular culture illustrate the prominence of contested values within individual families. When Woody Guthrie, the prolific writer of folk songs ("This Land Is Your Land"), was growing up in Oklahoma during the 1910s and 1920s, he received quite different signals from his parents. His mother was compassionate, concerned about the needs and welfare of others—a selfless communitarian—whereas his father was an aggressive individualist, a feisty wheeler-dealer in real estate, a man who sought personal recognition in his community.

Nina Simone, the African-American singer and musician, grew up in the 1940s in rural North Carolina where her mother was an itinerant preacher and the principal breadwinner. Her well-intentioned father was more of a home-person and was frequently unemployed, in part the victim of white southern mistreatment of black men during a period of severe racial repression. Simone recalls that "there were some things Daddy's pride would not allow him to face. . . . There was no question that his pride was hurt by the fact that Momma and the older children were the ones who provided much of the income that kept our family going. It made no difference that it wasn't his fault, that he had done nothing wrong. He felt he'd let us down, and it burnt inside him. At times there was a lot of conflict . . . between Daddy and Momma."[5]

The vocational and temperamental tensions between Simone's parents provide a partial variation on the conventional view of white families during the late nineteenth and early twentieth centuries: the home-centered religious world of women versus the commercial, secular, nondomestic sphere of men. To the extent that such a dichotomy actually did divide men and women, it has given way to a major and enduring conflict between the Puritan ethic of saving and the consumer ethos of spending. The intense development of advertising and public relations during the 1920s did much to tip the balance toward consumerism. Corporate capitalism stimulated not only wants and the production of goods, but also an economy whose very success depended on the persistence of consumer demand. In recent years we have become increasingly alarmed about the perils of personal debt, yet we continue to assume that widespread purchasing power is the very engine of a healthy capitalist economy.

No one would deny that the path to our present dilemma has been complex; yet the historical dimensions of that complexity can be intriguingly instructive. Take evangelical Protestantism, for example. We might be inclined to assume that it affirmed traditional values, ranging from strict temperance to the sanctity of home and family. That assumption is correct. And evangelical Protestant preachers, like Dwight L. Moody and Billy Sunday, opposed the Social Gospel movement because it seemed excessively rationalist and reform-minded.

Nevertheless, Moody and Sunday developed large organizations with highly specialized support staffs. They were exceedingly modern in their attentiveness to public relations, and they rationalized urban missionary work as a form of Christian consumerism. Not merely passing but filling the collection plates was critical to the economic success of their organizations. At their revivals enthusiasts could buy books, tracts, photographs, and other souvenirs. In short, consumerism was not simply a secular phenomenon. Billy Sunday, the most popular and influential preacher of the Progressive era (1900–18), was a shrewd and effective businessman who even loved to use commercial metaphors and analogies in his sermons.

Between the 1880s and the 1920s no battle in American culture was livelier or more heated than the one waged between the polite culture of genteel Victorianism and the mold-shattering exuberance of innovative modernism. At the level of high culture, or learned culture, we call that battle the "revolt against formalism." It involved new modes of philosophy, such as pragmatism; advocacy of educational reform, such as John Dewey's instrumentalism; legal realism as a replacement for time-honored but rigid law codes; and experimentalism in the arts, ranging from imagism in poetry to postimpressionism in painting.

If mere enumeration of such trends seems a little bit elusive, take the concrete case of an extremely popular song in which the contested values of tradition and modernism were deliberately pitted as contrapuntal opposites. The song is called "Play a Simple Melody," and it was written in

1914 for a music and dance revue on Broadway called *Watch Your Step*. The composer was Irving Berlin, the most successful writer of popular tunes in the history of Tin Pan Alley and Broadway. (Among many of his other songs are "Easter Parade," "White Christmas," and "There's No Business Like Show Business.")

Ragtime had emerged early in the twentieth century as the very essence of musical modernism, and Berlin rode the crest of that craze in 1911 when he composed "Alexander's Ragtime Band," the most popular piece of sheet music until his later hits surpassed it. In 1914, however, Berlin successfully incorporated in a single pop song the cultural contest between Victorian gentility and the desire for liberation and leisure. "Play a Simple Melody" would be the first of Berlin's "double songs" in which two different melodies and lyrics are counterpointed against one another. One melody is attached to a nostalgic call for a song "like my mother sang to me"; but that proper request is contrasted with a brassily colloquial and modish innovation.

> Won't you play me some rag[time]?
> Just change that classical nag
> To some sweet beautiful drag.

Berlin's intricately blended contest between two different voices, tradition and modernism, moved the whole concept of "ragging" to a new structural level.[6]

The complex simplicity of Berlin's achievement serves to remind us of a dynamic outcome to many contested values in American history: the fusion of binary opposites into a new attribute, attitude, or quality that would be very widely shared or valued. Take as one illustration "practical idealism," an apparent oxymoron that pops up in all sorts of texts during the earlier twentieth century. Americans had long prided themselves not only on their moralistic idealism, but also on their experimental practicality. Could they possibly have it both ways? Leaders like Theodore Roosevelt continually insisted that Americans should approach their ideals through practical measures. Henry Ford's famous announcement in 1914 of the five dollar per day minimum wage was welcomed as a splendid example of the kind of altruism that brings results—practical idealism at its best. Frederick W. Taylor firmly believed that his principles of scientific management (see Chapter 6) embodied the essence of practical idealism.

Carl Becker, one of the most distinguished American historians of the twentieth century, once described "an idealism that is immensely concrete and practical, requiring always some definite object upon which to expend itself with a restless, nervous energy . . . : whatever the object, it is pursued with the enthusiasm, the profound conviction given only to those who have communed with the Absolute."[7] That's a compelling vision of practical idealism made operational in its American setting.

Are all, or most, or even many of our contested values likely to be reconciled into hyphenated formulations of that kind? I think not, and for several reasons. First, the American people become ever more diverse with each passing decade. Although the concept of cultural pluralism dates back to Horace Kallen's classic 1915 essay (Chapter 7), it is an even more urgent message in the closing years of the twentieth century. His words not only echo, they resound: "the adage about the rolling stone is notorious, and the moss we call culture, even the culture of America, requires a broad and quiet back to grow on, when the back is native. How, when the back is foreign?" To appreciate the multiplicity of our society, its variegated components, mingled allegiances, and mixed emotions, we must update and adapt Kallen's thinking about cultural pluralism.[8]

Second, it has become an integral part of the American style to set our agendas in terms of contested values. Mabel Dodge, a prominent figure in the avant-garde of art and politics, started her famous salon discussions in 1913 in New York City. She would invite 100 or more guests each week, choose appropriate discussion leaders for the occasion, and select the most important and controversial issues of the day. Her purpose was to generate intellectual excitement through the clash of opposing ideologies, theories, and interests. Her salons personified the very essence of contested values, and by 1914 they had achieved national notoriety.

The "Fairness Doctrine" of the Federal Communications Commission, which regulated news broadcasting on American television for many years, developed from the assumption that all Americans do not share a single set of values. Consequently, opportunities *must* be provided for audiences to hear all sides of an issue.

(In practice, as with this book, that usually meant two sides of an issue. The positions of small minorities have never received an adequate hearing in the United States. We *seem* less fragmented than other societies because our fragments are not encouraged to be as visible or as vocal as those elsewhere. Many Americans regard that as a strength: a source of stability. Many others, however, regard it as a serious flaw: the marginalization of those who choose to think otherwise. The dissonance between those two views is yet another instance of contestation.)

Finally, in this age of mass culture, consider the deliberate format of *TV Guide*, the largest circulation magazine in all of American history. There are some twenty million copies in circulation each week, and more than forty million readers. The editors of *TV Guide*, a remarkably stable group since its genesis in 1953, are committed to a policy of "vigorous and visible debate." Once again, despite the prophets of gloom who warn against the homogenization of American values because of mass culture, we find the culture industry itself committed to contested values.

One other observation ought to be made. The role of government as a referee of contested values in the United States has ranged from modest to minimal. Given the historical heterogeneity of American society, and given our mandated system of federalism combined with checks and balances, perhaps government could not have played any other role. Still, the point needs to be developed just a bit because it helps to explain the persistence of contested values in America.

Government at all levels tends to respond hesitantly and slowly to the need for change—political rhetoric to the contrary notwithstanding. Government officials, appointed as well as elected, ordinarily hope that the ailing patient (such as the economy, or the political process, or social inequities) will somehow, miraculously, heal itself. For much of our history, with regard to most situations, officeholders have responded with all deliberate inertia and have applied to the American scene generally a formula that is supposed to suit our free enterprise system: the formula of laissez-faire, leave it alone. The application of that formula has been particularly evident when values have been in conflict.[9] Hence, we had decades of debate over national Prohibition, followed by indecisive enforcement and then political reversal. The Prohibition fiasco became an object lesson to many people in and out of government.

Those who pursue the suggested readings will make at least one other incidental discovery: namely, that historians also find themselves, quite often, in conflict with one another despite intellectual integrity and sincerity on all sides. As Harry S. Truman once quipped, "No two historians ever agree on what happened, and the damn thing is they both think they're telling the truth." I have to wonder whether that increases or reduces the potential for reconciliation among historians.

Notes

1. See Norman Mailer, "The White Negro" (1957) in Mailer, *Advertisements for Myself* (New York: Putnam, 1959), pp. 337–58; and James Baldwin, "The Black Boy Looks at the White Boy" (1961) in Baldwin, *Nobody Knows My Name: More Notes of a Native Son* (New York: Dial Press, 1961), pp. 169–90.
2. Ralph Ellison, *Going to the Territory* (New York: Random House, 1986), pp. 124–25.
3. The prospects for individualism in the United States continued to be contested in new ways during the 1920s and 1930s. Compare, for example, Herbert Hoover, *American Individualism* (Garden City, N.Y.: Doubleday, 1922) and Horace Kallen, *Individualism: An American Way of Life* (New York: Liveright, 1933).
4. See Lizabeth Cohen, *Making a New Deal: Industrial Workers in Chicago, 1919–1939* (New York: Cambridge University Press, 1990), ch. 4, "Contested Loyalty at the Workplace."
5. *I Put a Spell on You: The Autobiography of Nina Simone* (New York: Pantheon, 1991), pp. 20–21, 30.
6. See Philip Furia, "Irving Berlin: Troubador of Tin Pan Alley," in William R. Taylor, ed., *Inventing Times Square* (New York: Russell Sage, 1991), pp. 196–97.

7. Carl Becker, *Everyman His Own Historian: Essays on History and Politics* (New York: F. S. Crofts & Co., 1935), p. 17.
8. See, for starters, Laurence H. Fuchs, *American Kaleidoscope: Race, Ethnicity, and the Civic Culture* (Middletown, Conn.: Wesleyan University Press, 1990); James Davison Hunter, *Culture Wars: The Struggle to Define America* (New York: Basic Books, 1991); and Arthur M. Schlesinger, Jr., *The Disuniting of America: Reflections on a Multicultural Society* (New York: W. W. Norton, 1991).
9. For elaboration of this point and many others in the Introduction, see Daniel T. Rodgers, *Contested Truths: Keywords in American Politics since Independence* (New York: Basic Books, 1987).

I

✑

LOOKING BACK:
DIFFERING
PERCEPTIONS
OF THE CIVIL WAR

Jefferson Davis (1808–89) served as president of the Confederacy and survived the so-called Lost Cause by more than twenty-four years. In the speech that follows (1882) he urges his audience to be proud of the past because their cause was just. Like U. S. Grant, Davis declares that he does not regret the war because southerners commendably fought to defend their country, their families, and their constitutional rights. Unlike Grant, however, Davis does not mention the institution of slavery as a provocation or as a southern cause. Although he insists that southerners are not bitter or vengeful, he offers caustic comments about the behavior of federal troops and pleads that Confederate heroes must be remembered because their cause now "lies buried."

Ulysses S. Grant (1822–85) won major Union victories in 1862 and 1863 and then commanded all Union forces in 1864–65. He served two terms as president (1869–77) and wrote his military memoirs during his last years in order to provide financial security for his family. The final chapter, which appears here, was written just days before Grant died of cancer. The book, which became a national best-seller, looks hopefully to the future as an era of sectional harmony. Grant rather blandly believed that American culture had been nationalized and that the freedmen were entitled to remain in the United States. He anticipates the views of many in the next generation, such as Theodore Roosevelt, that the best way to maintain peace is by preparation for war.

The address given by Oliver Wendell Holmes, Jr. (1841–1935) in 1895 has an entirely different tone because it emphasizes the ephemeral nature of military service and the oblivion of soliders' experiences. (Holmes had been wounded in several battles.) It is interesting because Holmes differentiates between the experience of battle at the time it actually occurred and the way it was recalled in retrospect. The address by Holmes (who served on the U.S. Supreme Court, 1902–32) is also noteworthy because its Darwinian language (the struggle for life) anticipates no fewer than three of the dialogues that follow: Ward and Sumner, Carnegie and Addams, James and Roosevelt. We might take note of Holmes's lament that "we do not save our traditions in this country," and we might ask whether that is equally true of the stances taken by Davis and Grant.

An Address on Behalf of the Southern Historical Society Given at New Orleans, April 25, 1882

JEFFERSON DAVIS

Ladies and Gentlemen,—It would be more than superfluous to address to a New Orleans audience any argument in favor of the preservation of the history of our Confederate struggle. Your course is too well known, marked by too many deeds both in war and in peace, to render it at all doubtful that your hearts beat time to the cause for which so many of your bravest and best have died. . . .

At the very first call of the late war your citizens rushed forth to the defense of their country, and you gave of your sons the first who reduced the fort that threatened to blockade a Southern harbor. And he, in the first great battle of Manassas, so distinguished himself as to be promoted on the field to the highest grade in the Confederate army. Such was your Beauregard. (Applause.) . . .

. . . [W]hen the war was over, then the fair daughters of Louisiana (it is always the women who are first in good work), originated that plan of decorating the graves of the Confederate dead, paying to them annually a tribute of flowers, which, in their beauty and recurring vitality, best express the everlasting love you bear toward the dead.

Then here, in New Orleans, was organized the Historical Society, with a view to preserving the records of the Confederate war. That Society has been removed, but still looks back to this the place of its birth. Here, where more than in any other city, you had been swept by the besom of desolation—where you had been more terribly pillaged than any other town that had been overrun—here have arisen more monuments to the Confederate heroes than in any other city of the South. Glorious New Orleans! You have the right to be proud of the past, and we have the right to be expectant of you in the future, for there is yet a higher and more immediate duty to perform. Monuments may crumble, their inscriptions may be defaced by time, but the records, the little slips of paper which contain the memorial of what is past will live forever. To collect and preserve these records is, therefore, our highest duty. They are said to be in danger. The

Jefferson Davis, "An Address on Behalf of the Southern Historical Society Given at New Orleans, April 25, 1882," in *Jefferson Davis, Constitutionalist: His Letters, Papers and Speeches* Dunbar Rowland, ed. (Jackson, Miss.: Mississippi Department of Archives and History, 1923), IX, pp. 162–69.

Southern Historical Society appeals to you now. They appeal to you in the midst of your disaster, when your country has been overwhelmed by a flood, and when there is a want of means to supply the necessities of your people. Still the Historical Society comes to Louisiana as the first place, in which they ask that the Confederate records should be perfected and protected. I do not doubt that you will respond to the extent of your ability; that you will here inaugurate a movement which, growing and extending from city to city and year to year, will render certain the preservation of those archives, the value of which it is impossible to compute. It is a duty we owe to the dead—the dead who died for us, but whose memories can never die. It is a duty we owe to posterity to see that our children shall know the virtues and rise worthy of their sires; to see that the sons grow up worthy of their noble mothers—those mothers who never faltered through all the hours of trial through which we passed. (Applause.)

They who now sleep in the grave cannot be benefitted, it is true, by anything we may do; their cause has gone before a higher tribunal than any earthly judgment-seat, but their children and children's children are to be benefitted by preserving the record of what they did, and more than all, the moral with which they did it. As for me—I speak only for myself—our cause was so just, so sacred, that had I known all that has come to pass, had I known what was to be inflicted upon me, all that my country was to suffer, all that our posterity was to endure, I would do it all over again. (Great applause.) . . .

It is not necessary that we should have recorded what is conceded by all the world, that our men were brave, that they had a power of endurance and self-denial which was remarkable, but if you would have your children rise to the high plane you desire them to occupy, you must add the evidence of their father's chivalry and forbearance from that staining crime of the soldier, plunder, under all the circumstances of the war. True that we did not invade to any great extent, though we did to some. It is a fact which I am happy to remember that when our army invaded the enemy's country, their property was safe. I draw no comparisons, as I am speaking now of our people and of our country. If somebody else did not behave as well, let it rest. (Laughter.)

We had no army at the opening of the war; our defenders were not professional soldiers. They were men who left their wives, children and peaceful occupations, and, at the first call of their country, seized such arms as they could gather, and rallied around their flag like a wall of fire to defend the rights their fathers left them. Could there be cause more sacred than this? If there be anything that justifies human war, it is defense of country, of family, of constitutional rights. (Applause.) . . .

The highest quality of man is self-sacrifice.

The man who gives his life for another, who surrenders all his earthly prospects that his fellow men may be benefitted, has most followed that grand exemplar who was given as a model for weak humanity. That we had many men in the Confederate service who forgot self in the defense of right, it is the purpose of this Society, by collecting the evidence, to show to the world. . . .

The other side has written, and is writing, their statement of the case. We wish to present ours also, that the future historian by considering both may deduce the unbiased statement, which no contemporary could make. . . .

You all know how utterly unprepared we were when we engaged in the war, without money, without an army, without credit, without arms or ammunition, or factories to make them. We went into the struggle relying solely on brave hearts, strong arms, and, unfortunately many relying on deciding the issue by argument. When they found they were mistaken— that it was the dread ordeal of battle by which the question was to be settled—they shrank not from it, and I do contend their valor was equaled only by the moral of their conduct throughout the struggle. The unanimity of our people and the heroism of our soldiers has caused us to be the admiration of the world. They know the disadvantages under which we fought; they know the great achievements which we did. But there is much that is not known. . . .

It is our duty to keep the memory of our heroes green. Yet they belong not to us alone; they belong to the whole country; they belong to America. And we do not seek to deprive "Americans" of the glory of such heroes as we have produced. Nor were their services rendered in our war those only which claim grateful remembrance. There was pious Jackson, the man, who, when he was waiting for the troops to move up would, under a storm of bullets, be lost in ejaculatory prayer: the man who, when he bent over a wounded comrade, would feel a woman's weakness creep into his eyes: the man who came like a thunderbolt when his friends most needed him, and his enemies least expected his coming, was the same who had marched into the valley of Mexico to sustain the flag of the United States. That man who had been the terror of the enemy in the hour of battle but was as peaceful as a lamb after the conflict, when he found he was on a bed of death, calmly folded his arms, resigning his soul to God and saying: "Let us cross over the river and rest under the shade of the trees." We do not claim to appropriate all his glory, but we hold dear every part of him that nobody else wants.

And there was Lee, the calm, faithful, far-seeing, dauntless Lee. As a soldier and engineer he penetrated the Mexican pedrigal and discovered a route by which the army must be led. To him more than to anybody else must be ascribed the capture of the city of Mexico.

We do not wish to wholly appropriate the glory of Lee but will willingly share it with those who have an equal right to it, and we would rather they should claim some share of the grand conduct of Lee at Chancellorsville, Fredericksburg, the Wilderness, and everywhere that soldiers met soldiers against mighty odds.

There was the great General Sidney Johnston, distinguished in the Black Hawk war and the siege of Monterey, holding a position in the army with a rank beyond his age and prospects the most inviting to a soldier, he surrendered everything in order to vindicate the principles he believed to be true, and came with nothing but his right arm and his good sword to offer his services to the Confederacy.

Never was man more true to his duty, more devoted to his cause, or more sincere in his purpose, as was shown in the hour of his death, when, on the field of Shiloh, having driven the enemy from every position before him save one, which he saw must be carried to make the victory complete, he led a column to storm it, receiving a death wound from which the life-blood was pouring, he recked not of himself, but thinking, feeling only of his country and its cause, rode on until he fell lifeless from his horse. . . .

Though the gallantry and capacity of the Confederate troops was so often and so brilliantly exhibited as to be undeniable and undenied, yet we have been inconsistently charged with cruelty to prisoners. I say inconsistently, because brave men are never cruel to those who are helpless and in their power. The fact is, we used our best efforts to alleviate the sufferings of the prisoners held by us. That they languished and died in prison was their misfortune and ours also. There were physical and climatic causes which we could not alter. We were wanting in supplies of the proper medicines and the kind of food to which the prisoners were accustomed. As the number of prisoners accumulated beyond what could have been anticipated, there was not a sufficient shelter for them. Disease was the consequence, and the medicine required could not be obtained because the enemy had made it contraband. It is a burning shame that the slander was ever circulated which imputed to us cruelty to those who were in our power. Enough has been collected and published on this subject to convince any fair, disinterested mind, but let us not stop until the facts have been so established that not even malignity and slanderous falsehood can fail to be silenced and abashed. Let the testimony of reliable persons who were in our prisons be taken, especially the evidence of those who came to me as a delegation from the prisoners at Andersonville, and whom I sent on parole to Washington to plead for the execution of the cartel for the exchange of prisoners. In due time they came back to report that they could not get an audience. Their conduct in observing their parole proved their honorable character, and must entitle them to credence. Let these and all other pertinent facts be added to the testimony already of record, so that the odious accusations about Andersonville shall not be thrown in the faces of our children and our children's children.

Time's mellowing influence has been felt on both sides of the Susquehanna, and our people sincerely appreciate the kindness shown them in time of pestilence, and more recently in time of flood. It is the characteristic of the brave and generous always gratefully to acknowledge any kindness they receive. . . .

My friends, it is somewhat difficult for a Confederate whose heart-love lies buried in the grave of our cause, to speak to you on a subject which revives the memories of that period, and to speak with that forbearance which the occasion requires. . . .

Conclusion to Personal Memoirs

U. S. GRANT

The cause of the great War of the Rebellion against the United States will have to be attributed to slavery. For some years before the war began it was a trite saying among some politicians that "A state half slave and half free cannot exist." All must become slave or all free, or the state will go down. I took no part myself in any such view of the case at the time, but since the war is over, reviewing the whole question, I have come to the conclusion that the saying is quite true.

Slavery was an institution that required unusual guarantees for its security wherever it existed; and in a country like ours where the larger portion of it was free territory inhabited by an intelligent and well-to-do population, the people would naturally have but little sympathy with demands upon them for its protection. Hence the people of the South were dependent upon keeping control of the general government to secure the perpetuation of their favorite institution. They were enabled to maintain this control long after the States where slavery existed had ceased to have the controlling power, through the assistance they received from odd men here and there throughout the Northern States. They saw their power waning, and this led them to encroach upon the prerogatives and independence of the Northern States by enacting such laws as the Fugitive Slave Law. By this law every Northern man was obliged, when properly summoned, to turn out and help apprehend the runaway slave of a Southern man. Northern marshals became slave-catchers, and Northern courts had to contribute to the support and protection of the institution.

This was a degradation which the North would not permit any longer than until they could get the power to expunge such laws from the statute books. Prior to the time of these encroachments the great majority of the people of the North had no particular quarrel with slavery, so long as they were not forced to have it themselves. But they were not willing to play

---

U. S. Grant, "Conclusion," in *Personal Memoirs* (New York: Charles L. Webster & Co., 1886, copyright 1885), pp. 542–54.

the role of police for the South in the protection of this particular institution. . . .

It is probably well that we had the war when we did. We are better off now than we would have been without it, and have made more rapid progress than we otherwise should have made. The civilized nations of Europe have been stimulated into unusual activity, so that commerce, trade, travel, and thorough acquaintance among people of different nationalities, has become common; whereas, before, it was but the few who had ever had the privilege of going beyond the limits of their own country or who knew anything about other people. Then, too, our republican institutions were regarded as experiments up to the breaking out of the rebellion, and monarchical Europe generally believed that our republic was a rope of sand that would part the moment the slightest strain was brought upon it. Now it has shown itself capable of dealing with one of the greatest wars that was ever made, and our people have proven themselves to be the most formidable in war of any nationality.

But this war was a fearful lesson, and should teach us the necessity of avoiding wars in the future. . . .

To maintain peace in the future it is necessary to be prepared for war. There can scarcely be a possible chance of a conflict, such as the last one, occurring among our own people again; but, growing as we are, in population, wealth and military power, we may become the envy of nations which led us in all these particulars only a few years ago; and unless we are prepared for it we may be in danger of a combined movement being some day made to crush us out. Now, scarcely twenty years after the war, we seem to have forgotten the lessons it taught, and are going on as if in the greatest security, without the power to resist an invasion by the fleets of fourth-rate European powers for a time until we could prepare for them. . . .

It is possible that the question of a conflict between races may come up in the future, as did that between freedom and slavery before. The condition of the colored man within our borders may become a source of anxiety, to say the least. But he was brought to our shores by compulsion, and he now should be considered as having as good a right to remain here as any other class of our citizens. . . .

By the war with Mexico, we had acquired, as we have seen, territory almost equal in extent to that we already possessed. It was seen that the volunteers of the Mexican war largely composed the pioneers to settle up the Pacific coast country. Their numbers, however, were scarcely sufficient to be a nucleus for the population of the important points of the territory acquired by that war. After our rebellion, when so many young men were at liberty to return to their homes, they found they were not satisfied with the farm, the store, or the work-shop of the villages, but wanted larger fields. The mines of the mountains first attracted them; but afterwards they found that rich valleys and productive grazing and farming lands were there. This territory, the geography of which was not known to us at the close of the rebellion, is now as well mapped as any portion of our country. Railroads traverse it in every direction, north, south, east, and west. The mines are worked. The high lands are used for grazing purposes, and rich agricultural lands are found in many of the valleys. This is the work of the volunteer. It is probable that the Indians would have had control of these lands for a century yet but for the war. We must conclude, therefore, that wars are not always evils unmixed with some good.

Prior to the rebellion the great mass of the people were satisfied to remain near the scenes of their birth. In fact an immense majority of the whole people did not feel secure against coming to want should they move among entire strangers. So much was the country divided into small communities that localized idioms had grown up, so that you could almost tell what section a person was from by hearing him speak. Before, new territories were settled by a "class"; people who shunned contact with others; people who, when the country began to settle up around them, would push out farther from civilization. Their guns furnished meat, and the cultivation of a very limited amount of the soil, their bread and vegetables. . . .

Little was known of the topography of the country beyond the settlements of these frontiersmen. This is all changed now. The war begot a spirit of independence and enterprise. The feeling now is, that a youth must cut loose from his old surroundings to enable him to get up in the world. There is now such a commingling of the people that particular idioms and pronunciation are no longer localized to any great extent; the country has filled up "from the centre all around to the sea"; railroads connect the two oceans and all parts of the interior; maps, nearly perfect, of every part of the country are now furnished the student of geography.

The war has made us a nation of great power and intelligence. We have but little to do to preserve peace, happiness and prosperity at home, and the respect of other nations. Our experience ought to teach us the necessity of the first; our power secures the latter.

I feel that we are on the eve of a new era, when there is to be great harmony between the Federal and Confederate. I cannot stay to be a living witness to the correctness of this prophecy; but I feel it within me that it is to be so. The universally kind feeling expressed for me at a time when it was supposed that each day would prove my last, seemed to me the beginning of the answer to "Let us have peace." . . .

The Soldier's Faith

OLIVER WENDELL HOLMES, JR.

. . . Behind every scheme to make the world over, lies the question, What kind of world do you want? The ideals of the past for men have been drawn from war, as those for women have been drawn from motherhood. For all our prophecies, I doubt if we are ready to give up our inheritance. Who is there who would not like to be thought a gentleman? Yet what has that name been built on but the soldier's choice of honor rather than life? To be a soldier or descended from soldiers, in time of peace to be ready to give one's life rather than to suffer disgrace, that is what the world has meant; and if we try to claim it at less cost than a splendid carelessness for life, we are trying to steal the good will without the responsibilities of the place. We will not dispute about tastes. The man of the future may want something different. But who of us could endure a world, although cut up into five-acre lots and having no man upon it who was not well fed and well housed, without the divine folly of honor, without the senseless passion for knowledge outreaching the flaming bounds of the possible, without ideals the essence of which is that they never can be achieved? I do not know what is true. I do not know the meaning of the universe. But in the midst of doubt, in the collapse of creeds, there is one thing I do not doubt, that no man who lives in the same world with most of us can doubt, and that is that the faith is true and adorable which leads a soldier to throw away his life in obedience to a blindly accepted duty, in a cause which he little understands, in a plan of campaign of which he has no notions, under tactics of which he does not see the use.

Most men who know battle know the cynic force with which the thoughts of common sense will assail them in times of stress; but they know that in their greatest moments faith has trampled those thoughts under foot. If you have been in line, suppose on Tremont Street Mall, ordered simply to wait and to do nothing, and have watched the enemy bring their guns to bear upon you down a gentle slope like that from Beacon Street, have seen the puff of the firing, have felt the burst of the spherical case-shot as it came toward you, have heard and seen the shrieking fragments go tearing through your company, and have known that the next or the next shot carries your fate; if you have advanced in line and have seen ahead of you the spot which you must pass where the rifle bullets are striking; if you have ridden by night at a walk toward the blue line of fire at the dead angle of Spottsylvania, where for twenty-four hours

Oliver Wendell Holmes, Jr., "The Soldier's Faith," in *Speeches* (Boston: Little, Brown & Co., 1913), pp. 56–66.

the soldiers were fighting on the two sides of an earthwork, and in the morning the dead and dying lay piled in a row six deep, and as you rode have heard the bullets splashing in the mud and earth about you; if you have been on the picketline at night in a black and unknown wood, have heard the spat of the bullets upon the trees, and as you moved have felt your foot slip upon a dead man's body; if you have had a blind fierce gallop against the enemy, with your blood up and a pace that left no time for fear—if, in short, as some, I hope many, who hear me, have known, you have known the vicissitudes of terror and of triumph in war, you know that there is such a thing as the faith I spoke of. You know your own weakness and are modest; but you know that man has in him that unspeakable somewhat which makes him capable of miracle, able to lift himself by the might of his own soul, unaided, able to face annihilation for a blind belief. . . .

When I went to the war I thought that soldiers were old men. I remembered a picture of the revolutionary soldier which some of you may have seen, representing a white-haired man with his flintlock slung across his back. I remembered one or two living examples of revolutionary soldiers whom I had met, and I took no account of the lapse of time. It was not until long after, in winter quarters, as I was listening to some of the sentimental songs in vogue, such as—

Farewell, Mother, you may never
See your darling boy again,

that it came over me that the army was made up of what I now should call very young men. I dare say that my illusion has been shared by some of those now present, as they have looked at us upon whose heads the white shadows have begun to fall. But the truth is that war is the business of youth and early middle age. You who called this assemblage together, not we, would be the soldiers of another war, if we should have one. . . .

War, when you are at it, is horrible and dull. It is only when time has passed that you see that its message was divine. I hope it may be long before we are called again to sit at that master's feet. But some teacher of the kind we all need. In this snug, over-safe corner of the world we need it, that we may realize that our comfortable routine is no eternal necessity of things, but merely a little space of calm in the midst of the tempestuous untamed streaming of the world, and in order that we may be ready for danger. We need it in this time of individualist negations, with its literature of French and American humor, revolting at discipline, loving fleshpots, and denying that anything is worthy of reverence,—in order that we may remember all that buffoons forget. We need it everywhere and at all times. For high and dangerous action teaches us to believe as right beyond dispute things for which our doubting minds are slow to find words of proof. Out of heroism grows faith in the worth of heroism. The proof comes later, and even may never come. Therefore I rejoice at every dangerous sport which I see pursued. The students at Heidelberg, with their sword-slashed faces, inspire me with sincere respect. I gaze with delight upon our poloplayers. If once in a while in our rough riding a neck is broken, I regard it, not as a waste, but as a price well paid for the breeding of a race fit for headship and command.

We do not save our traditions, in this country. The regiments whose battle-flags were not large enough to hold the names of the battles they had fought, vanished with the surrender of Lee, although their memories inherited would have made heroes for a century. It is the more necessary to learn the lesson afresh from perils newly sought, and perhaps it is not vain for us to tell the new generation what we learned in our day, and what we still believe. That the joy of life is living, is to put out all one's powers as far as they will go; that the measure of power is obstacles overcome; to ride boldly at what is in front of you, be it fence or enemy; to pray, not for comfort, but for combat; to keep the soldier's faith against the doubts of civil life, more besetting and harder to overcome than all the misgivings of the battle-field, and to remember that duty is not to be proved in the evil day, but then to be obeyed unquestioning; to love glory more than the temptations of wallowing ease, but to know that one's final judge and only rival is oneself—with all our failures in act and thought, these things we learned from noble enemies in Virginia or Georgia or on the Mississippi, thirty years ago; these things we believe to be true. . . .

As for us, our days of combat are over. Our swords are rust. Our guns will thunder no more. The vultures that once wheeled over our heads are buried with their prey. Whatever of glory yet remains for us to win must be won in the council or the closet, never again in the field. I do not repine. We have shared the incommunicable experience of war; we have felt, we still feel, the passion of life to its top.

Three years ago died the old colonel of my regiment, the Twentieth Massachusetts. He gave our regiment its soul. No man could falter who heard his "Forward, Twentieth!" I went to his funeral. From a side door of the church a body of little choir-boys came in like a flight of careless doves. At the same time the doors opened at the front, and up the main aisle advanced his coffin, followed by the few gray heads who stood for the men of the Twentieth, the rank and file whom he had loved, and whom he led for the last time. The church was empty. No one remembered the old man whom we were burying, no one save those next to him, and us. And I said to myself, The Twentieth has shrunk to a skeleton, a ghost, a memory, a forgotten name which we other old men alone keep in our hearts. And then I thought: It is right. It is as the colonel would have had it. This also is part of the soldier's faith: Having known great things, to be content with silence. . . .

SUGGESTIONS FOR FURTHER READING

Paul D. Escott, *After Secession: Jefferson Davis and the Failure of Confederate Nationalism* (Baton Rouge, La.: Louisiana State University Press, 1978); Gaines M. Foster, *Ghosts of the Confederacy: Defeat, the Lost Cause, and the Emergence of the New South, 1865 to 1913* (New York: Oxford University Press, 1987); and for the dramatic circumstances under which U.S. Grant wrote his *Memoirs*, see William S. McFeely, *Grant: A Biography* (New York: W. W. Norton, 1981), ch. 28.

II

❧

CAN AMERICANS REFORM THEIR SOCIETY AND ECONOMIC SYSTEM?

The pros and cons of Social Darwinism agitated a generation of American thinkers from the mid-1870s through the 1910s. The issue was drawn with special sharpness among the founders of social science disciplines in the United States. Lester Frank Ward (1841–1913) was trained in the natural sciences but developed a strong interest in integrating sociology, psychology, and biology with other fields. In one of his major works, Dynamic Sociology *(1883, 2 vols.), Ward was critical of laissez-faire and argued that sociology could be useful in bringing about social improvement. In 1906 he became a professor of sociology at Brown University.*

The selection here is from Psychic Factors of Civilization *(1893), which many scholars regard as Ward's best and most important book. In this selection, notice in particular his belief that society in cooperation with a nonpartisan government could further its own interests. Ward considered social reformers to be necessary and legitimate because he believed that "psychic [mental] factors" could counterbalance and control natural forces. He saw subjective psychology as a potential philosophy of action.*

William Graham Sumner (1840–1910), an equally erudite social scientist who had been trained in theology, taught at Yale from 1872 until his death. Because of his belief in natural law and in very gradual evolution, things as they were seemed inevitable to him and he accepted the individual's inability to control social or economic change: humankind could only hope to understand them. In the essay that follows, however, Sumner's conservatism goes a step further. Industrial organization becomes an uncontrollable force, and Sumner contends, on behalf of plutocracy, that positive good is accomplished by large concentrations of capital in the hands of a few. Unlike Ward, Sumner is skeptical, if not hostile, toward democracy.

Therefore, Sumner accepts and defends the status quo, whereas Ward finds a place for human initiative, and even anticipates the welfare state by advocating activist cooperation between the private and public sectors. The lines of conflict over Social Darwinism were clearly drawn between these two influential intellectual giants.

Psychic Factors of Civilization

LESTER FRANK WARD

The history of man, if it should ever be written, would be an account of what man has done. The numerous changes that have been made in the position of certain imaginary lines on the earth's surface, called political boundaries, and the events that have given rise to such changes, would be recorded, but instead of making the bulk of human annals as they now do, they would occupy a very subordinate place. Such changes and their conditioning events are temporary, superficial, and unimportant. They leave no lasting impress and are soon swept by time completely from the real record of man's achievements. The major part of a true history of man would be devoted to the reproduction of this real record. Although it is written on the face of nature by the events themselves, very much as the cosmical history of the earth is written in the rocks, still the history of man needs to be studied from these natural records, interpreted by the facts there observed, and described in writing and by graphic representation as much as the history of the earth needs to be thus treated by the geologist. Human phenomena, or, as they are popularly called, social phenomena, differ in these respects from geological and other phenomena only in the nature of the forces which produce them. In these it is the psychic forces, as described in the last chapter. Man is the instrument through which these forces operate, and the immediate cause of the phenomena is human action. As man has been a social being during the greater part of his history, and as the principal results of his activities have been brought about by some form of social cooperation, it is customary and proper to designate such action as social action. The laws and principles of such action belong to social science, or sociology, and it thus becomes clear that sociology rests directly upon psychology, and especially upon subjective psychology.

Subjective psychology is a philosophy of action. Looked at retrospectively and from the standpoint of natural history it is seen that all the changes that have taken place either in the organism or the environment have been due to the action of the former under the influence of the psychic or vital forces, and that from the time that conscious desires began to determine action great transformations have taken place and are still going on. Not dwelling on the subhuman stage, it is obvious that man is the being that has most notably displayed this transforming power. An animal of rather inferior physical strength, endowed with few natural

Lester Frank Ward, *Psychic Factors of Civilization* (Boston: Ginn & Co., 1893), pp. 97–101, 323–27.

weapons of either offense or defense, lacking the powers of nocturnal vision, keen scent, fleetness in pursuit or escape, flight, or special skill in swimming, by which to aid him in migration, he has nevertheless almost completely changed the appearance and character of everything above ground over half the land surface of the earth and established himself supreme over all else in all the habitable parts of the globe. All this is commonly and properly attributed to mind. . . . But the present point of view is that of insisting that the motive power of mind has been his multiplied and ever-increasing wants, to supply which perpetual effort has been put forth and ceaseless activity has taken place. This purposeful activity is the middle term of the threefold psychologic succession, mediating between desire and feeling and the necessary condition to the satisfaction of the former in attaining the latter. Here more than anywhere else pleasure or happiness has been made an end, though only intended by nature as a means. But neither did the transformations wrought by man's activity constitute in any sense the purpose of that activity. The sum total of these transformations constitute what is meant by material civilization, but man never made civilization an end of his efforts. In so far as this has been a gain the sole beneficiary of that gain has been society. . . .

There are those who maintain that civilization can only be achieved through the action of the individual, unconscious of the end, doing that which will conduce to the end. The present state of progress is adduced as proof that this is the necessary result. But while it is admitted that this has resulted in some parts of the world and in past history, it must be denied that the effect has been beneficial in all parts of the world or wholly so in any part, and also that any guaranty exists that it will continue indefinitely to be so, even where the actual benefits have been greatest. It can also be legitimately argued that much greater benefits might be secured if society were the conscious agent and had its improvement for its clearly perceived end. But this is an anticipation. This much needs however to be said, that in predicating action as the object of society the time has not yet come when it can be said to be conscious of its end. Society has not yet begun to seek its end. . . . Yet none the less is society the beneficiary of the direct results of human action in so far as they are beneficial, albeit that action is directed solely toward the attainment of the object of the individual man, viz., happiness.

It is the essence of the doctrine of individualism that what is good for the individual must be good for society. This is based on the admitted fact that society exists only for the individual. Society is only an idea—a Platonic idea, like species, genus, order, etc., in natural history. The only real thing is the individual. And it is argued: Why strive to benefit that which has no feeling and therefore is incapable of being benefited? The argument is plausible. Only it proceeds from a misconception of what social reformers really mean when they talk of improving society. There are none so simple as literally to personify society and conceive it endowed with wants and passions. By the improvement of society they only mean such modifications in its constitution and structure as will in their opinion result in ameliorating the condition of its individual members. Therefore there is nothing illogical in their claim, and to answer them it must be shown in each case that the particular supposed reform that they are advocating will not as a matter of fact result in the alleged amelioration of the individual members of society. Arguments of this class are legitimate.

It would also be legitimate to argue that no possible alteration in the existing status of society can produce beneficial effects as thus defined, but I am not aware that anyone has ever taken that position. It is too obvious on the most superficial view that the evils that individuals suffer are often due to the constitution of society which entails them. This results from the constant changes that are going on in every direction through the activities of individuals seeking their ends, and from time to time causing the needs of the mass to outgrow the restrictions which society under very different previous circumstances was obliged to impose. So that if a state of perfect adaptation of the individual to society could be at any given moment conceived to exist it would not remain so very long, and new internal transformations would soon again throw the individual units out of harmony with the social aggregate. It is this inertia of society and its inability to keep pace with the growth of the living mass within it that gives rise to social reformers who are legitimate and necessary, nay, natural products of every country and age, and the ignoring of this fact by conservative writers who lay so great stress on the word *natural,* is one of the amusing absurdities of the present period.

So long, therefore, as society remains the unconscious product of the individual demands of each age, so long will the organized social state continue to be found out of accord with and lagging behind the real spirit of the age, often so intolerably so as to require more or less violent convulsions and social revolutions. But if ever an ideal social organization shall come to be a clearly defined conscious individual want, it will be possible to establish one that will have elements of flexibility sufficient to render it more or less permanent. But here, as everywhere else under the dominion of the psychic forces, the end of the individual or object of man, happiness, or some improvement in his personal condition, must be put vividly before him as the loadstone of desire and motive to action. . . .

The individual has reigned long enough. The day has come for society to take its affairs into its own hands and shape its own destinies. The individual has acted as best he could. He has acted in the only way he could. With a consciousness, will, and intellect of his own he could do nothing else than pursue his natural ends. He should not be denounced nor called any names. He should not even be blamed. Nay, he should be praised, and even *imitated.* Society should learn its great lesson from him, should follow the path he has so clearly laid out that leads to success. It should imagine itself an individual, with all the interests of an individual, and becoming fully *conscious* of these interests it should pursue them with the same indomitable *will* with which the individual pursues his interests. Not only this, it must be guided, as he is guided, by the social *intellect*, armed with all the knowledge that all individuals combined, with so great labor, zeal, and talent have placed in its possession, constituting the social intelligence.

Sociocracy will differ from all other forms of government that have been devised, and yet that difference will not be so radical as to require a revolution. Just as absolute monarchy passed imperceptibly into limited monarchy, and this, in many states without even a change of name has passed into more or less pure democracy, so democracy is capable of passing as smoothly into sociocracy, and without taking on this unfamiliar name or changing that by which it is now known. For, though paradoxical, democracy, which is now the weakest of all forms of government, at least in the control of its own internal elements, is capable of becoming the strongest. Indeed, none of the other forms of government would be capable of passing directly into a government by society. Democracy is a phase through which they must first pass on any route that leads to the ultimate social stage which all governments must eventually attain if they persist.

How then, it may be asked, do democracy and sociocracy differ? How does society differ from the people? If the phrase "the people" really meant the people, the difference would be less. But that shibboleth of democratic states, where it means anything at all that can be described or defined, stands simply for the majority of qualified electors, no matter how small that majority may be. There is a sense in which the action of a majority may be looked upon as the action of society. At least, there is no denying the right of the majority to act for society, for to do this would involve either the denial of the right of government to act at all, or the admission of the right of a minority to act for society. But a majority acting for society is a different thing from society acting for itself, even though, as must always be the case, it acts through an agency chosen by its members. All democratic governments are largely party governments. The electors range themselves on one side or the other of some party line, the winning side considers itself the state as much as Louis the Fourteenth did. The losing party usually then regards the government as something alien to it and hostile, like an invader, and thinks of nothing but to gain strength enough to overthrow it at the next opportunity. While various issues are always brought forward and defended or attacked, it is obvious to the looker-on that the contestants care nothing for these, and merely use them to gain an advantage and win an election.

From the standpoint of society this is child's play. A very slight awakening of the social consciousness will banish it and substitute something more business-like. Once get rid of this puerile gaming spirit and have attention drawn to the real interests of society, and it will be seen that upon nearly all important questions all parties and all citizens are agreed, and that there is no need of this partisan strain upon the public energies. This is clearly shown at every change in the party complexion of the government. The victorious party which has been denouncing the government merely because it was in the hands of its political opponents boasts that it is going to revolutionize the country in the interest of good government, but the moment it comes into power and feels the weight of national responsibility it finds that it has little to do but carry out the laws in the same way that its predecessors had been doing.

There is a vast difference between all this outward show of partisanship and advocacy of so-called principles, and attention to the real interests and necessary business of the nation, which latter is what the government must do. It is a social duty. The pressure which is brought to enforce it is the power of the social will. But in the factitious excitement of partisan struggles where professional politicians and demagogues on the one hand, and the agents of plutocracy on the other, are shouting discordantly in the ears of the people, the real interests of society are, temporarily at least, lost sight of, clouded and obscured, and men lose their grasp on the real issues, forget even their own best interests, which, however selfish, would be a far safer guide, and the general result usually is that these are neglected and nations continue in the hands of mere politicians who are easily managed by the shrewd representatives of wealth.

Sociocracy will change all this. Irrelevant issues will be laid aside. The important objects upon which all but an interested few are agreed will receive their proper degree of attention, and measures will be considered in a non-partisan spirit with the sole purpose of securing these objects. Take as an illustration the postal telegraph question. No one not a stockholder in an existing telegraph company would prefer to pay twenty-five cents for a message if he could send it for ten cents. Where is the room for discussing a question of this nature? What society wants is the cheapest possible system. It wants to know with certainty whether a national postal telegraph system would secure this universally desired object. It is to be expected that the agents of the present telegraph companies would try to show that it would not succeed. This is according to the known laws of psychology as set forth in this work. But why be influenced by the interests of such a small number of persons, however worthy, when all the rest of mankind are interested in the opposite solution? The investigation should be a disinterested and strictly scientific one, and should actually settle the question in one way or the other. If it was found to be a real benefit, the system should be adopted. There are to-day a great number of these strictly social questions before the American people, questions which concern every citizen in the country, aud whose solution would doubtless profoundly affect the state of civilization attainable on this continent. Not only is it impossible to secure this, but it is impossible to secure an investigation of them on their real merits. The same is true of other countries, and in general the prevailing democracies of the world are incompetent to deal with problems of social welfare.

The more extreme and important case referred to a few pages back may make the distinction still more clear. It was shown, and is known to all political economists, that the prices of most of the staple commodities consumed by mankind have no necessary relation to the cost of producing them and placing them in the hands of the consumer. It is always the highest price that the consumer will pay rather than do without. Let us suppose that price to be on an average double what it would cost to produce, transport, exchange, and deliver the goods, allowing in each of these transactions a fair compensation for all services rendered. Is there any member of society who would prefer to pay two dollars for what is thus fairly worth only one? Is there any sane ground for arguing such a question? Certainly not. The individual cannot correct this state of things. No democracy can correct it. But a government that really represented the interests of society would no more tolerate it than an individual would tolerate a continual extortion of money on the part of another without an equivalent.

And so it would be throughout. Society would inquire in a business way without fear, favor, or bias, into everything that concerned its welfare, and if it found obstacles it would remove them, and if it found opportunities it would improve them. In a word, society would do under the same circumstances just what an intelligent individual would do. It would further, in all possible ways, its own interests.

The Absurd Effort to Make the World Over

WILLIAM GRAHAM SUMNER

(1894)

It will not probably be denied that the burden of proof is on those who affirm that our social condition is utterly diseased and in need of radical regeneration. My task at present, therefore, is entirely negative and critical: to examine the allegations of fact and the doctrines which are put forward

William Graham Sumner, "The Absurd Effort to Make the World Over (1894)," in *War and Other Essays* Albert G. Keller, ed. (New Haven, Conn.: Yale University Press, 1911), pp. 195–210.

to prove the correctness of the diagnosis and to warrant the use of the remedies proposed.

The propositions put forward by social reformers nowadays are chiefly of two kinds. There are assertions in historical form, chiefly in regard to the comparison of existing with earlier social states, which are plainly based on defective historical knowledge, or at most on current stock historical dicta which are uncritical and incorrect. Writers very often assert that something never existed before because they do not know that it ever existed before, or that something is worse than ever before because they are not possessed of detailed information about what has existed before. . . .

When anyone asserts that the class of skilled and unskilled manual laborers of the United States is worse off now in respect to diet, clothing, lodgings, furniture, fuel, and lights; in respect to the age at which they can marry; the number of children they can provide for; the start in life which they can give to their children, and their chances of accumulating capital, than they ever have been at any former time, he makes a reckless assertion for which no facts have been offered in proof. Upon an appeal to facts, the contrary of this assertion would be clearly established. It suffices, therefore, to challenge those who are responsible for the assertion to make it good.

If it is said that the employed class are under much more stringent discipline than they were thirty years ago or earlier, it is true. It is not true that there has been any qualitative change in this respect within thirty years, but it is true that a movement which began at the first settlement of the country has been advancing with constant acceleration and has become a noticeable feature within our time. This movement is the advance in the industrial organization. The first settlement was made by agriculturists, and for a long time there was scarcely any organization. There were scattered farmers, each working for himself, and some small towns with only rudimentary commerce and handicrafts. As the country has filled up, the arts and professions have been differentiated and the industrial organization has been advancing. This fact and its significance has hardly been noticed at all; but the stage of the industrial organization existing at any time, and the rate of advance in its development, are the absolutely controlling social facts. Nine-tenths of the socialistic and semi-socialistic, and sentimental or ethical, suggestions by which we are overwhelmed come from failure to understand the phenomena of the industrial organization and its expansion. It controls us all because we are all in it. It creates the conditions of our existence, sets the limits of our social activity, regulates the bonds of our social relations, determines our conceptions of good and evil, suggests our life-philosophy, molds our inherited political institutions, and reforms the oldest and toughest customs, like marriage and property. I repeat that the turmoil of heterogeneous and antagonistic social whims and speculations in which we live is due to the failure to understand what the industrial organization is and its all-pervading control over human life, while the traditions of our school of philosophy lead us always to approach the industrial organization, not from the side of objective study, but from that of philosophical doctrine. Hence it is that we find that the method of measuring what we see happening by what are called ethical standards, and of proposing to attack the phenomena by methods thence deduced, is so popular.

The advance of a new country from the very simplest social coordination up to the highest organization is a most interesting and instructive chance to study the development of the organization. It has of course been attended all the way along by stricter subordination and higher discipline. All organization implies restriction of liberty. The gain of power is won by narrowing individual range. The methods of business in colonial days were loose and slack to an inconceivable degree. The movement of industry has been all the time toward promptitude, punctuality, and reliability. It has been attended all the way by lamentations about the good old times; about the decline of small industries; about the lost spirit of comradeship between employer and employee; about the narrowing of the interests of the workman; about his conversion into a machine or into a "ware," and about industrial war. These lamentations have all had reference to unquestionable phenomena attendant on advancing organization. In all occupations the same movement is discernible—in the learned professions, in schools, in trade, commerce, and transportation. It is to go on faster than ever, now that the continent is filled up by the first superficial layer of population over its whole extent and the intensification of industry has begun. The great inventions both make the intension of the organization possible and make it inevitable, with all its consequences, whatever they may be. I must expect to be told here, according to the current fashions of thinking, that we ought to control the development of the organization. The first instinct of the modern man is to get a law passed to forbid or prevent what, in his wisdom, he disapproves. A thing which is inevitable, however, is one which we cannot control. We have to make up our minds to it, adjust ourselves to it, and sit down to live with it. Its inevitableness may be disputed, in which case we must reexamine it; but if our analysis is correct, when we reach what is inevitable we reach the end, and our regulations must apply to ourselves, not to the social facts.

Now the intensification of the social organization is what gives us greater social power. It is to it that we owe our increased comfort and abundance. We are none of us ready to sacrifice this. On the contrary, we want more of it. We would not return to the colonial simplicity and the colonial exiguity if we could. If not, then we must pay the price. Our life is bounded on every side by conditions. We can have this if we will agree to submit to that. In the case of industrial power and product the great condition is combination of force under discipline and strict coordination. Hence the wild language about wage-slavery and capitalistic tyranny.

In any state of society no great achievements can be produced without great force. Formerly great force was attainable only by slavery aggregating the power of great numbers of men. Roman civilization was built on this. Ours has been built on steam. It is to be built on electricity. Then we are all forced into an organization around these natural forces and adapted to the methods or their application; and although we indulge in rhetoric about political liberty, nevertheless we find ourselves bound tight in a new set of conditions, which control the modes of our existence and determine the directions in which alone economic and social liberty can go. . . .

Another social function of the first importance in an intense organization is the solution of those crises in the operation of it which are called the conjuncture of the market. It is through the market that the lines of relation run which preserve the system in harmonious and rhythmical operation. The conjuncture is the momentary sharper misadjustment of supply and demand which indicates that a redistribution of productive effort is called for. The industrial organization needs to be insured against these conjunctures, which, if neglected, produce a crisis and catastrophe; and it needs that they shall be anticipated and guarded against as far as skill and foresight can do it. The rewards of this function for the bankers and capitalists who perform it are very great. The captains of industry and the capitalists who operate on the conjuncture, therefore, if they are successful, win, in these days, great fortunes in a short time. There are no earnings which are more legitimate or for which greater services are rendered to the whole industrial body. The popular notions about this matter really assume that all the wealth accumulated by these classes of persons would be here just the same if they had not existed. They are supposed to have appropriated it out of the common stock. This is so far from being true that, on the contrary, their own wealth would not be but for themselves; and besides that, millions more of wealth, many-fold greater than their own, scattered in the hands of thousands, would not exist but for them. . . .

But it is repeated until it has become a commonplace which people are afraid to question, that there is some social danger in the possession of large amounts of wealth by individuals. I ask, Why? I heard a lecture two years ago by a man who holds perhaps the first chair of political economy in the world. He said, among other things, that there was great danger in our day from great accumulations; that this danger ought to be met by taxation, and he referred to the fortune of the Rothschilds and to the great fortunes made in America to prove his point. He omitted, however, to state in what the danger consisted or to specify what harm has ever been done by the Rothschild fortunes or by the great fortunes accumulated in America. It seemed to me that the assertions he was making, and the measures he was recommending, ex-cathedra, were very serious to be thrown out so recklessly. It is hardly to be expected that novelists, popular magazinists, amateur economists, and politicians will be more responsible. It would be easy, however, to show what good is done by accumulations of capital in a few hands—that is, under close and direct management, permitting prompt and accurate application; also to tell what harm is done by loose and unfounded denunciations of any social component or any social group. . . .

Great figures are set out as to the magnitude of certain fortunes and the proportionate amount of the national wealth held by a fraction of the population, and eloquent exclamation-points are set against them. If the figures were beyond criticism, what would they prove? Where is the rich man who is oppressing anybody? If there was one, the newspapers would ring with it. The facts about the accumulation of wealth do not constitute a plutocracy, as I will show below. Wealth, in itself considered, is only power, like steam, or electricity, or knowledge. The question of its good or ill turns on the question how it will be used. To prove any harm in aggregations of wealth it must be shown that great wealth is, as a rule, in the ordinary course of social affairs, put to a mischievous use. This cannot be shown beyond the very slightest degree, if at all. . . .

Assuming, however, that the charges against the existing "capitalistic"—that is, industrial—order of things are established, it is proposed to remedy the ill by reconstructing the industrial system on the principles of democracy. Once more we must untangle the snarl of half ideas and muddled facts.

Democracy is, of course, a word to conjure with. We have a democratic-republican political system, and we like it so well that we are prone to take any new step which can be recommended as "democratic" or which will round out some "principle" of democracy to a fuller fulfillment. Everything connected with this domain of political thought is crusted over with false historical traditions, cheap philosophy, and undefined terms, but it is useless to try to criticize it. The whole drift of the world for five hundred years has been toward democracy. That drift, produced by great discoveries and inventions, and by the discovery of a new continent, has raised the middle class out of the servile class. In alliance with the crown they crushed the feudal classes. They made the crown absolute in order to do it. Then they turned against the crown and, with the aid of the handicraftsmen and peasants, conquered it. Now the next conflict which must inevitably come is that between the middle capitalist class and the proletariat, as the word has come to be used. If a certain construction is put on this conflict, it may be called that between democracy and plutocracy, for it seems that industrialism must be developed into plutocracy by the conflict itself. That is the conflict which stands before civilized society to-day. All the signs of the times indicate its commencement, and it is big with fate to mankind and to civilization.

Although we cannot criticize democracy profitably, it may be said of it, with reference to our present subject, that up to this time democracy never has done anything, either in politics, social affairs, or industry, to prove its power to bless mankind. If we confine our attention to the United States, there are three difficulties with regard to its alleged achievements, and they all have the most serious bearing on the proposed democratization of industry.

1. The time during which democracy has been tried in the United States is too short to warrant any inferences. A century or two is a very short time in the life of political institutions, and if the circumstances change rapidly during the period the experiment is vitiated.

2. The greatest question of all about American democracy is whether it is a cause or a consequence. It is popularly assumed to be a cause, and we ascribe to its beneficent action all the political vitality, all the easiness of social relations, all the industrial activity and enterprise which we experience and which we value and enjoy. I submit, however, that, on a more thorough examination of the matter, we shall find that democracy is a consequence. There are economic and sociological causes for our political vitality and vigor, for the ease and elasticity of our social relations, and for our industrial power and success. Those causes have also produced democracy, given it success, and have made its faults and errors innocuous. Indeed, in any true philosophy, it must be held that in the economic forces which control the material prosperity of a population lie the real causes of its political institutions, its social class-adjustments, its industrial prosperity, its moral code, and its world-philosophy. If democracy and the industrial system are both products of the economic conditions which exist, it is plainly absurd to set democracy to defeat those conditions in the control of industry. If, however, it is not true that democracy is a consequence, and I am well aware that very few people believe it, then we must go back to the view that democracy is a cause. That being so, it is difficult to see how democracy, which has had a clear field here in America, is not responsible for the ills which Mr. Bellamy and his comrades in opinion see in our present social state, and it is difficult to see the grounds of asking us to intrust it also with industry. The first and chief proof of success of political measures and systems is that, under them, society advances in health and vigor and that industry develops without causing social disease. If this has not been the case in America, American democracy has not succeeded. Neither is it easy to see how the masses, if they have undertaken to rule, can escape the responsibilities of ruling, especially so far as the consequences affect themselves. If, then, they have brought all this distress upon themselves under the present system, what becomes of the argument for extending the system to a direct and complete control of industry?

3. It is by no means certain that democracy in the United States has not, up to this time, been living on a capital inherited from aristocracy and industrialism. We have no pure democracy. Our democracy is limited

at every turn by institutions which were developed in England in connection with industrialism and aristocracy, and these institutions are of the essence of our system. While our people are passionately democratic in temper and will not tolerate a doctrine that one man is not as good as another, they have common sense enough to know that he is not; and it seems that they love and cling to the conservative institutions quite as strongly as they do to the democratic philosophy. They are, therefore, ruled by men who talk philosophy and govern by the institutions. Now it is open to Mr. Bellamy to say that the reason why democracy in America seems to be open to the charge made in the last paragraph, of responsibility for all the ill which he now finds in our society, is because it has been infected with industrialism (capitalism); but in that case he must widen the scope of his proposition and undertake to purify democracy before turning industry over to it. The socialists generally seem to think that they make their undertakings easier when they widen their scope, and make them easiest when they propose to remake everything; but in truth social tasks increase in difficulty in an enormous ratio as they are widened in scope.

The question, therefore, arises, if it is proposed to reorganize the social system on the principles of American democracy, whether the institutions of industrialism are to be retained. If so, all the virus of capitalism will be retained. It is forgotten, in many schemes of social reformation in which it is proposed to mix what we like with what we do not like, in order to extirpate the latter, that each must undergo a reaction from the other, and that what we like may be extirpated by what we do not like. We may find that instead of democratizing capitalism we have capitalized democracy— that is, have brought in plutocracy. Plutocracy is a political system in which the ruling force is wealth. The denunciation of capital which we hear from all the reformers is the most eloquent proof that the greatest power in the world to-day is capital. They know that it is, and confess it most when they deny it most strenuously. At present the power of capital is social and industrial, and only in a small degree political. . . .

We must not drop the subject of democracy without one word more. The Greeks already had occasion to notice a most serious distinction between two principles of democracy which lie at its roots. Plutarch says that Solon got the archonship in part by promising equality, which some understood of esteem and dignity, others of measure and number. There is one democratic principle which means that each man should be esteemed for his merit and worth, for just what he is, without regard to birth, wealth, rank, or other adventitious circumstances. The other principle is that each one of us ought to be equal to all the others in what he gets and enjoys. The first principle is only partially realizable, but, so far as it goes, it is elevating and socially progressive and profitable. The second is not capable of an intelligible statement. The first is a principle of industrialism. It proceeds from and is intelligible only in a society built on the industrial virtues, free endeavor, security of property, and repression of the baser vices; that is, in a society whose industrial system is built on labor and exchange. The other is only a rule of division for robbers who have to divide plunder or monks who have to divide gifts. If, therefore, we want to democratize industry in the sense of the first principle, we need only perfect what we have now, especially on its political side. If we try to democratize it in the sense of the other principle, we corrupt politics at one stroke; we enter upon an industrial enterprise which will waste capital and bring us all to poverty, and we set loose greed and envy as ruling social passions.

If this poor old world is as bad as they say, one more reflection may check the zeal of the headlong reformer. It is at any rate a tough old world. It has taken its trend and curvature and all its twists and tangles from a long course of formation. All its wry and crooked gnarls and knobs are therefore stiff and stubborn. If we puny men by our arts can do anything at all to straighten them, it will only be by modifying the tendencies of some of the forces at work, so that, after a sufficient time, their action may be changed a little and slowly the lines of movement may be modified. This effort, however, can at most be only slight, and it will take a long time. In the meantime spontaneous forces will be at work, compared with which our efforts are like those of a man trying to deflect a river, and these forces will have changed the whole problem before our interferences have time to make themselves felt. The great stream of time and earthly things will sweep on just the same in spite of us. It bears with it now all the errors and follies of the past, the wreckage of all the philosophies, the fragments of all the civilizations, the wisdom of all the abandoned ethical systems, the debris of all the institutions, and the penalties of all the mistakes. . . . [I]t is the greatest folly of which a man can be capable, to sit down with a slate and pencil to plan out a new social world.

SUGGESTIONS FOR FURTHER READING

Dorothy Ross, *The Origins of American Social Science* (New York: Cambridge University Press, 1991), especially ch. 3; Robert C. Bannister, *Sociology and Scientism: The American Quest for Objectivity, 1880–1940* (Chapel Hill, N. C.: University of North Carolina Press, 1987).

III

❦

THE PHILANTHROPIC IMPULSE: HELPING PEOPLE IN A DEMOCRACY

The private accumulation of surplus wealth during the Gilded Age, along with increased perceptions of poverty and social need, gave rise to diverse views concerning the most appropriate ways to provide charitable relief and humanitarian uplift. Andrew Carnegie (1835–1919), a poor Scottish immigrant who became a dominant figure in the steel industry, gave serious consideration to the obligations of rich people toward the less fortunate. His widely influential views, known as "the gospel of wealth," were based on certain explicit assumptions: that socioeconomic competition and inequality are inevitable; that individualism is desirable and must remain unimpeded; that the rich are wiser than the indigent and can make more prudent decisions for them than the poor could make for themselves; and that indiscriminate charity is foolish.

Jane Addams (1860–1935), a social reformer who came from a prosperous middle-class background, targets the truly poor, whereas Carnegie is really more concerned about cultural and economic uplift for middling Americans. Although both agree that the less privileged must learn to help themselves, Addams is concerned about the implications of a democratic ethos for charity—a connection that does not occur to Carnegie. Whereas he contemplates what to do with wealth, Addams worries more about how to help the needy—tactfully in terms of technique with due sensitivity to considerations of class. Addams wants to provide guidance for social workers, whereas Carnegie wants to articulate a philosophy of trusteeship based on noblesse oblige. He has less confidence than she that the unfortunate can ever make prudent decisions about their own lives.

The Gospel of Wealth

ANDREW CARNEGIE

The problem of our age is the proper administration of wealth, that the ties of brotherhood may still bind together the rich and poor in harmonious relationship. The conditions of human life have not only been changed, but revolutionized, within the past few hundred years. In former days there was little difference between the dwelling, dress, food, and environment of the chief and those of his retainers. The Indians are to-day where civilized man then was. When visiting the Sioux, I was led to the wigwam of the chief. It was like the others in external appearance, and even within the difference was trifling between it and those of the poorest of his braves. The contrast between the palace of the millionaire and the cottage of the laborer with us to-day measures the change which has come with civilization. This change, however, is not to be deplored, but welcomed as highly beneficial. It is well, nay, essential, for the progress of the race that the houses of some should be homes for all that is highest and best in literature and the arts, and for all the refinements of civilization, rather than that none should be so. Much better this great irregularity than universal squalor. Without wealth there can be no Mæcenas. The "good old times" were not good old times. Neither master nor servant was as well situated then as to-day. A relapse to old conditions would be disastrous to both—not the least so to him who serves—and would sweep away civilization with it. But whether the change be for good or ill, it is upon us, beyond our power to alter, and, therefore, to be accepted and made the best of. It is a waste of time to criticize the inevitable. . . .

The price which society pays for the law of competition, like the price it pays for cheap comforts and luxuries, is also great; but the advantages of this law are also greater still than its cost—for it is to this law that we owe our wonderful material development, which brings improved conditions in its train. But, whether the law be benign or not, we must say of it, as we say of the change in the conditions of men to which we have referred: It is here; we cannot evade it; no substitutes for it have been found; and while the law may be sometimes hard for the individual, it is best for the race, because it insures the survival of the fittest in every department. We accept and welcome, therefore, as conditions to which we must accommodate ourselves, great inequality of environment; the concentration of business, industrial and commercial, in the hands of a few; and the law of competition between these, as being not only beneficial, but essential to the future

Andrew Carnegie, "The Gospel of Wealth," ch. 2 in *The Gospel of Wealth and Other Timely Essays* (New York: Century Co., 1901).

progress of the race. Having accepted these, it follows that there must be great scope for the exercise of special ability in the merchant and in the manufacturer who has to conduct affairs upon a great scale. That this talent for organization and management is rare among men is proved by the fact that it invariably secures enormous rewards for its possessor, no matter where or under what laws or conditions. The experienced in affairs always rate the MAN whose services can be obtained as a partner as not only the first consideration, but such as render the question of his capital scarcely worth considering: for able men soon create capital; in the hands of those without the special talent required, capital soon takes wings. Such men become interested in firms or corporations using millions; and, estimating only simple interest to be made upon the capital invested, it is inevitable that their income must exceed their expenditure and that they must, therefore, accumulate wealth. Nor is there any middle ground which such men can occupy, because the great manufacturing or commercial concern which does not earn at least interest upon its capital soon becomes bankrupt. It must either go forward or fall behind; to stand still is impossible. It is a condition essential to its successful operation that it should be thus far profitable, and even that, in addition to interest on capital, it should make profit. It is a law, as certain as any of the others named, that men possessed of this peculiar talent for affairs, under the free play of economic forces must, of necessity, soon be in receipt of more revenue than can be judiciously expended upon themselves; and this law is as beneficial for the race as the others. . . .

We start, then, with a condition of affairs under which the best interests of the race are promoted, but which inevitably gives wealth to the few. Thus far, accepting conditions as they exist, the situation can be surveyed and pronounced good. The question then arises,—and if the foregoing be correct, it is the only question with which we have to deal,— What is the proper mode of administering wealth after the laws upon which civilization is founded have thrown it into the hands of the few? And it is of this great question that I believe I offer the true solution. It will be understood that fortunes are here spoken of, not moderate sums saved by many years of effort, the returns from which are required for the comfortable maintenance and education of families. This is not wealth, but only competence, which it should be the aim of all to acquire, and which it is for the best interests of society should be acquired.

There are but three modes in which surplus wealth can be disposed of. It can be left to the families of the decedents; or it can be bequeathed for public purposes; or, finally, it can be administered by its possessors during their lives. Under the first and second modes most of the wealth of the world that has reached the few has hitherto been applied. Let us in turn consider each of these modes. The first is the most injudicious. In monarchical countries, the estates and the greatest portion of the wealth are left to the first son, that the vanity of the parent may be gratified by the thought that his name and title are to descend unimpaired to succeeding generations. The condition of this class in Europe to-day teaches the failure of such hopes or ambitions. . . .

It is not suggested that men who have failed to educate their sons to earn a livelihood shall cast them adrift in poverty. If any man has seen fit to rear his sons with a view to their living idle lives, or, what is highly commendable, has instilled in them the sentiment that they are in a position to labor for public ends without reference to pecuniary considerations, then, of course, the duty of the parent is to see that such are provided for in moderation. There are instances of millionaires' sons unspoiled by wealth, who, being rich, still perform great services to the community. Such are the very salt of the earth, as valuable as, unfortunately, they are rare. It is not the exception, however, but the rule, that men must regard; and, looking at the usual result of enormous sums conferred upon legatees, the thoughtful man must shortly say, "I would as soon leave to my son a curse as the almighty dollar," and admit to himself that it is not the welfare of the children, but family pride, which inspires these legacies.

As to the second mode, that of leaving wealth at death for public uses, it may be said that this is only a means for the disposal of wealth, provided a man is content to wait until he is dead before he becomes of much good in the world. Knowledge of the results of legacies bequeathed is not calculated to inspire the brightest hopes of much posthumous good being accomplished by them. The cases are not few in which the real object sought by the testator is not attained, nor are they few in which his real wishes are thwarted. In many cases the bequests are so used as to become only monuments of his folly. It is well to remember that it requires the exercise of not less ability than that which acquires it, to use wealth so as to be really beneficial to the community. Besides this, it may fairly be said that no man is to be extolled for doing what he cannot help doing, nor is he to be thanked by the community to which he only leaves wealth at death. Men who leave vast sums in this way may fairly be thought men who would not have left it at all had they been able to take it with them. The memories of such cannot be held in grateful remembrance, for there is no grace in their gifts. It is not to be wondered at that such bequests seem so generally to lack the blessing. . . .

There remains, then, only one mode of using great fortunes; but in this we have the true antidote for the temporary unequal distribution of wealth, the reconciliation of the rich and the poor—a reign of harmony, another ideal, differing, indeed, from that of the Communist in requiring only the further evolution of existing conditions, not the total overthrow of our civilization. It is founded upon the present most intense Individualism, and the race is prepared to put it in practice by degrees whenever it pleases. Under its sway we shall have an ideal State, in which the surplus wealth of the few will become, in the best sense, the property of the many, because administered for the common good; and this wealth, passing through the hands of the few, can be made a much more potent force for the elevation of our race than if distributed in small sums to the people themselves. Even the poorest can be made to see this, and to agree that great sums gathered by some of their fellow-citizens and spent for public purposes, from which the masses reap the principal benefit, are more valuable to them than if scattered among themselves in trifling amounts through the course of many years.

If we consider the results which flow from the Cooper Institute, for instance, to the best portion of the race in New York not possessed of means, and compare these with those which would have ensued for the good of the masses from an equal sum distributed by Mr. Cooper in his lifetime in the form of wages, which is the highest form of distribution, being for work done and not for charity, we can form some estimate of the possibilities for the improvement of the race which lie embedded in the present law of the accumulation of wealth. Much of this sum, if distributed in small quantities among the people, would have been wasted in the indulgence of appetite, some of it in excess, and it may be doubted whether even the part put to the best use, that of adding to the comforts of the home, would have yielded results for the race, as a race, at all comparable to those which are flowing and are to flow from the Cooper Institute from generation to generation. Let the advocate of violent or radical change ponder well this thought. . . .

This, then, is held to be the duty of the man of wealth: To set an example of modest, unostentatious living, shunning display or extravagance; to provide moderately for the legitimate wants of those dependent upon him; and, after doing so, to consider all surplus revenues which come to him simply as trust funds, which he is called upon to administer, and strictly bound as a matter of duty to administer in the manner which, in his judgment, is best calculated to produce the most beneficial results for the community—the man of wealth thus becoming the mere trustee and agent for his poorer brethren, bringing to their service his superior wisdom, experience, and ability to administer, doing for them better than they would or could do for themselves.

We are met here with the difficulty of determining what are moderate sums to leave to members of the family; what is modest, unostentatious living; what is the test of extravagance. There must be different standards for different conditions. The answer is that it is as impossible to name exact amounts or actions as it is to define good manners, good taste, or the rules of propriety; but, nevertheless, these are verities, well known, although indefinable. Public sentiment is quick to know and to feel what offends these. So in the case of wealth. The rule in regard to good taste in dress of men or women applies here. Whatever makes one conspicuous offends the canon. If any family be chiefly known for display, for extravagance in home, table, or equipage, for enormous sums ostentatiously spent in any form upon itself—if these be its chief distinctions, we have no difficulty in estimating its nature or culture. So likewise in regard to the use or abuse of its surplus wealth, or to generous, free-handed cooperation in good public uses, or to unabated efforts to accumulate and hoard to the last, or whether they administer or bequeath. The verdict rests with the best and most enlightened public sentiment. The community will surely judge, and its judgments will not often be wrong.

The best uses to which surplus wealth can be put have already been indicated. Those who would administer wisely must, indeed, be wise; for one of the serious obstacles to the improvement of our race is indiscriminate charity. It were better for mankind that the millions of the rich were thrown into the sea than so spent as to encourage the slothful, the drunken, the unworthy. Of every thousand dollars spent in so-called charity to-day, it is probable that nine hundred and fifty dollars is unwisely spent—so spent, indeed, as to produce the very evils which it hopes to mitigate or cure. A well-known writer of philosophic books admitted the other day that he had given a quarter of a dollar to a man who approached him as he was coming to visit the house of his friend. He knew nothing of the habits of this beggar, knew not the use that would be made of this money, although he had every reason to suspect that it would be spent improperly. This man professed to be a disciple of Herbert Spencer; yet the quarter-dollar given that night will probably work more injury than all the money will do good which its thoughtless donor will ever be able to give in true charity. He only gratified his own feelings, saved himself from annoyance—and this was probably one of the most selfish and very worst actions of his life, for in all respects he is most worthy.

In bestowing charity, the main consideration should be to help those who will help themselves; to provide part of the means by which those who desire to improve may do so; to give those who desire to rise the aids by which they may rise; to assist, but rarely or never to do all. Neither the individual nor the race is improved by almsgiving. Those worthy of assistance, except in rare cases, seldom require assistance. The really valuable men of the race never do, except in case of accident or sudden change. Every one has, of course, cases of individuals brought to his own knowledge where temporary assistance can do genuine good, and these he will not overlook. But the amount which can be wisely given by the individual for individuals is necessarily limited by his lack of knowledge of the circumstances connected with each. He is the only true reformer who is as careful and as anxious not to aid the unworthy as he is to aid the worthy, and, perhaps, even more so, for in almsgiving more injury is probably done by rewarding vice than by relieving virtue.

The rich man is thus almost restricted to following the examples of Peter Cooper, Enoch Pratt of Baltimore, Mr. Pratt of Brooklyn, Senator Stanford, and others, who know that the best means of benefiting the community is to place within its reach the ladders upon which the aspiring can rise—free libraries, parks, and means of recreation, by which men are helped in body and mind; works of art, certain to give pleasure and improve the public taste; and public institutions of various kinds, which will improve the general conditon of the people; in this manner returning their surplus wealth to the mass of their fellows in the forms best calculated to do them lasting good.

Thus is the problem of rich and poor to be solved. The laws of accumulation will be left free, the laws of distribution free. Individualism will continue, but the millionaire will be but a trustee of the poor, entrusted for a season with a great part of the increased wealth of the community, but administering it for the community far better than it could or would have done for itself. The best minds will thus have reached a stage in the development of the race in which it is clearly seen that there is no mode of disposing of surplus wealth creditable to thoughtful and earnest men into whose hands it flows, save by using it year by year for the general good. This day already dawns. Men may die without incurring the pity of their fellows, still sharers in great business enterprises from which their capital cannot be or has not been withdrawn, and which is left chiefly at death for public uses; yet the day is not far distant when the man who dies leaving behind him millions of available wealth, which was free to him to administer during life, will pass away "unwept, unhonored, and unsung," no matter to what uses he leaves the dross which he cannot take with him. Of such as these the public verdict will then be: "The man who dies thus rich dies disgraced."

Such, in my opinion is the true gospel concerning wealth, obedience to which is destined some day to solve the problem of the rich and the poor, and to bring "Peace on earth, among men good will."

Charitable Effort

JANE ADDAMS

. . . Probably there is no relation in life which our democracy is changing more rapidly than the charitable relation—that relation which obtains between benefactor and beneficiary; at the same time there is no point of contact in our modern experience which reveals so clearly the lack of that equality which democracy implies. We have reached the moment when

Jane Addams, "Charitable Effort," ch. 2 in *Democracy and Social Ethics* (New York: Macmillan Co., 1902).

when democracy has made such inroads upon this relationship, that the complacency of the old-fashioned charitable man is gone forever; while, at the same time, the very need and existence of charity, denies us the consolation and freedom which democracy will at last give.

It is quite obvious that the ethics of none of us are clearly defined, and we are continually obliged to act in circles of habit, based upon convictions which we no longer hold. Thus our estimate of the effect of environment and social conditions has doubtless shifted faster than our methods of administrating charity have changed. Formerly when it was believed that poverty was synonymous with vice and laziness, and that the prosperous man was the righteous man charity was administered harshly with a good conscience; for the charitable agent really blamed the individual for his poverty, and the very fact of his own superior prosperity gave him a certain consciousness of superior morality. We have learned since that time to measure by other standards, and have ceased to accord to the money-earning capacity exclusive respect; while it is still rewarded out of all proportion to any other, its possession is by no means assumed to imply the possession of the highest moral qualities. We have learned to judge men by their social virtues as well as by their business capacity, by their devotion to intellectual and disinterested aims, and by their public spirit, and we naturally resent being obliged to judge poor people so solely upon the industrial side. Our democratic instinct instantly takes alarm. It is largely in this modern tendency to judge all men by one democratic standard, while the old charitable attitude commonly allowed the use of two standards, that much of the difficulty adheres. We know that unceasing bodily toil becomes wearing and brutalizing, and our position is totally untenable if we judge large numbers of our fellows solely upon their success in maintaining it. . . .

The only families who apply for aid to the charitable agencies are those who have come to grief on the industrial side; it may be through sickness, through loss of work, or for other guiltless and inevitable reasons; but the fact remains that they are industrially ailing, and must be bolstered and helped into industrial health. The charity visitor, let us assume, is a young college woman, well-bred and open-minded; when she visits the family assigned to her, she is often embarrassed to find herself obliged to lay all the stress of her teaching and advice upon the industrial virtues, and to treat the members of the family almost exclusively as factors in the industrial system. She insists that they must work and be self-supporting, that the most dangerous of all situations is idleness, that seeking one's own pleasure, while ignoring claims and responsibilities, is the most ignoble of actions. The members of her assigned family may have other charms and virtues—they may possibly be kind and considerate of each other, generous to their friends, but it is her business to stick to the industrial side. As she daily holds up these standards, it often occurs to the mind of the sensitive visitor, whose conscience has been made tender by much talk of brotherhood and equality, that she has no right to say these things; that her untrained hands are no more fitted to cope with actual conditions than those of her broken-down family.

The grandmother of the charity visitor could have done the industrial preaching very well, because she did have the industrial virtues and housewifely training. In a generation our experiences have changed, and our views with them; but we still keep on in the old methods, which could be applied when our consciences were in line with them, but which are daily becoming more difficult as we divide up into people who work with their hands and those who do not. The charity visitor belonging to the latter class is perplexed by recognitions and suggestions which the situation forces upon her. Our democracy has taught us to apply our moral teaching all around, and the moralist is rapidly becoming so sensitive that when his life does not exemplify his ethical convictions, he finds it difficult to preach.

Added to this is a consciousness, in the mind of the visitor, of a genuine misunderstanding of her motives by the recipients of her charity, and by their neighbors. Let us take a neighborhood of poor people, and test their ethical standards by those of the charity visitor, who comes with the best desire in the world to help them out of their distress. A most striking incongruity, at once apparent, is the difference between the emotional kindness with which relief is given by one poor neighbor to another poor neighbor, and the guarded care with which relief is given by a charity visitor to a charity recipient. The neighborhood mind is at once confronted not only by the difference of method, but by an absolute clashing of two ethical standards. . . .

The evolutionists tell us that the instinct to pity, the impulse to aid his fellows, served man at a very early period, as a rude rule of right and wrong. There is no doubt that this rude rule still holds among many people with whom charitable agencies are brought into contact, and that their ideas of right and wrong are quite honestly outraged by the methods of these agencies. When they see the delay and caution with which relief is given, it does not appear to them a conscientious scruple, but as the cold and calculating action of a selfish man. It is not the aid that they are accustomed to receive from their neighbors, and they do not understand why the impulse which drives people to "be good to the poor" should be so severely supervised. They feel, remotely, that the charity visitor is moved by motives that are alien and unreal. They may be superior motives, but they are different, and they are "agin nature." They cannot comprehend why a person whose intellectual perceptions are stronger than his natural impulses, should go into charity work at all. The only man they are accustomed to see whose intellectual perceptions are stronger than his tenderness of heart, is the selfish and avaricious man who is frankly "on the make." If the charity visitor is such a person, why does she pretend to like the poor? Why does she not go into business at once? . . .

We may say, of course, that it is a primitive view of life, which thus confuses intellectuality and business ability; but it is a view quite honestly held by many poor people who are obliged to receive charity from time to time. In moments of indignation the poor have been known to say: "What do you want, anyway? If you have nothing to give us, why not let us alone and stop your questionings and investigations?" "They investigated me for three weeks, and in the end gave me nothing but a black character," a little woman has been heard to assert. This indignation, which is for the most part taciturn, and a certain kindly contempt for her abilities, often puzzles the charity visitor. The latter may be explained by the standard of worldly success which the visited families hold. Success does not ordinarily go, in the minds of the poor, with charity and kindheartedness, but rather with the opposite qualities. The rich landlord is he who collects with sternness, who accepts no excuse, and will have his own. There are moments of irritation and of real bitterness against him, but there is still admiration, because he is rich and successful. The good-natured landlord, he who pities and spares his poverty-pressed tenants, is seldom rich. He often lives in the back of his house, which he has owned for a long time, perhaps has inherited; but he has been able to accumulate little. He commands the genuine love and devotion of many a poor soul, but he is treated with a certain lack of respect. In one sense he is a failure. The charity visitor, just because she is a person who concerns herself with the poor, receives a certain amount of this good-natured and kindly contempt, sometimes real affection, but little genuine respect. The poor are accustomed to help each other and to respond according to their kindliness; but when it comes to worldly judgment, they use industrial success as the sole standard. In the case of the charity visitor who has neither natural kindness nor dazzling riches, they are deprived of both standards, and they find it of course utterly impossible to judge of the motive of organized charity.

Even those of us who feel most sorely the need of more order in altruistic effort and see the end to be desired, find something distasteful in the juxtaposition of the words "organized" and "charity." We say in defense that we are striving to turn this emotion into a motive, that pity is capricious, and not to be depended on; that we mean to give it the dignity of conscious duty. But at bottom we distrust a little a scheme which substitutes a theory of social conduct for the natural promptings of the heart, even although we appreciate the complexity of the situation. . . .

The visitor says, sometimes, that in holding her poor family so hard to a standard of thrift she is really breaking down a rule of higher living which they formerly possessed; that saving, which seems quite commendable in a comfortable part of town, appears almost criminal in a poorer quarter where the next-door neighbor needs food, even if the children of the family do not.

She feels the sordidness of constantly being obliged to urge the industrial view of life. The benevolent individual of fifty years ago honestly believed that industry and self-denial in youth would result in comfortable possessions for old age. It was, indeed, the method he had practiced in his own youth, and by which he had probably obtained whatever fortune he possessed. He therefore reproved the poor family for indulging their children, urged them to work long hours, and was utterly untouched by many scruples which afflict the contemporary charity visitor. She says sometimes, "Why must I talk always of getting work and saving money, the things I know nothing about? . . ." But she finds it difficult to connect the experiences of her youth with the experiences of the visited family.

Because of this diversity in experience, the visitor is continually surprised to find that the safest platitude may be challenged. She refers quite naturally to the "horrors of the saloon," and discovers that the head of her visited family does not connect them with "horrors" at all. He remembers all the kindnesses he has received there, the free lunch and treating which goes on, even when a man is out of work and not able to pay up; the loan of five dollars he got there when the charity visitor was miles away and he was threatened with eviction. He may listen politely to her reference to "horrors," but considers it only "temperance talk." . . .

The charity visitor finds herself still more perplexed when she comes to consider such problems as those of early marriage and child labor; for she cannot deal with them according to economic theories, or according to the conventions which have regulated her own life. She finds both of these fairly upset by her intimate knowledge of the situation, and her sympathy for those into whose lives she has gained a curious insight. She discovers how incorrigibly bourgeois her standards have been, and it takes but a little time to reach the conclusion that she cannot insist so strenuously upon the conventions of her own class, which fail to fit the bigger, more emotional, and freer lives of working people. The charity visitor holds well-grounded views upon the imprudence of early marriages, quite naturally because she comes from a family and circle of professional and business people. . . .

The sense of prudence, the necessity for saving, can never come to a primitive, emotional man with the force of a conviction; but the necessity of providing for his children is a powerful incentive. He naturally regards his children as his savings-bank; he expects them to care for him when he gets old, and in some trades old age comes very early. . . .

The struggle for existence, which is so much harsher among people near the edge of pauperism, sometimes leaves ugly marks on character, and the charity visitor finds these indirect results most mystifying. Parents who work hard and anticipate an old age when they can no longer earn, take care that their children shall expect to divide their wages with them from the very first. Such a parent, when successful, impresses the immature nervous system of the child thus tyrannically establishing habits of obedience, so that the nerves and will may not depart from this control when the child is older. The charity visitor, whose family relation is lifted quite out of this, does not in the least understand the industrial foundation for this family tyranny. . . .

The young charity visitor who goes from a family living upon a most precarious industrial level to her own home in a prosperous part of the city, if she is sensitive at all, is never free from perplexities which our growing democracy forces upon her. . . .

We are singularly slow to apply this evolutionary principle to human affairs in general, although it is fast being applied to the education of children. We are at last learning to follow the development of the child; to expect certain traits under certain conditions; to adapt methods and matter to his growing mind. No "advanced educator" can allow himself to be so absorbed in the question of what a child ought to be as to exclude the discovery of what he is. But in our charitable efforts we think much more of what a man ought to be than of what he is or of what he may become; and we ruthlessly force our conventions and standards upon him, with a sternness which we would consider stupid indeed did an educator use it in forcing his mature intellectual convictions upon an undeveloped mind.

SUGGESTIONS FOR FURTHER READING

Joseph F. Wall, *Andrew Carnegie* (New York: Oxford University Press, 1970); Allen F. Davis, *The Life and Legend of Jane Addams* (New York: Oxford University Press, 1973); Edward Chase Kirkland, *Dream and Thought in the Business Community, 1860–1900* (Ithaca, N.Y.: Cornell University Press, 1956).

IV

⚬➤⚬

WHAT ROLE FOR THE NEGRO IN AMERICAN SOCIETY?

Booker T. Washington (1856–1915) was the son of a slave mother and a white father. Educated at the Hampton Institute in Virginia, he was appointed in 1881 to head a new Negro "normal school" at Tuskegee, Alabama, a school supported mainly by funds raised in the North. During the thirty-four years of his leadership, the school increased in size to 200 faculty and 1,500 students. Following his famous address at the opening of the Atlanta Exposition in 1895, Washington swiftly became the best known African-American leader in the United States.

Because of his prominence and moderate tone in race relations, Washington advised Presidents Theodore Roosevelt and William Howard Taft on various matters related to race and patronage. He also influenced the donations of Andrew Carnegie, John D. Rockefeller, and other wealthy whites to black schools and enterprises.

Washington urged Negroes to press for vocational education and economic opportunity rather than political rights and social equality. Because he believed that harmonious race relations were paramount, he did not want whites to perceive blacks as aggressive or threatening. Although many observers at the time considered his strategy to be the best hope for the Negro, North and South, it was attacked by various black leaders, most notably W. E. B. Du Bois (1868–1963).

Educated at Fisk and Harvard universities (Ph.D. in History, 1895), Du Bois taught sociology, economics, and history at Atlanta University. His book, The Philadelphia Negro *(1899), was a pioneering study of an urban black community. Active in the early civil rights movement, in 1909 Du Bois was a founding member of the National Association for the Advancement of Colored People. He would also be active in the Pan-African movement and wrote many other books and essays, including* The Souls of Black Folk *(1903),* Black Reconstruction *(1935), and* The World and Africa *(1947).*

The Atlanta Exposition Address

BOOKER T. WASHINGTON

Mr. President and Gentlemen of the Board of Directors and Citizens:

One-third of the population of the South is of the Negro race. No enterprise seeking the material, civil, or moral welfare of this section can disregard this element of our population and reach the highest success. I but convey to you, Mr. President and Directors, the sentiment of the masses of my race when I say that in no way have the value and manhood of the American Negro been more fittingly and generously recognized than by the managers of this magnificent Exposition at every stage of its progress. It is a recognition that will do more to cement the friendship of the two races than any occurrence since the dawn of our freedom.

Not only this, but the opportunity here afforded will awaken among us a new era of industrial progress. Ignorant and inexperienced, it is not strange that in the first years of our new life we began at the top instead of at the bottom; that a seat in Congress or the state legislature was more sought than real estate or industrial skill; that the political convention or stump speaking had more attractions than starting a dairy farm or truck garden. . . .

To those of my race who depend on bettering their condition in a foreign land or who underestimate the importance of cultivating friendly relations with the Southern white man, who is their next-door neighbor, I would say: "Cast down your bucket where you are"—cast it down in making friends in every manly way of the people of all races by whom we are surrounded.

Cast it down in agriculture, mechanics, in commerce, in domestic service, and in the professions. And in this connection it is well to bear in mind that whatever other sins the South may be called to bear, when it comes to business, pure and simple, it is in the South that the Negro is given a man's chance in the commercial world, and in nothing is this Exposition more eloquent than in emphasizing this chance. Our greatest danger is that in the great leap from slavery to freedom we may overlook the fact that the masses of us are to live by the productions of our hands, and fail to keep in mind that we shall prosper in proportion as we learn to dignify and glorify common labor and put brains and skill into the common occupations of life; shall prosper in proportion as we learn to draw the line between the superficial and the substantial, the ornamental gewgaws of life and the useful. No race can prosper till it learns that there is as much

Booker T. Washington, "The Atlanta Exposition Address," ch. 14 in *Up from Slavery: An Autobiography* (New York: Doubleday, Page & Co., 1901), pp. 217–27.

dignity in tilling a field as in writing a poem. It is at the bottom of life we must begin, and not at the top. Nor should we permit our grievances to overshadow our opportunities.

To those of the white race who look to the incoming of those of foreign birth and strange tongue and habits for the prosperity of the South, were I permitted I would repeat what I say to my own race, "Cast down your bucket where you are." Cast it down among the eight millions of Negroes whose habits you know, whose fidelity and love you have tested in days when to have proved treacherous meant the ruin of your firesides. Cast down your bucket among these people who have, without strikes and labor wars, tilled your fields, cleared your forests, builded your railroads and cities, and brought forth treasures from the bowels of the earth, and helped make possible this magnificent representation of the progress of the South. Casting down your bucket among my people, helping and encouraging them as you are doing on these grounds, and to education of head, hand, and heart, you will find that they will buy your surplus land, make blossom the waste places in your fields, and run your factories. While doing this, you can be sure in the future, as in the past, that you and your families will be surrounded by the most patient, faithful, law-abiding, and unresentful people that the world has seen. As we have proved our loyalty to you in the past, in nursing your children, watching by the sick-bed of your mothers and fathers, and often following them with tear-dimmed eyes to their graves, so in the future, in our humble way, we shall stand by you with a devotion that no foreigner can approach, ready to lay down our lives, if need be, in defense of yours, interlacing our industrial, commercial, civil, and religious life with yours in a way that shall make the interests of both races one. In all things that are purely social we can be as separate as the fingers, yet one as the hand in all things essential to mutual progress.

There is no defense or security for any of us except in the highest intelligence and development of all. If anywhere there are efforts tending to curtail the fullest growth of the Negro, let these efforts be turned into stimulating, encouraging, and making him the most useful and intelligent citizen. Effort or means so invested will pay a thousand per cent interest. These efforts will be twice blessed—"blessing him that gives and him that takes." . . .

Gentlemen of the Exposition, as we present to you our humble effort at an exhibition of our progress, you must not expect overmuch. Starting thirty years ago with ownership here and there in a few quilts and pumpkins and chickens (gathered from miscellaneous sources), remember the path that has led from these to the inventions and production of agricultural implements, buggies, steam-engines, newspapers, books, statuary, carving, paintings, the management of drug-stores and banks, has not been trodden without contact with thorns and thistles. While we take pride in what we exhibit as a result of our independent efforts, we do not for a moment forget that our part in this exhibition would fall far short of your expectations but for the constant help that has come to our educational life, not only from the Southern states, but especially from Northern philanthropists, who have made their gifts a constant stream of blessing and encouragement.

The wisest among my race understand that the agitation of questions of social equality is the extremest folly, and that progress in the enjoyment of all the privileges that will come to us must be the result of severe and constant struggle rather than of artificial forcing. No race that has anything to contribute to the markets of the world is long in any degree ostracized. It is important and right that all privileges of the law be ours, but it is vastly more important that we be prepared for the exercises of these privileges. The opportunity to earn a dollar in a factory just now is worth infinitely more than the opportunity to spend a dollar in an opera-house.

In conclusion, may I repeat that nothing in thirty years has given us more hope and encouragement, and drawn us so near to you of the white race, as this opportunity offered by the Exposition; and here bending, as it were, over the altar that represents the results of the struggles of your race and mine, both starting practically empty-handed three decades ago, I pledge that in your effort to work out the great and intricate problem which God has laid at the doors of the South, you shall have at all times the patient, sympathetic help of my race; only let this be constantly in mind, that, while from representations in these buildings of the product of field, of forest, of mine, of factory, letters, and art, much good will come, yet far above and beyond material benefits will be that higher good, that, let us pray God, will come, in a blotting out of sectional differences and racial animosities and suspicions, in a determination to administer absolute justice, in a willing obedience among all classes to the mandates of law. This, this, coupled with our material prosperity, will bring into our beloved South a new heaven and a new earth.

The first thing that I remember, after I had finished speaking, was that Governor Bullock rushed across the platform and took me by the hand, and that others did the same. I received so many and such hearty congratulations that I found it difficult to get out of the building. I did not appreciate to any degree, however, the impression which my address seemed to have made, until the next morning, when I went into the business part of the city. As soon as I was recognized, I was surprised to find myself pointed out and surrounded by a crowd of men who wished to shake hands with me. This was kept up on every street on to which I went, to an extent which embarrassed me so much that I went back to my boarding-place. The next morning I returned to Tuskegee. At the station in Atlanta, and at almost all of the stations at which the train stopped between that city and Tuskegee, I found a crowd of people anxious to shake hands with me.

The papers in all parts of the United States published the address in full, and for months afterward there were complimentary editorial references to it. . . .

I very soon began receiving all kinds of propositions from lecture bureaus, and editors of magazines and papers, to take the lecture platform, and to write articles. One lecture bureau offered me fifty thousand dollars, or two hundred dollars a night and expenses, if I would place my services at its disposal for a given period. To all these communications I replied that my life-work was at Tuskegee; and that whenever I spoke it must be in the interests of the Tuskegee school and my race, and that I would enter into no arrangements that seemed to place a mere commercial value upon my services.

Some days after its delivery I sent a copy of my address to the President of the United States, the Hon. Grover Cleveland. I received from him the following autograph reply:—

Gray Gables, Buzzard's Bay, Mass.,
October 6, 1895.

Booker T. Washington, Esq.:

My Dear Sir: I thank you for sending me a copy of your address delivered at the Atlanta Exposition.

I thank you with much enthusiasm for making the address. I have read it with intense interest, and I think the Exposition would be fully justified if it did not do more than furnish the opportunity for its delivery. Your words cannot fail to delight and encourage all who wish well for your race; and if our colored fellow-citizens do not from your utterances gather new hope and form new determinations to gain every valuable advantage offered them by their citizenship, it will be strange indeed.

Yours very truly,
Grover Cleveland.

Of Mr. Booker T. Washington and Others

W. E. B. Du BOIS

Easily the most striking thing in the history of the American Negro since 1876 is the ascendancy of Mr. Booker T. Washington. It began at the time when war memories and ideals were rapidly passing; a day of astonishing commercial development was dawning; a sense of doubt and hesitation overtook the freedmen's sons,—then it was that his leading began. Mr. Washington came, with a simple definite program, at the psychological moment when the nation was a little ashamed of having bestowed so much sentiment on Negroes, and was concentrating its energies on Dollars. His program of industrial education, conciliation of the South, and submission and silence as to civil and political rights, was not wholly original; the Free Negroes from 1830 up to war-time had striven to build industrial schools, and the American Missionary Association had from the first taught various trades; and Price and others had sought a way of honorable alliance with the best of the Southerners. But Mr. Washington first indissolubly linked these things; he put enthusiasm, unlimited energy, and perfect faith into this program, and changed it from a by-path into a veritable Way of Life. And the tale of the methods by which he did this is a fascinating study of human life.

It startled the nation to hear a Negro advocating such a program after many decades of bitter complaint; it startled and won the applause of the South, it interested and won the admiration of the North; and after a confused murmur of protest, it silenced if it did not convert the Negroes themselves.

To gain the sympathy and cooperation of the various elements comprising the white South was Mr. Washington's first task; and this, at the time Tuskegee was founded, seemed, for a black man, well-nigh impossible. And yet ten years later it was done in the words spoken at Atlanta: "In all things purely social we can be as separate as the five fingers, and yet one as the hand in all things essential to mutual progress." This "Atlanta Compromise" is by all odds the most notable thing in Mr. Washington's career. The South interpreted it in different ways: the radicals received it as a complete surrender of the demand for civil and political equality; the conservatives, as a generously conceived working basis for mutual understanding. So both approved it, and to-day its author is certainly the

---

W. E. B. Du Bois, "Of Mr. Booker T. Washington and Others," ch. 3 in *The Souls of Black Folk: Essays and Sketches* (Chicago: A. C. McClurg & Co., 1903), pp. 41–59.

most distinguished Southerner since Jefferson Davis, and the one with the largest personal following.

Next to this achievement comes Mr. Washington's work in gaining place and consideration in the North. Others less shrewd and tactful had formerly essayed to sit on these two stools and had fallen between them; but as Mr. Washington knew the heart of the South from birth and training, so by singular insight he intuitively grasped the spirit of the age which was dominating the North. . . .

. . . This very singleness of vision and thorough oneness with his age is a mark of the successful man. It is as though Nature must needs make men narrow in order to give them force. So Mr. Washington's cult has gained unquestioning followers, his work has wonderfully prospered, his friends are legion, and his enemies are confounded. To-day he stands as the one recognized spokesman of his ten million fellows, and one of the most notable figures in a nation of seventy millions. One hesitates, therefore, to criticize a life which, beginning with so little, has done so much. And yet the time is come when one may speak in all sincerity and utter courtesy of the mistakes and shortcomings of Mr. Washington's career, as well as of his triumphs, without being thought captious or envious, and without forgetting that it is easier to do ill than well in the world. . . .

Among his own people, however, Mr. Washington has encountered the strongest and most lasting opposition, amounting at times to bitterness, and even to-day continuing strong and insistent even though largely silenced in outward expression by the public opinion of the nation. Some of this opposition is, of course, mere envy; the disappointment of displaced demagogues and the spite of narrow minds. But aside from this, there is among educated and thoughtful colored men in all parts of the land a feeling of deep regret, sorrow, and apprehension at the wide currency and ascendancy which some of Mr. Washington's theories have gained. These same men admire his sincerity of purpose, and are willing to forgive much to honest endeavor which is doing something worth the doing. They cooperate with Mr. Washington as far as they conscientiously can; and, indeed, it is no ordinary tribute to this man's tact and power that, steering as he must between so many diverse interests and opinions, he so largely retains the respect of all.

But the hushing of the criticism of honest opponents is a dangerous thing. It leads some of the best of the critics to unfortunate silence and paralysis of effort, and others to burst into speech so passionately and intemperately as to lose listeners. Honest and earnest criticism from those whose interests are most nearly touched,—criticism of writers by readers, of government by those governed, of leaders by those led,—this is the soul of democracy and the safeguard of modern society. If the best of the American Negroes receive by outer pressure a leader whom they had not recognized before, manifestly there is here a certain palpable gain. Yet there is also irreparable loss,—a loss of that peculiarly valuable education which a group receives when by search and criticism it finds and commissions its own leaders. The way in which this is done is at once the most elementary and the nicest problem of social growth. History is but the record of such group-leadership; and yet how infinitely changeful is its type and character! And of all types and kinds, what can be more instructive than the leadership of a group within a group?—that curious double movement where real progress may be negative and actual advance be relative retrogression. All this is the social student's inspiration and despair. . . .

. . . Booker T. Washington arose as essentially the leader not of one race but of two,—a compromiser between the South, the North, and the Negro. Naturally the Negroes resented, at first bitterly, signs of compromise which surrendered their civil and political rights, even though this was to be exchanged for larger chances of economic development. The rich and dominating North, however, was not only weary of the race problem, but was investing largely in Southern enterprises, and welcomed any method of peaceful cooperation. Thus, by national opinion, the Negroes began to recognize Mr. Washington's leadership; and the voice of criticism was hushed.

Mr. Washington represents in Negro thought the old attitude of adjustment and submission; but adjustment at such a peculiar time as to make his program unique. This is an age of unusual economic development, and Mr. Washington's program naturally takes an economic cast, becoming a gospel of Work and Money to such an extent as apparently almost completely to overshadow the higher aims of life. Moreover, this is an age when the more advanced races are coming in closer contact with the less developed races, and the race-feeling is therefore intensified; and Mr. Washington's program practically accepts the alleged inferiority of the Negro races. Again, in our own land, the reaction from the sentiment of war time has given impetus to race-prejudice against Negroes, and Mr. Washington withdraws many of the high demands of Negroes as men and American citizens. In other periods of intensified prejudice all the Negro's tendency to self-assertion has been called forth; at this period a policy of submission is advocated. In the history of nearly all other races and peoples the doctrine preached at such crises has been that manly self-respect is worth more than lands and houses, and that a people who voluntarily surrender such respect, or cease striving for it, are not worth civilizing.

In answer to this, it has been claimed that the Negro can survive only through submission. Mr. Washington distinctly asks that black people give up, at least for the present, three things,—

First, political power,

Second, insistence on civil rights,

Third, higher education of Negro youth,—

and concentrate all their energies on industrial education, the accumulation of wealth, and the conciliation of the South. This policy has been courageously and insistently advocated for over fifteen years, and has been triumphant for perhaps ten years. As a result of this tender of the palm-branch, what has been the return? In these years there have occurred:

1. The disfranchisement of the Negro.
2. The legal creation of a distinct status of civil inferiority for the Negro.
3. The steady withdrawal of aid from institutions for the higher training of the Negro.

These movements are not, to be sure, direct results of Mr. Washington's teachings; but his propaganda has, without a shadow of doubt, helped their speedier accomplishment. The question then comes: Is it possible, and probable, that nine millions of men can make effective progress in economic lines if they are deprived of political rights, made a servile caste, and allowed only the most meager chance for developing their exceptional men? If history and reason give any distinct answer to these questions, it is an emphatic *No*. And Mr. Washington thus faces the triple paradox of his career:

1. He is striving nobly to make Negro artisans business men and property-owners; but it is utterly impossible, under modern competitive methods, for workingmen and property-owners to defend their rights and exist without the right of suffrage.
2. He insists on thrift and self-respect, but at the same time counsels a silent submission to civic inferiority such as is bound to sap the manhood of any race in the long run.
3. He advocates common-school and industrial training, and depreciates institutions of higher learning; but neither the Negro common-schools, nor Tuskegee itself, could remain open a day were it not for teachers trained in Negro colleges, or trained by their graduates.

This triple paradox in Mr. Washington's position is the object of criticism by two classes of colored Americans. One class is spiritually descended from Toussaint the Savior, through Gabriel, Vesey, and Turner, and they represent the attitude of revolt and revenge; they hate the white South blindly and distrust the white race generally, and so far as they agree on definite action, think that the Negro's only hope lies in emigration beyond the borders of the United States. And yet, by the irony of fate, nothing has more effectually made this program seem hopeless than the recent course of the United States toward weaker and darker peoples in the West Indies, Hawaii, and the Philippines,—for where in the world may we go and be safe from lying and brute force?

The other class of Negroes who cannot agree with Mr. Washington has hitherto said little aloud. They deprecate the sight of scattered counsels, of internal disagreement; and especially they dislike making their just criticism of a useful and earnest man an excuse for a general discharge of venom from small-minded opponents. Nevertheless, the questions involved are so fundamental and serious that it is difficult to see how men like the Grimkes, Kelly Miller, J. W. E. Bowen, and other representatives of this group, can much longer be silent. Such men feel in conscience bound to ask of this nation three things:

1. The right to vote.
2. Civic equality.
3. The education of youth according to ability.

They acknowledge Mr. Washington's invaluable service in counseling patience and courtesy in such demands; they do not ask that ignorant black men vote when ignorant whites are debarred, or that any reasonable restrictions in the suffrage should not be applied; they know that the low social level of the mass of the race is responsible for much discrimination against it, but they also know, and the nation knows, that relentless color-prejudice is more often a cause than a result of the Negro's degradation; they seek the abatement of this relic of barbarism, and not its systematic encouragement and pampering by all agencies of social power from the Associated Press to the Church of Christ. They advocate, with Mr. Washington, a broad system of Negro common schools supplemented by thorough industrial training; but they are surprised that a man of Mr. Washington's insight cannot see that no such educational system ever has rested or can rest on any other basis than that of the well-equipped college and university, and they insist that there is a demand for a few such institutions throughout the South to train the best of the Negro youth as teachers, professional men, and leaders.

This group of men honor Mr. Washington for his attitude of conciliation toward the white South; they accept the "Atlanta Compromise" in its broadest interpretation; they recognize, with him, many signs of promise, many men of high purpose and fair judgment, in this section; they know that no easy task has been laid upon a region already tottering under heavy burdens. But, nevertheless, they insist that the way to truth and right lies in straightforward honesty, not in indiscriminate flattery; in praising those of the South who do well and criticizing uncompromisingly those who do ill; in taking advantage of the opportunities at hand and urging their fellows to do the same, but at the same time in remembering that only a firm adherence to their higher ideals and aspirations will ever keep those ideals within the realm of possibility. They do not expect that the free right to vote, to enjoy civic rights, and to be educated, will come in a moment;

they do not expect to see the bias and prejudices of years disappear at the blast of a trumpet; but they are absolutely certain that the way for a people to gain their reasonable rights is not by voluntarily throwing them away and insisting that they do not want them; that the way for a people to gain respect is not by continually belittling and ridiculing themselves; that, on the contrary, Negroes must insist continually, in season and out of season, that voting is necessary to modern manhood, that color discrimination is barbarism, and that black boys need education as well as white boys. . . .

First, it is the duty of black men to judge the South discriminatingly. The present generation of Southerners are not responsible for the past, and they should not be blindly hated or blamed for it. Furthermore, to no class is the indiscriminate endorsement of the recent course of the South toward Negroes more nauseating than to the best thought of the South. The South is not "solid"; it is a land in the ferment of social change, wherein forces of all kinds are fighting for supremacy; and to praise the ill the South is to-day perpetrating is just as wrong as to condemn the good. Discriminating and broad-minded criticism is what the South needs,—needs it for the sake of her own white sons and daughters, and for the insurance of robust, healthy mental and moral development.

To-day even the attitude of the Southern whites toward the blacks is not, as so many assume, in all cases the same; the ignorant Southerner hates the Negro, the workingmen fear his competition, the money-makers wish to use him as a laborer, some of the educated see a menace in his upward development, while others—usually the sons of the masters— wish to help him to rise. National opinion has enabled this last class to maintain the Negro common schools, and to protect the Negro partially in property, life, and limb. Through the pressure of the money-makers, the Negro is in danger of being reduced to semi-slavery, especially in the country districts; the workingmen, and those of the educated who fear the Negro, have united to disfranchise him, and some have urged his deportation; while the passions of the ignorant are easily aroused to lynch and abuse any black man. To praise this intricate whirl of thought and prejudice is nonsense; to inveigh indiscriminately against "the South" is unjust; but to use the same breath in praising Governor Aycock, exposing Senator Morgan, arguing with Mr. Thomas Nelson Page, and denouncing Senator Ben Tillman, is not only sane, but the imperative duty of thinking black men.

It would be unjust to Mr. Washington not to acknowledge that in several instances he has opposed movements in the South which were unjust to the Negro; he sent memorials to the Louisiana and Alabama constitutional conventions, he has spoken against lynching, and in other ways has openly or silently set his influence against sinister schemes and unfortunate happenings. Notwithstanding this, it is equally true to assert that on the whole the distinct impression left by Mr. Washington's propaganda is, first, that the South is justified in its present attitude toward the Negro because of the Negro's degradation; secondly, that the prime cause of the Negro's failure to rise more quickly is his wrong education in the past; and, thirdly, that his future rise depends primarily on his own efforts. Each of these propositions is a dangerous half-truth. The supplementary truths must never be lost sight of: first, slavery and race-prejudice are potent if not sufficient causes of the Negro's position; second, industrial and common-school training were necessarily slow in planting because they had to await the black teachers trained by higher institutions,—it being extremely doubtful if any essentially different development was possible, and certainly a Tuskegee was unthinkable before 1880; and, third, while it is a great truth to say that the Negro must strive and strive mightily to help himself, it is equally true that unless his striving be not simply seconded, but rather aroused and encouraged, by the initiative of the richer and wiser environing group, he cannot hope for great success.

In his failure to realize and impress this last point, Mr. Washington is especially to be criticized. His doctrine has tended to make the whites, North and South, shift the burden of the Negro problem to the Negro's shoulders and stand aside as critical and rather pessimistic spectators; when in fact the burden belongs to the nation, and the hands of none of us are clean if we bend not our energies to righting these great wrongs.

The South ought to be led, by candid and honest criticism, to assert her better self and do her full duty to the race she has cruelly wronged and is still wronging. The North—her co-partner in guilt—cannot salve her conscience by plastering it with gold. We cannot settle this problem by diplomacy and suaveness, by "policy" alone. If worse come to worst, can the moral fiber of this country survive the slow throttling and murder of nine millions of men?

The black men of America have a duty to perform, a duty stern and delicate,—a forward movement to oppose a part of the work of their greatest leader. So far as Mr. Washington preaches Thrift, Patience, and Industrial Training for the masses, we must hold up his hands and strive with him, rejoicing in his honors and glorying in the strength of this Joshua called of God and of man to lead the headless host. But so far as Mr. Washington apologizes for injustice, North or South, does not rightly value the privilege and duty of voting, belittles the emasculating effects of caste distinctions, and opposes the higher training and ambition of our brighter minds,—so far as he, the South, or the Nation, does this,—we must unceasingly and firmly oppose them. By every civilized and peaceful method we must strive for the rights which the world accords to men, clinging unwaveringly to those great words which the sons of the Fathers would fain forget: "We hold these truths to be self-evident: That all men are created equal; that they are endowed by their Creator with certain unalienable rights; that among these are life, liberty, and the pursuit of happiness."

SUGGESTIONS FOR FURTHER READING

August Meier, *Negro Thought in America, 1880–1915* (Ann Arbor, Mich.: University of Michigan Press, 1963); Louis Harlan, *Booker T. Washington: The Making of a Black Leader, 1856–1901* (New York: Oxford University Press, 1972) and *Booker T. Washington: The Wizard of Tuskegee, 1901–1915* (New York: Oxford University Press, 1983); John Higham, ed., *Ethnic Leadership in America* (Baltimore: Johns Hopkins University Press, 1978), especially the chapter by Nathan I. Huggins, "Afro-Americans."

V

⚜

PACIFISM AND MILITARISM: IS PEACE BEST PRESERVED THROUGH MILITARY PREPAREDNESS?

Complex memories of the American Civil War and popular approval of national success in the Spanish-American War, 1898–99, meant that military strength as a precipitant or preventive measure would be widely discussed early in the twentieth century. In various forms the issue of preparedness has remained controversial throughout the century. There were many outspoken opponents of U.S. participation in World War I, such as Henry Ford, and others who opposed U.S. involvement in World War II, such as Charles Lindbergh. The Korean and Vietnam wars caused different kinds of controversy, and the Cold War generated an arms race that escalated wildly and provoked considerable discussion of military preparedness as the best way to prevent World War III.

William James (1842–1910) was trained in medicine, became deeply interested in psychology, and following 1890 became the best-known social philosopher in the United States. The Will to Believe *(1897) dealt with the personal need for religion, and* Varieties of Religious Experience *(1902) examined the psychology of religion.* Pragmatism *(1907) established James as the leader of an American school of philosophy. He also criticized imperialism, the Spanish-American War, and the brutality of war in general.*

Theodore Roosevelt (1858–1919) found much to admire in armed conflict. His books included The Naval War of 1812 *(1882) and his four-volume work,* The Winning of the West *(1889–96). As assistant secretary of the navy under President McKinley (1897–98), he urged war against Spain for imperialistic and humanitarian reasons. He then resigned, helped to organize the "Rough Riders," and as their colonel achieved laurels in the battle for San Juan.*

During his presidency (1901–9), Roosevelt issued his "Corollary" to the Monroe Doctrine. It asserted that under certain conditions the United States might intervene in the internal affairs of Latin American nations in order to prevent

European powers from interfering in the Western Hemisphere. In 1906 Roosevelt received the Nobel Peace Prize for mediating the Russo-Japanese War in order to influence a balance of power in the Far East. In the decade following his presidency, Roosevelt's romantic militarism became more prominent and enjoyed considerable influence.

The Moral Equivalent of War

WILLIAM JAMES

The war against war is going to be no holiday excursion or camping party. The military feelings are too deeply grounded to abdicate their place among our ideals until better substitutes are offered than the glory and shame that come to nations as well as to individuals from the ups and downs of politics and the vicissitudes of trade. There is something highly paradoxical in the modern man's relation to war. Ask all our millions, north and south, whether they would vote now (were such a thing possible) to have our war for the Union expunged from history, and the record of a peaceful transition to the present time substituted for that of its marches and battles, and probably hardly a handful of eccentrics would say yes. Those ancestors, those efforts, those memories and legends, are the most ideal part of what we now own together, a sacred spiritual possession worth more than all the blood poured out. Yet ask those same people whether they would be willing in cold blood to start another civil war now to gain another similar possession, and not one man or woman would vote for the proposition. In modern eyes, precious though wars may be, they must not be waged solely for the sake of the ideal harvest. Only when forced upon one, only when an enemy's injustice leaves us no alternative, is a war now thought permissible.

It was not thus in ancient times. The earlier men were hunting men, and to hunt a neighboring tribe, kill the males, loot the village and possess the females, was the most profitable, as well as the most exciting, way of living. Thus were the more martial tribes selected, and in chiefs and peoples a pure pugnacity and love of glory came to mingle with the more fundamental appetite for plunder.

Modern war is so expensive that we feel trade to be a better avenue to plunder; but modern man inherits all the innate pugnacity and all the love of glory of his ancestors. Showing war's irrationality and horror is of no effect upon him. The horrors make the fascination. War is the *strong* life; it is life *in extremis;* war-taxes are the only ones men never hesitate to pay, as the budgets of all nations show us. . . .

We inherit the warlike type; and for most of the capacities of heroism that the human race is full of we have to thank this cruel history. Dead men tell no tales, and if there were any tribes of other type than this they have left no survivors. Our ancestors have bred pugnacity into our bone and marrow, and thousands of years of peace won't breed it out of us. The popular imagination fairly fattens on the thought of wars. Let public

William James, "The Moral Equivalent of War" (February 1910), Association for International Conciliation, Leaflet No. 27.

opinion once reach a certain fighting pitch, and no ruler can withstand it. In the Boer war both governments began with bluff, but couldn't stay there, the military tension was too much for them. In 1898 our people had read the word WAR in letters three inches high for three months in every newspaper. The pliant politician McKinley was swept away by their eagerness, and our squalid war with Spain became a necessity.

At the present day, civilized opinion is a curious mental mixture. The military instincts and ideals are as strong as ever, but are confronted by reflective criticisms which sorely curb their ancient freedom. Innumerable writers are showing up the bestial side of military service. Pure loot and mastery seem no longer morally avowable motives, and pretexts must be found for attributing them solely to the enemy. England and we, our army and navy authorities repeat without ceasing, arm solely for "peace," Germany and Japan it is who are bent on loot and glory. "Peace" in military mouths to-day is a synonym for "war expected." The word has become a pure provocative, and no government wishing peace sincerely should allow it ever to be printed in a newspaper. Every up-to-date dictionary should say that "peace" and "war" mean the same thing, now *in posse*, now *in actu*. It may even reasonably be said that the intensely sharp competitive *preparation* for war by the nations *is the real war*, permanent, unceasing; and that the battles are only a sort of public verification of the mastery gained during the "peace"-interval.

It is plain that on this subject civilized man has developed a sort of double personality. If we take European nations, no legitimate interest of any one of them would seem to justify the tremendous destructions which a war to compass it would necessarily entail. It would seem as though common sense and reason ought to find a way to reach agreement in every conflict of honest interests. I myself think it our bounden duty to believe in such international rationality as possible. But, as things stand, I see how desperately hard it is to bring the peace-party and the war-party together, and I believe that the difficulty is due to certain deficiencies in the program of pacificism which set the militarist imagination strongly, and to a certain extent justifiably, against it. In the whole discussion both sides are on imaginative and sentimental ground. It is but one utopia against another, and everything one says must be abstract and hypothetical. Subject to this criticism and caution, I will try to characterize in abstract strokes the opposite imaginative forces, and point out what to my own very fallible mind seems the best utopian hypothesis, the most promising line of conciliation.

In my remarks, pacificist tho' I am, I will refuse to speak of the bestial side of the war-regime (already done justice to by many writers) and consider only the higher aspects of militaristic sentiment. Patriotism no one thinks discreditable; nor does any one deny that war is the romance of history. But inordinate ambitions are the soul of every patriotism, and the possibility of violent death the soul of all romance. The militarily patriotic and romantic-minded everywhere, and especially the professional military class, refuse to admit for a moment that war may be a transitory phenomenon in social evolution. The notion of a sheep's paradise like that revolts, they say, our higher imagination. Where then would be the steeps of life? If war had ever stopped, we should have to reinvent it, on this view, to redeem life from flat degeneration.

Reflective apologists for war at the present day all take it religiously. It is a sort of sacrament. Its profits are to the vanquished as well as to the victor; and quite apart from any question of profit, it is an absolute good, we are told, for it is human nature at its highest dynamic. Its "horrors" are a cheap price to pay for rescue from the only alternative supposed, of a world of clerks and teachers, of co-education and zoophily, of "consumer's leagues" and "associated charities," of industrialism unlimited, and feminism unabashed. No scorn, no hardness, no valor any more! Fie upon such a cattleyard of a planet!

So far as the central essence of this feeling goes, no healthy minded person, it seems to me, can help to some degree partaking of it. Militarism is the great preserver of our ideals of hardihood, and human life with no use for hardihood would be contemptible. Without risks or prizes for the darer, history would be insipid indeed; and there is a type of military character which every one feels that the race should never cease to breed, for every one is sensitive to its superiority. The duty is incumbent on mankind, of keeping military characters in stock—of keeping them, if not for use, then as ends in themselves and as pure pieces of perfection,—so that Roosevelt's weaklings and mollycoddles may not end by making everything else disappear from the face of nature.

This natural sort of feeling forms, I think, the innermost soul of army-writings. Without any exception known to me, militarist authors take a highly mystical view of their subject, and regard war as a biological or sociological necessity, uncontrolled by ordinary psychological checks and motives. When the time of development is ripe the war must come, reason or no reason, for the justifications pleaded are invariably fictitious. War is, in short, a permanent human *obligation*. . . .

. . . If we speak of the *fear of emancipation from the fear-regime*, we put the whole situation into a single phrase; fear regarding ourselves now taking the place of the ancient fear of the enemy.

Turn the fear over as I will in my mind, it all seems to lead back to two unwillingnesses of the imagination, one aesthetic, and the other moral: unwillingness, first to envisage a future in which army-life, with its many elements of charm, shall be forever impossible, and in which the destinies of peoples shall nevermore be decided quickly, thrillingly, and tragically, by force, but only gradually and insipidly by "evolution"; and, secondly, unwillingness to see the supreme theatre of human strenuousness closed, and the splendid military aptitudes of men doomed to keep always in a state of latency and never show themselves in action. These insistent unwillingnesses, no less than other aesthetic and ethical insistencies have, it seems to me, to be listened to and respected. One cannot meet them effectively by mere counter-insistency on war's expensiveness and horror. The horror makes the thrill; and when the question is of getting the extremest and supremest out of human nature, talk of expense sounds ignominious. The weakness of so much merely negative criticism is evident—pacificism makes no converts from the military party. The military party denies neither the bestiality nor the horror, nor the expense; it only says that these things tell but half the story. It only says that war is *worth* them; that, taking human nature as a whole, its wars are its best protection against its weaker and more cowardly self, and that mankind cannot *afford* to adopt a peace-economy.

Pacificists ought to enter more deeply into the aesthetical and ethical point of view of their opponents. Do that first in any controversy, says J. J. Chapman, *then move the point*, and your opponent will follow. So long as anti-militarists propose no substitute for war's disciplinary function, no *moral equivalent* of war, analogous, as one might say, to the mechanical equivalent of heat, so long they fail to realize the full inwardness of the situation. And as a rule they do fail. The duties, penalties, and sanctions pictured in the utopias they paint are all too weak and tame to touch the military-minded. Tolstoy's pacificism is the only exception to this rule, for it is profoundly pessimistic as regards all this world's values, and makes the fear of the Lord furnish the moral spur provided elsewhere by the fear of the enemy. But our socialistic peace-advocates all believe absolutely in this world's values; and instead of the fear of the Lord and the fear of the enemy, the only fear they reckon with is the fear of poverty if one be lazy. This weakness pervades all the socialistic literature with which I am acquainted. Even in Lowes Dickinson's exquisite dialogue, high wages and short hours are the only forces invoked for overcoming man's distaste for repulsive kinds of labor. Meanwhile men at large still live as they always have lived, under a pain-and-fear economy—for those of us who live in an ease-economy are but an island in the stormy ocean—and the whole atmosphere of present-day utopian literature tastes mawkish and dishwatery to people who still keep a sense for life's more bitter flavors. It suggests, in truth, ubiquitous inferiority. . . .

. . . I will now confess my own utopia. I devoutly believe in the reign of peace and in the gradual advent of some sort of a socialistic equilibrium. The fatalistic view of the war-function is to me nonsense, for I know that war-making is due to definite motives and subject to prudential checks and reasonable criticisms, just like any other form of enterprise. And when whole nations are the armies, and the science of destruction vies in intellectual refinement with the sciences of production, I see that war becomes absurd and impossible from its own monstrosity. Extravagant ambitions will have to be replaced by reasonable claims, and nations must make common cause against them. I see no reason why all this should not apply to yellow as well as to white countries, and I look forward to a future when acts of war shall be formally outlawed as between civilized peoples.

All these beliefs of mine put me squarely into the anti-militarist party. But I do not believe that peace either ought to be or will be permanent on this globe, unless the states pacifically organized preserve some of the old elements of army-discipline. A permanently successful peace-economy cannot be a simple pleasure-economy. In the more or less socialistic future towards which mankind seems drifting we must still subject ourselves collectively to those severities which answer to our real position upon this only partly hospitable globe. We must make new energies and hardihoods continue the manliness to which the military mind so faithfully clings. Martial virtues must be the enduring cement; intrepidity, contempt of softness, surrender of private interest, obedience to command, must still remain the rock upon which states are built—unless, indeed, we wish for dangerous reactions against commonwealths fit only for contempt, and liable to invite attack whenever a center of crystallization for military-minded enterprise gets formed anywhere in their neighborhood.

The war-party is assuredly right in affirming and reaffirming that the martial virtues, although originally gained by the race through war, are absolute and permanent human goods. Patriotic pride and ambition in their military form are, after all, only specifications of a more general competitive passion. They are its first form, but that is no reason for supposing them to be its last form. Men now are proud of belonging to a conquering nation, and without a murmur they lay down their persons and their wealth, if by so doing they may fend off subjection. But who can be sure that *other aspects of one's country* may not, with time and education and suggestion enough, come to be regarded with similarly effective feelings of pride and shame? Why should men not some day feel that it is worth a blood-tax to belong to a collectivity superior in *any* ideal respect? Why should they not blush with indignant shame if the community that owns them is vile in any way whatsoever? Individuals, daily more numerous, now feel this civic passion. It is only a question of blowing on the spark till the whole population gets incandescent, and on the ruins of the old morals of military honor, a stable system of morals of civic honor builds itself up. What the whole community comes to believe in grasps the individual as in a vise. The war-function has grasped us so far; but constructive interests may some day seem no less imperative, and impose on the individual a hardly lighter burden.

Let me illustrate my idea more concretely. There is nothing to make one indignant in the mere fact that life is hard, that men should toil and suffer pain. The planetary conditions once for all are such, and we can stand it. But that so many men, by mere accidents of birth and opportunity, should have a life of *nothing else* but toil and pain and hardness and inferiority imposed upon them, should have *no* vacation, while others natively no more deserving never get any taste of this campaigning life at all,—*this* is capable of arousing indignation in reflective minds. It may end by seeming shameful to all of us that some of us have nothing but campaigning, and others nothing but unmanly ease. If now—and this is my idea—there were, instead of military conscription a conscription of the whole youthful population to form for a certain number of years a part of the army enlisted against *Nature*, the injustice would tend to be evened out, and numerous other goods to the commonwealth would follow. The military ideals of hardihood and discipline would be wrought into the growing fiber of the people; no one would remain blind as the luxurious classes now are blind, to man's real relations to the globe he lives on, and to the permanently sour and hard foundations of his higher life. To coal and iron mines, to freight trains, to fishing fleets in December, to dish-washing, clothes-washing, and window-washing, to road-building, and tunnel-making, to foundries and stoke-holes, and to the frames of skyscrapers, would our gilded youths be drafted off, according to their choice, to get the childishness knocked out of them, and to come back into society with healthier sympathies and soberer ideas. They would have paid their blood-tax, done their own part in the immemorial human warfare against nature, they would tread the earth more proudly, the women would value them more highly, they would be better fathers and teachers of the following generation.

Such a conscription, with the state of public opinion that would have required it, and the many moral fruits it would bear, would preserve in the midst of a pacific civilization the manly virtues which the military party is so afraid of seeing disappear in peace. We should get toughness without callousness, authority with as little criminal cruelty as possible, and painful work done cheerily because the duty is temporary, and threatens not, as now, to degrade the whole remainder of one's life. I spoke of the "moral equivalent" of war. So far, war has been the only force that can discipline a whole community, and until an equivalent discipline is organized, I believe that war must have its way. But I have no serious doubt that the ordinary prides and shames of social man, once developed to a certain intensity, are capable of organizing such a moral equivalent as I have sketched, or some other just as effective for preserving manliness of type. It is but a question of time, of skillful propagandism, and of opinion-making men seizing historic opportunities.

The martial type of character can be bred without war. Strenuous honor and disinterestedness abound elsewhere. Priests and medical men are in a fashion educated to it, and we should all feel some degree of it imperative if we were conscious of our work as an obligatory service to the state. We should be *owned*, as soldiers are by the army, and our pride would rise accordingly. We could be poor, then, without humiliation, as army officers now are. The only thing needed henceforward is to inflame the civic temper as past history has inflamed the military temper. . . .

Every Hour is Lunch Hour at the Dreadnought Club: Peace—Waiting on a Crowd like This Is No Job for a Woman, by Joseph Keppler, Jr. (1872–1956)   The title refers to the proliferation of large-caliber battleships prior to World War I, beginning with the British ship *Dreadnought* in 1907. The artist idealizes women as the embodiment of peace and liberty, and attributes aggression and greed to men. In addition to the allegorization of Peace as female and War as male, Keppler presents people of various ethnic backgrounds seated around the table. Uncle Sam and Liberty represent the United States. The figures plead for their share of weapons, but Peace cannot accommodate the gluttony of War and the needs of individual nations. Despite her angelic features and wings, the female figure of Peace is too weak to prevent war.

Warlike Power—The Prerequisite for the Preservation of Social Values

THEODORE ROOSEVELT

In December last I was asked to address the American Sociological Congress on "the effect of war and militarism on social values." In sending my answer I pointed out that infinitely the most important fact to remember in connection with the subject in question is that if an unscrupulous, warlike, and militaristic nation is not held in check by the warlike ability of a neighboring non-militaristic and well-behaved nation, then the latter will be spared the necessity of dealing with its own "moral and social values" because it won't be allowed to deal with anything. Until this fact is thoroughly recognized, and the duty of national preparedness by justice-loving nations explicitly acknowledged, there is very little use of solemnly debating such questions as the one which the sociological congress assigned me—which, in detail, was "How war and militarism affect such social values as the sense of the preciousness of human life; care for child welfare; the conservation of human resources; upper-class concern for the lot of the masses; interest in popular education; appreciation of truth-telling and truth-printing; respect for personality and regard for personal rights." It seems to me positively comic to fail to appreciate, with the example of Belgium before our eyes, that the real question which modern peace-loving nations have to face is not how the militaristic or warlike spirit within their own borders will affect these "values," but how failure on their part to be able to resist the militarism of an unscrupulous neighbor will affect them. Belgium had a very keen sense of the "preciousness of human life" and of "the need for the care of child welfare and the conservation of human resources," and there was much "concern" by the Belgian "upper classes for the lot of the masses," great "interest in popular education and appreciation of truth-telling and truth-printing and a high respect for personality and regard for personal rights." But all these "social values" existed in Belgium only up to the end of July, 1914. Not a vestige of them remained in 1915. To discuss them as regards present-day Belgium is sheer prattle, simply because on August 4, 1914, Belgium had not prepared her military strength so that she could put on her frontiers at least half a million thoroughly armed and trained men of fighting spirit. In similar fashion the

Theodore Roosevelt, "Warlike Power—The Prerequisite for the Preservation of Social Values," a paper delivered before the American Sociological Congress, Washington, D.C., December 28–31, 1914. American Sociological Society, *Papers and Proceedings*, X (1915), 12–21.

question of the internal reformation of China at this moment is wholly secondary to the question whether any China will remain to be reformed internally. A Chinese gentleman wrote me the other day that he had formerly been absorbed in plans for bringing China abreast of the modern movement, but that the events of the past year had shown him that what he really ought to be absorbed in was the question whether or not China would be able by military preparation to save itself from the fate of Korea. Korean "social values" now have to be studied exclusively through a Japanese medium. At this moment the Armenians, who for some centuries have sedulously avoided militarism and war, and have practically applied advanced pacifist principles, are suffering a fate, if possible, worse than that of the Belgians; and they are so suffering precisely and exactly because they have been pacifists, whereas their neighbors, the Turks, have not been pacifists but militarists. They haven't the vestige of a "social value" left, to be "affected" by militarism or by anything else.

In the thirteenth century Persia had become a highly civilized nation, with a cultivated class of literary men and philosophers, with universities, and with great mercantile interests. These literary men and merchants took toward the realities of war much the same attitude that is taken in our own country by gentlemen of the stamp of Messrs. David Starr Jordan and Henry Ford. Unfortunately for these predecessors of the modern pacifists, they were within striking distance of Genghis Khan and his Mongols; and, as of course invariably happens in such a case, when the onrush came, the pacifists' theories were worth just about what a tissue-paper barrier would amount to against a tidal wave. Russia at that time was slowly struggling upward toward civilization. She had become Christian. She was developing industry and she was struggling toward individual freedom. In other words, she was in halting fashion developing the "social values" of which the foregoing extract speaks. But she had not developed military efficiency; she had not developed efficiency in war. The Mongols overwhelmed her as fire overwhelms stubble. For two centuries the Russians were trodden under foot by an alien dominion so ruthless, so brutal, that when they finally shook it off, all popular freedom had been lost and the soul of the nation seared by torment and degradation; and to this day the scars remain on the national life and character. The chief difficulties against which Russia has had to struggle in modern times are due ultimately to the one all-essential fact that in the early part of the thirteenth century she had not developed the warlike strength to enable her to hold her own against a militaristic neighbor. The Russian Jew of to-day is oppressed by the Russian Christian because that Christian's ancestor in the thirteenth century had not learned efficiency in war.

There are well-meaning people, utterly incapable of learning any lesson taught by history, utterly incapable even of understanding aright what has gone on before their very eyes during the past year or two, who nevertheless wish to turn this country into an Occidental China—the kind of China which every intelligent Chinaman of the present day is seeking to abolish. There are plenty of politicians, by no means as well-meaning, who find it to their profit to pander to the desire common to most men to live softly and easily and avoid risk and effort. Timid and lazy men, men absorbed in money-getting, men absorbed in ease and luxury, and all soft and slothful people naturally hail with delight anybody who will give them high-sounding names behind which to cloak their unwillingness to run risks or to toil and endure. Emotional philanthropists to whom thinking is a distasteful form of mental exercise enthusiastically champion this attitude. The faults of all these men and women are of a highly non-militaristic and unwarlike type; and naturally they feel great satisfaction in condemning misdeeds which are incident to lives that they would themselves be wholly unable to lead without an amount of toil and effort that they are wholly unwilling to undergo. These men and women are delighted to pass resolutions in favor of anything with a lofty name, provided always that no demand is ever made upon them to pay with their bodies to even the smallest degree in order to give effect to these lofty sentiments. It is questionable whether in the long run they do not form a less desirable national type than is formed by the men who are guilty of the downright iniquities of life; for the latter at least have in them elements of strength which, if guided aright, could be used to good purpose. . . .

The first thing to do is to make these citizens understand that war and militarism are terms whose values depend wholly upon the sense in which they are used. The second thing is to make them understand that there is a real analogy between the use of force in international and the use of force in intranational or civil matters; although of course this analogy must not be pushed too far.

In the first place, we are dealing with a matter of definition. A war can be defined as violence between nations, as the use of force between nations. It is analogous to violence between individuals within a nation— using violence in a large sense as equivalent to the use of force. When this fact is clearly grasped, the average citizen will be spared the mental confusion he now suffers because he thinks of war as *in itself* wrong. War, like peace, is properly a means to an end—righteousness. Neither war nor peace is in itself righteous, and neither should be treated as of itself the end to be aimed at. Righteousness is the end. Righteousness when triumphant brings peace; but peace may not bring righteousness. Whether war is right or wrong depends purely upon the purpose for which, and the spirit in which, it is waged. Here the analogy with what takes place in civil life is perfect. The exertion of force or violence by which one man masters another may be illustrated by the case of a black-hander who kidnaps a child, knocking down the nurse or guardian; and it may also be illustrated by the case of the guardian who by violence withstands and thwarts the black-hander in his efforts to kidnap the child, or by the case of the policeman who by force arrests the black-hander or white-slaver or whoever it is and takes his victim away from him. There are, of course, persons who believe that all force is immoral, that it is always immoral to resist wrong-doing by force. I have never taken much interest in the individuals who profess this kind of twisted morality; and I do not know the extent to which they practically apply it. But if they are right in their theory, then it is wrong for a man to endeavor by force to save his wife or sister or daughter from rape or other abuse, or to save his children from abduction and torture. It is a waste of time to discuss with any man a position of such folly, wickedness, and poltroonery. But unless a man is willing to take this position, he cannot honestly condemn the use of force or violence in war—for the policeman who risks and perhaps loses or takes life in dealing with an anarchist or white-slaver or black-hander or burglar or highwayman must be justified or condemned on precisely the same principles which require us to differentiate among wars and to condemn unstintedly certain nations in certain wars and equally without stint to praise other nations in certain other wars.

If the man who objects to war also objects to the use of force in civil life as above outlined, his position is logical, although both absurd and wicked. If the college presidents, politicians, automobile manufacturers, and the like, who during the past year or two have preached pacifism in its most ignoble and degrading form are willing to think out the subject and are both sincere and fairly intelligent, they must necessarily condemn a police force or a posse comitatus just as much as they condemn armies; and they must regard the activities of the sheriff and the constable as being essentially militaristic and therefore to be abolished. . . .

The really essential things for men to remember, therefore, in connection with war are, first, that neither war nor peace is immoral in itself, and, secondly, that in order to preserve the "social values" which were enumerated in the quotation with which I began this chapter it is absolutely essential to prevent the dominance in our country of the one form of militarism which is surely and completely fatal—that is, the military dominion of an alien enemy.

It is utterly impossible to appreciate social values at all or to discriminate between what is socially good and socially bad unless we appreciate the utterly different social values of different wars. The Greeks who triumphed at Marathon and Salamis did a work without which the world would have been deprived of the social value of Plato and Aristotle, of Aeschylus, Herodotus, and Thucydides. The civilization of Europe, America, and Australia exists to-day at all only because of the victories of civilized man over the enemies of civilization, because of victories stretching through the centuries from the days of Miltiades and Themistocles to those of Charles Martel in the eighth century and those of John Sobieski in the seventeenth century. During the thousand years that included the careers of the Frankish soldier and the Polish king, the Christians of Asia and Africa proved unable to wage successful war with the Moslem conquerors; and in consequence Christianity practically vanished from the two continents; and to-day nobody can find in them any "social values" whatever, in the sense in which we use the words, so far as the sphere of Mohammedan influence and the decaying native Christian churches are concerned. There are such "social values" to-day in Europe, America, and Australia only because during those thousand years the Christians of Europe possessed the warlike power to do what the Christians of Asia and Africa had failed to do—that is, to beat back the Moslem invader. It is of course worth while for sociologists to discuss the effect of this European militarism on "social values," but only if they first clearly realize and formulate the fact that if the European militarism had not been able to defend itself against and to overcome the militarism of Asia and Africa, there would have been no "social values" of any kind in our world to-day, and no sociologists to discuss them.

The Sociological Society meets at Washington this year only because the man after whom the city was named was willing to go to war. If he and his associates had not gone to war, there would have been no possibility of discussing "social values" in the United States, for the excellent reason that there would have been no United States. If Lincoln had not been willing to go to war, to appeal to the sword, to introduce militarism on a tremendous scale throughout the United States, the sociologists who listened to this chapter, when it was read to them, if they existed at all, would not be considering the "social values" enumerated above, but the "social values" of slavery and of such governmental and industrial problems as can now be studied in the Central American republics.

It is a curious fact that during the thirty years prior to the Civil War the men who in the Northern and especially the Northeastern States gradually grew to take most interest in the antislavery agitation were almost equally interested in antimilitaristic and peace movements. Even a casual glance at the poems of Longfellow and Whittier will show this. They were strong against slavery and they were strong against war. They did not take the trouble to think out the truth, which was that in actual fact slavery could be abolished only by war; and when the time came they had to choose between, on the one hand, the "social values" of freedom and of union and, on the other hand, the "social value" of peace, for peace proved incompatible with freedom and union. Being men fit to live in a free country, they of course chose freedom and union rather than peace. I say men; of course I mean women also. I am speaking of Julia Ward Howe and Harriet Beecher Stowe just exactly as I am speaking of Longfellow and Lowell and Whittier.

Now, during the thirty years preceding the Civil War these men and women often debated and occasionally in verse or prose wrote about the effect of war on what we now call "social values." I think that academically they were a unit in saying that this effect was bad; but when the real crisis came, when they were faced by the actual event, they realized that this academic discussion as to the effect of war on "social values" was of no consequence whatever. They did not want war. Nobody wants war who has any sense. But when they moved out of a world of dreams into a world of realities they realized that now, as always in the past has been the case, and as undoubtedly will be the case for a long time in the future, war may be the only alternative to losing, not merely certain "social values," but the national life which means the sum of all "social values." They realized that as the world is now it is a wicked thing to use might against right, and an unspeakably silly, and therefore in the long run also a wicked thing, to chatter about right without preparing to put might back of right. They abhorred a wanton or an unjust war and condemned those responsible for it as they ought always to be condemned; and, on the other hand, they realized that righteous war for a lofty ideal may and often does offer the only path by which it is possible to move upward and onward. There are unquestionably real national dangers connected even with a successful war for righteousness; but equally without question there are real national dangers connected even with times of righteous peace. There are dangers attendant on every course, dangers to be fought against in every kind of life, whether of an individual or of a nation. But it is not merely danger, it is death, the death of the soul even more than the death of the body, which surely awaits the nation that does not both cultivate the lofty morality which will forbid it to do wrong to others, and at the same time spiritually, intellectually, and physically prepare itself, by the development of the stern and high qualities of the soul and the will no less than in things material, to defend by its own strength its own existence, and, as I at least hope some time will be the case, also to fit itself to defend other nations that are weak and wronged, when in helpless misery they are ground beneath the feet of the successful militarism which serves evil. At present, in this world, and for the immediate future, it is certain that the only way successfully to oppose the might which is the servant of wrong is by means of the might which is the servant of right.

Nothing is gained by debate on non-debatable subjects. No intelligent man desires war. But neither can any intelligent man who is willing to think fail to realize that we live in a great and free country only because our forefathers were willing to wage war rather than accept the peace that spells destruction. No nation can permanently retain any "social values" worth having unless it develops the warlike strength necessary for its own defense.

SUGGESTIONS FOR FURTHER READING

Peter Brock, *Pacifism in the United States, From the Colonial Era to the First World War* (Princeton, N.J.: Princeton University Press, 1968), especially chs. 22 and 23; Charles Chatfield, *The American Peace Movement: Ideals and Activism* (New York: Twayne, 1992); Linda Schott, "Jane Addams and William James on Alternatives to War," *Journal of the History of Ideas* 54 (April 1993), 241–55.

VI

CAN INDUSTRIALIZATION BE EFFICIENT AND HUMANE? THE CONFLICT OVER SCIENTIFIC MANAGEMENT

Frederick W. Taylor (1856–1915) was trained as an engineer, became chief engineer at the Midvale Steel Company, and founded his own consulting firm in 1893 to provide technological advice and increase worker productivity. For more than a decade following 1901, he sought to develop a theory of industrial efficiency based on rational control. His influence spread to politics, household management, and other areas of concern during the Progressive era. When Herbert Croly founded the New Republic *magazine in 1914, for example, he hoped to make American politics more rational by spreading Taylor's theories. In 1915 a suburban New Jersey club woman, Mary Pattison, wrote the first book that applied Taylor's ideas to the home,* Principles of Domestic Engineering.

In response to growing labor unrest and major strikes, especially in 1911–12, Congress passed an act in August 1912 creating and defining a Commission on Industrial Relations. It included members of Congress, employers, representatives of organized labor, and a staff of investigators that included prominent academics. The commission's charge was notably comprehensive and concluded that it "shall seek to discover the underlying causes of dissatisfaction in the industrial situation and report its conclusions thereon."

Authorization to print its massive report came from Congress in 1916. The report included a lengthy statement prepared by Professor Robert F. Hoxie and others who were quite critical of the consequences of scientific management as envisioned by Frederick W. Taylor and several of his associates.

"Taylorism" became an international byword for social control and for programs designed to make men function like machines. During the 1930s, for example, the famous Italian social critic, Antonio Gramsci, devoted a section of his

Prison Notebooks *(the fascists under Mussolini imprisoned Gramsci for a decade)* to "Taylorism and the Mechanisation of the Worker." Gramsci observed that most workers refused to become automata. "Not only does the worker think, but the fact that he gets no immediate satisfaction from his work and realizes that they are trying to reduce him to a trained gorilla, can lead him into a train of thought that is far from conformist. That the industrialists are concerned about such things is made clear from a whole series of cautionary measures and 'educative' initiatives."[1]

---

[1]Quintin Hoare and Geoffrey Nowell Smith, eds. and trans. *Selections from the Prison Notebooks of Antonio Gramsci* (London: Lawrence and Wishart, 1971), p. 310.

The Principles of Scientific Management

FREDERICK WINSLOW TAYLOR

The writer has found that there are three questions uppermost in the minds of men when they become interested in scientific management.

First. Wherein do the principles of scientific management differ essentially from those of ordinary management?

Second. Why are better results attained under scientific management than under the other types?

Third. Is not the most important problem that of getting the right man at the head of the company? And if you have the right man cannot the choice of the type of management be safely left to him?

One of the principal objects of the following pages will be to give a satisfactory answer to these questions.

THE FINEST TYPE OF ORDINARY MANAGEMENT

Before starting to illustrate the principles of scientific management, or "task management" as it is briefly called, it seems desirable to outline what the writer believes will be recognized as the best type of management which is in common use. This is done so that the great difference between the best of the ordinary management and scientific management may be fully appreciated.

In an industrial establishment which employs say from 500 to 1,000 workmen, there will be found in many cases at least twenty to thirty different trades. The workmen in each of these trades have had their knowledge handed down to them by word of mouth, through the many years in which their trade has been developed from the primitive condition, in which our far-distant ancestors each one practiced the rudiments of many different trades, to the present state of great and growing subdivision of labor, in which each man specializes upon some comparatively small class of work.

The ingenuity of each generation has developed quicker and better methods for doing every element of the work in every trade. Thus the methods which are now in use may in a broad sense be said to be an evolution representing the survival of the fittest and best of the ideas

Frederick Winslow Taylor, *The Principles of Scientific Management* (New York: Harper & Brothers, 1911), pp. 30–39, 117–19, 142–43.

which have been developed since the starting of each trade. However, while this is true in a broad sense, only those who are intimately acquainted with each of these trades are fully aware of the fact that in hardly any element of any trade is there uniformity in the methods which are used. Instead of having only one way which is generally accepted as a standard, there are in daily use, say, fifty or a hundred different ways of doing each element of the work. And a little thought will make it clear that this must inevitably be the case, since our methods have been handed down from man to man by word of mouth, or have, in most cases, been almost unconsciously learned through personal observation. Practically in no instances have they been codified or systematically analyzed or described. The ingenuity and experience of each generation—of each decade, even, have without doubt handed over better methods to the next. This mass of rule-of-thumb or traditional knowledge may be said to be the principal asset or possession of every tradesman. Now, in the best of the ordinary types of management, the managers recognize frankly the fact that the 500 or 1,000 workmen, included in the twenty to thirty trades, who are under them, possess this mass of traditional knowledge, a large part of which is not in the possession of the management. The management, of course, includes foremen and superintendents, who themselves have been in most cases first-class workers at their trades. And yet these foremen and superintendents know, better than any one else, that their own knowledge and personal skill falls far short of the combined knowledge and dexterity of all the workmen under them. The most experienced managers therefore frankly place before their workmen the problem of doing the work in the best and most economical way. They recognize the task before them as that of inducing each workman to use his best endeavors, his hardest work, all his traditional knowledge, his skill, his ingenuity, and his good-will—in a word, his "initiative," so as to yield the largest possible return to his employer. The problem before the management, then, may be briefly said to be that of obtaining the best *initiative* of every workman. And the writer uses the word "initiative" in its broadest sense, to cover all of the good qualities sought for from the men.

On the other hand, no intelligent manager would hope to obtain in any full measure the initiative of his workmen unless he felt that he was giving them something more than they usually receive from their employers. Only those among the readers of this paper who have been managers or who have worked themselves at a trade realize how far the average workman falls short of giving his employer his full initiative. It is well within the mark to state that in nineteen out of twenty industrial establishments the workmen believe it to be directly against their interests to give their employers their best initiative, and that instead of working hard to do the largest possible amount of work and the best quality of work for their employers, they deliberately work as slowly as they dare while they at the same time try to make those over them believe that they are working fast.

The writer repeats, therefore, that in order to have any hope of obtaining the initiative of his workmen the manager must give some *special incentive* to his men beyond that which is given to the average of the trade. This incentive can be given in several different ways, as, for example, the hope of rapid promotion or advancement; higher wages, either in the form of generous piece-work prices or of a premium or bonus of some kind for good and rapid work; shorter hours of labor; better surroundings and working conditions than are ordinarily given, etc., and, above all, this special incentive should be accompanied by that personal consideration for, and friendly contact with, his workmen which comes only from a genuine and kindly interest in the welfare of those under him. It is only by giving a special inducement or "incentive" of this kind that the employer can hope even approximately to get the "initiative" of his workmen. Under the ordinary type of management the necessity for offering the workman a special inducement has come to be so generally recognized that a large proportion of those most interested in the subject look upon the adoption of some one of the modern schemes for paying men (such as piece-work, the premium plan, or the bonus plan, for instance) as practically the whole system of management. Under scientific management, however, the particular pay system which is adopted is merely one of the subordinate elements.

Broadly speaking, then, the best type of management in ordinary use may be defined as management in which the workmen give their best *initiative* and in return receive some *special incentive* from their employers. This type of management will be referred to as the management of *"initiative and incentive"* in contradistinction to scientific management, or task management, with which it is to be compared.

The writer hopes that the management of "initiative and incentive" will be recognized as representing the best type in ordinary use, and in fact he believes that it will be hard to persuade the average manager that anything better exists in the whole field than this type. The task which the writer has before him, then, is the difficult one of trying to prove in a thoroughly convincing way that there is another type of management which is not only better but overwhelmingly better than the management of "initiative and incentive."

The universal prejudice in favor of the management of "initiative and incentive" is so strong that no mere theoretical advantages which can be pointed out will be likely to convince the average manager that any other system is better. It will be upon a series of practical illustrations of the actual working of the two systems that the writer will depend in his efforts to prove that scientific management is so greatly superior to other types. Certain elementary principles, a certain philosophy, will however be recognized as the essence of that which is being illustrated in all of the practical examples which will be given. And the broad principles in which the scientific system differs from the ordinary or "rule-of-thumb" system are so simple in their nature that it seems desirable to describe them before starting with the illustrations.

Under the old type of management success depends almost entirely upon getting the "initiative" of the workmen, and it is indeed a rare case in which this initiative is really attained. Under scientific management the "initiative" of the workmen (that is, their hard work, their good-will, and their ingenuity) is obtained with absolute uniformity and to a greater extent than is possible under the old system; and in addition to this improvement on the part of the men, the managers assume new burdens, new duties, and responsibilities never dreamed of in the past. The managers assume, for instance, the burden of gathering together all of the traditional knowledge which in the past has been possessed by the workmen and then of classifying, tabulating, and reducing this knowledge to rules, laws, and formulæ which are immensely helpful to the workmen in doing their daily work. In addition to developing a *science* in this way, the management take on three other types of duties which involve new and heavy burdens for themselves.

These new duties are grouped under four heads:

First. They develop a science for each element of a man's work, which replaces the old rule-of-thumb method.

Second. They scientifically select and then train, teach, and develop the workman, whereas in the past he chose his own work and trained himself as best he could.

Third. They heartily cooperate with the men so as to insure all of the work being done in accordance with the principles of the science which has been developed.

Fourth. There is an almost equal division of the work and the responsibility between the management and the workmen. The management take over all work for which they are better fitted than the workmen, while in the past almost all of the work and the greater part of the responsibility were thrown upon the men.

It is this combination of the initiative of the workmen, coupled with the new types of work done by the management, that makes scientific management so much more efficient than the old plan.

Three of these elements exist in many cases, under the management of "initiative and incentive," in a small and rudimentary way, but they are, under this management, of minor importance, whereas under scientific management they form the very essence of the whole system.

The fourth of these elements, "an almost equal division of the responsibility between the management and the workmen," requires further explanation. The philosophy of the management of "initiative and incentive" makes it necessary for each workman to bear almost the entire responsibility for the general plan as well as for each detail of his work, and in many cases for his implements as well. In addition to this he must do all of the actual physical labor. The development of a science, on the other hand, involves the establishment of many rules, laws, and formulæ which replace the judgment of the individual workman and which can be effectively used only after having been systematically recorded, indexed, etc. The practical use of scientific data also calls for a room in which to keep the books, records, etc., and a desk for the planner to work at. Thus all of the planning which under the old system was done by the workman, as a result of his personal experience, must of necessity under the new system be done by the management in accordance with the laws of the science; because even if the workman were well suited to the development and use of scientific data, it would be physically impossible for him to work at his machine and at a desk at the same time. It is also clear that in most cases one type of man is needed to plan ahead and an entirely different type to execute the work.

The man in the planning room, whose specialty under scientific management is planning ahead, invariably finds that the work can be done better and more economically by a subdivision of the labor; each act of each mechanic, for example, should be preceded by various preparatory acts done by other men. And all of this involves, as we have said, "an almost equal division of the responsibility and the work between the management and the workman."

To summarize: Under the management of "initiative and incentive" practically the whole problem is "up to the workman," while under scientific management fully one-half of the problem is "up to the management."

Perhaps the most prominent single element in modern scientific management is the task idea. The work of every workman is fully planned out by the management at least one day in advance, and each man receives in most cases complete written instructions, describing in detail the task which he is to accomplish, as well as the means to be used in doing the work. And the work planned in advance in this way constitutes a task which is to be solved, as explained above, not by the workman alone, but in almost all cases by the joint effort of the workman and the management. This task specifies not only what is to be done but how it is to be done and the exact time allowed for doing it. And whenever the workman succeeds in doing his task right, and within the time limit specified, he receives an addition of from 30 per cent to 100 per cent to his ordinary wages. These tasks are carefully planned, so that both good and careful work are called for in their performance, but it should be distinctly understood that in no case is the workman called upon to work at a pace which would be injurious to his health. The task is always so regulated that the man who is well suited to his job will thrive while working at this rate during a long term of years and grow happier and more prosperous, instead of being overworked. Scientific management consists very largely in preparing for and carrying out these tasks. . . .

. . . In most trades, the science is developed through a comparatively simple analysis and time study of the movements required by the work-men to do some small part of his work, and this study is usually made by a man equipped merely with a stop-watch and a properly ruled notebook. Hundreds of these "time-study men" are now engaged in developing elementary scientific knowledge where before existed only rule of thumb. . . . The general steps to be taken in developing a simple law of this class are as follows:

> *First.* Find, say, 10 or 15 different men (preferably in as many separate es-tablishments and different parts of the country) who are especially skillful in doing the particular work to be analyzed.
>
> *Second.* Study the exact series of elementary operations or motions which each of these men uses in doing the work which is being investigated, as well as the implements each man uses.
>
> *Third.* Study with a stop-watch the time required to make each of these elementary movements and then select the quickest way of doing each element of the work.
>
> *Fourth.* Eliminate all false movements, slow movements, and useless move-ments.
>
> *Fifth.* After doing away with all unnecessary movements, collect into one series the quickest and best movements as well as the best implements.

This one new method, involving that series of motions which can be made quickest and best, is then substituted in place of the ten or fifteen inferior series which were formerly in use. This best method becomes standard, and remains standard, to be taught first to the teachers (or functional foremen) and by them to every workman in the establishment until it is superseded by a quicker and better series of movements. In this simple way one element after another of the science is developed.

In the same way each type of implement used in a trade is studied. Under the philosophy of the management of "initiative and incentive" each workman is called upon to use his own best judgment, so as to do the work in the quickest time, and from this results in all cases a large variety in the shapes and types of implements which are used for any specific purpose. Scientific management requires, first, a careful investigation of each of the many modifications of the same implement, developed under rule of thumb; and second, after a time study has been made of the speed attainable with each of these implements, that the good points of several of them shall be united in a single standard implement, which will enable the workman to work faster and with greater ease than he could before. This one implement, then, is adopted as standard in place of the many different kinds before in use, and it remains standard for all workmen to use until superseded by an implement which has been shown, through motion and time study, to be still better.

With this explanation it will be seen that the development of a science to replace rule of thumb is in most cases by no means a formidable undertaking, and that it can be accomplished by ordinary, every-day men without any elaborate scientific training; but that, on the other hand, the successful use of even the simplest improvement of this kind calls for records, system, and cooperation where in the past existed only individual effort. . . .

The general adoption of scientific management would readily in the future double the productivity of the average man engaged in industrial work. Think of what this means to the whole country. Think of the increase, both in the necessities and luxuries of life, which becomes available for the whole country, of the possibility of shortening the hours of labor when this is desirable, and of the increased opportunities for education, culture, and recreation which this implies. But while the whole world would profit by this increase in production, the manufacturer and the workman will be far more interested in the especial local gain that comes to them and to the people immediately around them. Scientific management will mean, for the employers and the workmen who adopt it—and particularly for those who adopt it first—the elimination of almost all causes for dispute and disagreement between them. What constitutes a fair day's work will be a question for scientific investigation, instead of a subject to be bargained and haggled over. Soldiering will cease because the object for soldiering will no longer exist. The great increase in wages which accompanies this type of management will largely eliminate the wage question as a source of dispute. But more than all other causes, the close, intimate cooperation, the constant personal contact between the two sides, will tend to diminish friction and discontent. It is difficult for two people whose interests are the same, and who work side by side in accomplishing the same object, all day long, to keep up a quarrel.

The low cost of production which accompanies a doubling of the output will enable the companies who adopt this management, particularly those who adopt it first, to compete far better than they were able to before, and this will so enlarge their markets that their men will have almost constant work even in dull times, and that they will earn larger profits at all times.

This means increase in prosperity and diminution in poverty, not only for their men but for the whole community immediately around them. . . .

Final Report of the Commission on Industrial Relations . . . and the Individual Reports and Statements of the Several Commissioners

The investigation of scientific management was conducted by Prof. Robert F. Hoxie, with the expert assistance and advice of Mr. Robert G. Valentine, representing the employer's interest in management, and Mr. John P. Frey, representing the interests of labor. The investigation grew out of public hearings held by the commission during the spring of 1914, at which the almost unqualified opposition of labor to scientific management was manifested. The purpose of the investigation was to test by the results of actual practice the claims of scientific management and the charges of the representatives of organized labor.

The investigation, which covered a period of more than a year, was made with the greatest care and thoroughness. Thirty-five shops and systematizing concerns were examined and interviews were had with a large number of scientific management leaders, experts, and employers. The shops visited were, almost without exception, those designated by authorities on scientific management, such as Messrs. Taylor, Gantt, and Emerson, as the best representatives of the actual results of scientific management. In other words, the examination was practically confined to the very best examples of scientific management. The defects and short-comings pointed out hereinafter are, therefore, characteristic of the system under the most favorable conditions.

As a result of their investigations, Prof. Hoxie, Mr. Valentine, and Mr. Frey submitted a report, agreed upon without exceptions, in which the statements and recommendations which follow are embodied. These statements constitute a very brief summary of the entire report, which should be read as a whole if a complete understanding of their results and findings is desired.

Throughout the report the term "scientific management" is understood to mean the system devised and applied by Frederick W. Taylor, H. L. Gantt, Harrington Emerson and their followers, with the object of promoting efficiency in shop management and operation.

The report, unanimously agreed upon by the commission's in-

Final Report of the Commission on Industrial Relations . . . , 64th Congress, 1916, Senate Document No. 415, pp. 127–43.

vestigator and his advisory experts, is the basis for the following statements.

POSSIBLE BENEFITS OF SCIENTIFIC
MANAGEMENT TO LABOR AND SOCIETY

1. As a system, scientific management presents certain possible benefits to labor and to society:

(a) A close causal relation exists between productive efficiency and
possible wages. Greater efficiency and output make possible higher wages
in general and better conditions of employment and labor.

In so far, then, as scientific management affords opportunities for
lower costs and increased production without adding to the burden of the
workers in exhaustive effort, long hours, or inferior working conditions, it
creates the possibility of very real and substantial benefits to labor and to
society.

(b) It is the policy of scientific management, as a preliminary to strictly
labor changes, to bring about improvement and standardization of the
material equipment and productive organization of the plant, particularly:

Machinery: Installation, repair, operation.

Tools: Storage, care, delivery.

Material equipment: Rearrangement to avoid delays, etc.

Product: Devices for economical and expeditious handling and routing.

Processes and methods: Elimination of waste motions, improvement of
accessories, etc.

Reorganization of managerial staff and improvement of managerial efficiency.

Reorganization of sales and purchasing departments with a view to broadening and stabilizing the market.

Improvements in methods of storekeeping and regulation of delivery, surplus
stock, etc.

All such improvements are to be commended, and investigation shows
that they are not only accepted by labor without opposition but are, in fact,
welcomed.

2. Scientific management in its direct relation to labor is not devoid of
beneficial aspects, inasmuch as it is to a large extent an attempt at immediate standardization of labor conditions and relations. It may also serve
labor by calling the attention of the employer to the fact that there are other
and more effective ways to meet severe competition than by "taking it out
of labor."

It is true that scientific management and organized labor are not
altogether in harmony in their attitude toward standardization of labor

conditions and relations. While both seek to have the conditions of work and pay clearly defined and definitely maintained at any given moment, they differ fundamentally as to the circumstances which may justly cause the substitution of new standards for old ones. Trade-unionism tends to hold to the idea that standards must not be changed in any way to the detriment of the workers. Scientific management, on the other hand, regards changes as justified and desirable if they result in increase of efficiency, and has provided methods, such as time study, for the constant suggestion of such changes.

3. The same may be said of many other major claims of scientific management. Whether the ideals advocated are attained or at present attainable, and whether scientific managers are to be found who purposely violate them, scientific management has in these claims and in the methods upon which they are based shown the way along which we may proceed to more advantageous economic results for labor and for society. It may not have succeeded in establishing a practical system of vocational selection and adaptation, but it has emphasized the desirability of it; it may not set the task with due and scientific allowance for fatigue so that the worker is guarded against overspeeding and overexertion, but it has undoubtedly developed methods which make it possible to better prevailing conditions in this respect; it has called attention most forcibly to the evils of favoritism and the rough and arbitrary decisions of foremen and others in authority. If scientific management be shown to have positive objectionable features, from both the standpoint of labor and the welfare of society, this constitutes no denial of these beneficial features, but calls rather for intelligent social action to eliminate that which is detrimental and to supplement and control that which is beneficial to all.

SCIENTIFIC MANAGEMENT IN PRACTICE— ITS DIVERSITIES AND DEFECTS

4. Conditions in actual shops do not conform to the ideals of the system, and show no general uniformity. Actual field investigations demonstrated beyond reasonable doubt that scientific management in practice is characterized by striking incompleteness and manifold diversity as compared with the theoretical exposition of its advocates. This incompleteness and diversity in practice apply not only to matters of detail but cover many of the essential features of scientific management even among those shops designated by Taylor, Gantt, and Emerson as representative of their work and influence. The following particular defects were observed:

(a) *Failure to carry into effect with any degree of thoroughness the general elements involved in the system.*—This may take the form of ignoring either the mechanical equipment and managerial organization, adopting simply a few routine features, such as time study and bonus payment, or the adoption of all mechanical features with a complete disregard of the spirit in which they are supposed to be applied.

(b) Failure to adopt the full system of "functional foremanship."—The results of prevailing practices do not support the claim that scientific management treats each workman as an independent personality and that it substitutes joint obedience to fact and law for obedience to personal authority.

(c) Lack of uniformity in the method of selecting and hiring help.—Upon the whole the range of excellence in methods of selection and hiring in "scientific" shops was the same as in other shops. The workers in scientific-management shops seem to be a select class when compared with the same classes of workers outside, but this result seems to be due to the weeding out of the less satisfactory material rather than to initial methods of selection.

(d) Failure to substantiate claims of scientific management with reference to the adaptation, instruction, and training of workers.—Scientific-management shops in general depend upon nothing in the way of occupational adaptation of the workers except the ordinary trial and error method. Investigation reveals little to substantiate the sweeping claims of scientific managers made in this connection, except that in the better scientific-management shops many workmen are receiving more careful instruction and a higher degree of training than is at present possible for them elsewhere. The most that can be said is that scientific management, as such, furthers a tendency to narrow the scope of the workers' industrial activity, and that it falls far short of a compensatory equivalent in its ideals and actual methods of instruction and training.

(e) Lack of scientific accuracy, uniformity, and justice in time study and task setting.—Far from being the invariable and purely objective matters that they are pictured, the methods and results of time study and task setting are in practice the special sport of individual judgment and opinion, subject to all the possibilities of diversity, inaccuracy, and injustice that arise from human ignorance and prejudice.

The objects of time study are: (1) Improvement and standardization of the methods of doing the work, without reference to a standard time for its accomplishment, and (2) fixing of a definite task time of efficiency scale.

Possibilities of great advantage exist in the use of time study for the first purpose. However, in a large number of shops, time study for this purpose is practically neglected.

In connection with the second purpose, setting of task time of efficiency scale, great variations are noted, and especially the part which fallible individual judgment and individual prejudice may and do play.

Detailed observations of the practice of making time studies and setting tasks showed great variations in methods and results. Seventeen separate sources of variation are pointed out, any one of which is sufficient to and in practice does greatly influence the results of time studies.

In face of such evidence it is obviously absurd to talk of time study as an accurate scientific method in practice or of the tasks set by means of it as objective scientific facts which are not possible or proper subjects of dispute and bargaining.

Furthermore, the time-study men upon whom the entire results depend were found to be prevailingly of the narrow-minded mechanical type, poorly paid, and occupying the lowest positions in the managerial organization, if they could be said to belong at all to the managerial group. Nor does the situation seem to promise much improvement, for the position and pay accorded to time-study men generally are such as to preclude the drawing into this work of really competent men in the broader sense. Aside from a few notable exceptions in the shops and some men who make a general profession of time study in connection with the installation of scientific management, this theoretically important functionary, as a rule, receives little more than good mechanic's wages and has little voice in determining shop policies. In fact, the time-study man, who, if scientific management is to make good the most important of its labor claims, should be among the most highly trained and influential officials in the shop, a scientist in viewpoint, a wise arbitrator between employer and workman, is in general a petty functionary, a specialist workman, a sort of clerk who has no voice in the counsels of the higher officials.

However, the method of time study is not necessarily impracticable or unjust to the workers. Under proper direction time study promises much more equitable results than can be secured by the ordinary methods. The greatest essential is a time-study man of exceptional knowledge, judgment, and tact. The average time-study man does not fulfill these requirements at present.

Finally, it is only in connection with standard products, requiring only moderate skill and judgment in layout and work, that economy seems to allow adequate application of the time-study method. Its natural sphere seems to be routine and repetitive work. As long as industry continues to be as complex and diversified as it is, this element of economy will without doubt continue to operate in a way to limit the legitimate scope of time study and task setting. Task setting as at present conducted is not satisfactory to workmen and creates dissatisfaction and jealousy.

(f) Failure to substantiate the claim of having established a scientific and equitable method of determining wage rates.—In analyzing the wage-fixing problem in connection with scientific management two matters are considered: (1) The "base rate," sometimes called the day wage, which constitutes for any group of workers the minimum earnings or indicates the general wage level for that group, and (2) added "efficiency payments," which are supposed to represent special additional rewards for special attainments.

The investigators sought in vain for any scientific methods devised or employed by scientific management for the determination of the base rate, either as a matter of justice between the conflicting claims of capital and labor, or between the relative claims of individuals and occupational groups.

Rates for women with reference to men are, as a rule, on the same basis in scientific-management shops as in other shops. One leader said, "There is to be no nonsense about scientific management. If by better organization and administration what is now regarded as man's work can be done by women, women will be employed and women's wages will be paid."

Scientific-management shops seem as ready as others to raise the rates as the wage level generally advances.

"Bewildering diversity" prevails in relation to the "efficiency payment" or reward for special effort. After a careful and extended analysis and investigation of the different ways of rewarding individual increases in output, it was concluded:

All of these systems definitely belie the claim that scientific management pays workers in proportion to their efficiency. One of them has the obvious intent of weeding out the lower grade of workers, while the other two are so constituted as to make such workers very unprofitable to the employers. Two of them lend themselves easily to the exploitation of mediocre workers—those who can deliver a medium output but can not attain to a standard task set high. All of them furnish a strong stimulus to high efficiency and output, but in themselves furnish no visible check on overspeeding and exhaustion. All of them are capable of being liberally applied, but all can also be used as instruments of oppression through the undue severity of task setting or efficiency rating.

There can be no doubt that under scientific management rates are cut. But to say positively that scientific management, on the whole, furthers the cutting of rates is quite another matter. The fact seems clear that at this point there is a conflict of tendencies within the thing itself. There is a strong inducement for scientific managers to maintain rates strictly, and the honest efforts of those who deserve the name to so maintain them can hardly be impugned. At the same time, however, the greatest advance toward efficiency, for which scientific management stands, is obtained by the constant alteration of conditions and tasks through time study. Such alterations almost of necessity mean constant rate cutting. Were industry once standardized for good and all, scientific management would undoubtedly operate as an unequivocal force tending to the maintenance of rates. As it is with industry in flux, what amounts to rate cutting seems to be almost of necessity an essential part of its very nature.

Finally, all of the systems of payment tend to center the attention of the worker on his individual interest and gain and to repress the development of group consciousness and interest. Where the work of one man is independent of another, the individual has no motive to consider his fellow, since his work and pay in no wise depend on the other man. What either does will not affect the other's task or rates. Where work is independent, the leader can not afford to slow down to accommodate his successor.

It must be admitted that these systems are admirably suited to stimulate the workers, but in so far as there may be virtue in the union principles of group solidarity and uniformity, and in so far as they lay claim to scientific accuracy or a special conformity to justice in reward, they must be judged adversely.

(g) *Failure to protect the workers from overexertion and exhaustion.*—It is claimed by scientific management that protection to workers is afforded by such devices as: Standardization of equipment and performance; substitution of exact knowledge of men and of machines for guesswork in the setting of the task and the determination of the hours and other conditions of work; careful studies of fatigue; elimination of the need for pace setters; transformation of speeders into instructors, and transfer of responsibility from the workers to the management for contriving the best methods of work; maintenance of the best conditions for performing work through furnishing the best tools and materials at the proper time and place; instruction of the workers in the most economical and easiest methods of performing operations; institution of rational rest periods and modes of recreation during working hours; and surrounding the workers with the safest and most sanitary shop conditions.

Investigation indicates that scientific management, in practice, furnishes no reasonable basis for the majority of these specific claims in the present, and little hope for their realization in the near future. In these matters, indeed, the utmost variation prevails in scientific management as in other shops. Several admirable cases were found with respect to all these matters, but shops were not wanting where the management exhibited the utmost suspicion of the workers, referring continually to their disposition to "beat the time-study man," although the time study in such shops was obviously based on the work of speeders and all sorts of inducements were offered for pace setting, where instruction and training of the workers were emphasized by their absence, and where the general conditions of the work were much in need of improvement.

The investigation seems to show clearly that practical scientific management has not materially affected the length of the working day. Aside from shops where the management was evidently imbued with a strong moral sense, the hours of labor in these shops were those common to the industry and the locality.

When we come to the matter of fatigue studies and their connection with speeding and exhaustion, the claims of scientific management seem to break down completely. No actual fatigue studies were found taking place in the shops, and the time-study men, who should be charged with such studies, seemed in general to be quite indifferent or quite ignorant in regard to this whole matter. This does not mean that no attention to fatigue is given in scientific management shops. Cases were found where the health and energy of the workers were carefully observed and attempts were made to adapt the work to their condition, but the methods employed were the rough-and-ready ones of common-sense observation. Rest periods and modes of recreation during the working hours are a regular institution on an extended scale in but one shop visited by the investigators. Isolated instances were encountered elsewhere, but managers in general apparently do not even entertain the idea of their institution.

Scientific management does not always surround the workers with the safest and most sanitary shop conditions. In general, scientific management shops seem to be good shops as shops go. The introduction of the system has the tendency without doubt to clean the shop up and to improve the condition of belting, machinery, and arrangement of material equipment generally. All this is in the direct line of efficiency and safety. Several very notable examples of excellence in safety and sanitation were found. On the other hand, several shops visited were below good standards in these respects, and flagrant specific violations of safety rules were encountered.

As a whole, the facts in nowise justify the assumption that scientific management offers any effective guaranty against overspeeding and exhaustion of workers. The investigation left a strong impression that scientific management workers in general are not overspeeded, but the challenge to show any overspeeded or overworked men in scientific management shops is very easily met. The situation in this respect varies much with the industry. Some instances of undoubted overspeeding were found, particularly in the case of girls and women. But these instances do not warrant a general charge. On the other hand, there appears to be nothing in the special methods of scientific management to prevent speeding up where the technical conditions make it possible and profitable, and there is much in these methods to induce it in the hands of unscrupulous employers.

(*h*) *Failure to substantiate the claim that scientific management offers exceptional opportunities for advancement and promotion on a basis of individual merit.*—While scientific management undoubtedly separates the efficient from the inefficient more surely and speedily than ordinary methods, it was shown by the investigation that scientific management often fails in the development of functional foremanship and in the elimination of favoritism. It tends to create a multitude of new tasks on which less skill is required and lower rates can be paid. It has developed no efficient system for the placing or adaptation of the workers. It is inclined in practice to regard a worker as adapted to his work and rightly placed when he succeeds in making the task. It tends to confine the mass of workmen to one or two tasks, and offers little opportunity, therefore, for the discovery and development of special aptitudes among the masses. It tends to divide the workers into two unequal classes—the few who rise to managerial positions and the many who seem bound to remain task workers within a narrow field. In the ideal it offers opportunity for promotion from the ranks, and this works out to a certain extent in practice, but not universally.

There is a great deal of exaggeration, too, in statements made concerning special rewards for usable suggestions. Few of the shops make any systematic rewards of this kind, and where this is the case the rewards are usually trivial. In one shop the investigator was shown an automatic machine invented by a workman, which did the work of several hand workers. "Did he receive a reward?" was asked. "Oh, yes," came the answer, "his rate of pay was increased from 17 to 22 cents per hour."

(*i*) *With reference to the alleged methods and severity of discipline under scientific management the "acrimonious criticism" from trade unions does not seem to be warranted.*—In theory, the scientific managers appear to have the best of the argument, and in practice the investigation showed an agreeable absence of rough and arbitrary disciplinary authority. When the tasks were liberally set, the workers were found generally operating without special supervision except where instructions or assistance were needed. Deductions were indeed made for poor work and destruction of materials, but in the better class of shops apparently with no greater and perhaps with less than ordinary severity.

While it should be remembered that the shops selected represented probably the best of the shops operating under this system, in general, it would seem that scientific management does lessen the rigors of discipline as compared with other shops where the management is autocratic and the workers have no organization.

(*j*) *Failure to substantiate the claim that workers are discharged only on just grounds and have an effective appeal to the highest managerial authority.*—This whole matter is one in which neither management claims nor union complaints seem susceptible of proof, but the investigation indicates that the unions have legitimate basis for charging that discharge is generally a matter of arbitrary managerial authority.

(*k*) *Lack of democracy under scientific management.*—As a result of the investigation, there can be little doubt that scientific management tends in practice to weaken the power of the individual worker as against the employer, setting aside all questions of personal attitude and the particular opportunities and methods for voicing complaints and enforcing demands. It gathers up and transfers to the management the traditional craft knowledge and transmits this again to the workers only piecemeal as it is needed in the performance of the particular job or task. It tends in practice to confine each worker to a particular task or small cycle of tasks. It thus narrows his outlook and skill to the experience and training which are necessary to do the work. He is therefore easier of displacement. Moreover, the changing of methods and conditions of work and the setting of tasks by time study with its assumption always of scientific accuracy puts the individual worker at a disadvantage in any attempt to question the justice of the demands made upon him. The onus of proof is upon him and the standards of judgment are set up by the employer, covered by the mantle of scientific accuracy.

It would seem also that scientific management tends, on the whole, to prevent the formation of groups of workers within the shop with recognized common interests, and to weaken the solidarity of those which exist. Almost everything points to the strengthening of the individualistic motive and the weakening of group solidarity. Each worker is bent on the attainment of his individual task. He can not combine with his fellows to determine how much that task shall be. If the individual slows down he merely lessens his wages and prejudices his standing without helping his neighbor. If he can beat the other fellow, he helps himself without directly affecting the other's task or pay. Assistance, unless the man is a paid instructor, is at personal cost. Special rewards, where offered, are for the individual. Rules of seniority are not recognized. Sometimes personal rivalry is stimulated by the posting of individual records or classification of the workers by name into "excellent," "good," "poor," etc. Potential groups are broken up by the constant changes in methods and reclassification of workers which are the mission of time study. The whole gospel of scientific management to the worker is to the individual, telling him how, by special efficiency, he can cut loose from the mass, and rise in wages or position.

With the power of the individual weakened and the chances lessened for the development of groups and group solidarity, the democratic possibility of scientific management, barring the presence of unionism, would seem to be scant. The individual is manifestly in no position to cope with the employer on a basis of equality. The claim to democracy based on the close association of the management and the men and the opportunities allowed for the voicing of complaints is not borne out by the facts; and in the general run of scientific-management shops, barring the presence of unionism and collective bargaining, the unionists are justified in the charge that the workers have no real voice in hiring and discharging, the setting of the task, the determination of the wage rates, or the general conditions of employment. This charge is true even where the employers have no special autocratic tendencies, much more so therefore where, as in many cases, they are thoroughly imbued with the autocratic spirit. With rare exceptions, then, democracy under scientific management can not and does not exist apart from unionism and collective bargaining.

Does the scientific manager, as a matter of fact, welcome the cooperation of unionism? Here, again, the facts should decide the contention. The fact is that while in numbers of scientific-management shops some unionists are employed, they are not generally employed as union men, and the union is rarely recognized and dealt with as such. The fact is that those who declare the willingness of scientific management to welcome the cooperation of unionism in general either know nothing about unionism and its rules and regulations or are thinking of a different kind of unionism from that to which the American Federation of Labor stands committed and a kind of cooperation foreign to its ideals and practices.

To sum up, scientific management in practice generally tends to weaken the competitive power of the individual worker and thwarts the formation of shop groups and weakens group solidarity; moreover, generally scientific management is lacking in the arrangements and machinery necessary for the actual voicing of the workers' ideas and complaints and for the democratic consideration and adjustment of grievances. Collective bargaining has ordinarily no place in the determination of matters vital to the workers, and the attitude toward it is usually tolerant only when it is not understood. Finally unionism, where it means a vigorous attempt to enforce the viewpoint and claims of the workers, is in general looked upon with abhorrence, and unions which are looked upon with complacency are not the kind which organized labor in general wants, while the union cooperation which is invited is altogether different from that which they stand ready to give. In practice scientific management must therefore be declared autocratic in tendency—a reversion to industrial autocracy, which forces the workers to depend on the employers' conception of fairness and limits the democratic safeguards of the workers.

5. Scientific management is still in its infancy or early trial stages, and immaturity and failure to attain ideals in practice are necessary accompaniments to the development of any new industrial or social movement. Doubtless many of its diversities and shortcomings will, therefore, be cured by time.

Before this can be brought about, however, certain potent causes of present evil must be eradicated:

(a) The first of these is a persistent attempt on the part of experts and managers to apply scientific management and its methods outside their natural sphere.

(b) A second chief source of danger and evil to labor in the application of scientific management is that it offers its wares in the open market, but it has developed no means by which it can control the use of these by the purchaser. In large part the practical departure of scientific management from its ideals is the result of special managerial or proprietorial aims and impatience of delay in their fulfillment. The expert is frequently called in because the establishment is in financial or industrial straits, and the chief concern of the management is quick increase of production and profits. It must meet its competitors here and now, and can not afford to expend more than is necessary to do this, or to forego immediate returns while the foundations are being laid for a larger but later success, and with careful regard to immediate justice and the longtime welfare of its working force. The outcome frequently is conflict between the systematizer and the management, resulting in the abandonment of the scheme only partially worked out on the retirement of the expert, leaving the management to apply crudely the methods partially installed, sometimes to the detriment of the workers and their interests.

It is true that the situation thus outlined is not of universal application. But bitter complaints were frequently heard from members of the small group of experts who represent the highest ideals and intelligence of the movement, in regard to the managerial opposition which they have encountered, and frequent apologies were offered for the conditions and results of their work, accompanied by the statement that they could go no further than the management would allow, or that things had been done by the management against their judgment and for which they could not stand. Moreover, scientific management is closely interlocked with the mechanism of production for profit and the law of economy rules. Many things which would be desirable from the ideal standpoint, and which are a practical necessity if the interests of the workers are to be fully protected, are not always or usually economical. This is specially true of time study, task setting, and rate making.

The arbitrary will of the employer and the law of economy are two potent special forces which contribute to the existing diversity, incompleteness, and crudity of scientific management as it is practiced, even where the systematizer is possessed of the highest intelligence and imbued with the best motives of his group.

(c) But to explain the situation as it exists at present, two other important factors must be taken into consideration. The first of these is the existence and practice of self-styled scientific management systematizers and time study experts who lack in most respects the ideals and the training essential to fit them for the work which they claim to be able to do. Scientific management as a movement is cursed with fakirs. The great rewards which a few leaders in the movement have secured for their services have brought into the field a crowd of industrial "patent medicine men." The way is open to all. No standards or requirements, private or public, have been developed by the application of which the goats can be separated from the sheep. Employers have thus far proved credulous. Almost anyone can show the average manufacturing concern where it can make some improvements in its methods. So the scientific management shingles have gone up all over the country, the fakirs have gone into the shops, and in the name of scientific management have reaped temporary gains to the detriment of both the employers and the workers.

(d) Fake scientific management experts, however, are not alone responsible for the lack of training and intelligence which contributes to the diversity and immaturity of scientific management in practice and its failure to make good the labor claims of its most distinguished leaders. The fact is that on the whole, and barring some notable exceptions, the sponsors and adherents of scientific management—experts and employers alike—are profoundly ignorant of very much that concerns the broader humanitarian and social problems which it creates and involves, especially as these touch the character and welfare of labor.

It is because of this ignorance and unwarranted assurance that there is a strong tendency on the part of scientific management experts to look upon the labor end of their work as the least difficult and requiring the least careful consideration. To their minds the delicate and difficult part of the task of installation is the solution of the material, mechanical, and organic problems involved. They tend to look upon the labor end of their work as a simple technical matter of so setting tasks and making rates that the workers will give the fullest productive cooperation. They tend naively to assume that when the productivity of the concern is increased and the laborers are induced to do their full part toward this end, the labor problem in connection with scientific management is satisfactorily solved. In short, in the majority of cases the labor problem appears to be looked at as one aspect of the general problem of production in the shop, and it is truthfully assumed that if it is solved with reference to this problem it must also be solved with due regard to labor's well-being and its just demands. This seems to have been the characteristic attitude of scientific management from the beginning. Labor was simply looked upon as one of the factors entering into production, like machinery, tools, stores, and other elements of equipment. The problem was simply how to secure an efficient coordination and functioning of these elements. It was only after the opposition of labor had been expressed that scientific management began to be conscious of any other aspect of the labor matter. And with some notable exceptions scientific management experts and employers still look upon the labor matter almost solely as an aspect of the general production problem, and have little positive interest or concern in regard to it otherwise.

It is probable that scientific managers will object to these statements, pleading that they are mainly variations and conditions due to the time element or to the necessity imposed by the law of costs. They will say, for example, that when a new and unusual job comes in, neither time nor economy will allow of careful time studies, and if careful studies were made of all the variations of a complicated task, the expense of such studies would wipe out the profit; that, in general, they are proceeding toward the full realization of the ideal of scientific management as fast as economy will allow. But such pleas would serve only to confirm the main contention that scientific managers and scientific management employers generally are necessarily ruled, like all members of the employing group, by the forces of cost and profits; that to them the labor problem is primarily an aspect of the problem of production, and that in the ends the needs and welfare of labor must be subordinated to these things. Beneath all other causes or shortcomings of scientific management, therefore, in its relation to labor, there seems to be the practical fact of an opposition of interests between the profit-taking and the labor group, which makes extremely doubtful the possibility that its shortcomings from the standpoint of labor are capable of elimination.

GENERAL LABOR PROBLEMS

6. *(a)* Scientific management at its best furthers the modern tendency toward the specialization of the workers. Its most essential features—functional foremanship, time study, task setting, and efficiency payment—all have this inherent effect.

Under the scientific management system fully developed, the ordinary mechanic is intended to be and is, in fact, a machine feeder and a machine feeder only, with the possibility of auxiliary operations clearly cut off and with means applied to discourage experimentation. And what applies to the machine feeder applies with more or less thoroughness to machine and hand operatives generally.

But it is not merely in stripping from the job its auxiliary operations that scientific management tends to specialize the work and the workmen. Time study, the chief cornerstone of all systems of scientific management, tends inherently to the narrowing of the job or task itself. As the final object of time study, so far as it directly touches the workers, is to make possible the setting of tasks so simple and uniform and so free from possible causes of interruption and variation that definite and invariable time limits can be placed upon them, and that the worker may be unimpeded in his efficient performance of them by the necessity for questioning and deliberation, the preponderating tendency of time study is to split up the work into smaller and simpler operations and tasks. Decidedly, then, time study tends to further the modern tendency toward specialization of the job and the task.

With functional foremanship lopping off from the job auxiliary operations, and time study tending to a narrowing of the task itself, task setting and efficiency methods of payment come into play as forces tending to confine the worker to a single task or a narrow range of operations. The worker is put upon the special task for which he seems best adapted, and he is stimulated by the methods of payment employed to make himself as proficient as possible at it. When he succeeds in this, to shift him to another task ordinarily involves an immediate and distinct loss to the employer, and the worker himself naturally resents being shifted to a new task since this involves an immediate loss in his earnings. Here worker and employer are as one in their immediate interest to have the job so simple that the operation can be quickly learned, and the task made, and that shifting of tasks be eliminated as far as possible. The employer besides has another motive for this, in that the shifting of the workers multiplies the records and renders more complex the system of wage accounting. It is true that the scientific management employer, like any other, must have a certain number of workers in the shop who are capable of performing a plurality of tasks. But the tendency is to have as few all-round workers as are necessary to meet these emergencies. The methods of scientific management operate most effectively when they break up and narrow the work of the individual, and the ends of scientific management are best served when the rank and file of the workers are specialists.

This inherent tendency of scientific management to specialization is buttressed, broadened in its scope and perpetuated by the progressive gathering up and systematizing in the hands of the employers of all the traditional craft knowledge in the possession of the workers. With this information in hand and functional foremanship to direct its use, scientific management claims to have no need of craftsmen, in the old sense of the term, and, therefore, no need for an apprenticeship system except for the training of functional foremen. It therefore tends to neglect apprenticeship except for the training of the few. And as this body of systematized knowledge in the hands of the employer grows, it is enabled to broaden the scope of its operation, to attack and specialize new operations, new crafts and new industries, so that the tendency is to reduce more and more to simple, specialized operations, and more and more workers to the positions of narrow specialists. Nor does scientific management afford anything in itself to check or offset this specialization tendency. The instruction and training offered is for specialist workmen. Selection and adaption are specializing in their tendencies. Promotion is for the relatively few. The whole system, in its conception and operation, is pointed toward a universally specialized industrial regime.

(b) But scientific management is not only inherently specializing; it also tends to break down existing standards and uniformities set up by the workmen, and to prevent the establishment of stable conditions of work and pay. Time study means constant and endless change in the method of operation. No sooner is a new and better method discovered and established and the condition of work and pay adapted to it than an improvement is discovered involving perhaps new machinery, new tools and materials, a new way of doing things, and a consequent alteration of the essential conditions of work and pay, and perhaps a reclassification of the workers.

(c) Ample evidence to support this analysis was afforded by the investigation. Where the system was found relatively completely applied, the mass of the workers were engaged in specialized tasks, there was little variation in the operations except in emergencies, apprenticeship for the many was abandoned or was looked upon as an investment which brought no adequate returns and was slated for abandonment; almost everywhere scientific management employers expressed a strong preference for specialist workmen, old crafts were being broken up and the craftsmen given the choice of retirement or of entering the ranks of specialized workmen; in the most progressive shops, the time-study men were preparing the way for a broader application of the system by the analytical study of the operations and crafts not yet systematized. Changes in methods and classification of workers were seen even during the short course of the investigation.

(d) What does this mean from the standpoint of labor and labor welfare? Certain conclusions are inevitable. Scientific management, fully and properly applied, inevitably tends to the constant breakdown of the established crafts and craftsmanship and the constant elimination of skill in the sense of narrowing craft knowledge and workmanship except for the lower orders of workmen. Some scientific management employers have asserted belief in their ability to get on a paying basis within three months, should they lose their whole working force except the managerial staff and enough others to maintain the organization, if they had to begin all over again with green hands. What this means in increased competition of workmen with workmen can be imagined. Were the scientific management ideal fully realized, any man who walks the street would be a practical competitor for almost any workman's job.

Such a situation would inevitably break down the basis of present-day unionism and render collective bargaining impossible in any effective sense in regard to the matters considered by the unions most essential. It has been proved by experience that unskilled workers generally find it most difficult to maintain effective and continuous organization for dealing with complicated industrial situations. Effective collective bargaining can not exist without effective organization. Moreover, we have already seen how scientific management, apart from the matter of skill, tends to prevent the formation and weakens the solidarity of groups within the shops.

But, beyond all this, time study strikes at the heart and core of the principles and conditions which make effective unionism and collective bargaining possible with respect to certain most essential matters. When the employer can constantly initiate new methods and conditions and reclassify the work and the workmen, he can evade all efforts of the union to establish and maintain definite and continuous standards of work and pay. Time study is in definite opposition to uniformity and stable classification. It enables the employer constantly to lop off portions of the work from a certain class and then to create new classifications of workers, with new conditions of work and pay. Add to all of this the advantage gained by the employers in the progressive gathering up and systematization of craft knowledge for their own uses, and the destruction of apprenticeship, which cuts the workers off from the perpetuation among them of craftsmanship, and the destructive tendencies of scientific management as far as present-day unionism and collective bargaining are concerned, seems inevitable.

(e) Under these circumstances the progressive degeneration of craftsmanship and the progressive degradation of skilled craftsmen also seems inevitable.

(f) The ultimate effects of scientific management, should it become universal, upon wages, employment, and industrial peace, are matters of pure speculation. During the period of transition, however, there can be little doubt of the results. The tendency will be first toward a realignment of wage rates. The craftsmen, the highly trained workers, can not hope to maintain their wage advantage over the semiskilled and less skilled workers. There will be a leveling tendency. Whether this leveling will be up or down, it is impossible to say. At present scientific management seems to be making the relatively unskilled more efficient than ever before, and they are in general receiving under it greater earnings than ever before. It is evident, however, that the native efficiency of the working class must suffer from the neglect of apprenticeship. Scientific managers have themselves complained bitterly of the poor material from which they must recruit their workers, compared with the efficient and self-respecting craftsman who applied for employment 20 years ago.

Moreover, it must not be overlooked that the whole scheme of scientific management, and especially the gathering up and systematizing of the knowledge formerly the possession of the workmen, tends enormously to add to the strength of capitalism. This fact, together with the greater ease of displacement shown above, must make the security and continuity of employment inherently more uncertain.

If generally increased efficiency is the result of scientific management, unemployment would in the end seem to become less of a menace. But during the period of transition its increase should be expected. Not only must the old craftsmen suffer as the result of the destruction of their crafts, but until scientific management finds itself able to control markets its increased efficiency must result in gluts in special lines, with resulting unemployment in particular trades and occupations. A leading scientific-management expert has stated that one shop of six in a certain industry systematized by him could turn out all the product that the market would carry. The result to the workers, if the statement be true, needs no explanation. Scientific management would seem to offer possibilities ultimately of better market control or better adaptation to market conditions, but the experience of the past year of depression indicates that at present no such possibilities generally exist.

Finally, until unionism as it exists has been done away with or has undergone essential modification, scientific management can not be said to make for the avoidance of strikes and the establishment of industrial peace. The investigation has shown several well-authenticated cases of strikes which have occurred in scientific-management shops. They are perhaps less frequent in this class of shop than elsewhere in similar establishments, owing largely to the fact that organized workmen are on the whole little employed. In its extension, however, it is certain that scientific management is a constant menace to industrial peace. So long as present-day unionism exists and unionists continue to believe, as they seem warranted in doing, that scientific management means the destruction of their organizations or their present rules and regulations, unionism will continue to oppose it energetically and whenever and wherever opportunity affords.

It has been said with much truth that scientific management is like the invention of machinery in its effect upon workers and social conditions and welfare generally—that it gives a new impulse to the industrial revolution which characterized the latter part of the eighteenth and nineteenth centuries and strengthens its general effects and tendencies. A chief characterization of this revolution has been the breakdown of craftsmanship, the destruction of crafts, and the carrying of the modern industrial world toward an era of specialized workmanship and generally semiskilled or unskilled workmen. Scientific management seems to be another force urging us forward toward this era.

CONCLUSIONS

7. Our industries should adopt all methods which replace inaccuracy with accurate knowledge and which systematically operate to eliminate economic waste. Scientific management at its best has succeeded in creating an organic whole of the several departments of an institution, establishing a coordination of their functions which has previously been impossible, and, in this respect, it has conferred great benefits on industry.

The social problem created by scientific management, however, does not lie in this field. As regards its social consequences neither organized nor unorganized labor finds in scientific management any adequate protection to its standards of living, any progressive means for industrial education, any opportunity for industrial democracy by which labor may create for itself a progressively efficient share in management. Therefore, as unorganized labor is totally unequipped to work for these human rights, it becomes doubly the duty of organized labor to work unceasingly and unswervingly for them, and, if necessary, to combat an industrial development which not only does not contain conditions favorable to their growth, but, in many respects, is hostile soil. . . .

SUGGESTIONS FOR FURTHER READING

Graham Adams, Jr., *Age of Industrial Violence, 1910–1915: The Activities and Findings of the United States Commission on Industrial Relations* (New York: Columbia Univ. Pr., 1966); Abraham Bisno, *Abraham Bisno: Union Pioneer* (Madison, Wis.: University of Wisconsin Press, 1967), especially pp. 211–17 for a critique of scientific management from the workers' point of view; and Samuel Haber, *Efficiency and Uplift: Scientific Management in the Progressive Era, 1890–1920* (Chicago: University of Chicago Press, 1964).

VII

❦

AMERICANIZATION VERSUS CULTURAL PLURALISM

The heavy influx of immigrants to the United States during the decades prior to 1915 prompted a broad array of responses, ranging from harsh rejection by old-stock nativists to ambivalent enthusiasm from manufacturers who welcomed the supply of cheap labor. Less readily noticed are the contrasting positions of various Progressives. Although these positions were not 180 degrees apart, they were vigorously contested and they set the agenda for an intense dialogue that continues to this day.

Edward A. Ross (1866–1961) became a pioneer in the discipline of sociology and taught at the University of Wisconsin from 1906 until his retirement in 1937. His major book, Social Control (1901), attempted to explain the sociological concept of order in a mass society. Subsequent work helped to transform American social thought from a deterministic and conservative mode to a reformist, environmentalist one.

Despite that Progressive outlook, however, Ross believed in British racial superiority and opposed unlimited immigration because it was not good for the native labor force. In 1898 he wrote from Paris to Lester Frank Ward that "the general result of my studies has been to convince me of the existence of moral varieties in the human species and to lead me to take as my problem the explanation of social order in the Aryan type of man, particularly the Celto-German stock." In 1913–14 he published a long series of monthly essays in The Century magazine—the most popular middlebrow monthly in the United States—in which he passed judgment on which groups of foreigners could best assimilate and contribute to American life and which could not. Ultimately, the ability to adapt and Americanize was essential in Ross's thinking.

Horace M. Kallen (1882–1974) was born in Silesia (eastern Germany) as a Russian subject. His Latvian father, having been expelled by Bismarck's Prussian government as an alien Jew, moved his family to Boston in 1887 where he found a position as rabbi to a German-speaking Orthodox congregation. Kallen rebelled against his father's traditional and (to him) coercive, disciplinary education. On occasion he ran away from home, but in the streets of Boston he encountered brutal manifestations of anti-Semitism. After he entered Harvard College in 1900, Kallen was deeply influenced by a stellar galaxy of teachers, particularly Barrett Wendell, a *pioneer in American literature. After teaching English at Princeton for a few years, Kallen returned to Harvard and completed a Ph.D. in English and philosophy in 1908 with a dissertation supervised by the philosopher William James. From 1911 until 1918 Kallen taught philosophy and psychology at the University of Wisconsin, where Edward A. Ross also taught. Despite its reputation as the most liberal university in the United States, Wisconsin was affected by the loyalty hysteria prompted by World War I. In 1918 Kallen resigned over issues involving academic freedom. The next year he was invited to join the original faculty of the New School for Social Research in New York. Kallen taught there until his retirement in 1970 at the age of 82.*

During his long and distinguished career, Kallen developed a social philosophy that reconciled his Jewishness and his Americanness. He generalized from his personal dilemmas to the society as a whole that "the tension between an ancient authoritarian monism [singularity] of culture and the free cultural pluralism intrinsic to the American Idea has been the vital spring of the nation's history." As a result of his personal struggle with contested values during his young manhood, quite early in his career Kallen developed a social philosophy that rejected the "melting pot" ideal of Israel Zangwill (1908) and Edward A. Ross. In so doing, he anticipated the multiculturalism that is widely advocated today.

American Blood and Immigrant Blood

EDWARD A. ROSS

. . . The conditions of settlement of this country caused those of uncommon energy and venturesomeness to outmultiply the rest of the population. Thus came into existence the pioneering breed; and this breed increased until it is safe to estimate that fully half of white Americans with native grandparents have one or more pioneers among their ancestors. Whatever valuable race traits distinguish the American people from the parent European stocks are due to the efflorescence of this breed. Without it there would have been little in the performance of our people to arrest the attention of the world. Now we confront the melancholy spectacle of this pioneer breed being swamped and submerged by an overwhelming tide of latecomers from the old-world hive. In Atlanta still seven out of eight white men had American parents; in Nashville and Richmond, four out of five; in Kansas City, two out of three; and in Los Angeles, one out of two; but in Detroit, Cleveland, and Paterson one man out of five had American parents; in Chicago and New York, one out of six; in Milwaukee, one out of seven; and in Fall River, one out of nine. Certainly never since the colonial era have the foreign-born and their children formed so large a proportion of the American people as at the present moment. I scanned 368 persons as they passed me in Union Square, New York, at a time when the garment-workers of the Fifth Avenue lofts were returning to their homes. Only thirty-eight of these passers-by had the type of face one would find at a county fair in the West or South.

In the six or seven hundred thousand strangers that yearly join themselves to us for good and all, there are to be found, of course, every talent and every beauty. Out of the steerage come persons as fine and noble as any who have trodden American soil. Any adverse characterization of an immigrant stream implies, then, only that the trait is relatively frequent, not that it is universal.

In this sense it is fair to say that the blood now being injected into the veins of our people is "sub-common." To one accustomed to the aspect of the normal American population, the Caliban type shows up with a frequency that is startling. Observe immigrants not as they come travel-wan up the gang-plank, nor as they issue toil-begrimed from pit's mouth or mill gate, but in their gatherings, washed, combed, and in their Sunday best.

Edward A. Ross, "American Blood and Immigrant Blood," ch. 12 in *The Old World in the New: The Significance of Past and Present Immigration to the American People* (New York: Century Co., 1914).

You are struck by the fact that from ten to twenty per cent are hirsute, low-browed, big-faced persons of obviously low mentality. Not that they suggest evil. They simply look out of place in black clothes and stiff collar, since clearly they belong in skins, in wattled huts at the close of the Great Ice Age. These oxlike men are descendants of those *who always stayed behind*. Those in whom the soul burns with the dull, smoky flame of the pine-knot stuck to the soil, and are now thick in the sluiceways of immigration. Those in whom it burns with a clear, luminous flame have been attracted to the cities of the home land and, having prospects, have no motive to submit themselves to the hardships of the steerage.

To the practiced eye, the physiognomy of certain groups unmistakably proclaims inferiority of type. I have seen gatherings of the foreign-born in which narrow and sloping foreheads were the rule. The shortness and smallness of the crania were very noticeable. There was much facial asymmetry. Among the women, beauty, aside from the fleeting, epidermal bloom of girlhood, was quite lacking. In every face there was something wrong—lips thick, mouth coarse, upper lip too long, cheek-bones too high, chin poorly formed, the bridge of the nose hollowed, the base of the nose tilted, or else the whole face prognathous. There were so many sugar-loaf heads, moon-faces, slit mouths, lantern-jaws, and goose-bill noses that one might imagine a malicious jinn had amused himself by casting human beings in a set of skew-molds discarded by the Creator.

Our captains of industry give a crowbar to the immigrant with a number nine face on a number six head, make a dividend out of him, and imagine that is the end of the matter. They overlook that this man will beget children in his image—two or three times as many as the American— and that these children will in turn beget children. They chuckle at having opened an inexhaustible store of cheap tools and, lo! the American people is being altered for all time by these tools. Once before, captains of industry took a hand in making this people. Colonial planters imported Africans to hoe in the sun, to "develop" the tobacco, indigo, and rice plantations. Then, as now, business-minded men met with contempt the protests of a few idealists against their way of "building up the country."

Those promoters of prosperity are dust, but they bequeathed a situation which in four years wiped out more wealth than two hundred years of slavery had built up, and which presents today the one unsolvable problem in this country. Without likening immigrants to negroes, one may point out how the latter-day employer resembles the old-time planter in his blindness to the effects of his labor policy upon the blood of the nation. . . .

The Northerners seem to surpass the southern Europeans in innate ethical endowment. Comparison of their behavior in marine disasters shows that discipline, sense of duty, presence of mind, and consideration for the weak are much more characteristic of northern Europeans. The southern Europeans, on the other hand, are apt, in their terror, to forget discipline, duty, women, children, everything but the saving of their own lives. In shipwreck it is the exceptional Northerner who forgets his duty, and the exceptional Southerner who is bound by it. . . .

NATURAL ABILITY

The performance of the foreign-born and their children after they have had access to American opportunities justifies the democrat's faith that latent capacity exists all through the humbler strata of society. On the other hand, it also confirms the aristocrat's insistence that social ranks correspond somewhat with the grades of natural ability existing within a people. The descendants of Europe's lowly are to be met in all the upper levels of American society, *but not so frequently* as the descendants of those who were high or rising in the land they left.

In respect to the value it contains, a stream of immigrants may be *representative*, *super-representative*, or *sub-representative* of the home people. When it is a fair sample, it is *representative;* when it is richer in wheat and poorer in chaff, it is *super-representative;* when the reverse is the case, it is *sub-representative.* What counts here, of course, is not the value the immigrants may have acquired by education or experience, but that fundamental worth which does not depend on opportunity, and which may be transmitted to one's descendants. Now, in the present state of our knowledge, it is perhaps risky to make a comparison in ability between the races which contributed the old immigration and those which are supplying the new immigration. Though backward, the latter may contain as good stuff. But it is fair to assume that a *super-representative* immigration from one stock is worth more to us than a *sub-representative* immigration from another stock, and that an influx which sub-represents a European people will thin the blood of the American people.

Many things have decided whether Europe should send America cream or skimmed milk. Religious or political oppression is apt to drive out the better elements. Racial oppression cannot be evaded by mere conformity; hence the emigration it sets up is apt to be representative. An unsubdued and perilous land attracts the more bold and enterprising. The seekers of homesteads include men of better stuff than the job-seekers attracted by high wages for unskilled labor. Only economic motives set in motion the sub-common people, but even in an economic emigration the early stage brings more people of initiative than the later. The deeper, straighter, and smoother the channels of migration, the lower the stratum they can tap.

It is not easy to value the early elements that were wrought into the American people. Often a stream of immigration that started with the best drained from the lower levels after it had worn itself a bed. It is therefore only in a broad way that I venture to classify the principal colonial migrations as follows:

Super-representative: English Pilgrims, Puritans, Quakers, Catholics, Scotch Covenanters, French Huguenots, German sectaries.

Representative: English of Virginia, Maryland, and the Carolinas, Scotch-Irish, Scotch Highlanders, Dutch, and Swedes.

Sub-representative: English of early Georgia, transported English, eighteenth-century Germans.

In our national period the Germans of 1848 stand out as a *super-representative* flow. The Irish stream has been *representative*, as was also the early German migration. The German inflow since 1870 has brought us very few of the elite of their people, and I have already given reasons for believing that the Scandinavian stream is not altogether *representative*. Our immigration from Great Britain has distinctly fallen off in grade since the chances in America came to be less attractive than those in the British Empire.

Oppression is now out of fashion over most of Europe, and our public lands are gone. Economic motives more and more bring us immigrants, and such motives will not uproot the educated, the propertied, the established, the well connected. The children of success are not migrating, which means that we get few scions from families of proved capacity. Europe retains most of her brains, but sends multitudes of the common and the sub-common. There is little sign of an intellectual element among the Magyars, Russians, South Slavs, Italians, Greeks, or Portuguese. This does not hold, however, for currents created by race discrimination or oppression. The Armenian, Syrian, Finnish, and Russo-Hebrew streams seem *representative*, and the first wave of Hebrews out of Russia in the eighties was superior. The Slovaks, German Poles, Lithuanians, Esthonians, and other restive subject groups probably send us a fair sample of their quality. . . .

When a more-developed element is obliged to compete on the same economic plane with a less-developed element, the standards of cleanliness or decency or education cherished by the advanced element act on it like a slow poison. William does not leave as many children as 'Tonio, because he will not huddle his family into one room, eat macaroni off a bare board, work his wife barefoot in the field, and keep his children weeding onions instead of at school. Even moral standards may act as poison. Once the women raisin-packers at Fresno, California, were American-born. Now the American women are leaving because of the low moral tone that prevails in the working force by reason of the coming in of foreigners with lax notions of propriety. The coarseness of speech and behavior among the packers is giving raisin-packing a bad name, so that American women are quitting the work and taking the next best job. Thus the very decency of the native is a handicap to success and to fecundity. . . .

Democracy versus
the Melting Pot

HORACE M. KALLEN

All immigrants and their offspring are by the way of undergoing "Americanization" if they remain in one place in the country long enough—say six or seven years. The general notion of "Americanization" appears to signify the adoption of the American variety of English speech, American clothes and manners, the American attitude in politics. "Americanization" signifies, in short, the disappearance of the external differences upon which so much race-prejudice often feeds. It appears to imply the fusion of the various bloods, and a transmutation by "the miracle of assimilation" of Jews, Slavs, Poles, Frenchmen, Germans, Hindus, Scandinavians and so on into beings similar in background, tradition, outlook and spirit to the descendants of the British colonists, the "Anglo-Saxon" stock. Broadly speaking, these elements of Americanism are somewhat external, the effect of environment; largely internal, the effect of heredity, social and personal. Thus American economic individualism, American traditional *laissez-faire* policy is largely the effect of environment; where nature offers more than enough potential wealth to go round, there is no immediate need for regulating distribution. . . .

. . . At his core, no human being, even in a "state of nature," is a mere mathematical unit of action like the "economic man." Behind him in time and tremendously in him in quality, are his ancestors; around him in space are his relatives and kin, carrying in common with him the inherited organic set from a remoter common ancestry. In all these he lives and moves and has his being. They constitute his, literally, *natio*, the inwardness of his nativity, and in Europe every inch of his non-human environment wears the effects of their action upon it and breathes their spirit. The America he comes to, beside Europe, is Nature virgin and inviolate: it does not guide him with ancestral blazings: externally he is cut off from the past. Not so internally: whatever else he changes, he cannot change his grandfather. Moreover, he comes rarely alone; he comes companioned with his fellow nationals; and he comes to no strangers, but to kin and friends who have gone before. If he is able to excel, he soon achieves a local habitation. There he encounters the native American to whom he is merely a Dutchman, a Mick, a frog, a wop, a dago, a hunky, or a sheeny and no more; and he encounters these others who are unlike him, dealing with him as a lower and outlandish creature. Then, be he even the rudest and most

Horace M. Kallen, "Democracy versus the Melting Pot," *The Nation*, 100 (February 18 and 25, 1915). Copyright © 1915 The Nation Company, Inc.

primeval peasant, heretofore totally unconscious of his nationality, of his categorical difference from many men and similarity to some, he must inevitably become conscious of it. Thus, in the industrial and congested towns of the United States, where there are real and large contacts between immigrant nationalities, the first effect appears to be an intensification of spiritual dissimilarities, always to the disadvantage of the dissimilarities.

The second generation, consequently, devotes itself feverishly to the attainment of similarity. The social tradition of its parents is lost by attrition or thrown off for advantage. The merest externals of the new one are acquired—via the street and the public school. But as the public school imparts it, or as the social settlement imparts it, it is not really a *life;* it is an abstraction, an arrangement of words. America is a word: as a historic fact, or as a democratic ideal of life, it is not realized at all. At best and at worst—now that the captains of industry are showing disturbance over the mess they have made, and "vocational training" is becoming a part of the public educational program—the prospective American learns a trade, acquiring at his most impressionable age the habit of being a cog in the industrial machine. . . .

The array of forces for and against that likemindedness which is the stuff and essence of nationality seems to align itself as follows. For it there work social imitations of the upper by the lower classes, the facility of communications, the national pastimes of baseball and motion-picture, the mobility of population, the cheapness of printing and the public schools. Against it there work the primary ethnic and cultural differences with which the population starts, its stratification over an enormous extent of country, and most powerfully, its industrial and economic stratification. The United States are an English-speaking country but in no intimate and utter way, as is New Zealand or Australia or even Canada. English seems to Americans what Latin used to be to the Roman provinces and to the middle ages—the language of the upper and dominant class, the vehicle and symbol of culture: for much of the population it is a sort of Esperanto or Ido, a *lingua franca* necessary less in the free than the business contacts of the daily life. The American mass is composed of elementals, peasants— Mr. Ross speaks of their menacing American life with "peasantism"—with, in a word, the proletarian foundation material of all forms of civilization. Their self-consciousness as groups is comparatively weak, although their organization and control of their individual members are often very strong. This is a factor which favors their "assimilation," for the more cultivated a group is the more it is aware of its individuality, and the less willing it is to surrender that individuality—one need think only of the Puritans them- selves, leaving Holland for fear of absorption into the Dutch population; of the Creoles and the Pennsylvania Germans of this country, or of the Jews, anywhere. Peasants, on the other hand, having nothing much consciously to surrender in taking over a new culture, feel no necessary break and find the transition easy. They accomplish it, other things being equal, in a generation. It is the shock of confrontation with other ethnic groups and the natural feeling of aliency reinforced by social discrimination and economic exploitation that generate in them an intenser group-consciousness, which then militates against "Americanization" by rendering more important than ever the two factors to which the spiritual expression of the proletarian has been largely confined. These factors are language and religion. Religion is, of course, no more a "universal" than language. The history of Christianity makes evident enough how religion is modified, even inverted, by race, place and time. It becomes a principle of separation, often the sole repository of the national spirit, almost always the conservator of the national language and of the tradition that is passed on with the language to succeeding generations. Among immigrants, hence, religion and language tend to be coordinate: a single expression of the spontaneous and instinctive cultural life of the masses, and the primary inward factors making against assimilation. Writers like Mr. Ross, one notes, tend to grow shrill over the competition of the parochial school with the public school, at the same time that they belittle the fact that "on Sunday Norwegian is preached in more churches in America than in Norway." . . .

. . . At the present time there seems to be no dominant American mind other than the industrial and theological. The spirit of the land is inarticulate, not a voice but a chorus of many voices each singing a rather different tune. How to get order into this cacophony is the question for all persons who are concerned about those things which alone justify wealth and power; for all who are concerned about justice, the arts, literature, philosophy, science. What must, what can, what *shall* this cacaphony become—a unison or a harmony?

For decidedly, the older America, whose voice and whose spirit were New England, has, by virtue of business, of communications, of the immigrant, gone beyond recall. Americans of British stock still are prevailingly the artists and thinkers of the land, but they work, each for himself, without common vision or ideals. They have no *ethos* any more. The older tradition has passed from a life into a memory, and the newer one, so far as it has an Anglo-Saxon base, is holding its own beside more and more formidable competitors, the expression in appropriate form of the national inheritances of the various populations concentrated in various states of the Union, populations of whom their national self-consciousness is perhaps the chief spiritual asset, as their labor-power is their chief economic asset. Think of the Creoles in the south and the French-Canadians in the north, clinging to French for countless generations and maintaining, however weakly, spiritual and social contacts with the mother-country; of the Germans with their *Deutschtum*, their *Männerchore*, *Turnvereine*, and *Schützenfeste;* of the generally separate Jews; of the intensely nationalistic Irish; of the Pennsylvania Germans; of the indomitably narrow Poles and even more indomitably flexible Bohemians; of the 30,000 Belgians in Wisconsin with their "Belgian" language, a mixture of Walloon and Flemish welded by reaction to a strange social environment. Except in such cases as the town of Lead, South Dakota, the great ethnic groups of proletarians, thrown upon themselves in a new setting, generate from among themselves the other social classes which Mr. Ross and his kind so sadly miss among them: their shopkeepers, their physicians, their attorneys, their journalists and their national and political leaders, who form the links between them and the greater American society. They develop their own literature or become conscious of that of the mother country. As they grow more prosperous and "Americanized," as they become freed from the stigma of "foreigner," they develop group self-respect: the wop changes into a proud Italian, the hunky into an intensely nationalist Slav. They learn, or they recall, the spiritual heritage of their nationality. Their cultural abjectness gives way to cultural pride and the public schools, the libraries and the clubs become beset with demands for texts in the national language and literature. . . .

Immigrants appear to pass through four phases in the course of being automatically Americanized. In the first phase they exhibit economic eagerness, the greedy hunger of the unfed. Since external differences are a handicap in the economic struggle, they "assimilate," seeking thus to facilitate the attainment of economic independence. Once the proletarian level of such independence is reached, the process of assimilation slows down and tends to come to a stop. The immigrant group is still a national group, modified, sometimes improved, by environmental influences, but otherwise a solidary spiritual unit, which is seeking to find its way out on its own social level. This search brings to light permanent group distinctions and the immigrant, like the Anglo-Saxon American, is thrown back upon himself and his ancestry. Then a process of dissimilation begins. The arts, life and ideals of the nationality become central and paramount; ethnic and national differences change in status from disadvantages to distinctions. All the while the immigrant has been uttering his life in the English language and behaving like an American in matters economic and political, and continues to do so. The institutions of the Republic have become the liberating cause and the background for the rise of the cultural consciousness and social autonomy of the immigrant Irishman, German, Scandinavian, Jew, Pole or Bohemian. On the whole, the automatic processes of Americanization have not repressed nationality. These processes have liberated nationality, and more or less gratified it.

Hence, what troubles Mr. Ross and so many other American citizens of British stock is not really inequality; what troubles them is *difference.* Only things that are *alike* in fact and not abstractly, and only men that are alike in origin and in feeling and not abstractly, can possess the equality which maintains that inward unanimity of sentiment and outlook which make a homogeneous national culture. The writers of the American Declaration of Independence and of the Constitution of the United States were not confronted by the practical fact of ethnic dissimilarity among the whites of the country. Their descendants are confronted by it. Its existence, acceptance and development are some of the inevitable consequences of the democratic principle on which the American theory of government is based, and the result at the present writing is to many worthies very unpleasant. Democratism and the federal principle have worked together with economic greed and ethnic snobbishness to people the land with all the nationalities of Europe, and to convert the early American nationality into the present American *nation*. For in effect the United States are in the process of becoming a federal state not merely as a union of geographical and administrative unities, but also as a cooperation of cultural diversities, as a federation or commonwealth of national cultures. . . .

The problems which these conditions give rise to are important, but not of primary importance. Although they have occupied the minds of all American political theorists, they are problems of means, of instruments, not of ends. They concern the conditions of life, not the *kind of life*, and there appears to have been a general assumption that only one kind of human life is possible in the United States of America. But the same democracy which underlies the evils of the economic order underlies also the evils, and the promise, of the cultural order. Because no individual is merely an individual, the political autonomy of the individual has presaged and is beginning to realize in these United States the spiritual autonomy of his group. The process is as yet far from fruition. America is, in fact, at the parting of the ways. Two genuine social alternatives are before Americans, either of which they may realize if they will. In social construction the will is father to the fact, for the fact is hardly ever anything more, under the grace of accident and luck, than the concord or conflict of wills. What do Americans *will* to make of the United States—a unison, singing the old British theme "America," the America of the New England School? or a harmony, in which that theme shall be dominant, perhaps, among others, but one among many, not the only one?

The mind reverts helplessly to the historic attempts at unison in Europe—the heroic failure of the pan-Hellenists, of the Romans, the disintegration and the diversification of the Christian church, for a time the most successful unison in history; the present-day failures of Germany and of Russia. In the United States, however, the whole social situation is favorable as it has never been at any time elsewhere—everything is favorable but the basic law of America itself, and the spirit of the American institutions. To achieve unison—it can be achieved—would be to violate these. For the end determines the means and the means transmute the end, and this end would involve no other means than those used by Germany in Poland, in Schleswig-Holstein, and Alsace-Lorraine; by Russia in the Jewish Pale, in Poland, in Finland; by Austria among the Slavs; by Turkey among the Arabs, Armenians and Greeks. Fundamentally it would require the complete nationalization of education, the abolition of every form of parochial and private school, the abolition of instruction in other tongues than English, and the concentration of the teaching of history and literature upon the English tradition. The other institutions of society would require treatment analogous to that administered by Germany to her European acquisitions. And all of this, even if meeting with no resistance, would not completely guarantee the survival as a unison of the older Americanism. For the program would be applied to diverse ethnic types under changing conditions, and the reconstruction that, with the best will, they might spontaneously make of the tradition would more likely than not be a far cry from the original. It is, already.

The notion that the program might be realized by radical and even forced miscegenation, by the creation of the melting-pot by law, and thus by the development of the new "American race" is, as Mr. Ross points out, as mystically optimistic as it is ignorant. . . . There is nothing more to be said to the pious stupidity that identifies recency with goodness. The unison to be achieved cannot be a unison of ethnic types. It must be, if it is to be at all, a unison of social and historic interests, established by the complete cutting-off of the ancestral memories of the American populations, the enforced, exclusive use of the English language and English and American history in the schools and in the daily life.

The attainment of the other alternative, a harmony, also requires concerted public action. But the action would do no violence to the ideals of American fundamental law and the spirit of American institutions nor to the qualities of men. It would seek simply to eliminate the waste and the stupidity of the social organization, by way of freeing and strengthening the strong forces actually in operation. Taking for its point of departure the existing ethnic and cultural groups it would seek to provide conditions under which each might attain the cultural perfection that is *proper to its kind*. The provision of such conditions has been said to be the primary intent of American fundamental law and the function of American institutions. And all of the various nationalities which compose the American nation must be taught first of all this fact, which used perhaps to be, to patriotic minds, the outstanding ideal content of "Americanism"—that democracy means self-realization through self-control, self-discipline, and that one is impossible without the other. . . .

. . . What is inalienable in the life of mankind is its intrinsic positive quality—its psycho-physical inheritance. Men may change their clothes, their politics, their wives, their religions, their philosophies, to a greater or lesser extent; they cannot change their grandfathers. Jews or Poles or Anglo-Saxons, in order to cease being Jews or Poles or Anglo-Saxons, would have to cease to be, while they could cease to be citizens or church members or carpenters or lawyers without ceasing to be. The selfhood which is inalienable in them, and for the realization of which they require "inalienable" liberty is ancestrally determined, and the happiness which they pursue has its form implied in ancestral endowment. This is what, actually, democracy in operation assumes. There are human capacities which it is the function of the state to liberate and to protect in growth: and the failure of the state as a government to accomplish this automatically makes for its abolition. Government, the state, under the democratic conception is, it cannot be too often repeated, merely an instrument, not an end. That it is often an abused instrument, that it is often seized by the powers that prey, that it makes frequent mistakes and considers only secondary ends, surface needs, which vary from moment to moment, of course is obvious: hence the social and political messes government is always getting into. But that it is an instrument, flexibly adjustable to changing life, changing opinion and needs, the whole modern electoral organization and party system declare. And as intelligence and wisdom prevail over "politics" and special interests, as the steady and continuous pressure of the "inalienable" qualities and purposes of human groups more and more dominate the confusion of their common life, the outlines of a possible great and truly democratic commonwealth become discernible. Its form would be that of the federal republic; its substance a democracy of nationalities, cooperating voluntarily and autonomously through common institutions in the enterprise of self-realization through the perfection of men according to their kind. The common language of the commonwealth, the language of its great tradition, would be English, but each nationality would have for its emotional and involuntary life its own peculiar dialect or speech, its own individual and inevitable esthetic and intellectual forms. The political and economic life of the commonwealth is a single unit and serves as the foundation and background for the realization of the distinctive individuality of each *natio* that composes it and of the pooling of these in a harmony above them all. Thus "American civilization" may come to mean the perfection of the cooperative harmonies of "European civilization"—the waste, the squalor and the distress of Europe being eliminated—a multiplicity in a unity, an orchestration of mankind. As in an orchestra every type of instrument has its specific *timbre* and *tonality*, founded in its substance and form; as every type has its appropriate theme and melody in the whole symphony, so in society, each ethnic group may be the natural instrument, its temper and culture may be its theme and melody and the harmony and dissonances and discords of them all may make the symphony of civilization. With this difference: a musical symphony is written before it is played; in the symphony of civilization the playing is the writing, so that there is nothing so fixed and inevitable about its progressions as in music, so that within the limits set by nature and luck they may vary at will, and the range and variety of the harmonies may become wider and richer and more beautiful—or the reverse.

But the question is, do the dominant classes in America want such a society? The alternative is actually before them. Can they choose wisely?

Or will vanity blind them and fear constrain, turning the promise of freedom into the fact of tyranny, and once more vindicating the ancient habit of men and aborting the hope of the world?

SUGGESTIONS FOR FURTHER READING

Julius Weinberg, *Edward Alsworth Ross and the Sociology of Progressivism* (Madison, Wis.: University of Wisconsin Press, 1972); Susanne Klingenstein, *Jews in the American Academy, 1900–1940: The Dynamics of Intellectual Assimilation* (New Haven, Conn.: Yale University Press, 1991), pp. 34–50; Philip S. Gleason, *Speaking of Diversity: Language and Ethnicity in Twentieth-Century America* (Baltimore: Johns Hopkins University Press, 1992), chs. 1 and 3.

VIII

BIRTH CONTROL:
NAY AND YEA

Anthony Comstock (1844–1915) was a Puritan by both temperament and personal descent. His temperance crusade, which targeted saloons that violated the Sunday closing law in New York, ultimately led him to report shopowners who sold smutty or erotic literature. Comstock loved to make citizen arrests, sometimes as many as six per day. Because he testified so often in courts, Comstock played a key role in broadening the definition of obscenity used to secure conviction in marginal or questionable cases: "anything having a tendency to suggest impure and libidinous thoughts to the young and inexperienced."

In 1873 Comstock figured prominently in the Congressional passage of a law making it a crime to send obscene material through the mail. The wording of that bill included, for the first time, materials "for the prevention of conception." In that same year he helped organize the New York Society for the Suppression of Vice. Two years later Comstock received a commission from the federal post office to be a special agent combatting obscene matter. In his view, any reference to the body or its functions—or any challenge to the social regulations concerning those functions—was sinful.

Charlotte Perkins Gilman (1860–1935) came from an old New England family that fell on hard times. Her own marriage, like her parents', failed and reduced her to genteel poverty. After a significant respite in California, she earned a modest living as a lecturer. In 1898 she published Women and Economics, a feminist manifesto that remains her best-known book. She used the work of Lester Frank Ward, especially his Dynamic Sociology (1883), to develop her argument for female economic independence. Ward had insisted that the status of women was not an irremediable fact of nature but could be adjusted for the good of society through rational and ethical analysis. Building on that notion, Gilman insisted that women had become excessively dependent on men for food and shelter. Consequently, women's capacity to contribute to community affairs had diminished, to the detriment of human progress. The obvious remedy was for the livelihood of women to be independent of men. In her view, that goal of financial autonomy was a more radical project than women's suffrage.

From 1909 until 1916 Gilman wrote, edited, and published her own monthly magazine, the Forerunner. It included diverse pieces—fiction, news, editorials, and poems—on feminist causes and on the need to reorder society. She was widely considered the leading intellectual of the women's movement.

Birth Control and Public Morals: An Interview with Anthony Comstock

MARY ALDEN HOPKINS

"Have read your articles. Self control and obedience to Nature's laws, you seem to overlook. Let men and women live a life above the level of the beasts. I see nothing in either of your articles along these lines. Existing laws are an imperative necessity in order to prevent the downfall of youths of both sex," wrote Mr. Anthony Comstock, secretary of the New York Society for the Suppression of Vice, replying to my request for an interview on the subject of Birth Control.

During the interview which he kindly allowed me, he reiterated his belief in the absolute necessity of drastic laws.

"To repeal the present laws would be a crime against society," he said, "and especially a crime against young women."

Although the name Anthony Comstock is known all over the country and over most of the civilized world, comparatively few people know for exactly what Mr. Comstock stands and what he has accomplished. It has been the policy of those who oppose his work to speak flippantly of it and to minimize its results. The Society for the Suppression of Vice was formed to support Mr. Comstock, from the beginning he has been its driving force, and it is giving him only the credit which is due him to say that the tremendous accomplishments of the society in its fight against vicious publications for the last forty years have been in reality the accomplishments of Mr. Comstock.

Up to 1914, Mr. Comstock had caused to be arraigned in state and federal courts 3,697 persons, of whom 2,740 were either convicted or pleaded guilty. On these were imposed fines to the extent of $237,134.30 and imprisonments to the length of 565 years, 11 months, and 20 days.

To this remarkable record of activity can be added since that date 176 arrests and 141 convictions.

The story of how Mr. Comstock began his unusual profession is as interesting as the story of any of the famous captains of industry. He has, if one may borrow a stage term, "created" his unique position.

"My attention was first drawn to the publication of vile books forty-three years ago when I was a clerk here in New York City," said Mr. Comstock.

Mary Alden Hopkins, "Birth Control and Public Morals: An Interview with Anthony Comstock," *Harper's Weekly*, 60 (May 22, 1915), pp. 489–90.

"There was in existence at that time a kind of circulating library where my fellow clerks went, made a deposit, and received the vilest of literature, and after reading it, received back the deposit or took other books. I saw young men being debauched by this pernicious influence.

"On March 2nd, 1872, I brought about the arrest of seven persons dealing in obscene books, pictures, and articles. I found that there were 169 books some of which had been in circulation since before I was born and which were publicly advertised and sold in connection with articles for producing abortion, prevention of conception, articles to aid seductions, and for indiscreet and immoral use. I had four publishers dealing in these arrested and the plates for 167 of these books destroyed. The other two books dropped out of sight. I have not seen a copy of one of them for forty years."

From this time on Mr. Comstock devoted his attention to this work, although it was, as he once said, like standing at the mouth of a sewer. Several times men whom he has arrested, have later tried to kill him.

There were no laws covering this ostracized business at that time. In March, 1873, Mr. Comstock secured the passage of stringent federal laws closing the mails and the ports to this atrocious business. Two days afterwards, upon the request of certain Senators, Mr. Comstock was appointed Special Agent of the Post Office Department to enforce these laws. He now holds the position of Post Office Inspector. The federal law as it at present stands is as follows:

United States Criminal Code, Section 211.

(Act of March 4th, 1909, Chapter 321, Section 211, United States Statutes at Large, vol. 35, part 1, page 1088 et seq.)

Every obscene, lewd, or lascivious and every filthy book, pamphlet, picture, paper, letter, writing, print, or other publication of an indecent character, and every article or thing designated, adapted or intended for preventing conception or procuring abortion, or for any indecent or immoral use; and every article, instrument, substance, drugs, medicine, or thing which is advertised or described in a manner calculated to lead another to use or apply it for preventing conception or producing abortion, or for any indecent or immoral purpose; and every written or printed card, circular, book, pamphlet, advertisement or notice of any kind giving information, directly, or indirectly, where or how, or by what means any of the hereinbefore mentioned matters, articles or things may be obtained or made, or where or by whom any act or operation of any kind for the procuring or producing of abortion will be done or performed, or how or by what means conception may be prevented or abortion produced, whether sealed or unsealed; and every letter, packet or package or other mail matter containing any filthy, vile or indecent thing, device or substance; and every paper, writing, advertisement or representation that any article, instrument, substance, drug, medicine or thing may, or can be used or applied for preventing conception or producing abortion, or for any indecent or immoral purpose; and every description calculated to induce or incite a person to so use or apply any such article, instrument, substance, drug, medicine or thing, is hereby declared to be non-mailable matter, and shall not be conveyed in the mails or delivered from any post office or by any letter carrier. Whosoever shall knowingly deposit or cause to be deposited for mailing or delivery, anything declared by this section to be non-mailable, or shall knowingly take, or cause the same to be taken, from the mails for the purpose of circulating or disposing thereof, or of aiding in the circulation or disposition of the same, shall be fined not more than $5000, or imprisoned not more than five years, or both.

Any one who has the patience to read through this carefully drawn law will see that it covers—well, everything. The detailed accuracy with which it is constructed partly explains Mr. Comstock's almost uniform success in securing convictions. One possible loophole suggested itself to me.

"Does it not," I asked, "allow the judge considerable leeway in deciding whether or not a book or a picture, is immoral?"

"No," replied Mr. Comstock, "the highest courts in Great Britain and the United States, have laid down the test in all such matters. What he has to decide is *whether or not it might arouse in young and inexperienced minds, lewd or libidinous thoughts.*"

In these words lies the motive of Mr. Comstock's work—the protection of children under twenty-one. If at times his ban seems to some to be too sweepingly applied it is because his faith looks forward to a time when there shall be in all the world not one object to awaken sensuous thoughts in the minds of young people. He expressed this sense of the terrible danger in which young people stand and his society's duty toward them in his fortieth annual report:

> . . . we first of all return thanks to Almighty God, the giver of every good and perfect gift, for the opportunities of service for Him in defense of the morals of the more than forty-two million youths and children twenty-one years of age, or under, in the United States of America. His blessings upon our efforts during the past year call for profound thanksgiving to Almighty God and for grateful and loyal service in the future.
>
> This Society in a peculiar manner is permitted to stand at a vital and strategic point where the foes to moral purity seek to concentrate their most deadly forces against the integrity of the rising generation. We have been assigned by the Great Commander to constantly face some of the most insidious and deadly forces for evil that Satan is persistently aligning against the integrity of the children of the present age.

And in a letter read at the fortieth anniversary he expresses himself thus:

> There are three points of special importance to be emphasized:
>
> 1. Every child is a character-builder.

2. In the heart of every child there is a chamber of imagery, memory's storehouse, the commissary department in which is received, stored up and held in reserve every good or evil influence for future requisition.

3. "Be not deceived, God is not mocked. For whatsoever a man soweth that he shall also reap." "Keep thy heart with all diligence, for out of it are the issues of life."

The three great crime-breeders of today are intemperance, gambling, and evil reading. The devil is sowing his seed for his future harvest. There is no foe so much to be dreaded as that which perverts the imagination, sears the conscience, hardens the heart, and damns the soul.

If you allow the devil to decorate the Chamber of Imagery in your heart with licentious and sensual things, you will find that he has practically thrown a noose about your neck and will forever after exert himself to draw you away from the "Lamb of God which taketh away sins of the world." You have practically put rope on memory's bell and placed the other end of the rope in the devil's hands, and, though you may will out your mind, the memory of some vile story or picture that you may have looked upon, be assured that even in your most solitary moments the devil will ring memory's bell and call up the hateful thing to turn your thoughts away from God and undermine all aspirations for holy things.

Let me emphasize one fact, supported by my nearly forty-two years of public life in fighting this particular foe. My experience leads me to the conviction that once these matters enter through the eye and ear into the chamber of imagery in the heart of the child, nothing but the grace of God can ever erase or blot it out.

Finally, brethren, "let us not be weary in well doing, for in due season we shall reap if we faint not." Raise over each of your heads the banner of the Lord Jesus Christ. Look to Him as your Commander and Leader.

I was somewhat confused at first that Mr. Comstock should class contraceptives with pornographic objects which debauch children's fancies, for I knew that the European scientists who advocate their use have no desire at all to debauch children. When I asked Mr. Comstock about this, he replied—with scant patience of "theorizers" who do not know human nature:

"If you open the door to anything, the filth will all pour in and the degradation of youth will follow."

The federal law, which we have quoted, covers only matter sent by post. This would leave large unguarded fields were it not for the state laws. The year following the passage of the federal law, Mr. Comstock obtained the passage of drastic laws in several states, and later in all states. The New York state law reads as follows:

Section 1142 of the Penal Law:

A person who sells, lends, gives away, or in any manner exhibits or offers to sell, lend or give away, or has in his possession with intent to sell, lend or give away, or advertises, or offers for sale, loan or distribution, any instrument or article, or any recipe, drug or medicine for the prevention of conception or for causing unlawful abortion, or purporting to be for the prevention of conception, or for causing unlawful abortion, or advertises, or holds out representations that it can be so used or applied, or any such description as will be calculated to lead another to so use or apply any such article, recipe, drug, medicine or instrument, or who writes or prints, or causes to be written or printed, a card, circular, pamphlet, advertisement or notice of any kind, or gives information orally, stating when, where, how, of whom, or by what means such an instrument, article, recipe, drug or medicine can be purchased or obtained, or who manufactures any such instrument, article, recipe, drug or medicine, is guilty of a misdemeanor, and shall be liable to the same penalties as provided in section eleven hundred and forty-one of this chapter.

This punishment is a sentence of not less than ten days nor more than one year's imprisonment or a fine not less than fifty dollars or both fine and imprisonment for each offense.

"Do not these laws handicap physicians?" I asked, remembering that this criticism is sometimes made.

"They do not," replied Mr. Comstock emphatically. "No reputable physician has ever been prosecuted under these laws. Have you ever known of one?" I had not, and he continued, "Only infamous doctors who advertise or send their foul matter by mail. A reputable doctor may tell his patient in his office what is necessary, and a druggist may sell on a doctor's written prescription drugs which he would not be allowed to sell otherwise."

This criticism of the laws interfering with doctors is so continuously made that I asked again:

"Do the laws never thwart the doctor's work; in cases, for instance, where pregnancy would endanger a woman's life?"

Mr. Comstock replied with the strongest emphasis:

"A doctor is allowed to bring on an abortion in cases where a woman's life is in danger. And is there anything in these laws that forbids a doctor's telling a woman that pregnancy must not occur for a certain length of time or at all? Can they not use self-control? Or must they sink to the level of the beasts?"

"But," I protested, repeating an argument often brought forward, although I felt as if my persistence was somewhat placing me in the ranks of those who desire evil rather than good, "If the parents lack that self-control, the punishment falls upon the child."

"It does not," replied Mr. Comstock. "The punishment falls upon the parents. When a man and woman marry they are responsible for their children. You can't reform a family in any of these superficial ways. You have to go deep down into their minds and souls. The prevention of conception would work the greatest demoralization. God has set certain natural barriers. If you turn loose the passions and break down the fear you bring worse disaster than the war. It would debase sacred things, break down the health of women and disseminate a greater curse than the plagues and diseases of Europe."

Birth Control

CHARLOTTE PERKINS GILMAN

The time will come when every nation must face the question, "How many people can live comfortably, healthfully, happily, upon this land?" That is the ultimate reason why we must learn that "the pressure of population" is not an unavoidable fate, but a result of our own irresponsible indulgence.

This time is still a long way off. At present the main reasons advanced in advocacy of the conscious limitation of offspring are these: the economic pressure which often makes it difficult, if not impossible, to rear large families without degradation of the stock from injurious conditions; the injury to women of a continuous repetition of maternity, especially when combined with hard work and lack of comfort; and back of these, less freely stated, a desire for "safe" and free indulgence of the sex instinct without this natural consequence.

Of the first reason it may be said that the economic pressure is our own making and may be removed when we choose. That a race of our intelligence should sink into conditions so miserable that it is difficult to raise healthy children; and then, instead of changing those miserable conditions, should weakly renounce parentage, is not creditable to that intelligence. While we have not come within centuries of "the limit of subsistence"; while there is land enough and water enough to feed a vast population as yet unapproached; it is contemptible for us to accept mere local and temporary injustice as if it were a natural condition. That the more ignorant masses should do this would not be strange; but they are not the main culprits. So far they have faced the evils around them with nature's process—the less chance of a living, the more young ones.

Wiser people, more far-seeing, with a higher standard of living to keep up, have accepted their restrictions as final, and sought to limit their own numbers as to maintain that standard for the few.

Charlotte Perkins Gilman, "Birth Control," *The Forerunner*, 6 (July 1915), pp. 177–80.

If we would apply our reasoning power and united force to secure a fair standard of living for all of us, we could go on enjoying our families for many centuries.

In the meantime, accepting our present limitations, we do have to face the very practical and personal problem—how many children ought a woman to have whose husband's wages average $600 a year[?] That is the average for millions, even in our country.

Face this fairly: $2.00 a day for all but the fifty-two Sundays, say three holidays, and a most modest allowance of ten days' unemployment—less than $12.00 a week the year around, with rent and food prices what they are now. How many children *ought* a woman to have under these circumstances?

Then, either for this woman, overworked and underfed; or for the professor's wife, also overworked in the demands of her environment; and, though having enough to eat, also underfed in the rest and relaxation she needs; we must face the limitations of physical strength.

Here again, in a large sense, our position is pusillanimous. Maternity is a natural process. It should benefit and not injure the mother. That women have allowed themselves to sink into a condition where they are unfit to perform the very functions for which their bodies are specially constructed, is no credit to their intelligence. Instead of accepting the limitations and saying: "We are not strong enough to bear children," the wise and noble thing to do is to say: "Our condition of health is shameful. We must become strong and clean again that we may function naturally as mothers."

In spite of this, the practical and personal problem confronts the individual mother: "I have had three children in three years. I am a wreck already. If I have another I may die or become a hopeless invalid. Is it not my duty for the sake of those I have, to refuse to have more?"

The third reason, by no means so outspoken, but far more universal than the others, is at once the strongest force urging us toward birth control, and the strongest ground of opposition to it.

The prejudice against the prevention of conception and the publication of knowledge as to the proper methods, is based partly on religious conviction, and partly on an objection to the third reason above given. The religious objection is neither more nor less difficult to meet than others of the same class. A wider enlightenment steadily tends to disabuse our minds of unthinking credulity as to ancient traditions. We are beginning at last to have a higher opinion of God than we used to entertain. The modern mind will not credit an Infinite Wisdom, an Infinite Love, with motives and commands unworthy of the love and wisdom of a mere earthly father. Still, for those who hold this objection, and upon whom it is enforced by their Church, it is a very serious one.

The other is still more serious; so much so that no one can rightly judge the question without squarely facing this, its biological base—what is sex union for. No one can deny its original purpose through all the millions of years of pre-human life on earth. But when human life is under consideration there are two opinions.

The first holds that the human species is sui generis in this regard; that we differ from all other animals in this process; that it has, for us, both a biological use quite aside from reproduction, and a psychological use entirely beyond that.

The second is to the effect that for our race, as for others, this is a biological process for the perpetuation of the species, and that its continuous indulgence with no regard to reproduction or in direct exclusion of reproduction indicates an abnormal development peculiar to our species.

The first opinion is held by practically everyone; the second by a mere handful. To those who have watched the growth of ideas in the human mind this disproportion proves nothing whatever. Of course a few people are as likely to be wrong as a great many people. Of course a small minority of people have held views as absurd as those of large majorities. Nevertheless it remains true that every advance in all human history has been begun by the ideas of a few, even of one perhaps, and opposed with cheerful unanimity by all the rest of the world.

An idea must be discussed on its merits, not measured by the numbers of people who "believe" this, or "think" that, or "feel" so and so. Especially as to feeling. The emotional responses of the mass of people are invariably reactionary. "Feelings" which belong to a more advanced state are always hard to find. Even in one's own mind, the intellectual perception comes first, the settled conviction later, and the appropriate emotional response later still.

One may be fairly forced by sheer reason and logic to admit the justice and expedience of equal suffrage for men and women; one may accept this as a strong belief and act accordingly. Yet the swift warm sense of approval for what is still called a "womanly woman," the cold aversion to what we have for long assumed to be "unwomanly," remain.

Because of these simple and common phenomena we must not be swayed too much in our judgment on this question as to the true use and purpose and the legitimate limits of the sex function, by the overwhelming mass of sentiment on the side of continuous indulgence.

For clear discussion it will be well to state definitely the thesis here advanced, which is:

That with the human species as with others the normal purpose of sex-union is reproduction;

That its continuous repetition, wholly disassociated with this use, results in a disproportionate development of the preliminary sex emotions and functional capacities, to the detriment of the parental emotions and capacities, and to the grave injury of the higher processes of human development;

That our present standard of "normal indulgence" is abnormal; this by no means in the sense of any individual abnormality, but in the sense of a whole race thus developed by thousands of generations of over-indulgence;

That, when the human species, gradually modifying its conduct by the adoption of changed ideas, becomes normal in this regard, it will show a very different scale of emotional and functional demand; the element of sex-desire greatly reduced in proportion to the higher development of parental activities worthy of our race; and of a whole range of social emotions and functions now impossible because of the proportionate predominance of this one process and its emotions;

That this change will necessarily be a slow one; and involves, not the pious struggles of a convicted sinner against a sin, but the wise gradual efforts of a conscious race to so change its habits, to so modify itself, as to breed out the tendency to excessive indulgence, and allow the re-assumption of normal habits;

That the resultant status is not of an emasculate or efeminate race; or of one violently repressing its desires; but rather that of a race whose entire standard has changed; in physical inclination, in emotion, and in idea; so that the impulse to that form of sex-expression comes only in a yearly season, as with other species of the same gestative period.

The opposing thesis is so universally held as hardly to need statement, but may be fairly put in this way:

That it is "natural" for the human species to continually indulge sex-emotion and its physical expression, with no regard whatever to reproduction.

That this indulgence has "a higher function" in no way associated with so crude a purpose as bringing forth children, but is (a) an expression of pure and lofty affection; (b) a concomitant of all noble creative work; (c) a physical necessity to maintain the health of men—some say also of women.

This position is reinforced not only by the originally strong sex instinct in all animals, and by the excessive force of that instinct in the human race; but by the world's accumulated psychology on the subject—its pictures, statues, stories, poems, music, drama, even its religions, all of which have been elaborated by the sex which has the most to gain and the least to lose by upholding such a standard.

Without expecting to make much impression upon such a measureless mass of instinct, sentiment, habit, and tradition, we may offer this much consideration of the above position.

First, as to the use of the word "natural." The forces of nature tend to preserve life—under any conditions. Up to the last limits of possibility, the form, size, and structure, habits and feelings of a living species, will change and change and change again in order that it may live. Anything will be sacrificed—so that the one main necessity is maintained—that the creature be not extinct. "Nature," in the sense of creatures below mankind, often failed in this effort, and many species did become extinct. Our human conditions, which are natural too, but not in this special sense, are so favorable that human life is maintained where less able creatures would die.

It is quite possible for a part of society to so conduct itself as would inevitably cause its own destruction if it were not meanwhile fed and clothed and sheltered by another part. It is possible for quite a small fraction of society to promote ideas, theories and habits which would corrupt and degrade the whole if they were not offset by other tendencies. In the specific matter in question the one absolute condition of life was merely this: that enough women reached the bearing age and produced enough children to maintain the race in existence. . . .

As to the "higher function," we should be clear in our minds about the relation between the "height" of the function and its frequence. It may be advanced, similarly, that eating with us has a "higher function," being used as a form of hospitality, a medium of entertainment, of aesthetic as well as gustatory pleasure. All that may be true of the preparation, service, and consumption of food which is perfectly suited to the needs of the body, and for which one has a genuine appetite. One would hardly seek to justify a ceaseless gluttony, or even an erratic consumption of unnecessary food, on those grounds.

It remains further to be discussed in detail whether noble and lofty affection may not be otherwise expressed; whether it is true that the highest creative work, or the most, or even any great part, is associated with our present degree of indulgence on this line; and whether that claim of "physical necessity" really holds good for either sex.

It may be shown that a person, to-day, is in better health if free to gratify his present degree of desire; but that is not the real point at issue, which is—is it normal for the human race to have this degree of desire?

Against the visible sum of our noble achievements, which may be urged as justification of our peculiarities, may be set the visible sum of our shameful diseases, sufferings, poverty, crime, degeneracy. As a race we do not show such an exceptionally high average of health and happiness in the sex relation as to indicate a "higher" method. Rather, on the contrary, the morbid phenomena with which this area of life is associated, plainly show some wrong condition.

Upon which general bias, returning to the subject of birth control, it is advanced:

That the normal sex relation is a periodic one, related to the reproductive process;

That the resultant "natural" product of a child a year is being gradually reduced by the action of that biological law—"reproduction is in inverse proportion to industrialization";

That when we are all reared in suitable conditions for the highest individual development, we shall only crave this indulgence for a brief annual period, and that, with no efforts at "prevention," our average birth rate will be but two or three to a family;

That, in the meantime, under specially hard conditions, it is right for a woman to refuse to bear more than that, or possibly to bear any;

That for reputable physicians or other competent persons to teach proper methods of such restrictions, is quite right.

As for needing a "safe," free and unlimited indulgence in the exercises of this function, I hold that to be an abnormal condition. . . .

SUGGESTIONS FOR FURTHER READING

Nancy F. Cott, *The Grounding of Modern Feminism* (New Haven, Conn.: Yale University Press, 1987); Paul S. Boyer, *Purity in Print: The Vice-Society Movement and Book Censorship in America* (New York: Scribner's, 1968), especially chs. 1 and 2; Ellen Chesler, *Woman of Valor: Margaret Sanger and the Birth Control Movement in America* (New York: Simon & Schuster, 1992); Ann J. Lane, *To Herland and Beyond: The Life and Work of Charlotte Perkins Gilman* (New York: Pantheon, 1990).

IX

❧

THE SCOPES TRIAL: EVOLUTION VERSUS SCRIPTURAL CHRISTIANITY

Clarence Darrow (1857–1938) was trained as an attorney and always sympathized with the underdog in civil and criminal cases. After defending Socialist Eugene V. Debs, and then the United Mine Workers in a famous coal strike (1902), as well as Big Bill Haywood and the Western Federation of Miners, he became the most famous trial lawyer in the United States. Because Darrow opposed capital punishment, in 1924 he defended Nathan Leopold and Richard Loeb for the ruthless murder of a fourteen-year-old boy. By introducing psychiatric evidence, Darrow persuaded the jury that his clients suffered from temporary insanity, thereby "winning" a sentence of life in prison rather than death.

In 1925 Darrow joined the defense team in the famous "monkey trial" of John Thomas Scopes, who admitted that he had violated a recent Tennessee state law by teaching the theory of evolution in a public school. The trial took place in Dayton, Tennessee, amidst a circuslike atmosphere as the nation followed media reports closely.

The emotional drama of the trial peaked when Darrow cross-examined William Jennings Bryan (1860–1925), one of the prosecuting attorneys. Bryan, a strict fundamentalist, acknowledged that he accepted the Bible literally.

Bryan had achieved national fame in the 1890s when he supported the prosilver bloc in Congress and won the Democratic presidential nomination following his "Cross of Gold" speech in which he embraced the populist agrarian cause and spoke in favor of government backing for silver purchase and price supports. He also received the nomination and ran unsuccessfully in 1900 and 1908, but served as secretary of state under President Woodrow Wilson. For most of his political career, Bryan was regarded as an ardent reformer who helped to keep the broadly based Democratic Party supportive of such reforms as direct election of senators, progressive tax legislation, an excess profits tax, legislation for maximum hour limitations and minimum wage requirements, women's suffrage, and government aid to farmers.

During the 1920s, Bryan became identified with Prohibition, real estate speculation in Florida, the Ku Klux Klan (at the 1924 Democratic convention he opposed denouncing the Klan by name), and opposition to the teaching of evolution. Bryan died just a few days after his intense cross-examination by Darrow in the Scopes trial.

For the Defense

CLARENCE DARROW

MR. DARROW ON THE BIBLE, LAW, AND SCIENCE

. . . "This case we have to argue is a case at law," Mr. Darrow continued, "and hard as it is for me to bring my mind to conceive it, almost impossible as it is to put my mind back into the sixteenth century, I am going to argue it as if it were serious, and as if it were a death struggle between two civilizations.

"Now, let us see what there is to it. We have been informed that the Legislature has the right to prescribe the course of study in the public schools. Within reason they, no doubt, have. They could not prescribe it, I am inclined to think, under your Constitution, if it omitted arithmetic and geography and writing; neither, under the rest of the Constitution, if it shall remain in force in the State, could they prescribe it if the course of study was only to teach religion.

"Several hundred years ago, when our people believed in freedom, and when no men felt so sure of their own sophistry that they were willing to send a man to jail who did not believe them, the people of Tennessee adopted a Constitution, and they made it broad and plain, and they said that the people of Tennessee should always enjoy religious freedom in its broadest terms. So I assume that no Legislature could fix a course of study which violated that.

"For instance, suppose the Legislature should say, 'We think the religious privileges and duties of the citizens of Tennessee are much more important than education.' We agree with the distinguished Governor of the State. If religion must go, or learning must go, why let learning go. I do not know how much of it would have to go, but let it go and, therefore, we will establish a course in the public schools teaching that the Christian religion as unfolded in the Bible is true, and that every other religion or modern system of ethics is false; and to carry that out, no person in the public schools shall be permitted to read or hear anything except Genesis, 'Pilgrim's Progress,' Baxter's 'Saints' Rest' and 'In His Image.' Would that be constitutional? If it is, the Constitution is a lie and a snare and the people have forgot what liberty means. . . .

Leslie H. Allen, comp., *Bryan and Darrow at Dayton: The Record and Documents of the "Bible-Evolution Trial"* (New York: Arthur Lee & Co., 1925), pp. 15–32.

"Now let us see what we claim with reference to this law. If this proceeding, both in form and substance, can prevail in this court, then, your Honor, any law, no matter how foolish, wicked, ambiguous, or ancient, can come back to Tennessee. All the guarantees go for nothing. All of the past has gone to waste, been forgotten, if this can succeed.

"I am going to begin with some of the simpler reasons why it is absolutely absurd to think that this statute, indictment, or any part of the proceedings in this case are legal; and I think the sooner we get rid of it in Tennessee the better for the people of Tennessee, and the better for the pursuit of knowledge in the world; so let me begin at the beginning. . . .

"Lots of things are put through the Legislature in the night time. Everybody does not read all of the statutes, even members of the Legislature—I have been a member of the Legislature myself, and I know how it is. They may vote for them without reading them, but the substance of the act is put in the caption, so it may be seen and read, and nothing may be in the act that is not contained in the caption. There is not any question about it, and only one subject shall be legislated on at once. Of course, the caption may be broader than the act. They may make a caption and the act may fall far short of it, but the substance of the act must be in the caption, and there can be no variance.

"Now let us see what they have done. There is not much dispute about the English language, I take it. Here is the caption:

"'Public Act, Chapter 37, 1925, an act prohibiting the teaching of the evolution theory in all the universities, normals, and all the public schools of Tennessee which are supported in whole or in part by the public school funds of the State, and to prescribe penalties for the violation thereof.'

"Now what is it—an act to prohibit the teaching of the evolution theory in Tennessee? Is this the act? Is this statute to prevent the teaching of the evolution theory? There is not a word said in the statute about evolution. There is not a word said in the statute about preventing the teaching of the theory of evolution—not a word.

"This caption says what follows is an act forbidding the teaching of evolution, and the Catholic could have gone home without any thought that his faith was about to be attacked. The Protestant could have gone home without any thought that his religion could be attacked. The intelligent, scholarly Christians, who by the millions in the United States find no inconsistency between evolution and religion, could have gone home without any fear that a narrow, ignorant, bigoted shrew of religion could have destroyed their religious freedom and their right to think and act and speak; and the nation and the State could have laid down peacefully to sleep that night without the slightest fear that religious hatred and bigotry were to be turned loose in a great State.

"Any question about that? Anything in this caption whatever about religion, or anything about measuring science and knowledge and learning by the Book of Genesis, written when everybody thought the world was flat? Nothing.

"They went to bed in peace, probably, and they woke up to find this, which has not the slightest reference to it; which does not refer to evolution in any way; which is, as claimed, a religious statute.

"That is what they found and here is what it is:

"'Be it enacted by the General Assembly of the State of Tennessee, that it shall be unlawful for any teacher in any of the universities, normals, and all other public schools in the State, which are supported in whole or in part by the public school funds of the State, to teach'—what, teach evolution? Oh, no.—'To teach the theory that denies the story of the divine creation of man as taught in the Bible, and to teach instead that man has descended from a lower order of animals.'

"That is what was foisted on the people of this State, under a caption which never meant it, and could give no hint of it; that it should be a crime in the State of Tennessee to teach any theory,—not evolution, but any theory of the origin of man, except that contained in the divine account as recorded in the Bible.

"But the State of Tennessee, under an honest and fair interpretation of the Constitution, has no more right to teach the Bible as the Divine Book than that the Koran is one, or the Book of Mormon, or the Book of Confucius, or the Buddha, or the Essays of Emerson, or any one of the 10,000 books to which human souls have gone for consolation and aid in their troubles.

"They will have to arrange their cohorts and come back for another fight if the courts of Tennessee stand by their own Constitution, and I presume they will. It is binding on all the courts of Tennessee, and on this court among the rest, and it would be a travesty that a caption such as this is, and a body such as this is, would be declared valid law in the State of Tennessee.

"Now as to the statute itself. It is full of weird, strange, impossible, and imaginary provisions. Driven by bigotry and narrowness, they come together and make this statute and bring this litigation. . . .

"Does this statute state what you shall teach and what you shall not?

"Not at all.

"Does it say you cannot teach the earth is round, because Genesis says it is flat? No.

"Does it say you cannot teach that the earth is millions of ages old, because the account in Genesis makes it less than 6,000 years old? Oh, no. It doesn't state that. If it did, you could understand it. It says you shan't teach any theory of the origin of man that is contrary to the divine theory contained in the Bible. . . .

"I know there are millions of people in the world who derive consolation in their times of trouble and solace in times of distress from the Bible. I would be pretty near the last one in the world to do anything or take any action to take it away. I feel exactly the same toward the religious creed of every human being who lives.

"If anybody finds anything in this life that brings them consolation and health and happiness, I think they ought to have it, whatever they get. I haven't any fault to find with them at all.

"But what is it? The Bible is not one Book. The Bible is made up of sixty-six books written over a period of about 1,000 years, some of them very early and some of them comparatively late. It is a book primarily of religion and morals. It is not a book of science—never was and was never meant to be. Under it, there is nothing prescribed that would tell you how to build a railroad or a steamboat or to make anything that would advance civilization.

"It is not a textbook or a text on chemistry; it is not big enough to be. It is neither a textbook nor primer on geology; its authors knew nothing about geology. It is not a work on evolution; that is a mystery. It is not a work on astronomy; the man who looked out at the universe and studied the heavens had no thought but that the earth was the center of the universe. But we know better; we know better than that. We know that the sun is the center of the solar system, and that there are an infinity of other systems around about us. They thought the sun went around the earth and gave us light and gave us night. We know better. We know the earth turns on its axis to produce days and nights.

"They thought the earth was 4,004 years old before the Christian era. We know better. I doubt if there is a person in Tennessee who does not know better. They told it as best they knew, and, while suns may change, there are no doubt certain primitive, elemental instincts in the organs of man that remain the same. He finds out what he can and yearns to know more and supplements his knowledge with hope and faith.

"That is the province of religion; and I haven't the slightest fault to find with it, not the slightest in the world. One has one thought and one another, and instead of fighting each other as in the past, they should support and help each other.

"Let's see now. Can your Honor tell what is given as the origin of man as shown in the Bible? Is there any human being who can tell us?

"There are two conflicting accounts in the first two chapters. There are scattered all through it various acts and ideas, but to pass that up for the sake of argument, no teacher in any school in the State of Tennessee can know that he is violating a law, but must test every one of its doctrines by the Bible, must he not?

"You cannot say 'two times two equals four' or make a man an educated man, if evolution is forbidden. It does not specify what you cannot teach, but says you cannot teach anything that conflicts with the Bible. Then just imagine making it a criminal code that is so uncertain and impossible that every man must be sure that he has read everything in the

Bible and not only read it, but understood it, or he might violate the criminal code.

"Who is the chief mogul that can tell us what the Bible means? He or they should write a book and make it plain and distinct, so we would know.

"Let us look at it. There are in America at least 500 different sects or churches, all of which quarrel with each other on the importance and non-importance of certain things or the construction of certain passages. All along the line they do not agree among themselves and cannot agree among themselves. They never have and probably never will.

"There is a great division between the Catholics and the Protestants. There is such a disagreement that my client, who is a school teacher, not only must know the subject he is teaching, but he must know everything about the Bible in reference to evolution. And he must be sure that he expresses it right or else some fellow will come along here, more ignorant perhaps than he, and say, 'You made a bad guess and I think you have committed a crime.'

"No criminal statute can rest that way. There is not a chance for it, for this is a criminal statute, and every criminal statute must be plain and simple.

"If Mr. Scopes is to be indicted and prosecuted because he taught a wrong theory of the origin of life, why not tell him what he must teach? Why not say that you must teach that man was made of the dust; and, still stranger, not directly from the dust, without taking any chances on it whatever, that Eve was made out of Adam's rib? You will know what I am talking about.

"Now my client must be familiar with the whole book, and must know all about all of these warring sects of Christians, and know which of them is right and which wrong, in order that he will not commit a crime.

"Nothing was heard of all that until the Fundamentalists got into Tennessee. I trust that when they prosecute their wildly made charge upon the intelligence of some other sect they may modify this mistake and state in simple language what was the account contained in the Bible that could not be taught. So unless other sects have something to do with it, we must know just what we are charged with doing. . . .

"Now, Mr. Scopes, on April 24 did unlawfully and willfully teach in a public school of Rhea County, Tennessee, which public school is supported in whole and in part by the public school fund of the State, certain theories that deny the story of the divine creation of man. What did he teach? Who is it that can tell us that John Scopes taught certain theories that denied the story of the divine—the divine story of creation as recorded in the Bible? How did he know? What textbooks did he teach from? Whom did he teach? Why did he teach?

"Not a word—all is silent. He taught, oh, yes, the place is mentioned, in Rhea County. Well, that is some county—maybe all over it; I don't know where he taught. He might have taught in a half-dozen schools in Rhea County on the one day, and if he is indicted next year, if this trial is over, for teaching in District No. 1, in Rhea County, he cannot plead that he has already been convicted, because this was over there in another district and at another place. . . .

"The Constitution of Tennessee, as I understand it, was copied from the one that Jefferson wrote—so clear, simple, direct—to encourage the freedom of religious opinion. It said in substance that no act shall ever be passed to interfere with complete religious liberty.

"Now, wait—is this it or not? What do you say? What does it do?

"We will say I am a scientist. No, I will take that back—I am a pseudo-scientist, because I believe in evolution,—pseudo-scientist, named by somebody, who neither knows or cares what science is, except to grab it by the throat and throttle it to death. I am a pseudo-scientist, and I believe in evolution. Can a legislative body say, 'You cannot read a book or take a lesson, or make a talk on science until you first find out whether you are saying anything against Genesis'? Can it? It can, unless that constitutional provision protects me. . . .

"That takes care even of the despised Modernist, who dares to be intelligent.

"'That no man can of right be compelled to attend, erect, or support any place of worship, or to maintain any minister against his consent; that no human authority can in any case whatever control or interfere with the rights of conscience in any case whatever.'

"Let us see. Here is the State of Tennessee, living peacefully, surrounded by its beautiful mountains, each one of which contains evidence that the earth is millions of years old. Here is a state going along in its own business, teaching evolution for years: state boards handing out books on evolution, professors in colleges, teachers in schools, lawyers at the bar, physicians, ministers,—a great percentage of the intelligent citizens of the State of Tennessee, evolutionists, have not even thought it was necessary to leave their Church.

"They believed that they could appreciate and understand and make their own simple and human doctrine of the Nazarene, to love their neighbors, be kindly with them, not to place a fine on and not to try to send to jail some man who did not believe as they believed. And they got along all right with it, too, until something happened.

"They have not thought it necessary to give up their Church because they believed that all that was here was not made on the first six days of creation, or that it had come by a slow process of developments extending over the ages, or that one thing grew out of another.

"They are people who believed that organic life and the plants and the animals and man, and the mind of man, and the religion of man are the subjects of evolution, and they have not got through, and that the God in which they believed did not finish creation on the first day, but that he is still working to make something better and higher still out of human beings, who are next to God, and that evolution has been working forever and will work forever—they believe it.

"And along comes somebody who says we have got 'to believe it as I believe it; it is a crime to know more than I know.' And they publish a law to inhibit learning. Now what is in the way of it?

"First, what does the law say? This law says that it shall be a criminal offense to teach in the public schools any account of the origin of man that is in conflict with the divine account in the Bible. It makes the Bible the yardstick to measure every man's intellect, to measure every man's intelligence, and to measure every man's learning. . . .

"I do not imagine evolution hurts the health of anyone, probably not the morals, excepting as all enlightenment may, and the ignorant think of course that it does. But it is not passed for them, your Honor. Oh, no; it is not passed because it is best for the public morals that they shall not know anything about evolution, but because it is contrary to the divine account contained in Genesis. That is all—that is the basis of it.

"Here is a law which makes it a crime to teach evolution in the caption. I don't know whether we have discussed that or not, but it makes it a crime in the body of the act to teach any theory of the origin of man excepting that contained in the divine account, which we find in the Bible. All right. Now that applies to what? Teachers in the public schools.

"Now, I have seen somewhere a statement of Mr. Bryan's that the fellow that made the pay check had a right to regulate the teachers. All right. Let us see. I do not question the right of the Legislature to fix the courses of study, but the State of Tennessee has no right under the police power of the State to carve out a law which applies to school teachers, a law which is a criminal statute and nothing else; which makes no effort to prescribe the school law or course of study. It says that John Smith, who teaches evolution, is a criminal if he teaches it in the public schools.

"There is no question about this act; there is no question where it belongs; there is no question of its origin. Nobody would claim for a minute that the act could be passed excepting that teaching evolution was in the nature of a criminal act; and that therefore the State should forbid it.

"Now, if this is the subject of a criminal act, then it cannot make a criminal out of a teacher in the public schools and [at the same time] leave a man free to teach it in a private school.

"It cannot make it criminal for this teacher to teach evolution and permit books upon evolution to be sold in every store in the State of Tennessee, and to permit the newspapers from foreign cities to bring into your peaceful community the horrible utterances of evolution. Oh, no, nothing like that. . . .

"If today you can take a thing like evolution and make it a crime to teach it in the public schools, tomorrow you can make it a crime to teach it in the private schools, and next year you can make it a crime to teach it to the hustings or in the church. At the next session you may ban books and the newspapers. Soon you may set Catholic against Protestant, and Protestant against Protestant, and try to foist your own religion upon the minds of men.

"If you can do one, you can do the other. Ignorance and fanaticism are ever busy and need feeding. Always they are feeding and gloating for more. Today it is the public school teachers, tomorrow the private, the next day the preachers and the lecturers, the magazines, the books, the newspapers.

"After a while, your Honor, it is the setting of man against man and creed against creed, until with flying banners and beating drums we are marching backward to the glorious ages of the sixteenth century when bigots lighted fagots to burn the men who dared to bring any intelligence and enlightenment and culture to the human mind."

For the Prosecution

WILLIAM JENNINGS BRYAN

MR. BRYAN ON THE ISSUES

William Jennings Bryan delivered his one speech of the trial on the fifth day, adding his protest to that of his son and Mr. McKenzie, against admitting scientific testimony.

"If the Court holds, as we believe the Court should hold," stated Mr. Bryan, "that the testimony the defense is now offering is not competent and not proper testimony, then I assume we are near the end of this trial, and because the question involved is not confined to local questions, but is the broadest that will possibly arise, I have felt justified in submitting my views on the case for the consideration of the Court.

"I have been tempted to speak at former times, but I have been able to withstand the temptation. I have been drawn into the case by, I think, nearly all the lawyers on the other side.

"The principal attorney has often suggested that I am the arch-conspirator and that I am responsible for the presence of this case, and I have almost been credited with leadership of the ignorance and bigotry which he thinks could alone inspire a law like this. . . .

Leslie H. Allen, comp. *Bryan and Darrow at Dayton: The Record and Documents of the "Bible-Evolution Trial"* (New York: Arthur Lee & Co., 1925), pp. 63–66, 69–70, 72–79, 103–108.

"Our position is that the statute is sufficient. The statute defines exactly what the people of Tennessee decided and intended and did declare unlawful, and it needs no interpretation.

"The caption speaks of the evolutionary theory, and the statute specifically states that teachers are forbidden to teach in the schools supported by taxation in this State any theory of creation of man that denies the Divine record of man's creation as found in the Bible, and that there might be no difference of opinion—there might be no ambiguity—that there might be no such confusion of thought as our learned friends attempt to inject into it. The Legislature was careful to define what is meant by the first of the statute.

"It says 'to teach that man is a descendant of any lower form of life.' If that had not been there, if the first sentence had been the only sentence in the statute, then these gentlemen might come and ask to define what that meant or to explain whether the thing that was taught was contrary to the language of the statute in the first sentence. But the second sentence removes all doubt, as has been stated by my colleague.

"The second sentence points out specifically what is meant, and that is the teaching that man is the descendant of any lower form of life; and if the defendant taught that, as we have proved by the textbook that he used and as we have proved by the students that went to hear him, if he taught that man is a descendant of any lower form of life, he violated the statute, and more than that, we have his own confession that he knew he was violating the statute."

After summarizing the evidence, Mr. Bryan continued:

"We do not need any expert to tell us what the law means. An expert cannot be permitted to come in here and try to defeat the enforcement of a law by testifying that it isn't a bad law, and it isn't—I mean a bad doctrine—no matter how these people phrase that doctrine, no matter how they eulogize it. This is not the place to try to prove that the law ought never to have been passed. The place to prove that was at the Legislature.

"If these people were so anxious to keep the State of Tennessee from disgracing itself, if they were so afraid that by this action taken by the Legislature, the State would put itself before the people of the nation as ignorant people and bigoted people—if they had half the affection for Tennessee that you would think they had as they come here to testify—they would have come at a time when their testimony would have been valuable, and not at this time to ask you to refuse to enforce a law because they did not think the law ought to have been passed.

"And if the people of Tennessee were to go into a state, into New York, the one from which this impulse comes to resist this law, or go into any state . . . and try to convince the people that a law they had passed ought not to be enforced (just because the people who went there didn't think it ought to have been passed), don't you think it would be resented as an impertinence? . . .

"The people of this State passed this law. The people of this State knew what they were doing when they passed the law, and they knew the dangers of the doctrine that they did not want it taught to their children. And, my friends, it isn't proper to bring experts in here to try to defeat the purpose of the people of this State by trying to show that this thing that they denounce and outlaw is a beautiful thing that everybody ought to believe in. . . .

"The question is, Can a minority in this State come in and compel a teacher to teach that the Bible is not true and make the parents of these children pay the expenses of the teacher to tell their children what these people believe is false and dangerous?

"Has it come to a time when the minority can take charge of a state like Tennessee and compel the majority to pay their teachers while they take religion out of the heart of the children of the parents who pay the teachers?

"This is the book that is outlawed, if we can judge from the questions asked by the counsel for the defense. They think, because the Board of Education selected this book four or five years ago, that therefore he had to teach it, that he would be guilty if he didn't teach it, and punished if he does.

"Certainly not one of these gentlemen are unlearned in the law, and if I, who have not practiced law for twenty-eight years, know enough to know it I think those who have been as conspicuous in the practice as these gentlemen have been certainly ought to know it—and that is no matter when that law was passed, no matter what the Board of Education had done, no matter whether they put their stamp of approval on this book or not, the moment that law became a law, anything in these books contrary to that law was prohibited, and nobody knew it better than Mr. Scopes himself. . . .

"Tell me that the parents of this day have not any right to declare that children are not to be taught this doctrine—shall not be taken down from the high plane upon which God put man? Shall we be detached from the throne of God and be compelled to link their ancestors with the jungle,— tell that to these children?

"Why, my friend, if they believe it, they go back to scoff at the religion of their parents. And the parents have a right to say that no teacher paid by their money shall rob their children of faith in God and send them back to their homes, skeptical, infidels, or agnostics, or atheists.

"This is the doctrine that they want taught, this doctrine that they would force upon the schools, that they will not let the Bible be read!

"Why, up in the State of New York they are now trying to keep the schools from adjourning for one hour in the afternoon, not that any teacher shall teach them the Bible, but that the children may go to the churches to which they belong and there have instruction in the work. . . ."

JUDGE RAULSTON—Let me ask you a question. Do you understand the evolution theory to involve the divine birth or divinity of Christ's virgin birth in any way or not?

MR. BRYAN—I am perfectly willing to answer the question. My contention is, that the evolutionary hypothesis is not a theory, your honor.

"The Legislature has actually paid evolution a higher honor than it deserves. Evolution is not a theory, but a hypothesis. Huxley said it could not rise to the dignity of a theory until they found some species that had developed according to the hypothesis, and at that time, Huxley's time, there had never been found a single species the origin of which could be traced to another species.

"Darwin himself said he thought it was strange that with two or three million species they had not been able to find one that they could trace to another. About three years ago, Bateson of London, who came all the way to Toronto, at the invitation of the American Academy for the Advancement of Science, which (if the gentlemen will brace themselves for a moment) I will say I am a member of. They invited Mr. Bateson to come over and speak to them on evolution, and he came and his speech on evolution was printed in Science Magazine. After having taken up every effort that had been made to show the origin of species and find it, Bateson told those people that every one had failed—every one, every one.

"And it is true today. Never have they traced one single species to any other, and that is why it was that this so-called expert stated that, while the fact of evolution they think is established, every theory has failed, and today there is not a scientist in all the world who can trace one single species to any other. And yet they call us ignoramuses and bigots, because we do not throw away our Bible and accept it as proved that out of two or three million species not one is traceable to another. . . .

"Now, my friends, I want you to know that they not only have no proof, but they cannot find the beginning. I suppose this distinguished scholar who came here shamed them all by his number of degrees. He did not shame me, for I have more than he has, but I can understand how my friends felt when he unrolled degree after degree. . . ."

JUDGE RAULSTON—Before it could be recognizable with the Bible, it would have to be admitted that God created the cell?

MR. BRYAN—There would be no contention about that, but our contention is, even if they put God back there, it does not make it harmonious with the Bible.

"The Court is right, that unless they put God back there it must dispute the Bible, and this witness who has been questioned, whether he has qualified or not—and they could ask him every question they wanted to, but they did not ask him how life began; they did not ask whether back of all, whether if in the beginning, there was God.

"They did not tell us where immortality began. They did not tell us where, in this long period of time, between the cell at the bottom of the sea and man, where he became endowed with the hope of immortality.

"And Your Honor asked me whether it has anything to do with the Virgin Birth. Yes, because this principle of evolution disputes the miracle.

"There is no place for the miracle in this train of evolution, and the Old Testament and the New are filled with miracles; if this doctrine is true, this logic eliminates every mystery in the Old Testament and the New. And eliminates everything supernatural. And that means they eliminate the Virgin Birth. That means that they eliminate resurrection of the body, and that means that they eliminate the doctrine of atonement.

"And they believe that man has been rising all the time, that man never fell, that when the Savior came there was not any reason for His coming. They believe there was no reason why He should not go as soon as He could, that He was born of Joseph or some other co-respondent, and that He lies in His grave. . . .

MR. BRYAN—Your Honor, we first pointed out that we do not need any experts in science. Here is one plain fact, and the statute defines itself, and it tells the kind of evolution it does not want taught, and the evidence says that this is the kind of evolution that was taught; and no number of scientists could come in here, my friends, and override that statute or take from the jury its right to decide this question. So that all the experts that they could bring would mean nothing. And, when it comes to Bible experts, every member of the jury is as good an expert on the Bible as any man that they could bring, or that we could bring.

"The one beauty about the word of God is, it does not take an expert to understand it. They have translated the Bible into five hundred languages. They have carried it into nations where but few can read a word, or write, to people who never saw a book, who never read and yet can understand that Bible, and they can accept the salvation that that Bible offers; and they can know more about that book by accepting Jesus and feeling in their hearts the sense of their sins forgiven, than all of the skeptical outside Bible experts that could come in here to talk to the people of Tennessee about the construction that they place upon the Bible.

"Therefore, your Honor, we believe that this evidence is not competent. This is not a mock trial. This is not a convocation brought here to allow men to come and stand for a time in the limelight and speak to the world from the platform at Dayton. If we must have a mock trial to give these people a chance to get before the public with their views, then let us convene it after this case is over, and let people stay as long as they want to listen. . . .

"The Bible is the word of God. The Bible is the only expression of man's hope of salvation. The Bible, the record of the Son of God, the Saviour of the world, born of the Virgin Mary, crucified and risen again— that Bible is not going to be driven out of this court by experts who come hundreds of miles to testify that they can reconcile evolution with its ancestor in the jungle, or man made by God in His image and put here for purposes as a part of the divine plan.

"No, we are not going to settle that question here, and I think we ought to confine ourselves to the law and to the evidence that can be admitted in accordance with the law.

"Your court is an office of this State, and we who represent the State as counsel are officers of the State, and we cannot humiliate the great State of Tennessee by admitting for a moment that people can come from anywhere and protest against the enforcement of this State's laws on the ground that it does not conform with their ideas, or because it banishes from our schools a thing that they believe in and think ought to be taught, in spite of the protest of those who employ the teacher and pay him his salary.

"The facts are simple, the case is plain, and if these gentlemen want to enter upon a larger field of educational work on the subject of evolution, let us get through with this case and then convene a mock court, or it will deserve the title of mock court if its purpose is to banish from the hearts of the people the Word of God as revealed." (Prolonged applause)

BRYAN VS. DARROW

During the second week-end, the scene of battle was shifted from the courtroom to the lawn in front of the house where Mr. Bryan was lodging, and to the Mansion, Mr. Darrow's headquarters. With about two miles as the range, each aimed his verbal shafts at the other on Saturday, while Dayton, relieved of the necessity of pushing its way into the courtroom or lounging about under the loud speaker, went about its business with something of its customary calm.

Mr. Bryan's statement, issued first, renewed hostilities thus:

"We are making progress. The Tennessee case has uncovered the conspiracy against the Bible Christianity; those who worship the Bible God, trust the Bible as the word of God, and believe in the Bible Christ are opening their eyes to what evolution really is and to its effect when accepted and followed as an interpretation of man and a philosophy of life.

"Multitudes have been deceived by the use of the term 'evolution' to define things that are not evolution. In one of the science books taught in the Dayton High School and referred to in the trial there is a chapter on the 'evolution of machinery.' Machinery does not evolve; it is an inanimate thing that man designs and improves. The various forms of growth, like the growth of a plant from a seed, the growth of a chicken from an egg or the growth of a human being from a small beginning—all these are carelessly described as 'evolution.'

"The world is now learning—most of the world for the first time—that evolution, as the scientists teach it, is an imaginary process, wholly unproved, that begins with life but does not attempt to explain life, and represents man as the climax of a series of changes coming up from a simple cell through millions of forms of life different from man.

"This hypothesis makes every living thing known in animal life a blood relative of every other living thing in animal life, and makes man a blood relative of them all—either an ancestor or a cousin. If this hypothesis were true, we would all be murderers if we swatted a fly or killed a bedbug, for we would be killing our kin, and we would be cannibals whenever we ate any of the mammals that, according to Mr. Scopes' teaching, are included with man in the little circle of the diagram of the biology taught by Scopes.

"But that is not all. If the evolutionary hypothesis is true, man has come up through the animals below him by a cruel law under which the strong kill off the weak. Darwin argues that the race was necessarily impaired by the suspension of this cruel law. He commended by implication the savages who are eliminating the weak, saying that it left the survivors strong.

"He even suggested that vaccination had saved the lives of thousands who would otherwise have succumbed because of weak constitutions—the implication being that the race would have been benefited by allowing them to die instead of prolonging their lives and permitting them to propagate. He complained that civilized society and medical men attempt to prolong life every last moment.

"No more cruel doctrine was ever promulgated. Those who believe it are robbed of the pity and the mercy that comes of civilization.

"To show that Darwin's heartless doctrine has not been abandoned one has only to read a book that came out about three years ago. I will not give the name of the author, for I do not care to advertise his name.

"In his preface, he says that he is indebted to some twenty eminent scientists, 'professors and doctors,' and he singled out for special gratitude a young man recently elected president of a great state university, a man whose career the author predicts will 'be one of the world's events of the coming generation.' This eminent educator read the manuscript over twice and 'made many invaluable suggestions.'

"On page 34 of this book we are told that 'evolution is a bloody business, but civilization tries to make it a pink tea.' Then he adds:

"'Barbarism is the only process by which man has organically progressed and civilization is the only process by which he has organically declined. Civilization is the most dangerous enterprise on which man ever set out. For when you take man out of the bloody, brutal but beneficent hand of natural selection, you place him at once in the soft, perfumed, daintily gloved but far more dangerous hand of artificial selection.' Here we have evolution unmasked.

"The evolutionists have not been honest with the public. Even ministers who believe in evolution have assured their congregations that there is no inconsistency between Darwinism and Christianity. Do they know its effect on Darwin, or, knowing its effect, do they dare conceal it from their congregations?

"The ministers should tell their congregations that evolution leads logically to agnosticism; they should tell them of the wail of Romanes, sometimes called the successor of Darwin, who said in his book, written to prove that there is no God:

"'I am not ashamed to confess that with this virtual negation of God, the universe to me has lost its soul of loveliness, yet when at times I think, as think at times I must, of the appalling contrast between the hallowed glory of that creed that once was mine and the lonely mystery of existence as now I find it—at such times, I shall ever feel it impossible to avoid the sharpest pang of which my nature is susceptible.'

"But this trial has another important effect. The presence of Mr. Darrow here, an avowed agnostic, both as to God and as to immortality—he has so stated in court before the Judge—represents the most militant anti-Christian sentiment in the country. He protested against opening the court with prayer and has lost no opportunity to slur the intelligence of those who believe in orthodox Christianity, and to hurl the charge of bigotry against every one who objects to the teaching of evolution in the schools.

"Mr. Darrow in the celebrated Leopold-Loeb trial boldly argued that the boys were not responsible for what they did, laying the blame upon their ancestors and their environment, and relieving them of all personality or power to decide between good and evil.

"The Christian world is not going to give up its belief in God or its belief in the Bible as our only standard of morals or in Christ as our only Savior and wisest guide. The Christian world will not give up these sacred things at the demand of these intolerant champions—not of science but of an unproven guess—the logical tendency of which is to rob man of his moral standards in this world and of hope of immortal life in the world to come.

"Yes, we are making progress, and we can acknowledge our indebtedness to quite a number for unintentional aid.

"First, we are indebted to Professor Scopes, whose devotion to the doctrine that gives him a jungle ancestry is so passionate that, though a school teacher, he was willing to become a violator of the law in order to test its constitutionality.

"But our indebtedness is much greater to Mr. Darrow, Mr. Scopes's chief attorney. Mr. Darrow was chosen by Mr. Scopes himself to represent his interests, if not his views. Mr. Darrow's hostility to Christianity, proclaimed for a generation, and his conduct in this case are now known to the world and will arouse the devout Christians of a nation whose prayers ascend in gratitude for the courage of the State of Tennessee; and Mr. Darrow's attitude will also compel the Christians who take sides with him to explain to their Christian brothers why they defend a doctrine that strikes at the root not only of Christianity but of civilization.

"Do they know what evolution means? If so, do they prefer it to the Bible?"

After reading Mr. Bryan's statement, Mr. Darrow issued this reply:

"Before the trial of this case I had no idea that there was only one interpretation of religion in the world. Christianity has had in its ranks thousands of able and intelligent men in all the countries of the world, but these are now all satisfied, and Mr. Bryan is to be the one and only judge of what the Bible and Christianity means.

"The theory of evolution as a scientific theory was only announced about seventy years ago, and since that time it has been accepted by almost every scientist in the world. It is true that how evolution came about has always been a matter of discussion and investigation by scientific men, but none of them questioned the truth of the theory.

"The believers in evolution are by no means confined to heretics, for the realms of religion and science are entirely separate. Among the most prominent evolutionists of the world are multitudes of men in high standing in all the Christian churches. All of these are pronounced heretics by Mr. Bryan.

"No doubt the law of life, through all the past, has been cruel. As the great naturalist, Fabre, says: 'Each man is in turn a guest and a dish. Life lives upon the vegetable world and upon the animal world. Different forms of life kill and devour each other. This is the law of nature, and nothing can change it. And Christianity has not yet succeeded in taking barbarism out of the world.'

"We have just emerged from a great war, where Christians have been busy killing each other, a war which shed an ocean of blood that was not even dreamed of on the earth before. Not only this, but ministers of all sorts were each praying that their side might succeed, and seeking to align God with their cause.

"Man has a bloody past, and he has a bloody present. What his future will be cannot safely be prophesied.

"It is perfectly plain that the scientist is as kind and humane and tolerant as the fundamentalist. In fact, no one ever heard a scientific man who ever sought to call the aid of the law to enforce belief in his theories. The scientific man has always welcomed the fullest investigation, and he himself has been the first to consider the way over objection, and modify and change his theory to conform to the facts.

"Men's religious views are involved in this prosecution. It is true that on the subject of God and immortality I am willing to confess that I am an agnostic. I do not know. I fancy that this is a much higher position than that of Mr. Bryan, who says that God was made in his image, and is sure that this is true. It is hard to understand how an intelligent man can believe that a photograph of a human being needs only to be enlarged to give us a picture of God. On this subject I am not agnostic. I do not believe it; but, as to the first cause and the power that is at the heart of the universe, it seems to me that most men must confess that they do not know.

"It is true also that I believe that man is largely, if not entirely, controlled by forces back of him and around him. I hope this has made me more understanding of my fellow-men and more kindly and charitable to them. However, this idea is not so far removed from that of the founder of Mr. Bryan's sect, John Calvin, who believed that man was predestined for ages to do exactly what he did.

"I have no desire to have the Christian world give up its belief in God or its Bible, but at least a very large portion of the Christian world do not regard the Bible as a book of science.

"Whether man should be proud of his ancestry is not a question for science, so long as one is interested in the truth, and no one needs to seek the truth unless he wants to find it.

"The scientists think that it is more to man's credit to believe that he began with a lower form of life than to believe that he was made out of hand from dust; every animal form is higher than dust.

"The scientist does not believe that man has ever fallen, but that he has steadily grown forward. It is the Fundamentalist only that believes man was once perfect and that he afterward fell.

"I did object to daily praying in court. Praying is rare in court, even in the South. I objected to it because of the peculiar situation wherein Mr. Bryan had sought to make this trial a contest between religion and science. I thought, of all cases, this was one where the court should stand perfectly free from bias. Even the Judge who presides had not followed the regular habit of opening court with prayer until this case arose.

"We are interested in two things: First, that a higher court shall pass upon this case, and second, that in other States, those who wish to pursue truth shall be left free to think and investigate and teach and learn.

"We know that the great majority of the intelligent Christians do not accept the literal interpretation for the whole Bible. We have learned here, both from laymen and clergymen, that a large part of the Fundamentalists do not accept it. This doctrine is a doctrine of the literalists, and we are perfectly satisfied that the majority of the Christian Church has long since passed beyond that." . . .

SUGGESTIONS FOR FURTHER READING

Ray Ginger, *Six Days or Forever? Tennessee* v. *John Thomas Scopes* (New York: Oxford University Press, 1958); Lawrence W. Levine, *Defender of the Faith: William Jennings Bryan, The Last Decade, 1915–1925* (New York: Oxford University Press, 1965).

X

DO WOMEN WANT NATIONAL PROHIBITION?

The so-called Prohibition era spans the period from January 1920 until April 1933 when the National Prohibition Enforcement Act made it illegal to produce and sell beverages with an alcohol content larger than 0.5 percent. Prohibition on a state-by-state and even a county-by-county basis began during the later nineteenth century. The temperance crusade actually dates back to the 1830s and 1840s, however, and in many respects remains the longest running, most heatedly contested reform movement in all of American history.

During the 1840s a businessman in Portland, Maine, Neal Dow, ascribed a great variety of antisocial behavior—family violence, poverty, crime, and poor performance in the workplace—to excessive use of alcohol encouraged by long-standing local custom and aggressive competition by saloons. When informal persuasion failed to make a difference, Dow and others became convinced that the state legislature had to take action. The famous "Maine Law" of 1851 prohibited the manufacture and sale of intoxicating liquors. Within four years, thirteen of the thirty-one states then existing had passed similar laws.

Because women especially suffered the consequences of alcohol abuse by men—family absenteeism, economic nonsupport, beatings, etc.—women became particularly prominent as leaders of the temperance movement. Frances Willard became the dynamic head of the Women's Christian Temperance Union, eventually an international organization, and in 1895 the Anti-Saloon League of America held its first annual convention. Carry Nation of Kansas began her town-by-town crusade during the 1880s, fearlessly smashing saloons with her notorious hatchet. By the early twentieth century she became a prominent figure in Washington, D.C., working for reform at the national level.

Although the Volstead Act passed in 1919 and provided for enforcement of the recently ratified Eighteenth Amendment, it remained intensely controversial throughout the 1920s, and for diverse reasons. Because it was so difficult to enforce, many recognized that Prohibition only served as a stimulus to organized crime. Gangsters got rich supplying booze to speakeasies, restaurants, and private individuals who could not imagine life without it. Others who felt strongly opposed to alcohol use (and abuse) opposed national prohibition because they were conservatives committed to state sovereignty. They feared that such legislation as the

Volstead Act would encourage the growing centralization of power in the federal government.

Calls for repeal of the Eighteenth Amendment emerged as early as 1923 and became increasingly intense during the next six years. Women's organizations debated it, and a division within the Democratic Party concerning Prohibition nearly split the party in 1928. By 1931 the Hoover administration acknowledged that Prohibition was not working. The following year the Democrats campaigned for repeal and won.

In 1928 Louise Gross was chair of the Women's Committee for the Repeal of the Eighteenth Amendment, whereas Mrs. Henry W. Peabody was chair of the Woman's National Committee for Law Enforcement. Their debate on the issue of repeal appeared in Current History. *The same issue of this journal also contained a dialogue between two male attorneys, experts on constitutional issues, titled "Prohibition and the Constitution."*

Why Women Desire Repeal

LOUISE GROSS

Do the women of America want National Prohibition? No. Do the women of America want temperance? Yes. Do they want saloons, as in pre-Volstead days? No. Then, what do they want? These are questions which are being asked and answered in various ways today all over the world— and I say all over the world because I recently returned from a European trip where these questions were put to me by governmental officials and leaders of the social and civic life of France, Germany, Switzerland and England.

American women believe in temperance which means voluntary abstinence, self-control, but not coerced abstinence or abstinence forced from the outside, which can never be obtained by passing useless laws. The American women believe in tolerance and fair play, they are noted for their good sportsmanship and courage to fight for ideals and changes in laws that will bring better conditions to the less fortunate, but they will not stand for hypocrisy, sham or misrepresentation. If they make a mistake they are quick to realize it and anxious to rectify it. That is why I do not hesitate to say that the majority of the women of America do not favor National Prohibition, because after eight years' trial it has proved a mistake and a costly experiment to the nation.

The majority of the women in America favored National Prohibition when it was first talked about, thinking that it might improve temperance, and we were willing to try it, but each year since it has become the law of the land we realize that it is not the cure for the ills of the nation, and that conditions in this country are gradually getting worse and worse as a result of the adoption of the Eighteenth Amendment, and being women, we want to know why.

The majority of the women of the country cannot reconcile the fact that the Anti-Saloon League proclaims in one breath that Prohibition is a great success, and in the next breath asks for five million dollars to carry on its propaganda with, when the Federal Government is spending millions of dollars yearly to try and enforce the law. What the average woman cannot figure out is, if Prohibition is such a success why does a group of plain citizens have to raise five million dollars to watch it? If Prohibition is the blessing to the country and the success its proponents would have us believe, why is it the chief topic of conversation, why does it occupy the

Louise Gross, "Why Women Desire Repeal," *Current History* (July 1928), pp. 537–42. Reprinted with permission from *Current History* magazine. Copyright © 1928 Current History, Inc.

most prominent space in the newspapers, why must this Government use the army, the navy, the courts and a large enforcement department, local officials and anything they can get a hold of, to help enforce the law?

These are a few of the questions the women of America are asking. Then we reason, that with the Prohibitionists themselves in control of all branches of the Federal Government and a majority in the House and Senate, why do we not have 100 per cent. enforcement, and why is it not a success? If Prohibition were a success and respected like the laws against stealing, murder, arson, and so forth, there would be no need for private individuals to raise money to help the Government to enforce something that never has been enforced, and never will be enforced, as long as the United States is as it now is with respect to geographical location and the temperament of its citizens. Good laws are automatically enforced and respected by the majority of the people, but laws such as the Eighteenth Amendment will always be regarded with suspicion and distrust by a free people.

PROHIBITION NOT A SUCCESS

Do you wonder, therefore, that the women of America are beginning to change their minds about the so-called benefits of National Prohibition? We reason further that if the anti-Prohibitionists controlled Congress and the Senate, there might be an excuse for the present conditions, but with the "Drys" in control, there must be something wrong somewhere, in that Prohibition is not the success some people would have us believe. Therefore, as the Eighteenth Amendment is the source and root of the evil, the natural conclusion the women arrive at is to remove the root—or the Eighteenth Amendment.

One of the real reasons why the women of America are beginning to feel apprehensive about Prohibition is its effect upon the young people of the land who are now indulging in drinking hard liquor, such as never was known in the days before Prohibition. Young people in this country exchange recipes for home brew, they carry hip flasks, and have drinking parties at their school and college dances and socials which are a disgrace to civilization. They think it is smart to drink. The increase of crime among youths between the ages of 14 and 21 may be laid to Prohibition, and is not the result of the World War, as the Drys are trying to make us believe, because these youths were small children ten years ago and not old enough to go to war. This is another source of worry to the women of America which is causing them to question the good of Prohibition.

The women of America are now studying ways of changing the situation brought about through the adoption of the Eighteenth Amendment and the Volstead Act. They are studying the laws pertaining to the question, they are studying the various remedies offered as a solution, they are asking questions and reading all available information on the subject, and a large group of them who do not believe in Prohibition have come to the conclusion that the only remedy is in the repeal of the Eighteenth Amendment. As long as this un-American doctrine remains a part of our Federal Constitution any bills which might be passed to modify the Volstead Act would be declared unconstitutional as conflicting with the Eighteenth Amendment, and with that intuition which women are supposed to possess we do not hesitate to advocate the repeal of this amendment.

Women who advocate the repeal of the Eighteenth Amendment consider that this question involves a greater issue than that of National Prohibition. It involves nothing less than the self-governing capacity of every citizen in this country, because it puts the question directly up to the people of the country themselves, to vote upon it. It involves the question whether or not all proposed Constitutional amendments which may affect the personal habits of the people of the entire United States should not be required by law to be submitted to a vote of the people themselves, and whether in the future the Constitution of the United States should not be strengthened to provide that no such amendment shall be made to it unless upon the consent of the people themselves.

A PATRIOTIC CAUSE

The women opposed to the Eighteenth Amendment and advocating its repeal consider, therefore, that they are working for one of the highest and most patriotic causes that have ever been presented to the country.

The women advocating repeal of the Eighteenth Amendment have discovered that there is at present in the United States Senate (peacefully sleeping in committee, where it will remain until there is a Wet majority in Congress) a Joint Resolution known as S. J. No. 2, which provides for the submission of the repeal of the Eighteenth Amendment to Conventions in the several States. This is the nearest thing to a national referendum on Prohibition that it is possible to have under our Federal Constitution. . . .

BILL OF RIGHTS VIOLATED

This referendum should be welcomed by the "Drys" as well as the anti-Prohibitionists, and if the people themselves vote in favor of National Prohibition there will be no reason for any more agitation against it. Many women realize that the Eighteenth Amendment violates the Bill of Rights in some of its articles, and we all know that it was not put into the Constitution by the direct vote of the people themselves, but by their representatives in Congress and the Legislatures of more than three-quarters of the States; therefore there has always been dissatisfaction with the law. Many women now realize that the fundamental mistake of the Eighteenth Amendment is that it established a precedent under which, by amending the Constitution through State Legislatures, other rights of liberty, which should reside wholly within the States themselves, may be gradually transferred to Congress, thereby paving the way for a highly centralized government, from which may spring all kinds of tyrannous laws, commissions and bureaucracies and their manifold rulings and decisions which should have no place in the government of our country.

After the Eighteenth Amendment is repealed it will devolve upon each State to regulate its own liquor traffic. The Federal Government now has the legal right under said Amendment to control this traffic, but the women who have studied this question contend that it is not wise or advisable to give this right to the Federal Government; that the right to control the liquor traffic and to regulate it should be left exclusively to the several States.

Many women cannot see where it involves any moral turpitude or sin to take a drink. People all through the Ages and in nearly all civilized countries in the world have been permitted to drink, and they are just as good as we are. I noticed particularly in the countries I visited in Europe that in no city were the night life and after-theatre parties or house parties as "wet" and as productive of drunkenness as similar life in America is since prohibition. I spent several hours in a London "pub" in the very worst section of London and noticed no drunkenness or evil consequences such as exist here today in our speakeasies and unlicensed public houses, soft-drink emporiums, and so forth, which flourish all over this country since the Eighteenth Amendment became the law of the land.

NEED OF A NATIONAL REFERENDUM

. . . The women of this country all know that some members of Congress vote "Dry" and live "Wet," that paid Reformers urge Prohibition and drink themselves, that Prohibition agents paid to enforce the law are seizing, killing and jailing people who are violating the law, and then taking the liquor away from them and selling it to others; we know that public officials who should enforce the law drink themselves, therefore we are opposed to Prohibition and to being called a nation of hypocrites.

The majority of the American women are tired of hearing representatives of the Anti-Saloon League and self-styled women's leaders shout that they represent ten or twenty million women of the country who stand like the Rock of Gibraltar for Prohibition when we know such is not the case. There are about 120,000,000 people in this country, of whom about 60,000,000 are women. If the "Drys" claim 20,000,000 for Prohibition, what is to prevent the rest of us from saying that the balance, or 40,000,000 women, are opposed to Prohibition? Has any one ever made an actual count? Then why not settle the question with a national referendum such as provided for in the present Senate resolution known as S. J. No. 2?

REFERENDUM VOTES AGAINST PROHIBITION

In every State where a referendum was held the majority has always been in favor of repealing the enforcement acts or against Prohibition, and in each case just as many women voted as men, and if women were in favor of Prohibition these referendums could never have succeeded as they did. In one or two instances, as in California, which always votes "Dry," the women understand that there are local conditions such as higher prices for grapes and larger quantities sold for home-brew making than in pre-Volstead days; therefore, it is a question of "self-preservation being the first law of nature," and not one of principle, and the rest of the country understands it; but aside from these cases, and regardless of what numbers the "Wets" or the "Drys" claim for or against Prohibition, the women of America would welcome a national referendum on the subject, and would then abide by the will of the majority. . . .

Women's Crusade against Repeal or Modification

MRS. HENRY W. PEABODY

That genial philosopher, Chauncey M. Depew, when asked if the Eighteenth Amendment would be repealed, answered, "No," and gave the reason in one word, "Women."

What do the women themselves say regarding it? Is there any possibility of knowing their collective mind?

Through the Woman's National Committee for Law Enforcement ten great national organizations of women have spoken, first in their own delegated bodies and then through their representatives who form the Executive Committee of this National Committee. They have spoken, not once, but repeatedly, without wavering, and they affiliated six years ago for cooperative expression and action. They number, on a conservative estimate, 12,000,000 women above the average in character, intellect and patriotism. These are the organizations:

General Federation of Women's Clubs.

Young Women's Christian Association.

Mrs. Henry W. Peabody, "Women's Crusade against Repeal or Modification," *Current History* (July 1928), pp. 542–47. Reprinted with permission from *Current History* magazine. Copyright © 1928 Current History, Inc.

National Congress of Parents and Teachers.

Lend-a-Hand Society.

International Order of King's Daughters.

Federation of Women's Boards of Foreign Missions of North America.

Council of Women for Home Missions.

Woman's Christian Temperance Union.

National Woman's Democratic Law Enforcement League.

The aggregate membership, as stated, is more than 12,000,000, but as there is some duplication we will take another numerical test. Protestant church women number approximately 20,000,000. At least 12,000,000 of these are for the Eighteenth Amendment, as indicated by the action in their own church groups. Do not from this suppose, as a reporter ingenuously inferred, that some 8,000,000 church women—Methodists, Baptists, Presbyterians, North and South, with Congregationalists, and others—are opposed to Prohibition. We doubt whether there would be a half million of that type. When we deduct 40 per cent. we are setting our opponents a noble example of restrained statement. Women of the Catholic Church are not organized with us, but Kathleen Norris is typical of a great host who declare with Cardinal Mercier: "If universal Prohibition could be introduced more lives would be saved than by universal disarmament. Alcohol kills more men than war, and does it less honorably." Some of the finest Jewish women are on our committee.

RESOLUTIONS OF WOMEN'S ORGANIZATIONS

It may be of interest to know the type of resolution adopted by some of the great organizations of women. We give only two out of many:

1—General Federation of Women's Clubs (3,000,000 Members) Biennial Council, Grand Rapids, Mich., June, 1927.

Resolution

Whereas, the Eighteenth Amendment prohibiting the manufacture, transportation and sale of intoxicating liquor, together with Federal and State enforcing laws, all adopted with large majorities, continue to be the subject of a vigorous onslaught for the purpose of reducing such majorities and of encouraging a sentiment favorable to the lax enforcement and nullification of such amendment and laws; now, therefore,

Be It Resolved, that the General Federation of Women's Clubs in Biennial Council assembled renews its allegiance to the Constitution of the United States of America and every part thereof; that we reaffirm our belief in the wisdom of national and State prohibition of the use of intoxicating liquor; that we oppose any weakening to the national or State enforcement laws; and that we favor adequate appropriations of such enforcement.

2—Platform Adopted Unanimously by the Woman's National Committee for Law Enforcement, Providence, R.I., May, 1927.

As members of our respective political parties we shall require for our votes Presidential candidates whose public pledges and private performance uphold the Eighteenth Amendment.

We shall require all platforms and all candidates to stand unequivocally for the support of the Constitution of the United States.

We shall require clean records of every Administration, Federal, State and local, of enforcement honestly carried out free from bribery, patronage and corruption by men who are for the law and are given sufficient power to be able to fulfill their duty. If this means making the Eighteenth Amendment the issue in the 1928 elections, then we are prepared to make it the issue.

This was endorsed January, 1928, by the Federation of Women's Foreign Mission Boards of all denominations.

Of the Woman's Christian Temperance Union, great and successful pioneer, there is no question.

MILLIONS OF WOMEN AGAINST REPEAL

There will be little question regarding Democratic women of the solid South and the liquid North, since a strong group, growing rapidly, has separated from party leaders and formed the National Woman's Democratic Law Enforcement League, with a fearless periodical, *The Woman Voter*. The chairman, Mrs. Jesse Nicholson of Chevy Chase, Md., was formerly high in office in the regular Democratic organization. These women repudiate all Wet candidates.

In addition to these affiliated groups are the militant Salvation Army, women of the Granges, patriotic organizations which can hardly evade an issue involving an attack on the Constitution. The League of Women Voters recently passed a strong enforcement resolution. *These millions of women have registered definitely by vote in favor of the Eighteenth Amendment and against repeal or modification.*

The National Committee for Law Enforcement has no salaried officials. It has sixteen State organizations, with offices in Massachusetts, New York and Ohio. Its work, mainly educational, is carried on through conventions, textbooks, literature, posters, and a monthly paper, *The Spotlight*, published in New York. Local organizations through every State down to the last little town are reached through the ten organizations represented in its executive.

CONVICTIONS REGISTERED AT POLLS

Women have also registered their convictions at the polls. Before the Federal Amendment 33 States had acted favorably for Prohibition. In many of these States women voted. Federal action on the Eighteenth Amendment and the Volstead Act was ratified with the hearty cooperation of women in 46 States. The Supreme Court has rendered favorable decisions in forty cases bearing on the Eighteenth Amendment and the Volstead Act. Therefore, the great majority in Congress must remain politically Dry if they continue to represent the electorate. Their oath of office requires that they "support and defend the Constitution without *mental reservation* or *purpose of evasion.*"

But Wet political optimists are saying, "The women will not vote." In certain States candidates have been presented for whom no reputable woman could vote. The women are not excited over the tariff, taxes or other masculine political pawns. They understand that the rallying cry, "Turn the Rascals Out," is reversible, equally applicable to both parties. But here comes their own issue and they will vote.

CHARACTER OF GROUPS OPPOSED

It would not be fair, however, to say that all women want Prohibition. There are certain groups opposed. Among these is a group who reflect the influence of unceasing propaganda in press and magazines. They really believe that only fanatics are back of Prohibition, that it cannot be enforced, though it is in two-thirds of the States. They understand that the Anti-Saloon League controls the Supreme Court, Congress, State Legislatures, manufacturing interests, railroads and educational institutions. They argue for Temperance versus Prohibition, forgetting that in the long years when temperance was the objective it was always possible for Wet border forces to "put the Wet into Dry States," while the temperance hosts could not "put the Dry into Wet States." Since State lines are imaginary, a Federal Amendment was essential to Dry States' Rights which, after all, are as legitimate as Wet States' Rights.

The second group includes women of the underworld, with illiterate aliens from wine-growing countries who cannot be counted on for moral or patriotic issues. These classes were much larger in old saloon days, and will grow less with education.

There is also the small privileged class. Few reforms start on Fifth Avenue or Beacon Street. Special privilege often breeds a type of self-centered women who hold themselves above moral or civil law; patriotic in war when the flag is in fashion, they are disloyal to the Constitution which daily protects them, their property and rights.

THE THOUGHTLESS AND THE CORRUPT

Then there are parrots, who talk but do not think. They say glibly, "More drinking than ever," without ability to reason that it takes "a great many hip flasks to make a saloon," or they declare "it was put over," which is untrue, though even so, it would stand with the Ten Commandments, the Declaration of Independence, the Constitution and the Bill of Rights, from which we are not exempt and which we are not proposing to repeal.

We must also deal with a certain type of woman politician and women paid to serve corrupt political interests. States which send disloyal men to Congress or Legislature will secure women to match. The remedy will not come through developing "women bosses," as Mrs. Franklin Roosevelt has suggested. This would create a worse political situation than we have in Mrs. Roosevelt's own State and party, where Tammany controls. Women are learning. The nation will rise as Chicago rose. The Chicago Woman's Law Enforcement Committee asks in a questionnaire, "Can you change the mind of your dripping Wet Senator?" Answer, "No; but you can change your Senator." They did, following the example of women in New York State.

Why do so many women stand for the Eighteenth Amendment and its enforcement? Women are accustomed to enforcing laws, essential in home and school, as in city and State government. They are not at all afraid of prohibitions. They recognize the demand for personal liberty as that of a four-year-old mentality, sometimes found in intellectuals. Then there were fewer alcoholics among women than among men, and women never feel the strain of giving up an old habit as men do, who cling fondly even to ancient garments, while most women readily adjust themselves to new. But back of these reasons is a great underlying natural law which will control the normal woman if human society continues. Men think logically, women biologically. The preservation of the race rests with the woman. Her instinct to protect the child leads her to deny herself privileges and liberties that injure the child. The woman's major reason for no repeal or modification of the Eighteenth Amendment is found also in one word, "Children."

Alcoholism is a disease as real as tuberculosis, more dangerous to body, soul and mind. The health motive appeals to women. They have seen the galloping type of the disease of alcoholism and the slow decline. They agree with thousands of eminent physicians and with great insurance companies who face the health risk in their business that alcohol, a habit-forming drug, is a menace to health. In 22 States alcohol is not allowed even as a medicine. These are States with the highest health rate. Most of the medicinal alcohol released is used in New York and Illinois, where the health rate is low.

Alcohol and vice have always gone hand in hand. The danger to youth from beer and wine is far greater than from distilled liquor. "No harm to take a drink," "Who has a right to interfere with my personal habits?" are Wet axioms which are dangerous to flaming youth. Indulgence in alcohol is accountable for political debauchery, for nearly every brutal crime and excess, for vast unhappiness and shame. Public safety in this mechanical age demands clear heads and steady hands, which alcohol will not furnish.

PROSPERITY UNDER PROHIBITION

A century ago Richard Cobden, a noted British economist, visited America. He declared that the two great Race Destroyers are liquor and war, and the battle against them would be won in this new Republic unless it became "choked with prosperity." Notwithstanding our boasted prosperity the nation, South and West, is still able to breathe, and there the fight against these destroyers is on.

Considerable credit for prosperity should be granted to Prohibition, which released billions of dollars wasted in alcohol for useful trades, home building, insurance, travel, automobiles, education, radios. Formerly a large part of the family wage supported 177,000 licensed saloons and hotel bars, with numberless speakeasies, for illicit selling did not come with the Eighteenth Amendment. . . .

Women citizens see no possibility of clean politics until the outlaw liquor traffic is really outlawed in every State. The situation in New York, Chicago and Philadelphia is typical of our great city governments. The feminine housecleaning instinct is rapidly taking possession. It will inevitably reach politics.

Women are not only for the Eighteenth Amendment, they are as strongly in favor of real enforcement. A man left alone with a lively family of children for a week is ready to repeal the Ten Commandments and to swear that woman's place is in the home. Who enforces the law in the family? Men are not better disciplinarians in government.

The present situation would be ludicrous if the results were not so tragic. It is evident that in Washington and vast States there has been no real intention to enforce law when it interferes with politics, patronage and pleasant friendships. Men whose honor was outraged by oil and election frauds still break their solemn oath of office in the Capitol, we are told, and other men make no protest. Patronage accounts for slipping outstanding Wets into enforcement departments, the appointment of doubtful Judges and Prohibition officials, the situation regarding sacramental wine in New York and the open defiance of certain clubs and resorts. It is not a failure of the Eighteenth Amendment, but largely a failure of honor in men sworn to support and defend that Amendment. This is a shocking example for youth, and a constant encouragement of lawlessness.

Perhaps no law ever met such propaganda and opposition because no law was ever more needed. When the personal liberty of father meant the personal slavery of mother and the children two great amendments came—the Eighteenth and Nineteenth, Emancipation Acts. They will stand together. The rights of women are as definitely linked with the Eighteenth as with the Nineteenth Amendment. Democratic and Republican women in great numbers are absolutely agreed on this issue, and their principle will prevail over party in the coming election.

The methods of those opposed are the familiar old saloon methods— enormous propaganda through Wet city press to control election of candidates who will later do the bidding of the bosses. . . .

Women, half the electorate, have little place or power in the game of politics, but they have great influence for right issues. American men are fair, and knowing what good women want and why, they will see that their cause has fair representation. If only "Mother's Day" could be changed to Election Day and men would "say it with votes," instead of with flowers and orations, it would mean much to many mothers and homes.

Women are afraid of drunken drivers of automobiles, locomotives and ships. They will choose a sober captain for our Titanic Ship of State and they will help elect him, unless it be true that the decision will be made by one or two men. . . .

Women believe that our Government needs a moral revival based on the Ten Commandments or *Prohibitions*, leading up to the greatest Commandment, "Thou shalt love the Lord thy God with all thy heart and thy neighbor as thyself," with its social implications.

The "hypocrites" are those who pray, "Lead us not into temptation, but deliver us from evil," while they fight unfairly to keep temptation and evil legalized.

In this crusade women will vote as they pray. They are singing, too, a new song, not the old wail, "Father, dear father, come home with me now," but a marching song, "Mother, dear mother, come down to the polls." Men do not yet understand this type of woman, a very old type. Men pride themselves on standing for party. Women will stand for the cause. The twentieth century Barbara Frietchie is another Southern woman, dauntless Mrs. Clem Shaver, wife of the National Democratic Committee Chairman, who in her Mayflower address "took up the flag the men hauled down" at the Jackson Dinner in January. Again in an address before the Woman's National Law Enforcement Convention in the Senate Chamber of the Capitol in Columbus, Ohio, she represented both Republican and Democratic women, and we believe the majority of good men, declaring: "Candidates for office in the coming election must take a decided stand on the liquor question. Those who hedge or stand with the

Wet side will have to fight the combined forces of the Dry women's organizations. They will not tolerate a Wet ticket in 1928."

Against this declaration we read in our morning paper of great accessions to the Society Opposed to Prohibition, with its triumphant statement that these men control organizations possessing funds that total $40,000,000,000. Even that does not intimidate the women, who reply to this challenge: "Gentlemen, the Constitution is not for sale."

SUGGESTIONS FOR FURTHER READING

Norman H. Clark, *Deliver Us from Evil: An Interpretation of American Prohibition* (New York: W. W. Norton, 1976); Ross E. Paulson, *Women's Suffrage and Prohibition: A Comparative Study of Equality and Social Control* (Glenview, Ill.: Scott, Foresman, 1973), especially ch. 8, "Social Control, Equality, and Social Cohesion"; Joseph R. Gusfield, *Symbolic Crusade: Status Politics and the American Temperance Movement* (Urbana, Ill.: University of Illinois Press, 1963).

XI

❧

THE QUALITY OF AMERICAN CULTURE COMPARED TO OTHER CULTURES: TWO VIEWS

During the 1920s and 1930s, in particular, an intense discussion took place concerning the nature and quality of national culture in the United States. Although no clear resolution of this fascinating conflict occurred, several aspects and outcomes seem clear. One aspect involved the impulse to judge American culture by European norms or standards of achievement. (In this chapter, the reader will notice that H. L. Mencken and Booth Tarkington disagree in many ways but share a decided hostility to English culture.) Another outcome is that most men and women who wrote about such matters were far more chauvinistic about the United States by 1938 than they had been following World War I. In that respect, an important change of mood had occurred, and it is reflected in these two pieces written in 1922 and 1929, respectively.

Henry L. Mencken (1880–1956) was a Baltimore-based journalist, who also served as coeditor of the Smart Set *magazine (1914–23) and the* American Mercury *(1924–33). His savagely critical and iconoclastic style helped to set a distinctive tone for American discourse in the 1920s, especially in college communities, and for more than a decade he reigned as the best-known and most outrageous cultural critic in the United States. His anti-Semitism and his use of words like "Japs" were commonplace at the time and elicited little protest. His pro-German sentiments and his steady shift toward conservatism made him much less influential as a pundit during the 1930s and 1940s.*

Booth Tarkington (1869–1946) achieved wide popularity with novels set largely in the Middle West. The Gentleman from Indiana *(1899), for example, concerned the crusade by a country editor against political corruption, a popular theme during the Progressive era.* The Magnificent Ambersons *(1918) narrated three generations of a leading Indiana family and its decline.* Alice Adams *(1921) described an ordinary girl whose illusions are destroyed when a love affair with a man above her social level is ended when he meets her mediocre family. Both* The Magnificent Ambersons *and* Alice Adams *won a Pulitzer Prize. Tarkington*

177

also wrote numerous books for and about adolescent boys, such as **Penrod** *and its sequels (1914–29), and popular essays on aspects of American culture, like the one that follows. His commitment to his native land was much more positive than Mencken's.*

On Being an American

H. L. MENCKEN

. . . The United States is essentially a commonwealth of third-rate men—that distinction is easy here because the general level of culture, of information, of taste and judgment, or ordinary competence is so low. No sane man, employing an American plumber to repair a leaky drain, would expect him to do it at the first trial, and in precisely the same way no sane man, observing an American Secretary of State in negotiation with Englishmen and Japs, would expect him to come off better than second best. Third-rate men, of course, exist in all countries, but it is only here that they are in full control of the state, and with it of all the national standards. The land was peopled, not by the hardy adventurers of legend, but simply by incompetents who could not get on at home, and the lavishness of nature that they found here, the vast ease with which they could get livings, confirmed and augmented their native incompetence. . . . The immigrants who have come in since those early days have been, if anything, of even lower grade than their forerunners. The old notion that the United States is peopled by the offspring of brave, idealistic and liberty-loving minorities, who revolted against injustice, bigotry and medievalism at home—this notion is fast succumbing to the alarmed study that has been given of late to the immigration of recent years. The truth is that the majority of non-Anglo-Saxon immigrants since the Revolution, like the majority of Anglo-Saxon immigrants before the Revolution, have been, not the superior men of their native lands, but the botched and unfit: Irishmen starving to death in Ireland, Germans unable to weather the *Sturm und Drang* of the post-Napoleonic reorganization, Italians weed-grown on exhausted soil, Scandinavians run to all bone and no brain, Jews too incompetent to swindle even the barbarous peasants of Russia, Poland and Rumania. Here and there among the immigrants, of course, there may be a bravo, or even a superman—e.g., the ancestors of Volstead, Ponzi, Jack Dempsey, Schwab, Daugherty, Debs, Pershing—but the average newcomer is, and always has been simply a poor fish.

Nor is there much soundness in the common assumption, so beloved of professional idealists and wind-machines, that the people of America constitute "the youngest of the great peoples." The phrase turns up endlessly; the average newspaper editorial writer would be hamstrung if the

H. L. Mencken, "On Being an American," in *Prejudices: Third Series* (New York: Alfred A. Knopf, 1922), pp. 22–32. Reprinted by permission of the Enoch Pratt Free Library in accordance with the terms of the will of H. L. Mencken. Copyright © 1922 by Alfred A. Knopf, Inc. Copyright renewed 1949 by H. L. Mencken.

post office suddenly interdicted it, as it interdicted "the right to rebel" during the war. What gives it a certain specious plausibility is the fact that the American Republic, compared to a few other existing governments, is relatively young. But the American Republic is not necessarily identical with the American people; they might overturn it tomorrow and set up a monarchy, and still remain the same people. The truth is that, as a distinct nation, they go back fully three hundred years, and that even their government is older than that of most other nations, e.g., France, Italy, Germany, Russia. Moreover, it is absurd to say that there is anything properly describable as youthfulness in the American outlook. It is not that of young men, but that of old men. All the characteristics of senescence are in it: a great distrust of ideas, an habitual timorousness, a harsh fidelity to a few fixed beliefs, a touch of mysticism. The average American is a prude and a Methodist under his skin, and the fact is never more evident than when he is trying to disprove it. His vices are not those of a healthy boy, but those of an ancient paralytic escaped from the *Greisenheim*. If you would penetrate to the causes thereof, simply go down to Ellis Island and look at the next shipload of immigrants. You will not find the spring of youth in their step; you will find the shuffling of exhausted men. From such exhausted men the American stock has sprung. It was easier for them to survive here than it was where they came from, but that ease, though it made them feel stronger, did not actually strengthen them. It left them what they were when they came: weary peasants, eager only for the comfortable security of a pig in a sty. Out of that eagerness has issued many of the noblest manifestations of American *Kultur:* the national hatred of war, the pervasive suspicion of the aims and intents of all other nations, the short way with heretics and disturbers of the peace, the unshakable belief in devils, the implacable hostility to every novel idea and point of view.

All these ways of thinking are the marks of the peasant—more, of the peasant long ground into the mud of his wallow, and determined at last to stay there—the peasant who has definitely renounced any lewd desire he may have ever had to gape at the stars. The habits of mind of this dull, sempiternal *fellah*—the oldest man in Christendom—are, with a few modifications, the habits of mind of the American people. The peasant has a great practical cunning, but he is unable to see any further than the next farm. He likes money and knows how to amass property, but his cultural development is but little above that of the domestic animals. He is intensely and cocksurely moral, but his morality and his self-interest are crudely identical. He is emotional and easy to scare, but his imagination cannot grasp an abstraction. He is a violent nationalist and patriot, but he admires rogues in office and always beats the tax-collector if he can. He has immovable opinions about all the great affairs of state, but nine-tenths of them are sheer imbecilities. He is violently jealous of what he conceives to be his rights, but brutally disregardful of the other fellow's. He is religious, but his religion is wholly devoid of beauty and dignity. This man, whether city or country bred, is the normal Americano—the 100 per cent Methodist, Odd Fellow, Ku Kluxer, and Know-Nothing. He exists in all countries, but here alone he rules—here alone his anthropoid fears and rages are accepted gravely as logical ideas, and dissent from them is punished as a sort of public offense. Around every one of his principal delusions—of the sacredness of democracy, of the feasibility of sumptuary law, of the incurable sinfulness of all other peoples, of the menace of ideas, of the corruption lying in all the arts—there is thrown a barrier of taboos, and woe to the anarchist who seeks to break it down!

The multiplication of such taboos is obviously not characteristic of a culture that is moving from a lower plane to a higher—that is, of a culture still in the full glow of its youth. It is a sign, rather, of a culture that is slipping downhill—one that is reverting to the most primitive standards and ways of thought. . . .

The Fathers of the Republic, I am convinced, had a great deal more prevision than even their most romantic worshipers give them credit for. They not only sought to create a governmental machine that would be safe from attack without; they also sought to create one that would be safe from attack within. They invented very ingenious devices for holding the mob in check, for protecting the national polity against its transient and illogical rages, for securing the determination of all the larger matters of state to a concealed but none the less real aristocracy. Nothing could have been further from the intent of Washington, Hamilton and even Jefferson than that the official doctrines of the nation, in the year 1922, should be identical with the nonsense heard in the chautauqua, from the evangelical pulpit, and on the stump. But Jackson and his merry men broke through the barbed wires thus so carefully strung, and ever since 1825 *vox populi* has been the true voice of the nation. Today there is no longer any question of statesmanship, in any real sense, in our politics. The only way to success in American public life lies in flattering and kowtowing to the mob. A candidate for office, even the highest, must either adopt its current manias *en bloc*, or convince it hypocritically that he has done so, while cherishing reservations *in petto*. The result is that only two sorts of men stand any chance whatever of getting into actual control of affairs—first, glorified mob-men who genuinely believe what the mob believes, and secondly, shrewd fellows who are willing to make any sacrifice of conviction and self-respect in order to hold their jobs. . . .

As I have pointed out in a previous work, this dominance of mob ways of thinking, this pollution of the whole intellectual life of the country by the prejudices and emotions of the rabble, goes unchallenged because the old landed aristocracy of the colonial era has been engulfed and almost obliterated by the rise of the industrial system, and no new aristocracy has arisen to take its place, and discharge its highly necessary functions. An upper class, of course, exists, and of late it has tended to increase in power, but it is culturally almost indistinguishable from the mob: it lacks absolutely anything even remotely resembling an aristocratic point of view. One searches in vain for any sign of the true *Junker* spirit in the Vanderbilts, Astors, Morgans, Garys, and other such earls and dukes of the plutocracy; their culture, like their aspiration, remains that of the pawnshop. One searches in vain, too, for the aloof air of the don in the official *intelligentsia* of the American universities; they are timorous and orthodox, and constitute a reptile Congregatio de Propaganda Fide to match Bismarck's *Reptilienpresse.* Everywhere else on earth, despite the rise of democracy, an organized minority of aristocrats survives from a more spacious day, and if its personnel has degenerated and its legal powers have decayed it has at least maintained some vestige of its old independence of spirit, and jealously guarded its old right to be heard without risk of penalty. Even in England, where the peerage has been debauched to the level of a political baptismal fount for Jewish moneylenders and Wesleyan soap-boilers, there is sanctuary for the old order in the two ancient universities, and a lingering respect for it in the peasantry. But in the United States it was paralyzed by Jackson and got its death blow from Grant, and since then no successor to it has been evolved. Thus there is no organized force to oppose the irrational vagaries of the mob. The legislative and executive arms of the government yield to them without resistance; the judicial arm has begun to yield almost as supinely, particularly when they take the form of witch-hunts; outside the official circle there is no opposition that is even dependably articulate. . . .

I often wonder, indeed, if there would be any intellectual life at all in the United States if it were not for the steady importation in bulk of ideas from abroad, and particularly, in late years, from England. What would become of the average American scholar if he could not borrow wholesale from English scholars? How could an inquisitive youth get beneath the surface of our politics if it were not for such anatomists as Bryce? Who would show our statesmen the dotted lines for their signatures if there were no Balfours and Lloyd Georges? . . . On certain levels this naive subservience must needs irritate every self-respecting American, and even dismay him. When he recalls the amazing feats of the English war propagandists between 1914 and 1917—and their even more amazing confessions of method since—he is apt to ask himself quite gravely if he belongs to a free nation or to a crown colony. The thing was done openly, shamelessly, contemptuously, cynically, and yet it was a gigantic success. The office of the American Secretary of State, from the end of Bryan's grotesque incumbency to the end of the Wilson administration, was little more than an antechamber of the British Foreign Office. . . .

. . . The average American of the Anglo-Saxon majority, in truth, is simply a second-rate Englishman, and so it is no wonder that he is spontaneously servile, despite all his democratic denial of superiorities, to what he conceives to be first-rate Englishmen. He corresponds, roughly, to an English Nonconformist of the better-fed variety, and he shows all the familiar characters of the breed. He is truculent and cocksure, and yet he knows how to take off his hat when a bishop of the Establishment passes. He is hot against the dukes, and yet the notice of a concrete duke is a singing in his heart. It seems to me that this inferior Anglo-Saxon is losing his old dominance in the United States—that is, biologically. But he will keep his cultural primacy for a long, long while, in spite of the overwhelming inrush of men of other races, if only because those newcomers are even more clearly inferior than he is. . . .

When Continental ideas, whether in politics, in metaphysics or in the fine arts, penetrate to the United States they nearly always travel by way of England. Emerson did not read Goethe; he read Carlyle. The American people, from the end of 1914 to the end of 1918, did not read first-handed statements of the German case; they read English interpretations of those statements. In London is the clearing house and transformer station. There the latest notions from the mainland are sifted out, carefully diluted with English water, and put into neat packages for the Yankee trade. The English not only get a chance to ameliorate or embellish; they also determine very largely what ideas Americans are to hear of at all. Whatever fails to interest them, or is in any way obnoxious to them, is not likely to cross the ocean. . . .

This wholesale import and export business in Continental fancies is of no little benefit, of course, to the generality of Americans. If it did not exist they would probably never hear of many of the salient Continentals at all, for the obvious incompetence of most of the native and resident introducers of intellectual ambassadors makes them suspicious even of those who, like Boyd and Nathan, are thoroughly competent. To this day there is no American translation of the plays of Ibsen; we use the William Archer Scotch-English translations, most of them atrociously bad, but still better than nothing. So with the works of Nietzsche, Anatole France, Georg Brandes, Turgeniev, Dostoevsky, Tolstoi, and other moderns after their kind. I can think of but one important exception: the work of Gerhart Hauptmann, done into English by and under the supervision of Ludwig Lewisohn. But even here Lewisohn used a number of English translations of single plays: the English were still ahead of him, though they stopped half way. He is, in any case, a very extraordinary American, and the Department of Justice kept an eye on him during the war. The average American professor is far too dull a fellow to undertake so difficult an enterprise. Even when he sports a German Ph.D. one usually finds on examination that all he knows about modern German literature is that a *Mass* of Hofbräu in Munich used to cost 27 *Pfennig* downstairs and 32 *Pfennig* upstairs. The German universities were formerly very tolerant of foreigners. Many an American, in preparation for professing at Harvard, spent a couple of years roaming from one to the other of them without picking up enough German to read the *Berliner Tageblatt*. Such frauds swarm in all our lesser universities, and many of them, during the war, became eminent authorities upon the crimes of Nietzsche and the errors of Treitschke. . . .

America and Culture

BOOTH TARKINGTON

It is a general habit of mind for people to think they see what they have expected to see and what they have been trained to see and what it is the fashion to see. There is an old story about someone's asking Columbus if he'd ever seen any mermaids, and he said yes, but they weren't nearly so good-looking as they were cracked up to be; he was honest; he believed what he said, but what he'd seen and thought were mermaids were seals.

A great many people believe that the Wild West still exists, that Chinamen are reliable in business, that Japanese are unreliable, that Frenchmen are excitable, that Englishmen are phlegmatic, that Italians are passionate, that Germans are stolid, that negroes are lazy and that Irishmen love a fight. Many of us Americans believe, more or less, that such things are true; though of course true with modifications and exceptions; we should not be surprised, therefore, if certain traditional characterizations of ourselves persist upon foreign soil, as they undoubtedly do. To the Frenchman, the Briton, for decades, appeared to be epitomized as John Bull in loud tweeds and a monocle, bellowing "Ros' bif! Goddam!" and, to both Briton and Frenchman, the caricature of Uncle Sam, lank and nasal, drawling "Wal, I swan!" seemed not too exaggerated to be representative of something actual.

Pleasant traditions are difficult to establish and unpleasant ones are more difficult to destroy. . . .

The European and British tradition that America is the land of the Almighty Dollar, and of no culture, still prevails abroad, not only among the unlearned and untraveled but also among the sophisticated; undoubtedly it will prevail for a long time to come. It is a tradition that was established almost a century ago; Charles Dickens and Mrs. Trollope did much to build its foundation, and many successive waves of our newly rich, traveling abroad conspicuously, have helped to give it substance. So have our expatriate apologists, as well as our expatriate detractors; and when we are tempted to defend ourselves we are at once in peril of adding

Booth Tarkington, "America and Culture," *The Saturday Evening Post*, 201 (March 2, 1929), pp. 25, 120. Copyright 1929, renewed © 1957. Reprinted by permission of Brandt & Brandt Literary Agents.

weight to the tradition that we are an uncultured race. "Bragging again!" the opposition may so easily retort, and laugh in our faces. If cleanliness is nearer to godliness than is culture, and we point to American plumbing and hygiene, the opposition may laugh again and remind us that the topic is not godliness but culture; when we bring forth statistics concerned with universities, with libraries, with publications, with galleries of works of art, with symphony orchestras, the opera and conservatories of music, with our new tremendous impetus in architecture, with scientific institutions, with learned societies, with honorary degrees, with medals and prizes, with popular education, with philanthropic bequests, with scholastic attainment and scientific research and invention, the opposition may continue to laugh, and might pertinently inquire if culture is a thing ever demonstrable by statistics.

On the other hand, we shan't get along very well if we assume the offensive ourselves and say to our detractors, "Where's your own culture? How are you going to prove it without statistics?" The reply of the Briton, the Frenchman, the German and the Italian would be one of imperturbable serenity: "Ours has never been questioned. If you seek to prove your own culture by questioning ours, you ruin your case, since the question itself is a perfect demonstration that you are an ignoramus." When a British painter asks us "Who looks at an American picture?" we convince him of nothing when we retort with the names of Whistler and Sargent; and in reply to the antique gibe of a British writer, "Who reads an American book?" we might find it best to say, "Should you have asked it? We read yours."

Two people who dispute the question, "Which of us is the more peaceful?" are not peaceful people; and I think it could be maintained that two people who would dispute the question, "Which of us is the more cultured?" would not be cultured people. If this is true, it might seem to follow that we needlessly disturb ourselves by being sensitive to the foreign view, sometimes expressed, that American culture is of an inferior quality, or indeed does not exist. The fact remains, however, that we still do exhibit some sensitiveness upon this point.

We know that our country is respected abroad, or feared perhaps, or in some quarters possibly envied and detested for its power and its riches; we have no sensitiveness here, and if a foreign critic called us weak or poor or commercially unprogressive we should suppose him a little mad and forget him. But when Mr. Norman Douglas informs us, even in the kindliest manner, that "progress is not civilization," we begin to be a little hurt with him and feel that he has not wholly understood us. Mr. Douglas is not condescending, because condescension is not a part of his individual nature; but when most of his British fellow countrymen, in friendly mood, speak of American civilization, there is that note, as of adult graciousness toward adolescent effort; and when amiable Continental Europeans speak upon that topic, the condescension is likely to be more marked, even when they defend us against the attacks of their compatriots. It is somewhat as if they said, "Oh, no, you must have patience; this good little fellow is doing his best to be cultured."

This foreign graciousness does not make us happy and allows us to feel that we have not been much more accurately observed by those who thus benignantly defend us than by our assailants. In fact, we seem to have reached the point at which we no longer care to be defended; we are not delighted to have it thought that we are consciously struggling to be cultured, and in the defense of us we detect something resembling that classical fragment of song perpetuated for us by the late Mr. Dan Daly: "Of course you can never be like us, but be as like us as you possibly can be!" We might, indeed, respond to our foreign defenders that we are not disposed to be like them; on the contrary, we are disposed to be like ourselves. The imitation of culture is not culture, and as a people we are not imitative. But we must be grateful for the good will that prompts defense of us, and also we should be tolerant of both defenders and assailants; especially because most of them have had little opportunity to know us well, and even when such opportunity exists, we are a people extremely difficult for a foreigner to know well. The size of us, alone, would make that sure, of course, and although there are other things more intricate that make it true, we need not here enumerate or discuss them. It is enough to take into account the fact that we are less simple and infinitely less of a pattern than foreigners suppose; and to aid our tolerance we should recall that critics and defenders are often betrayed into generalizations and conclusions by Americans who are not representative of America, but exceptions.

A great many of our fellow countrymen and countrywomen, finding congeniality and charm in a life abroad, enthusiastically become more Royalist than the king; and the foreigner in contact with them, perceiving them to be imitative of himself and engaged in the adulatory task of trying to absorb his own kind of culture, will easily believe that in them he sees the best of us doing the best that the best of us can do. Moreover, he will obviously receive from them not the most accurate account of the country from which they are emancipating themselves. Indeed, he will hear not only a great many things gratifying to his *amour propre* but a great deal of nonsense concerning American manners, customs and lack of culture. He finds the nonsense readily plausible, however; and few little social scenes are, for instance, pleasanter, to an observer possessed of some favor on the part of the Comic Muse, than that of an interview between a French gentleman and an American lady who is telling him that "no American knows how to enter a drawing-room." This particular art—or perhaps it should be spoken of as a ceremony—is probably the one most often denied by expatriate ladies to their compatriots who know no more cultured way of getting into any room than by walking into it.

But it is not only the expatriate who adds obliquity to the foreign scrutiny of us; the foreigner traveling in this country—perhaps intending the subsequent publication of a critique—is also likely to receive from various quarters an oversympathetic confirmation of the foreign view that we have much money and little culture. He may encounter sophisticates and their sharp contempt for the "one hundred per cent American," and since he himself is perhaps a one hundred per cent Frenchman or a one hundred per cent Italian—for nearly all Frenchmen and Italians are of that percentage—he will be extremely susceptible to the derogatory information offered him; also, if he meets the painfuller kind of one hundred per cent Americans, he will not be happily impressed—the proud boasts of alien nationals are seldom ingratiating—and he may be misled, too, by our habit of making fun of ourselves, a custom not usually intelligible to people of the Latin races and less constantly congenial to our British cousins than to ourselves.

For it is easy to be misled or to become confused upon so elusive a topic as culture. The word itself is subject to disputatious definitions; it is almost as difficult to define as "gentleman" or "art." It is one of those words for the meaning of which the dictionaries fail to represent a court of final appeal, because these authorities are reduced to definitions in terms likewise subject to argument and opinion. Thus, a dictionary may tell us that culture consists in part of "refinement of mind, morals, or taste; enlightenment"; and that cultured means "educated, refined"; whereupon we are at once on disputatious ground and must seek agreement upon the meanings of "refinement," "taste," "enlightenment" and "educated." And also, it seems possible that a cultured Arab may differ from a cultured Spanish cardinal upon the meaning of "morals." However, although there may always hang upon our use of the words some vagueness of outline, we may be clear, at least, that it means cultivation, and cultivation with results—that is to say, the ground cultivated is rich enough to respond with fruition, and the fruition reaches a rather definite degree of opulence. Practically speaking, a cultured person must have had intelligence to begin with, and his intelligence must have been cultivated until it has attained a fine kind of enlightenment—for we are forced back upon this term, itself so shadowy. . . .

. . . American culture must grow upon American soil; it has grown there, of course, and is not represented by an Anglicized American or by a Gallicized American. What might confuse the Briton seeking for evidences of culture in America may be a natural but localized conception of all culture as being of the British kind. . . .

Provincial or even national definitions of the nature of culture must ever prove fallible. There is perceptible in the writings of some scholarly English authors, not all of the distant past, a conviction that no one deserved to be called cultured who could not speak Latin or read Greek; but this excludes the cultured Chinese, no matter how profound their knowledge of their own classics, as of course it would exclude the more ancient Greeks themselves. That is to say, any definition of culture that demands a specialized knowledge or a specialized education proves itself absurd, for surely a salient component of any person's culture is his awareness of other kinds of culture than his own. Probably a voluminous history could be written of illusions concerning culture and what constitutes it; fashion is mistaken for it continually—even to speak in the fashion has often been mistaken for a sign of culture. There is undoubtedly a quality of voice recognizable as cultivated, or regulated with some regard to the auricular comfort of listeners and also with respect to the better traditions of pronunciation; but these traditions are many, and often they are disputable.

Pronunciation is comparable to costume in the fashions it has followed and follows; our ears are probably the most provincial of our organs in their love for native sounds and dislike of the alien. As a race, we have been accused abroad of being nasal, and it is true that some of our American climates have produced a great deal of catarrh, but that is a physical token and not a cultural one. The pronunciation of Matthew Arnold was at times almost unintelligible to his American audiences, and no doubt he found our Midland short *a* and burred *r* surprising and perhaps disagreeable to his ear; but even the type to which we sometimes rather loosely allude as the Oxford Don may not with safety to his own culture deny the culture of those whose quality of voice and method of pronunciation differ from his own; not the American would here die hardest, but the Scot.

A specialist, then, even in art or a branch of learning, is not necessarily cultured, but may be, in the realm of the mind, a provincial; and cosmopolitanism in point of view is a requisite of the kind of enlightenment that constitutes culture. A people progressive in their own civilization will seek to understand and appreciate the civilization of other peoples; they will pay the tribute of pilgrimage to the cultural altars of other peoples; nor would this mean that they have no cultural altars of their own. Even in the seventeenth century, cultured English gentlemen, like Evelyn, were not content to rest on the English cathedrals, but went to Rome. Such pilgrimages have been made by Americans in numbers so increasing from generation to generation that our patriots and railroads and hotel keepers have raised the cry, in which there seems to sound a note almost of desperation, "See America first"; and even they do not entreat us to see America only. Our enormously multitudinous pilgrimages do not prove that we are a cultured nation, for it is the mind that sees, and not the eye, and a cultured person may have traveled only mentally; nevertheless, the pilgrimages do suggest that we may to a degree possess the cosmopolitanism of point of view, and also the awareness of the culture of others, that are requisite components of culture.

If these components are requisites—as they seem to be—and if we possess them to the degree that we seem to possess them, it appears to follow that we need not feel injured by the criticisms of our culture, or the patronizing defenses of it, made by persons who thus reveal themselves to be lacking in those same requisites. When an Englishman is disappointed in us because he does not find among us an English kind of culture, the time has come for us to feel entertained, not indignant, as he would himself be entertained and not indignant if the positions were reversed. We need be sensitive on this point no longer, not even to the foreign traveler's time-worn discovery that we are in too great a hurry, too busy in the rush for the Almighty Dollar to have acquired culture. A rolling stone gathers no moss, but culture is not necessarily mossy; it can grow in a living and ever-quickened soil, and grow there in a bright and living profusion.

A living and growing culture, eager to discern and appreciate the kinds of culture other than its own, has the vigor and generosity that will save it from self-worship; for self-worship means stagnation. American culture is still moving, and more than ever appreciative of other culture; it has not crystallized into rigidity or turned back upon itself to become decadent. It lives and is safe even from its defenders.

SUGGESTIONS FOR FURTHER READING

Warren I. Susman, *Culture as History: The Transformation of American Society in the Twentieth Century* (New York: Pantheon, 1984), especially ch. 7, "Culture and Civilization: The Nineteen-Twenties"; Charles C. Alexander, *Here the Country Lies: Nationalism and the Arts in Twentieth-Century America* (Bloomington, Ind.: University of Indiana Press, 1980); Casey Nelson Blake, *Beloved Community: The Cultural Criticism of Randolph Bourne, Van Wyck Brooks, Waldo Frank, & Lewis Mumford* (Chapel Hill, N.C.: University of North Carolina Press, 1990).

XII

◦◦◦

INTERNATIONALISM VERSUS ISOLATIONISM: ENTERING WORLD WAR II

From the outbreak of war in Europe in 1939 until the Japanese bombed Pearl Harbor in December 1941, a great debate raged in the United States between isolationists and interventionists. One of the latter, publisher Henry R. Luce, believed that in 1940–41 Americans were already unacknowledged partisans on the Allied side but had neglected to fulfill their role as a world force. Although the twentieth century was the first in which the United States emerged as a dominant power, the country had failed to assess and implement its ultimate values for the rest of the world. Believing that isolationism was morally and practically bankrupt, Luce regarded himself as an internationalist rather than merely an interventionist. His views would have notable influence in the decades after 1945, the Cold War era.

Charles A. Lindbergh, Jr. (1902–74), a leading spokesman for the isolationists, pleaded for a policy of international disengagement, for a separate civilization whose destiny would be independent of Europe's. Lindbergh had become an international hero in 1927 when he flew The Spirit of St. Louis *alone from Long Island to Paris. Later that year he made the first nonstop flight from Washington, D.C., to Mexico City. In 1939 Lindbergh went on duty with the Army Air Corps as a colonel. After World War II began, he became active with the America First Committee and crisscrossed the country pleading against American intervention. Later, in 1941, Lindbergh resigned his Air Corps reserve commission. During the war, however, he served as a consultant with the United Aircraft and Ford Motor companies, and as a civilian technician attached to the Army Air Corps in the Pacific theater. Following the war, he served the Defense Department as an occasional adviser on aviation matters. He also contributed in significant ways to natural resource conservation.*

Henry R. Luce (1898–1967) entered journalism following his graduation from Yale. In 1923 he established a weekly newsmagazine, Time, *and in 1930 a successful business journal called* Fortune. *In 1936 he entered photojournalism with the creation of* Life, *and in 1954 he added* Sports Illustrated. *Luce also purchased radio and television stations, and produced movie, radio, and TV programs. The most successful of the programs was the "March of Time" newsreel series (1928–43).*

Ideologically, Luce was passionately committed to the free enterprise system, the Republican party, and anticommunism. He believed that the United States could serve as a model for all nations—indeed, he stated that perhaps it had been divinely ordained to do so—and that the "American way" should spread overseas. As an entrepreneur, patriot, and ideologue, Luce became one of the most influential figures in twentieth-century America.

The American Century

HENRY R. LUCE

We Americans are unhappy. We are not happy about America. We are not happy about ourselves in relation to America. We are nervous—or gloomy—or apathetic.

As we look out at the rest of the world we are confused; we don't know what to do. "Aid to Britain short of war" is typical of halfway hopes and halfway measures.

As we look toward the future—our own future and the future of other nations—we are filled with foreboding. The future doesn't seem to hold anything for us except conflict, disruption, war. . . .

In this whole matter of War and Peace especially, we have been at various times and in various ways false to ourselves, false to each other, false to the facts of history and false to the future.

In this self-deceit our political leaders of all shades of opinion are deeply implicated. Yet we cannot shove the blame off on them. If our leaders have deceived us it is mainly because we ourselves have insisted on being deceived. Their deceitfulness has resulted from our own moral and intellectual confusion. In this confusion, our educators and churchmen and scientists are deeply implicated.

Journalists, too, of course, are implicated. But if Americans are confused it is not for lack of accurate and pertinent information. The American people are by far the best informed people in the history of the world. . . .

AMERICA IS IN THE WAR . . . BUT ARE WE IN IT?

Where are we? We are *in* the war. All this talk about whether this or that might or might not get us into the war is wasted effort. We are, for a fact, *in* the war.

If there's one place we Americans did not want to be, it was *in* the war. We didn't want much to be in any kind of war but, if there was one kind of war we most of all didn't want to be in, it was a European war. Yet, we're in a war, as vicious and bad a war as ever struck this planet, and, along with being worldwide, a European war.

Of course, we are not technically at war, we are not painfully at war, and we may never have to experience the full hell that war can be. Nevertheless the simple statement stands: we are *in* the war. The irony is that Hitler knows it—and most Americans don't. It may or may not be an advantage to continue diplomatic relations with Germany. But the fact that

Henry R. Luce, *The American Century* (New York: Farrar & Rinehart, Inc., 1941), pp. 3, 6–10, 16–18, 22–27, 32–40. Reprinted by permission of *Life*, Time Warner, Inc.

a German embassy still flourishes in Washington beautifully illustrates the whole mass of deceits and self-deceits in which we have been living.

Perhaps the best way to show ourselves that we are in the war is to consider how we can get out of it. Practically, there's only one way to get out of it and that is by a German victory over England. If England should surrender soon, Germany and America would not start fighting the next day. So we would be out of the war. For a while. Except that Japan might then attack in the South Seas and the Philippines. We could abandon the Philippines, abandon Australia and New Zealand, withdraw to Hawaii. And wait. We would be out of the war.

We say we don't want to be in the war. We also say we want England to win. We want Hitler stopped—more than we want to stay out of the war. So, at the moment, we're in.

WHAT ARE WE FIGHTING FOR? . . . AND WHY WE NEED TO KNOW

Having now, with candor, examined our position, it is time to consider, to better purpose than would have been possible before, the larger issue which confronts us. Stated most simply, and in general terms, that issue is: What are we fighting for?

Each of us stands ready to give our life, our wealth, and all our hope of personal happiness, to make sure that America shall not lose any war she is engaged in. But we would like to know what war we are trying to win—and what we are supposed to win when we win it?

This questioning reflects our truest instincts as Americans. But more than that. Our urgent desire to give this war its proper name has a desperate practical importance. If we know what we are fighting for, then we can drive confidently toward a victorious conclusion and, what's more, have at least an even chance of establishing a workable Peace.

Furthermore—and this is an extraordinary and profoundly historical fact which deserves to be examined in detail—America and only America can effectively state the war aims of this war.

Almost every expert will agree that Britain cannot win complete victory—cannot even, in the common saying, "stop Hitler"—without American help. Therefore, even if Britain should from time to time announce war aims, the American people are continually in the position of effectively approving or not approving those aims. On the contrary, if America were to announce war aims, Great Britain would almost certainly accept them. And the entire world including Adolf Hitler would accept them as the gauge of this battle.

Americans have a feeling that in any collaboration with Great Britain we are somehow playing Britain's game and not our own. Whatever sense there may have been in this notion in the past, today it is an ignorant and foolish conception of the situation. In any sort of partnership with the

British Empire, Great Britain is perfectly willing that the United States of America should assume the role of senior partner. This has been true for a long time. Among serious Englishmen, the chief complaint against America (and incidentally their best alibi for themselves) has really amounted to this—that America has refused to rise to the opportunities of leadership in the world. . . .

Friends and allies of America? Who are they, and for what? This is for us to tell them.

DONG DANG OR DEMOCARY . . . BUT WHOSE DONG DANG, WHOSE DEMOCRACY?

But how can we tell them? And how can we tell ourselves for what purposes we seek allies and for what purposes we fight? Are we going to fight for dear old Danzig or dear old Dong Dang? Are we going to decide the boundaries of Uritania? Or, if we cannot state war aims in terms of vastly distant geography, shall we use some big words like Democracy and Freedom and Justice? Yes, we can use the big words. The President has already used them. And perhaps we had better get used to using them again. Maybe they do mean something—about the future as well as the past.

Some amongst us are likely to be dying for them—on the fields and in the skies of battle. Either that, or the words themselves and what they mean die with us—in our beds.

But is there nothing between the absurd sound of distant cities and the brassy trumpeting of majestic words? And if so, whose Dong Dang and whose Democracy? Is there not something a little more practically satisfying that we can get our teeth into? Is there no sort of understandable program? A program which would be clearly good for America, which would make sense for America—and which at the same time might have the blessing of the Goddess of Democracy and even help somehow to fix up this bothersome matter of Dong Dang?

Is there none such? There is. And so we now come squarely and closely face to face with the issue which Americans hate most to face. It is that old, old issue with those old, old battered labels—the issue of Isolationism versus Internationalism.

We detest both words. We spit them at each other with the fury of hissing geese. We duck and dodge them.

Let us face that issue squarely now. If we face it squarely now—and if in facing it we take full and fearless account of the realities of our age—then we shall open the way, not necessarily to peace in our daily lives but to peace in our hearts.

Life is made up of joy and sorrow, of satisfactions and difficulties. In this time of trouble, we speak of troubles. There are many troubles. There are troubles in the field of philosophy, in faith and morals. There are troubles of home and family, of personal life. All are interrelated but we speak here especially of the troubles of national policy.

In the field of national policy, the fundamental trouble with America has been, and is, that whereas their nation became in the 20th Century the most powerful and the most vital nation in the world, nevertheless Americans were unable to accommodate themselves spiritually and practically to that fact. Hence they have failed to play their part as a world power—a failure which has had disastrous consequences for themselves and for all mankind. And the cure is this: to accept wholeheartedly our duty and our opportunity as the most powerful and vital nation in the world and in consequence to exert upon the world the full impact of our influence, for such purposes as we see fit and by such means as we see fit.

"For such purposes as we see fit" leaves entirely open the question of what our purposes may be or how we may appropriately achieve them. Emphatically our only alternative to isolationism is not to undertake to police the whole world nor to impose democratic institutions on all mankind. . . .

America cannot be responsible for the good behavior of the entire world. But America is responsible, to herself as well as to history, for the world-environment in which she lives. Nothing can so vitally affect America's environment as America's own influence upon it, and therefore if America's environment is unfavorable to the growth of American life, then America has nobody to blame so deeply as she must blame herself.

In its failure to grasp this relationship between America and America's environment lies the moral and practical bankruptcy of any and all forms of isolationism. It is most unfortunate that this virus of isolationist sterility has so deeply infected an influential section of the Republican Party. For until the Republican Party can develop a vital philosophy and program for America's initiative and activity as a world power, it will continue to cut itself off from any useful participation in this hour of history. And its participation is deeply needed for the shaping of the future of America and of the world.

. . .[U]nder Franklin Roosevelt we ourselves have failed to make democracy work successfully. Our only chance now to make it work is in terms of a vital international economy and in terms of an international moral order.

. . . Our job is to help in every way we can, for our sakes and our children's sakes, to ensure that Franklin Roosevelt shall be justly hailed as America's greatest President.

Without our help he cannot be our greatest President. With our help he can and will be. Under him and with his leadership we can make isolationism as dead an issue as slavery, and we can make a truly *American* internationalism something as natural to us in our time as the airplane or the radio. . . .

THE 20TH CENTURY IS THE AMERICAN CENTURY . . . SOME FACTS ABOUT OUR TIME

Consider the 20th Century. It is ours not only in the sense that we happen to live in it but ours also because it is America's first century as a dominant power in the world. So far, this century of ours has been a profound and tragic disappointment. No other century has been so big with promise for human progress and happiness. And in no one century have so many men and women and children suffered such pain and anguish and bitter death.

AMERICA'S VISION OF OUR WORLD . . . HOW IT SHALL BE CREATED

What can we say and foresee about an American Century? It is meaningless merely to say that we reject isolationism and accept the logic of internationalism. What internationalism? Rome had a great internationalism. So had the Vatican and Genghis Khan and the Ottoman Turks and the Chinese Emperors and 19th Century England. After the first World War, Lenin had one in mind. Today Hitler seems to have one in mind—one which appeals strongly to some American isolationists whose opinion of Europe is so low that they would gladly hand it over to anyone who would guarantee to destroy it forever. But what internationalism have we Americans to offer?

Ours cannot come out of the vision of any one man. It must be the product of the imaginations of many men. It must be a sharing with all peoples of our Bill of Rights, our Declaration of Independence, our Constitution, our magnificent industrial products, our technical skills. It must be an internationalism of the people, by the people and for the people. . . .

Once we cease to distract ourselves with lifeless arguments about isolationism, we shall be amazed to discover that there is already an immense American internationalism. American jazz, Hollywood movies, American slang, American machines and patented products, are in fact the only things that every community in the world, from Zanzibar to Hamburg, recognizes in common. Blindly, unintentionally, accidentally and really in spite of ourselves, we are already a world power in all the trivial ways—in very human ways. But there is a great deal more than that. America is already the intellectual, scientific and artistic capital of the world. Americans—Midwestern Americans—are today the least provincial people in the world. They have traveled the most and they know more about the world than the people of any other country. America's worldwide experience in commerce is also far greater than most of us realize. . . .

No narrow definition can be given to the American internationalism of the 20th Century. It will take shape, as all civilizations take shape, by the living of it, by work and effort, by trial and error, by enterprise and adventure and experience.

And by imagination!

As America enters dynamically upon the world scene, we need most of all to seek and to bring forth a vision of America as a world power which is authentically American and which can inspire us to live and work and fight with vigor and enthusiasm. And as we come now to the great test, it may yet turn out that in all our trials and tribulations of spirit during the first part of this century we as a people have been painfully apprehending the meaning of our time and now in this moment of testing there may come clear at last the vision which will guide us to the authentic creation of the 20th Century—our Century.

Consider four areas of life and thought in which we may seek to realize such a vision:

First, the economic. It is for America and for America alone to determine whether a system of free economic enterprise—an economic order compatible with freedom and progress—shall or shall not prevail in this century. We know perfectly well that there is not the slightest chance of anything faintly resembling a free economic system prevailing in this country if it prevails nowhere else. What then does America have to decide? Some few decisions are quite simple. For example: we have to decide whether or not we shall have for ourselves and our friends freedom of the seas—the right to go with our ships and our ocean-going airplanes where we wish, when we wish and as we wish. The vision of America as the principal guarantor of the freedom of the seas, the vision of America as the dynamic leader of world trade, has within it the possibilities of such enormous human progress as to stagger the imagination. Let us not be staggered by it. Let us rise to its tremendous possibilities. Our thinking of world trade today is on ridiculously small terms. For example, we think of Asia as being worth only a few hundred millions a year to us. Actually, in the decades to come Asia will be worth to us exactly zero—or else it will be worth to us four, five, ten billions of dollars a year. And the latter are the terms we must think in, or else confess a pitiful impotence.

Closely akin to the purely economic area and yet quite different from it, there is the picture of an America which will send out through the world its technical and artistic skills. Engineers, scientists, doctors, movie men, makers of entertainment, developers of airlines, builders of roads, teachers, educators. Throughout the world, these skills, this training, this leadership is needed and will be eagerly welcomed, if only we have the imagination to see it and the sincerity and good will to create the world of the 20th Century.

But now there is a third thing which our vision must immediately be concerned with. We must undertake now to be the Good Samaritan of the entire world. It is the manifest duty of this country to undertake to feed all the people of the world who as a result of this worldwide collapse of civilization are hungry and destitute—all of them, that is, whom we can from time to time reach consistently with a very tough attitude toward all hostile governments. For every dollar we spend on armaments, we should spend at least a dime in a gigantic effort to feed the world—and all the world should know that we have dedicated ourselves to this task. Every farmer in America should be encouraged to produce all the crops he can, and all that we cannot eat—and perhaps some of us could eat less—should forthwith be dispatched to the four quarters of the globe as a free gift, administered by a humanitarian army of Americans, to every man, woman and child on this earth who is really hungry.

But all this is not enough. All this will fail and none of it will happen unless our vision of America as a world power includes a passionate devotion to great American ideals. We have some things in this country which are infinitely precious and especially American—a love of freedom, a feeling for the equality of opportunity, a tradition of self-reliance and independence and also of co-operation. In addition to ideals and notions which are especially American, we are the inheritors of all the great principles of Western civilization—above all Justice, the love of Truth, the ideal of Charity. The other day Herbert Hoover said that America was fast becoming the sanctuary of the ideals of civilization. For the moment it may be enough to be the sanctuary of these ideals. But not for long. It now becomes our time to be the powerhouse from which the ideals spread throughout the world and do their mysterious work of lifting the life of mankind from the level of the beasts to what the Psalmist called a little lower than the angels.

America as the dynamic center of ever-widening spheres of enterprise, America as the training center of the skillful servants of mankind, America as the Good Samaritan, really believing again that it is more blessed to give than to receive, and America as the powerhouse of the ideals of Freedom and Justice—out of these elements surely can be fashioned a vision of the 20th Century to which we can and will devote ourselves in joy and gladness and vigor and enthusiasm. . . .

Throughout the 17th Century and the 18th Century and the 19th Century, this continent teemed with manifold projects and magnificent purposes. Above them all and weaving them all together into the most exciting flag of all the world and of all history was the triumphal purpose of freedom.

It is in this spirit that all of us are called, each to his own measure of capacity, and each in the widest horizon of his vision, to create the first great American Century.

Lindbergh's Isolationist Speech

CHARLES A. LINDBERGH

There are many viewpoints from which the issues of this war can be argued. Some are primarily idealistic. Some are primarily practical. One should, I believe, strive for a balance of both. But, since the issues that can be covered in a single address are limited, tonight I shall discuss the war from a viewpoint which is primarily practical. It is not that I believe ideals are unimportant, even among the realities of war; but if a nation is to survive in a hostile world, its ideals must be backed by the hard logic of military practicability. If the outcome of war depended upon ideals alone, this would be a different world than it is today.

I know I will be severely criticized by the interventionists in America when I say we should not enter a war unless we have a reasonable chance of winning. That, they will claim, is far too materialistic a standpoint. They will advance again the same arguments that were used to persuade France to declare war against Germany in 1939. But I do not believe that our American ideals, and our way of life, will gain through an unsuccessful war. And I know that the United States is not prepared to wage war in Europe successfully at this time. We are no better prepared today than France was when the interventionists in Europe persuaded her to attack the Siegfried Line.

I have said before, and I will say again, that I believe it will be a tragedy to the entire world if the British Empire collapses. That is one of the main reasons why I opposed this war before it was declared, and why I have constantly advocated a negotiated peace. I did not feel that England and France had a reasonable chance of winning. France has now been defeated; and, despite the propaganda and confusion of recent months, it is now obvious that England is losing the war. I believe this is realized even by the British Government. But they have one last desperate plan remaining. They hope that they may be able to persuade us to send another American

---

Charles A. Lindbergh, speech at Madison Square Garden, April 23, 1941, *New York Times*, April 24, 1941, p. 12.

Expeditionary Force to Europe and to share with England militarily, as well as financially, the fiasco of this war.

I do not blame England for this hope, or for asking for our assistance. But we now know that she declared a war under circumstances which led to the defeat of every nation that sided with her from Poland to Greece. We know that in the desperation of war England promised to all these nations armed assistance that she could not send. We know that she misinformed them, as she has misinformed us, concerning her state of preparation, her military strength, and the progress of the war.

In time of war, truth is always replaced by propaganda. I do not believe we should be too quick to criticize the actions of a belligerent nation. There is always the question whether we, ourselves, would do better under similar circumstances. But we in this country have a right to think of the welfare of America first, just as the people in England thought first of their own country when they encouraged the smaller nations of Europe to fight against hopeless odds. When England asks us to enter this war, she is considering her own future, and that of her empire. In making our reply, I believe we should consider the future of the United States and that of the Western Hemisphere.

It is not only our right, but it is our obligation as American citizens to look at this war objectively and to weigh our chances for success if we should enter it. I have attempted to do this, especially from the standpoint of aviation; and I have been forced to the conclusion that we cannot win this war for England, regardless of how much assistance we send.

I ask you to look at the map of Europe today and see if you can suggest any way in which we could win this war if we entered it. Suppose we had a large army in America, trained and equipped. Where would we send it to fight? The campaigns of the war show only too clearly how difficult it is to force a landing, or to maintain an army, on a hostile coast.

Suppose we took our Navy from the Pacific, and used it to convoy British shipping. That would not win the war for England. It would, at best, permit her to exist under the constant bombing of the German Air fleet. Suppose we had an air force that we could send to Europe. Where could it operate? Some of our squadrons might be based in the British Isles; but it is physically impossible to base enough aircraft in the British Isles alone to equal in strength the aircaft that can be based on the Continent of Europe.

I have asked these questions on the supposition that we had in existence an Army and an air force large enough and well enough equipped to send to Europe; and that we would dare to remove our Navy from the Pacific. Even on this basis, I do not see how we could invade the Continent of Europe successfully as long as all of that Continent and most of Asia is under Axis domination. But the fact is that none of these suppositions are correct. We have only a one-ocean Navy. Our Army is still untrained and inadequately equipped for foreign war. Our air force is deplorably lacking in modern fighting planes because most of them have already been sent to Europe.

When these facts are cited, the interventionists shout that we are defeatists, that we are undermining the principles of democracy, and that we are giving comfort to Germany by talking about our military weakness. But everything I mention here has been published in our newspapers, and in the reports of congressional hearings in Washington. Our military position is well known to the governments of Europe and Asia. Why, then, should it not be brought to the attention of our own people?

I say it is the interventionist in America, as it was in England and in France, who gives comfort to the enemy. I say it is they who are undermining the principles of democracy when they demand that we take a course to which more than 80 per cent of our citizens are opposed. I charge them with being the real defeatists, for their policy has led to the defeat of every country that followed their advice since this war began. There is no better way to give comfort to an enemy than to divide the people of a nation over the issue of foreign war. There is no shorter road to defeat than by entering a war with inadequate preparation. Every nation that has adopted the interventionist policy of depending on some one else for its own defense has met with nothing but defeat and failure.

When history is written, the responsibility for the downfall of the democracies of Europe will rest squarely upon the shoulders of the interventionists who led their nations into war uninformed and unprepared. With their shouts of defeatism, and their disdain of reality, they have already sent countless thousands of young men to death in Europe. From the campaign of Poland to that of Greece, their prophesies have been false and their policies have failed. Yet these are the people who are calling us defeatists in America today. And they have led this country, too, to the verge of war.

There are many such interventionists in America, but there are more people among us of a different type. That is why you and I are assembled here tonight. There is a policy open to this nation that will lead to success— a policy that leaves us free to follow our own way of life, and to develop our own civilization. It is not a new and untried idea. It was advocated by Washington. It was incorporated in the Monroe Doctrine. Under its guidance, the United States has become the greatest nation in the world.

It is based upon the belief that the security of a nation lies in the strength and character of its own people. It recommends the maintenance of armed forces sufficient to defend this hemisphere from attack by any combination of foreign powers. It demands faith in an independent American destiny. This is the policy of the America First Committee today. It is a policy not of isolation, but of independence; not of defeat, but of courage. It is a policy that led this nation to success during the most trying years of our history, and it is a policy that will lead us to success again.

We have weakened ourselves for many months, and still worse, we have divided our own people by this dabbling in Europe's wars. While we should have been concentrating on American defense we have been forced to argue over foreign quarrels. We must turn our eyes and our faith back to our own country before it is too late. And when we do this, a different vista opens before us. Practically every difficulty we would face in invading Europe becomes an asset to us in defending America. Our enemy, and not we, would then have the problem of transporting millions of troops across the ocean and landing them on a hostile shore. They, and not we, would have to furnish the convoys to transport guns and trucks and munitions and fuel across three thousand miles of water. Our battleships and . . . submarines would then be fighting close to their home bases. We would then do the bombing from the air and the torpedoing at sea. And if any part of an enemy convoy should ever pass our navy and our air force, they would still be faced with the guns of our coast artillery and behind them the divisions of our Army.

The United States is better situated from a military standpoint than any other nation in the world. Even in our present condition of unpreparedness no foreign power is in a position to invade us today. If we concentrate on our own defenses and build the strength that this nation should maintain, no foreign army will ever attempt to land on American shores.

War is not inevitable for this country. Such a claim is defeatism in the true sense. No one can make us fight abroad unless we ourselves are willing to do so. No one will attempt to fight us here if we arm ourselves as a great nation should be armed. Over a hundred million people in this nation are opposed to entering the war. If the principles of democracy mean anything at all, that is reason enough for us to stay out. If we are forced into a war against the wishes of an overwhelming majority of our people, we will have proved democracy such a failure at home that there will be little use fighting for it abroad.

The time has come when those of us who believe in an independent American destiny must band together and organize for strength. We have been led toward war by a minority of our people. This minority has power. It has influence. It has a loud voice. But it does not represent the American people. During the last several years I have traveled over this country from one end to the other. I have talked to many hundreds of men and women, and I have letters from tens of thousands more, who feel the same way as you and I.

Most of these people have no influence or power. Most of them have no means of expressing their convictions, except by their vote which has always been against this war. They are the citizens who have had to work too hard at their daily jobs to organize political meetings. Hitherto, they have relied upon their vote to express their feelings; but now they find that it is hardly remembered except in the oratory of a political campaign. These people—the majority of hard-working American citizens, are with us. They are the true strength of our country. And they are beginning to realize, as you and I, that there are times when we must sacrifice our normal interests in life in order to insure the safety and the welfare of our nation.

Such a time has come. Such a crisis is here. That is why the America First Committee has been formed—to give voice to the people who have no newspaper, or newsreel, or radio station at their command to give voice to the people who must do the paying, and the fighting, and the dying if this country enters the war.

Whether or not we do enter the war rests upon the shoulders of you in this audience, upon us here on this platform, upon meetings of this kind that are being held by Americans in every section of the United States today. It depends upon the action we take, and the courage we show at this time. If you believe in an independent destiny for America, if you believe that this country should not enter the war in Europe, we ask you to join the America First Committee in its stand. We ask you to share our faith in the ability of this nation to defend itself, to develop its own civilization, and to contribute to the progress of mankind in a more constructive and intelligent way than has yet been found by the warring nations of Europe. We need your support, and we need it now. The time to act is here. I thank you.

SUGGESTIONS FOR FURTHER READING

Richard M. Ketchum, *The Borrowed Years, 1938–1941: America on the Way to War* (New York: Random House, 1989); James L. Baughman, *Henry R. Luce and the Rise of the American News Media* (Boston: Twayne, 1987); W. A. Swanberg, *Luce and His Empire* (New York: Scribner's, 1972).

XIII

ᑐᕵᑐ

THE EXPERIENCE OF JAZZ: PROVENANCE AND PERFORMANCE

Duke Ellington (1899–1974) and Louis Armstrong (1900–71) were both great musicians and popular entertainers. Late in their lives each one provided a revealing interview. Although they shared some attitudes—skepticism about music serving a political cause and about the overrated role of "improvisation" in jazz—their contrasting personal styles are even more interesting and revealing. Ellington's approach to music was much more cerebral; Armstrong's intuitive and impulsive. Ellington's music was cool; Armstrong's hot. Ellington denied any desire to please the masses; Armstrong believed in showmanship, and he put the audience first. Their differences of class and style are self-evident. What marks them especially, as men who came of age in the 1920s and 1930s, is a restraint in their perspective about the relationship between music and race. For Armstrong, if his fans felt the music was "Real Negroid. That's all right." In contrast, Ellington didn't believe in "categories" and insisted on seeing the African-American contributions in a broader cultural perspective. Nevertheless, he titled some of his best-known compositions "Mood Indigo" (1930), "Symphony in Black," a short film suite (1935), and "Black and Tan Fantasy" (1927).

Although these two remarkable performers surely must have respected one another, the profound contrast in their responses reminds us that "jazz," even black jazz, was not a singular phenomenon sustained by some consensus of musical and social values. Jazz has meant different things to different people.

Ralph Ellison, a distinguished novelist and essayist, observed in 1980 that jazz, "which is an amalgam of past musical styles, may be seen as a rejection of a music which expressed the values of a social elite, but let me say that although jazz musicians are practitioners of a vernacular style, they are also unreconstructed elitists when it comes to maintaining the highest standards of the music which expresses their sense of the American experience."[1]

---

[1]Ralph Ellison, *Going to the Territory* (New York: Random House, 1986), p. 140.

Interview with Louis Armstrong

RICHARD MERYMAN

. . . When I got to New York there in 1928, everybody was playing frantic, screaming and everything, so I get frantic right with them. Stay with the trend—get along with everybody. I was young—blowing, blowing, blowing—any chops left, blow some more. Four shows a day. And always that cat beating on the drum, saying one more chorus. How many trumpet players been put out of business by that "one more"?

Got a job playing at Connie's Inn—and the crazy things I did with that horn. Pretty soon I was playing at Connie's Hot Chocolate downtown at the Hudson Theater, then rushing up to Connie's Inn, 131st and 7th Ave., play the show there, and then go over to the Lafayette Theater right next door. Had to get my sleep coming through the park in the cab. It was 1929 and I was only 29 years old. Didn't exactly feel I had the world at my feet, but was very nice everybody was picking up on the things I was doing and all the band leaders wanted me. Pretty soon I had to get in front of my own band, nothing else I could do.

But I wasn't thinking about nothing in those days. Just idling away all day and blasting all night. Just trying to please the musicians. And they the ones with passes, ain't putting out nothing. Those cats would bring their sandwiches, sit there and catch four more shows a day. And I used to come off the stage—almost had to be carried to the dressing room from running up and down just blowing and blowing and blowing—and the first thing those cats ask, "Was you high? She was blowing man, was you high?" That's all the appreciation you get from a cat. You try to show your art-tis-try, and this son-of-a-bitch come up with a bust right off the reel and drag you.

And the audience, the ordinary public, thought I was a maniac or something, running amuck. I was only standing on my head, blowing my brains out, to please the musicians. I forgot about the audience—and it didn't do me no good.

See, I think when I commenced to put a little showmanship in with the music, people appreciated me better. Always used to play one number after another, one after another—what the hell, just another blasting band—and pretty soon you got everybody's backs. But in New York, I began having to get out there to the mike and tell the people what we're going to play and what's happening. And I got to be around great actors

Richard Meryman, "Interview with Louis Armstrong," *Time* (April 15, 1966), reprinted as *Louis Armstrong—A Self-Portrait* (New York: Eakins Press, 1971), pp. 41–44, 53–57. Copyright © 1966 Time Warner, Inc. Reprinted with permission.

like Bill Robinson. So I found out, the main thing is live for that audience, live for the public. If the people ain't sick of it, I ain't. It's a pleasure. The minute you sing, "He-l-lo, Dol-ly!" there always some cats out there saying, "Yeeeeaaaah!"

Like the old timer told me when I left New Orleans, "Stay before them people. Please the public." Well, I'm with *him.*

I guess I've done *Hello, Dolly!* about a million times. But if I do a program and don't put it in, right away everybody "You didn't do *Hello, Dolly!*" It's been years since I recorded that, and all over the world still get the same response—Budapest, Rumania, everywhere. Prague.

All over the world, in Europe, behind the Iron Curtain, the people like a little gesture to what you're doing—instead of just standing there like a stiff shirt. It's all show business. And I don't think I'd want to be one of them serious kind. Take *Black and Blue:* you know, *Why am I so black and blue?* It's a serious thing, and I used to sing it serious—like shame on you for this and that. But I don't want to do nothing that would ask people to look at the song and be depressed and thinking about marching and equal rights. We all have our moments for them problems, but—well, the song's a pretty thing. Way I sing it now with a little chuckle, get a *big* reaction.

In *Hello, Dolly!* the movements and the jive with the audience clapping—aw, it's all in the fun. The people expect all that from me—coming out all chesty, making faces. That's me and I don't want to be nobody else. They know I'm there in the cause of happiness. And I don't worry what anybody thinks. There's an old saying. "I'll be the horse's head—and you be yourself."

I do that song *Hello, Dolly!* the same way every night 'cause that's the way the people like it. And even back in the old days it was like that— when everybody was supposed to be improvising. Who knows who's improvising? All trumpet players can hear what you play and they can play the same notes. That's why it was so silly when Freddie Keppard in all his ego there in New Orleans used to keep a handkerchief over his valves so nobody could see what he was doing. And always, once you got a certain solo that fit in the tune, and that's it, you keep it. Only vary it two or three notes every time you play it—specially if the record was a hit. There's always different people there every night, and they just want to be entertained.

I guess it's possible there's people who wish I'd just play like the old days in Chicago—and there ain't come a time when I can't play anything I ever did. Still play a few of those fine old tunes—but mostly I don't never think about them any more. I say, people got all those records and let them play 'em. Haven't heard 'em by now, shame on them. So let the other fellow have some pleasure now. Those records aren't why I'm popular today. More people know me since *Hello, Dolly!* than *ever.* And all my biggest hits are things like *Mack the Knife* and *Blueberry Hill.*

But all songs display my life somewhat, and you got to be thinking and feeling about something as you watch them notes and phrase that music—got to see the life of the song. *Blueberry Hill,* that could be some chick I ain't seen for twenty years, which chick, who cares. . . .

Touring England I had an English boy look after my clothes and everything. After a show I'm resting there—and here comes this boy saying, "Mister Armstrong, Lord Dishrag is now approaching and. . . ." And I say, "Man, let the man in." And this cat come in, uniform and everything, stood up straight and salute, clicking his heels—so protocol-fied. And I say, "Stash it, Daddy." And he say, "Good!" And we stood up there all day long talking about jazz and all the cats he got records of.

And traveling to Africa, that trip was fantastic. They wait for you at the airport and do a dance for you—and I danced with them, blowing with their musicians. One afternoon I never saw so many Africans in my life—no place to sit down, all standing up. It was real nice 'cause my ancestors came from Africa. I felt at home there, man. But I never did make no notations about all of it. Just everyday life to me.

People like to think of me as a "good will ambassador" and that's very nice, but I never think too much about things like that. Just try to do my job, please the public. And Satchmo have nice crowds everywhere. Never worry about crowds.

To me wherever you go—even behind the Iron Curtain—it's just another city. All hotels are alike—bed, bureau, two pillows. Maybe after a show, you try to make one or two joints, have a ball, get stoned, and that's it for the night. That's my life.

It's a funny thing, but I never was too much carried away by anything in my whole career. I never read no writeups. Nobody. What they say about the old days is corny. They form their own opinions, they got so many words for things and make everything soooo big—and it turns out a—what you call it—a fictitious story.

And when these writers come up so great they know every goddam thing, telling you how you should blow your horn. That's when I want to shoot the son-of-a-bitch. Just because they went to Harvard or Yale, got to make the public realize how superior they are, so what they do to plain old jazz! Bring up terms, goddam, the people reading it got to have a dictionary.

I still don't know what bop is, and they don't either. What is bop? What is progressive? What is modern? There's a trumpet exercise book you practice to realize you are a good sight reader—called *Arban Method.* Those exercises aren't nothing but the rudiments of bop. Cats come out of school, they know it all by heart, so they play a tune, put all those notes in there and now that's a style.

When I was a kid in New Orleans, I used to do a whole lot of figurations. Man I was crazy on that. Joe Oliver tell me, play the lead, boy, play the lead so people can know what you're doing. These cats today couldn't play a straight lead to save their lives. Old Scott Joplin used to make up all them rags. When I was coming up all you had to do was play what you see on them cards and you was a hell of a musician; you were swinging. Nowadays cats try to make the music as hard as possible so you think they're really playing. They ain't.

How many musicians today could play a funeral march or a blues like they did when I was a kid? Had to be beautiful, 'cause they were thinking as they watch those notes and phrasing that music. Like when I play, maybe *Back o'Town Blues*, I'm thinking about one of the old, low-down moments—when maybe your woman didn't treat you right. That's a hell of a moment when a woman tell you, "I got another mule in my stall."

These cool cats that say my music's old fashioned. They say they *study* music. Funny they got to and I didn't have to go into no rudimentals. More power to them. If I'm out of style now, I was a flying cat when I was in—so to hell with it now. If a son-of-a-bitch came to the conclusion, "We don't ever want to see Louis Armstrong again"—Thank you! 'cause I can get in a corner, look at TV for days and take my shower, sleep, and let the maid come in, don't even look out the window for six months. I'll still be Satchmo. Ain't never going to move. That's the way I can enjoy life. I don't sigh for nothing. Sixty years is a long time and there ain't going to be no more cats in the game that long.

Jazz is all the same—isn't anything new. At one time they was calling it levee camp music, then in my day it was ragtime. When I got up North I commenced to hear about jazz, Chicago style, Dixieland, swing. All refinements of what we played in New Orleans. But every time they change the name, they got a bigger check. And all these different kinds of fantastic music you hear today—course it's all guitars now—used to hear that way back in the old sanctified churches where the sisters used to shout till their petticoats fell down. There ain't nothing new. Old soup used over.

And who'd have thought the same tempo, same music would be named go-go. That was the sign the policeman used in New Orleans for you to cross the street. He turn that sign—"Go go," "Stop stop."

So now a lot of stars picking up the old records, and phrasing from them, and making hits. Ain't a trumpet player alive that don't play a little something I used to play. Makes them feel like they're getting hot or something. Real Negroid. That's all right. Makes me feel good.

I don't think you should analyze music. . . .

Music Is My Mistress

DUKE ELLINGTON

Q. Do you consider yourself as a forerunner in the advanced musical trends derived from jazz?

A. There were many wonderful musicians who established themselves and the word "jazz" many years before my time. "Jazz" is only a word and really has no meaning. We stopped using it in 1943. To keep the whole thing clear, once and for all, I don't believe in categories of any kind.

Q. In the music you compose now, is there some survival of what was once characterized as "jungle style" in your performances?

A. We write from the same perspective as before. We write to fit the tonal personalities of the individual instrumentalists who have the responsibility of interpreting our works.

Q. How do you regard the phenomenon of the black race's contribution to U.S. and world culture?

A. Regarding the Negro influence on culture generally, I imagine other people too found it agreeable to their senses.

Q. Do you enjoy composing music, or do you prefer performing? And have you a magic formula for attracting audiences?

A. I like any and all of my associations with music—writing, playing, and listening. We write and play from our perspective, and the audience listens from its perspective. If and when we agree, I am lucky.

Q. Do you think your performances in the jazz field can be connected with those of other writers and artists in the U.S.?

A. I try not to conform to vogues.

Q. Do you think jazz is having a kind of revival now?

A. The word "jazz" is still being used with great success, but I don't know how such great extremes as now exist can be contained under the one heading.

Q. Why do so many people, above all abroad, consider jazz intellectual music?

A. We enjoy freedom of expression in presenting our music, and some people prefer to accept it in their own fashion.

Duke Ellington, *Music Is My Mistress* (New York: Doubleday, 1973), pp. 452–56, 464–66. Copyright © 1973 by Duke Ellington, Inc. Used by permission of Doubleday, a division of Bantam Doubleday Dell Publishing Group, Inc.

211

Q. When you work with symphony orchestras, what is the greatest hurdle in conducting their musicians and yours? Do the symphony men dig your way easily?

A. There is no hurdle at all in the case of our musicians. The music is mostly all in tempo and the responsibility for togetherness rests in the main with the symphony orchestra. It's more or less a matter of establishing an understandable beat, whether it's in two-four, four-four, or five-four. They can play anything they can see, and the conductor's responsibility is to *know* thoroughly the piece he is conducting. . . .

Q. Do you hear your music mentally first? Does it work out in a pattern from a beginning? And do you hear it in single notes, chords, phrases, or larger, whole parts?

A. Each and all the ways. Acceptance is unconditional.

Q. Do you think a composer will ever be able to figure out mathematically what he wants, feed it to a computer, and let *it* compose?

A. They had the player piano years ago. . . .

Q. What do you think of the new music?

A. I think that music is neither new or old.

Q. I mean the young people's music.

A. I don't think the age of the performer should be considered one way or the other. If it sounds good, it's good music, and if it doesn't, then it is the other kind. The question of new and old music, young and old musicians, always seems to be designed to defeat me. It is usually asked by someone who is not aware of what is going on today, who, I imagine, has in mind the kids in the Top 40 who get the most publicity, like the kids who are rebellious, smoke pot, or indulge themselves in various unlawful ways. The naughty kids, in other words, always get their picture on television, in newspapers and magazines. The constructive youngsters, who are doing something normal and behaving like clean, progressive individuals in preparation for responsible positions in the society of tomorrow—they are never mentioned.

Q. Does this apply to music?

A. Of course it does. There is a whole world of college and school bands where youngsters are very diligently preparing for careers in music, and a lot of extremely talented musicians are devoting themselves to their tuition. . . .

Q. Don't these people and the bands they put together get publicity?

A. Yes, some, but it is generally at a local level, or in specialist magazines like *Down Beat* and *Music Journal*. Charles Suber, the publisher of *Down Beat*, told me that they estimated there would be nearly sixty school jazz festivals in 1971, with an involvement of around 35,000 school musicians at all levels within 1,750 big bands and two hundred combos. They also estimated that the total for all school and college jazz ensembles in the country is approximately 16,500 big bands and 2,500 combos. Now that's incredible when you translate it into a total of musically educated youngsters, and you have to consider it not merely from the viewpoint of educated performers, but also from that of educated listeners and educated ears. If this process compounds itself, as it seems to be doing, we could end up with a remarkably literate nation, musically speaking. Meanwhile, how interested are the media in, say, a twenty-year-old girl who plays first trumpet in the Cincinnati Symphony Orchestra, or the 138 kids of all ages between eleven and eighteen who compose the California Youth Symphony in Palo Alto? Not very much. Not, that is, as compared with their interest in pot-smoking, abortion, and pollution.

Q. Yet the current trend in music is surely anything but conservative?

A. Conservative is a word and a category, and when a good musician compromises on his aim in music and descends to what the brainwashed masses expect, then he is not being honest with himself. An artist must be true to himself. If money is more important to him than his music, then he is indulging in prostitution. Now I don't say that everybody who listens to music, or uses it as an atmospheric background, really knows or cares about what is being played, but a real musician cannot be swayed from his natural groove by those who believe the listings of the Top Forty indicate what sounds good or best. In any case, if the listener is to make the decision, we are all in a pretty bad situation. With the exception of movie-scoring and theatre and television backgrounds, consonance is considered desirable as agreeable to the normal ear, but there are, of course, artists who resort to shock in desperation. There are those, too, who truly dig distortion of everything. A clinker in a symphony is no less bad than a clinker in jazz or rock, so once again—why the category?

Q. How do you rate composition, arrangement, and performance in importance?

A. All are interdependent on each other. Composition depends a great deal on the subsequent arrangement, but neither should burden the performers, for if the performance fails all is lost.

Q. Was there any special reason why you set out to develop a particularly strong left hand at the piano?

A. When I started out, the left hand was considered the first step toward acknowledgment.

Q. When you began composing as a very young man, did you draw from your environment, real experiences, or what you experienced through reading and listening? Where did the initial inspiration come from?

A. The driving power was a matter of wanting to be—and to be heard—on the same level as the best.

Q. Am I wrong in assuming your aural sense is more acute than your other senses? And how strong a part do the other senses play?

A. Composers try to parallel observations made through all the senses.

Q. How does a performer "tune in" to a particular audience, to its receptiveness, reaction, or mood? People in one section of the country may want to hear something completely different to those in another.

A. There is no geographical scale for appraising audiences. When the artist encounters a sensitive audience—jackpot! If he plays to the audience according to geography, nationality, race, or creed, he is condescending, and this is the world's worst social offense. . . .

Q. What does America mean to you?

A. It's where I was born. It's *home*. Its music world has been an extremely competitive scene, and that in itself incites drive. Without competition you wouldn't have it. Then I've been very lucky in America. I've been allowed to live well, and in many instances I've been spoiled. My friends and relatives live well, too. I've learned a lot there, where there are so many great musicians to learn from. Opportunity and luck are so important. You have to be in the right place at the right time. A gambler in a lucky streak can't get lucky unless he's shooting dice or doing what he does best.

Q. Don't you get tired of doing what you're doing year in and year out?

A. You're talking from the perspective either of someone who doesn't love music, or who doesn't do what he enjoys most for a living. To be frank, that question annoys me very much, and not merely because it recurs so often. Millions and millions of dollars are spent building big vacation places for people to escape to from their daily chores, but they are the people who don't enjoy what they are doing for a living. Nobody else does what we do for fifty-two weeks of the year, every day of the week. It's our unique thing. Nobody does anything every day like we do, and nobody does it in so many places as we do. Doctors, surgeons, football players, bankers—you name it—they all take vacations. We go to many countries and we fly more than pilots do! We live in an entirely different climate. Three days ago we crossed the equator. Yesterday we went through a blizzard. Everybody else takes a day off, but not us. We're not captive, but we're built in. . . .

Q. What is music to you?

A. My mistress. I live with music.

Q. What is the audience?

A. The audience is the other side of the realm that serves the same muse I do.

Q. While performing, what do you insist on from the audience?

A. I don't insist on anything. I play for the audience, and if I'm lucky they have the same taste I have. It's rather like that word "swing": when two people are together, and my pulse and your pulse are together, then we're swinging.

Q. What do you think of the narcotics problem?

A. Why ask me? You are not a doctor, a detective, or a junkie, are you?

Q. How important is improvisation in jazz?

A. The word "improvisation" has great limitations, because when musicians are given solo responsibility they already have a suggestion of a melody written for them, and so before they begin they already know more or less what they are going to play. Anyone who plays anything worth hearing knows what he's going to play, no matter whether he prepares a day ahead or a beat ahead. It has to be with intent.

Q. How is it that you have not flirted with commercial music?

A. This is where the categorization of jazz gets washed away. We may play something of our own creation like *The Latin-American Suite* or *The New Orleans Suite*, but a great artist like Sidney Bechet will play "Love for Sale," or Coleman Hawkins will play "Body and Soul," so where does it end? We've all worked and fought under the banner of jazz for many years, but the word really has no meaning. What is the relationship between Guy Lombardo, Stan Kenton, Count Basie, and Louis Armstrong—all of whom people regard as playing jazz? Music is limitless. . . .

Q. What about the future of jazz?

A. You've got to call it music whether you want to or not. A class graduates from a conservatory—say Juilliard, Eastman, or Berklee—and they've been through the whole history, every great composer, and every great orchestrator. They've mastered all the techniques, and they can't be put into a little category called jazz. Out of such a class, a fourth may go into movies, a fourth into radio and television, a fourth to teach music or lead a church choir, and the other fourth to play what some people want to call jazz.

Q. You don't see a need for divisions of taste, but only of necessity?

A. Billy Strayhorn and I did the arrangements on the *Peer Gynt Suite*. We liked what we did, and we had fun doing it, but we did not try to do better than the symphony people. There was a certain amount of humor in it, and unfortunately the Grieg Society in Norway barred it. I don't think Grieg would have barred it.

Q. Once born, do you leave a number alone?

A. The original framework remains the same. Sometimes people come in the band who see it from a different perspective, and they do something that is a little zesty in accordance with their own personality. You're never satisfied, of course. You say to yourself, "I should have done this here, and that there." You know greater development is possible, but then we went through the conditioning of a period when we were limited to three minutes.

Q. When jam sessions could not be recorded?

A. No. A jam session is like a polite encounter, or an exchange of compliments, but in the old days they had cutting contests where you defended your honor with your instrument. I remember a great night at the Comedy Club. We arrived late one Sunday morning, but Sidney Bechet and Coleman Hawkins had hooked up, and they went at it all night long. They just happened to have their horns with them! Without them, they would have been like knights walking around without swords or armor. . . .

Q. Is there such a thing as Black Culture in American music?

A. There was when I was a child in school. I agree, incidentally, with something that William Grant Still said in a letter to *Music Journal* in February 1971. I quote:
     "In actual fact, American Negro music (which is indeed a fusion of African and various European elements) encompasses a great deal more than jazz, and any teacher who claims to teach the subject should be aware of all its forms, from the Negro folk product to the advances now being made in serious music.
     "The only reason there has been such great emphasis on jazz is that it has been pushed by commercial interests, and this doesn't mean that it is the *only*—or even the most important—form in existence."

Q. It has been said that you and your orchestra have been chosen as one of five cultural attractions to represent this country in the U.S.S.R. in 1971. How do you feel about a tour there?

A. The vibrations were very good when we were in Czechoslovakia.

Russia is the same place from which the Fabulous Five came: Tchaikovsky, Rimsky-Korsakov, Borodin, Prokofiev, and Shostakovich. So you know I want to breathe some of that air!

Q. Who are your favorite singers?

A. It is always a matter of the one I am enjoying at the moment.

Q. Do you think jazz should be subsidized?

A. I don't think so. The minute you start subsidizing it, you are going to get yourself a bastard product. It started as a competitive thing, and if you take away the competition, where a guy must fight to eat, it's going to become something else. Of course, if people *want* to take care of people—crazy! . . .

SUGGESTIONS FOR FURTHER READING

Gary Giddins, *Satchmo* (New York: Doubleday, 1988); Gunther Schuller, *Early Jazz: Its Roots and Musical Development* (New York: Oxford University Press, 1968), especially ch. 7, "The Ellington Style"; Leonard Feather, *From Satchmo to Miles* (New York: Da Capo, 1972).

XIV

⚘

AMERICA ON FILM: DISTORTED IMAGES AND DISMAL PROSPECTS?

Each of the next three selections examines the uses of myth by Hollywood's film industry. Each one acknowledges that Hollywood creates illusions, including illusions about itself. The second and third selections engage in a direct debate about the future of the film industry and the role of film in American culture. Novelist and critic Ralph Ellison (1914–94) also reveals his concerns on that subject.

Ellison observes that while Hollywood did not create a malevolent stereotype of African Americans, it manipulated such stereotypes in ways that seemed to be socially acceptable to whites and commercially viable. He does acknowledge some overall improvement in the depiction of blacks in Hollywood films by midcentury. Ultimately, however, films that appeared to be about Negroes were actually about white perceptions of them and failed to depict the Negro's humanity in a three-dimensional way.

Gilbert Seldes (1893–1970) was a prominent critic of the popular arts who wrote extensively about movies and the film industry from the 1920s to the 1950s. He had been a great fan of silent film during the 1920s, lavishing praise on such performers as Charlie Chaplin and the Keystone Kops. A generation later, however, Seldes became increasingly critical of Hollywood for depending so heavily on a small cluster of mythic subjects, and he warned repeatedly that Hollywood's audience was diminishing because of the film studios' shortsightedness.

Arthur L. Mayer (1886–1979) was executive vice president of the Council of Motion Picture Organizations, 1950–52, and president of the Independent Motion Pictures Distributors Association, 1951–57. For fifteen years he operated the prestigious Rialto Theater in New York City (1933–48), and he became a major importer of foreign films to the United States. Although he agreed with Seldes that Americans did not go to the movies as much as they once had, he did not share Seldes's pessimism about the future of the film industry or the commercial prospects for movie theaters. If only the public would support good films, Mayer insisted, "we can make our motion pictures a symbol and token of all striving humanity."

In the years 1949 to 1951, when these three essays appeared, the film industry faced an uncertain future because commercial television was just beginning to emerge as a successful form of stay-at-home entertainment. Those with a stake in Hollywood simply could not agree on how serious a threat television presented or what to do about it.

The Shadow and the Act

RALPH ELLISON

Faulkner has given us a metaphor. When, in the film *Intruder in the Dust*, the young Mississippian Chick Mallison falls into an ice-coated creek on a Negro's farm, he finds that he has plunged into the depth of a reality which constantly reveals itself as the reverse of what it had appeared before his plunge. Here the ice—white, brittle and eggshell-thin—symbolizes Chick's inherited views of the world, especially his Southern conception of Negroes. Emerging more shocked by the air than by the water, he finds himself locked in a moral struggle with the owner of the land, Lucas Beauchamp, the son of a slave, who, while aiding the boy, angers him by refusing to act toward him as Southern Negroes are expected to act.

To Lucas, Chick is not only a child but his guest. Thus he not only dries the boy's clothes, he insists that he eat the only food in the house, Lucas's own dinner. When Chick (whose white standards won't allow him to accept the hospitality of a Negro) attempts to pay him, Lucas refuses to accept the money. What follows is one of the most sharply amusing studies of Southern racial ethics to be seen anywhere. Asserting his whiteness, Chick throws the money on the floor, ordering Lucas to pick it up; Lucas, disdaining to quarrel with a child, has Chick's young Negro companion, Aleck Sander, return the coins.

Defeated but still determined, Chick later seeks to discharge his debt by sending Lucas and his wife a gift. Lucas replies by sending Chick a gallon of molasses by—outrage of all Southern Negro outrages!—a white boy on a mule. He is too much, and from that moment it becomes Chick's passion to repay his debt and to see Lucas for once "act like a nigger." The opportunity has come, he thinks, when Lucas is charged with shooting a white man in the back. But instead of humbling himself, Lucas (from his cell) tells, almost orders, Chick to prove him innocent by violating the white man's grave.

In the end we see Chick recognizing Lucas as the representative of those virtues of courage, pride, independence and patience that are usually attributed only to white men—and, in his uncle's words, accepting the Negro as "the keeper of our [the whites'] consciences." This bit of dialogue, coming after the real murderer is revealed as the slain man's own

Ralph Ellison, "The Shadow and the Act," in *Shadow and Act* (New York: Random House, 1964), pp. 273–81. Copyright © 1953, 1964 by Ralph Ellison. Reprinted by permission of Random House, Inc.

brother, is, when viewed historically, about the most remarkable concerning a Negro ever to come out of Hollywood.

With this conversation, the falling into creeks, the digging up of corpses and the confronting of lynch mobs that mark the plot, all take on a new significance: Not only have we been watching the consciousness of a young Southerner grow through the stages of a superb mystery drama, we have participated in a process by which the role of Negroes in American life has been given what, for the movies, is a startling new definition.

To appreciate fully the significance of *Intruder in the Dust* in the history of Hollywood we must go back to the film that is regarded as the archetype of the modern American motion picture, *The Birth of a Nation*.

Originally entitled *The Clansman*, the film was inspired by another Southern novel, the Reverend Thomas Dixon's work of that title, which also inspired Joseph Simmons to found the Knights of the Ku Klux Klan. (What a role these malignant clergymen have played in our lives!) Re-entitled *The Birth of a Nation* as an afterthought, it was this film that forged the twin screen image of the Negro as bestial rapist and grinning, eye-rolling clown—stereotypes that are still with us today. Released during 1915, it resulted in controversy, riots, heavy profits and the growth of the Klan. Of it Terry Ramsaye, a historian of the American motion-picture industry writes: "The picture . . . and the K.K.K. secret society, which was the afterbirth of a nation, were sprouted from the same root. In subsequent years they reacted upon each other to the large profit of both. The film presented predigested dramatic experience and thrills. The society made the customers all actors in costume."

Usually *The Birth of a Nation* is discussed in terms of its contributions to cinema technique, but, as with every other technical advance since the oceanic sailing ship, it became a further instrument in the dehumanization of the Negro. And while few films have gone so far in projecting Negroes in a malignant light, few before the 1940s showed any concern with depicting their humanity. Just the opposite. In the struggle against Negro freedom, motion pictures have been one of the strongest instruments for justifying some white Americans' anti-Negro attitudes and practices. Thus the South, through D. W. Griffith's genius, captured the enormous myth-making potential of the film form almost from the beginning. While the Negro stereotypes by no means made all white men Klansmen the cinema did to the extent that audiences accepted its image of Negroes, make them participants in the South's racial ritual of keeping the Negro "in his place."

After Reconstruction the political question of what was to be done with Negroes, "solved" by the Hayes-Tilden deal of 1876, came down to the psychological question: "How can the Negro's humanity be evaded?" The problem, arising in a democracy that holds all men as created equal, was a highly moral one: democratic ideals had to be squared with anti-Negro practices. One answer was to *deny* the Negro's humanity—a pattern set long before 1915. But with the release of *The Birth of a Nation* the propagation of subhuman images of Negroes became financially and dramatically profitable. The Negro as scapegoat could be sold as entertainment, could even be exported. If the film became the main manipulator of the American dream, for Negroes that dream contained a strong dose of such stuff as nightmares are made of.

We are recalling all this not so much as a means of indicting Hollywood as by way of placing *Intruder in the Dust,* and such recent films as *Home of the Brave, Lost Boundaries* and *Pinky,* in perspective. To direct an attack upon Hollywood would indeed be to confuse portrayal with action, image with reality. In the beginning was not the shadow, but the act, and the province of Hollywood is not action, but illusion. Actually, the anti-Negro images of the films were (and are) acceptable because of the existence throughout the United States of an audience obsessed with an inner psychological need to view Negroes as less than men. Thus, psychologically and ethically, these negative images constitute justifications for all those acts, legal, emotional, economic and political, which we label Jim Crow. The anti-Negro image is thus a ritual object of which Hollywood is not the creator, but the manipulator. Its role has been that of justifying the widely held myth of Negro unhumanness and inferiority by offering entertaining rituals through which that myth could be reaffirmed.

The great significance of the definition of Lucas Beauchamp's role in *Intruder in the Dust* is that it makes explicit the nature of Hollywood's changed attitude toward Negroes. Form being, in the words of Kenneth Burke, "the psychology of the audience," what is taking place in the American movie patron's mind? Why these new attempts to redefine the Negro's role? What has happened to the audience's mode of thinking?

For one thing there was the war; for another there is the fact that the United States' position as a leader in world affairs is shaken by its treatment of Negroes. Thus the thinking of white Americans is undergoing a process of change, and reflecting that change, we find that each of the films mentioned above deals with some basic and unusually negative assumption about Negroes: Are Negroes cowardly soldiers? (*Home of the Brave*); are Negroes the real polluters of the South? (*Intruder in the Dust*); have mulatto Negroes the right to pass as white, at the risk of having black babies, or if they have white-skinned children, of having to kill off their "white" identities by revealing to them that they are, alas, Negroes? (*Lost Boundaries*); and, finally, should Negro girls marry white men or—wonderful non sequitur—should they help their race? (*Pinky*).

Obviously these films are not *about* Negroes at all; they are about what whites think and feel about Negroes. And if they are taken as accurate reflectors of that thinking, it becomes apparent that there is much confusion. To make use of Faulkner's metaphor again, the film makers fell upon the eggshell ice but, unlike the child, weren't heavy enough to break it. And, being unable to break it, they were unable to discover the real direction of their film narratives. In varying degree, they were unwilling to dig into the grave to expose the culprit, and thus we find them using ingenious devices for evading the full human rights of their Negroes. The result represents a defeat not only of drama, but of purpose.

In *Home of the Brave*, for instance, a psychiatrist tells the Negro soldier that his hysterical paralysis is like that of any other soldier who has lived when his friends have died; and we hear the soldier pronounced cured; indeed, we see him walk away prepared to open a bar and restaurant with a white veteran. But here there is an evasion (and by *evasion* I refer to the manipulation of the audience's attention away from reality to focus it upon false issues), because the guilt from which the Negro is supposed to suffer springs from an incident in which, immediately after his friend has called him a "yellowbelly nigger," he has wished the friend dead—only to see the wish granted by a sniper's bullet.

What happens to this racial element in the motivation of his guilt? The psychiatrist ignores it, and becomes a sleight-of-hand artist who makes it vanish by repeating again that the Negro is like everybody else. Nor, I believe, is this accidental, for it is here exactly that we come to the question of whether Negroes can rightfully be expected to risk their lives in an army in which they are slandered and discriminated against. Psychiatry is not, I'm afraid, the answer. The soldier suffers from concrete acts, not hallucinations.

And so with the others. In *Lost Boundaries* the question evaded is whether a mulatto Negro has the right to practice the old American pragmatic philosophy of capitalizing upon one's assets. For after all, whiteness *has* been given an economic and social value in our culture; and for the doctor upon whose life the film is based "passing" was the quickest and most certain means to success.

Yet Hollywood is uncertain about his right to do this. The film does not render the true circumstances. In real life Dr. Albert Johnson, the Negro doctor who "passed" as white, purchased the thriving practice of a deceased physician in Gorham, New Hampshire, for a thousand dollars. Instead, a fiction is introduced in the film wherein Dr. Carter's initial motivation for "passing" arises after he is refused an internship by dark Negroes in an Atlanta hospital—because of his color! It just isn't real, since there are thousands of mulattoes living as Negroes in the South, many of them Negro leaders. The only functional purpose served by this fiction is to gain sympathy for Carter by placing part of the blame for his predicament upon black Negroes. Nor should the irony be missed that part of the sentiment evoked when the Carters are welcomed back into the community is gained by painting Negro life as horrible, a fate worse than a living death. It would seem that in the eyes of Hollywood, it is only "white" Negroes who ever suffer—or is it merely the "white" corpuscles of their blood?

Pinky, for instance, is the story of another suffering mulatto, and the suffering grows out of a confusion between race and love. If we attempt to reduce the heroine's problem to sentence form we'd get something like this: "Should white-skinned Negro girls marry white men, or should they inherit the plantations of old white artistocrats (provided they can find any old aristocrats to will them their plantations) or should they live in the South and open nursery schools for black Negroes?" It doesn't follow, but neither does the action. After sitting through a film concerned with interracial marriage, we see it suddenly become a courtroom battle over whether Negroes have the right to inherit property.

Pinky wins the plantation, and her lover, who has read of the fight in the Negro press, arrives and still loves her, race be hanged. But now Pinky decides that to marry him would "violate the race" and that she had better remain a Negro. Ironically, nothing is said about the fact that her racial integrity, whatever that is, was violated before she was born. Her parents are never mentioned in the film. Following the will of the white aristocrat, who, before dying, advises her to "be true to herself," she opens a school for darker Negroes.

But in real life the choice is not between loving or denying one's race. Many couples manage to intermarry without violating their integrity, and indeed their marriage becomes the concrete expression of their integrity. In the film Jeanne Crain floats about like a sleepwalker, which seems to me to be exactly the way a girl so full of unreality would act. One thing is certain: no one is apt to mistake her for a Negro, not even a white one.

And yet, despite the absurdities with which these films are laden, they are all worth seeing, and if seen, capable of involving us emotionally. That they do is testimony to the deep centers of American emotion that they touch. Dealing with matters which, over the years, have been slowly charging up with guilt, they all display a vitality which escapes their slickest devices. And, naturally enough, one of the most interesting experiences connected with viewing them in predominantly white audiences is the profuse flow of tears and the sighs of profound emotional catharsis heard on all sides. It is as though there were some deep relief to be gained merely from seeing these subjects projected upon the screen.

It is here precisely that a danger lies. For the temptation toward self-congratulation which comes from seeing these films and sharing in their emotional release is apt to blind us to the true nature of what is unfolding—or failing to unfold—before our eyes. As an antidote to the sentimentality of these films, I suggest that they be seen in predominantly Negro audiences. For here, when the action goes phony, one will hear derisive laughter, not sobs. (Perhaps this is what Faulkner means about Negroes keeping the white man's conscience.) Seriously, *Intruder in the Dust* is the only film that could be shown in Harlem without arousing unintended laughter. For it is the only one of the four in which Negroes can make complete identification with their screen image. Interestingly, the factors that make this identification possible lie in its depiction not of racial but of human qualities.

Yet in the end, turning from art to life, we must even break with the definition of the Negro's role given us by Faulkner. For when it comes to conscience, we know that in this world each of us, black and white alike, must become the keeper of his own. This, in the deepest sense, is what these four films, taken as a group, should help us realize.

Faulkner himself seems to realize it. In the book *Intruder in the Dust,* Lucas attempts not so much to be the keeper of anyone else's conscience as to preserve his own life. Chick, in aiding Lucas, achieves that view of truth on which his own conscience depends.

Myth and Movies

GILBERT SELDES

. . . At the time Congressman Hoffman spoke, the Supreme Court of the United States was on his side and against the foreign ideologists. The Court has never actually reversed its decision that the movies are entertainment and not a form of persuasion. The issue was brought before the Court in 1916, in a case involving censorship which the Mutual Film Corporation believed to be a violation of the First Amendment. The Court held that as the movies were "spectacles" made for entertainment, they were not entitled to freedom of expression and could not be considered "as part of the press of the country or as organs of public opinion." On the other hand, the Pope and Lenin saw in the movies a form of communication— not an organ of public opinion, perhaps, but a powerful way to *influence* public opinion. The position of the Court has implied that they were wrong.

The question of free expression has not yet been settled, but it probably will be by the time this is read, because the authority of the censors in Atlanta, Georgia, is being challenged by the producers of *Lost Boundaries,* which treats sympathetically the plight of a Negro who has passed as white. The Court has indicated its frame of mind in a sort of aside delivered in an antitrust suit against the major studios; the essential words are: "We have no doubt that moving pictures, like newspapers and radio, are in-

Gilbert Seldes, *The Great Audience* (New York: Viking Press, 1950), pp. 9–24. Reprinted by permission.

cluded in the press, whose freedom is guaranteed by the First Amendment." In the thirty-three years between the two decisions many things have happened to the movies, but the doctrine of "entertainment" (commonly considered as another word for "amusement") has not been overthrown.

In business to create illusion, Hollywood has imposed a compound illusion about itself on the American people: that the production of movies is the prime occupation of the movie companies; that movies are America's fourth or fifth largest industry; and that everybody goes to the movies. None of these things is true: a mere fraction of the money invested in the movie business goes into the making of pictures; the industry ranks nearer the forty-sixth place than the sixth; and nearly everybody stops going to the movies. Nevertheless they are a proper subject for a statesman to think about. If the Pope and Lenin are right, and the movies are a supremely powerful instrument for influencing people, a statesman should decide whether it is good for the country to have the movies continue in the service of a small mass minority prodigiously important because it is composed largely of the adolescent; whether the movies should be encouraged publicly to destroy the audience they create; whether the country can afford a movie industry which hardly ever functions in the service of the majority of its citizens. . . .

. . . One fact is established: after they reach the age of twenty or so, people go less and less to the movies. The movies live on children from the ages of ten to nineteen, who go steadily and frequently and almost automatically to the pictures; from the ages of twenty to twenty-five people still go, but less often; after thirty, the audience begins to vanish from the movie houses. Checks made by different researchers at different times and places turn up minor variations in percentages; but it works out that between the ages of thirty and fifty, more than half of the men and women in the United States, steady patrons of the movies in their earlier years, do not bother to see more than one picture a month; after fifty, more than half see virtually no pictures at all.

This is the ultimate, essential, overriding fact about the movies; around it crystallize all the problems—personal, financial, social, moral, and aesthetic—of the motion-picture industry, from the "frustration" of its writers to the "glamour" of its stars. The detailed statistics were presented to the studios by such organizations as the Audience Research Institute, a special branch of the Gallup organization. Their significance has been made clear by outsiders, myself and others, for several years; but it has had no effect on the studios. The dazzling (and inflated) figure of four billion paid admissions a year dwindles into a probable thirty million separate moviegoers, chiefly young people, many of whom go several times a week; and at the end of the statistical hocus-pocus stands the gaunt figure of a mere thirteen to fifteen million individuals who actually see the basic staple commodity of Hollywood, the A feature-picture. (This is three million less than in 1946—a drop of twenty per cent.) The Audience Research Institute estimates that eight of these thirteen million people are under thirty, so that something like two-thirds of the population is contributing only one-third of the A-picture audience.

Face to face with the prime economic fact that the movies kill off their own audiences and live truly on the unearned increment of a steady birth rate, I confess to a sense of shock at the spectacle of an industry, financed by the shrewdest of bankers, contenting itself with a mere third, or at most half, of its potential income. The actual figures have been worked out: if the forty million who have stopped going to the movies would be brought back for only one picture a week, the gain at the box-office would be nearly half a billion dollars a year, after taxes; the share of the studios would be a hundred and fifty million dollars. Moreover, with these strays returned to the fold, American movies would, for the first time in years, be making a profit in the domestic market alone and be able to live without the export trade. In recent years about one out of every ten pictures has been able to do this.

It does not follow that we would have better pictures or that richer studios would be more daring in their experiments. All we can be sure of is that to attract a large audience the movies would be compelled to satisfy many more *kinds* of interest; they would have to become a genuinely democratic, instead of a mass-minority, entertainment; and in a democracy like ours, encouragement of individual interests and satisfaction of many various desires are the surest protection against the constant threat of robotization and the ultimate emergence of the mass man.

It will presently appear that so long as the movies neglect the majority of citizens they must actually contribute to the creation of a robotized society; and that is the primary reason for examining the structure that makes this inevitable. But the fact itself is so incredible that we have to inquire why the financiers of movie production have either failed to notice it or considered it insignificant. No other manufacturer of a mass-consumption commodity—cigarettes, soaps, cereals, motorcars—has deliberately cut himself off from the larger part of his market. Why have the movies done so? . . .

Financing the movies is done in one of two ways: a bank may put up a large part of the cost of a single picture, on the strength of an independent producer's reputation, the stars he has signed, the story he proposes to make, and particularly the guarantees he can give that his picture will be released by one of the major distributors; or a financial organization—a bank, a holding corporation—may invest in a major studio by making loans or acquiring stock. In the second case, the actual profit of any single picture is unimportant; the studio acts as producer of pictures, but the company of which the studio is one part is also distributor and exhibitor—it owns theaters. At the end of ten years of litigation, two major companies have yielded to the government and agreed to "divorcement"; Paramount, for instance, will be divided into two totally separate companies, one to produce films, the other to own about six hundred and fifty of the fifteen hundred theaters now controlled by the corporation. (The rest must be sold.) In preparation for this fission, Paramount acquainted its stockholders with the facts of life: in recent years two-thirds of its total profit was made by the theaters, one-third by the pictures produced. No other studio has controlled more than five hundred theaters, and a breakdown of balance sheets has not been made public; however, it has been generally assumed that Warners and Twentieth Century-Fox earn between fifty and sixty per cent of their profit as exhibitors, and only MGM definitely made more than half its income in the studios. The importance of the theaters can be measured in another way: in recent years the total investment in the movie business has been around two billion dollars, nearly all of it in theaters; only five per cent of the total was invested in the manufacture of films. An investor in a movie company has been paid dividends out of real estate more often than out of productions in the studio. The bookkeeping is intricate, but the simple fact is that a theater can make money while the picture it shows does not; the exhibitor, who takes as much as sixty-five per cent of the box-office receipts, prefers a smash hit, but he can make a profit by showing less successful pictures for brief runs, while the picture itself may never, out of the thirty-five per cent given to the studio, repay the cost of the negative. The investor in a single picture is vitally concerned with its fate; the backer of a studio, the holder of its stock, doesn't care where his profits come from. He hasn't, in the past, been worried by the fact that out of every hundred average-cost pictures made, only ten have actually made a profit on their domestic rentals alone. He was interested in annual dividends and he got them. He didn't know, or didn't care if he knew, that without its function as a real-estate operator, the company he invested in might be heading for bankruptcy.

The major studios do not completely monopolize either production or distribution, but their influence is predominant. There are many small companies, and from time to time independent producers manage to get backing for a single picture at a time; and there are nearly seven hundred circuits of theaters ranging in size from four houses to several hundred, as well as some seven thousand individuals or small companies managing less than four houses each. But the major studios and the large circuits which depend on them dominate the business of exhibiting pictures, because they control almost all the big city showcases, and, with less than half the theaters in the country, they have about two-thirds of all the seats. The remaining third of the seats, in the hands of small operators, are cheap ones, so that seven thousand small enterprisers, with more than half of the movie houses in the country, contribute only a small fraction of the total revenue and are consequently negligible in influence.

The large circuits are closely allied to the producing studios and form the channel through which pressure is brought to bear; exhibitors subscribe to annual reports on "marquee value"—estimating the drawing power of a star's name, all by itself—and they also make known their preference as to the kind of pictures they want. As one-third of the box-office receipts goes to the producing studio, these expressions are treated with respect. The small independent exhibitor has to trail along with the big operators, conscious of his service to the community and perhaps wondering whether influence must always be in proportion to income. These small exhibitors have not, in the past, been precisely free in their enterprise; contracts with the studios have bound them in many ways, and the system of distribution has by-passed the free competitive market.

The exhibitors make their wants known by criticism of the current product and at times are shrewd in their comments (which are liberally quoted in the *Motion Picture Herald*); as when, during the fatuous cycle of historical movies, one wrote, "Don't send me any more pictures where the hero signs his name with a feather." The most conspicuous instance occurred when a chain of theaters denounced Katharine Hepburn as "box-office poison"; her spirited reaction to this was to buy *The Philadelphia Story*, in which she had returned to the stage; she helped finance the movie version and restored herself as a first-rate "marquee" property. A great many exhibitors complain that they are without influence, that the studios make pictures without studying the needs of the exhibitor, and that the system of block-booking has forced them to play pictures they did not want in order to get the studios' superior products. The system is now being abandoned, in the interests of free competition, and it is generally assumed that the studios will have to make better pictures since each one will be sold on its merits. However, one realistic observer, after twenty years of experience as an exhibitor, has expressed grave doubts, saying that by block-booking the studios often forced the exhibitor to show their finer products and that now they may not make any exceptional pictures since they cannot be sure that exhibitors will take the risk of showing them. This gloomy reasoning is supported by the action of small operators throughout the country who declared that the slump in attendance in 1948–49 was due to the production of too many pictures "for sophisticated Broadway audiences" and the New York critics. They called for a return to pictures which would please the mass audience, darkly warning Hollywood that "some other form of entertainment" (a euphemism for television) might supplant the movies if they became a "class medium." Since the routine studio product, not the exceptional pictures, had in effect destroyed the audience, this comment was notably pointless.

Denouncing the exhibitor is a commonplace of all discussion of the movies. In *Life*'s Round Table on the subject in 1949, Joseph Manckiewicz, who has been responsible for many successful pictures as writer, director, or producer, asked, "Who controls the movies? . . . Isn't it true that a real-estate operator whose chief concern should be taking gum off carpets,

. . . isn't it true that this man is in control? . . . Here is . . . the real undercover man in the motion-picture industry—the exhibitor." In this indictment no distinction is made between the real-estate department of a major studio, which runs several hundred big-city theaters, and the owner of two or three houses in small towns. If the major companies follow the example of Paramount in "divorcing" production from exhibition, each one will create a powerful chain of theaters—the one developed from Paramount will control six hundred and fifty theaters—and many smaller ones; the owners of medium-size chains will gain in relative importance; but it isn't likely that the individual taste of the exhibitors will influence the production of movies to any revolutionary extent.

From time to time the studios have tried to convince exhibitors that a picture would make money. Pictures have been pretested by telling a selected group of people the story, the title, the names of the stars, and noting the degrees of enthusiasm they express. (As pretesting is more completely developed in the radio business, I will discuss it fully in that connection.)

The Johnston office makes its own sampling of information. It works with committees in the General Federation of Women's Clubs, the DAR, and Protestant, Catholic, and Jewish groups; it learns from them what objectionable features there may be in pictures previewed by its committees, and also gets "suggestions as to pictures not yet in production," which it transmits directly to the producers. By pretesting and getting the criticism before pictures are made, the producers manage to stand the pyramid of creativeness on its head. The imagination functions only after its effects are known.

Pacifying the exhibitor by pretesting is perhaps a symptom of uneasiness in the minds of producers, an awareness that all's not quite right in the movie world. The known facts seem to indicate that the movies subsist on the movie-going habit and that the habit breaks down; neither of these circumstances has ever been fully accepted by producers, who have obstinately held to the principle that people go to the movies to see stars and listen to stories and watch brilliant productions—and that they never stop going.

"LET'S GO TO THE MOVIES"

Since we now know how few separate individuals make up the movie audience, it is clear that repetitive, unselective, almost automatic attendance at the movies is a prime economic factor. In the formation of any habit, sameness of stimulant and confidence in the effect are required; within the over-all sameness there can be some minor variety—the baseball fan doesn't want to see the Giants play the Dodgers every day; and even some variation of effect is tolerated. A definite additional thrill comes from the appearance of a new sensation, especially when it delivers the faithful and wanted reaction in the end. The reader of mysteries, of Westerns, of comic strips expects the familiar response and is satisfied to delay its coming when material new in its outward appearance takes the place of the old. The simplest stage—of the child insisting that stories be repeated verbatim—gives place to the more sophisticated pleasure of watching the old emerge from a new disguise.

The basic audience, from the start, went to a movie because it was a novelty—and was playing around the corner. They went to all the movies. Later, the sprouting of many movie houses, with small admission charges, ministered to all the inclinations of the addict; he could be sure of getting a seat, he knew more or less what he was likely to get, and he would rather have a bad movie than none. Even the exploitation of the star system did not alter this habit. People went to see Chaplin or Pickford, probably both, when these two were racing through the headlines to see which would sign the first million-a-year contract in the movies; they also went to see the competitors and imitators of these two. There seemed to be an irreducible minimum who went to the movies because they were movies, regardless of stars or story.

Long after the movies had ceased to be a novelty, people continued to go because they were movies; this was true in the movies' first twenty years, when stories might be trifling episodes inflated to five reels or major classics reduced to one; when players were anonymous or stage stars were imported, exploited, and rejected; when famous novelists condescended to write for the screen or actors improvised their plots as they went along. The basic forms of the movies were established in those days: the chase picture (Western or criminal), the historical romance, the biography, the problem play, the slapstick comedy, the spectacle; even polite comedy existed by 1914, with a certain satiric wit; with *The Birth of a Nation* in 1916 the spectacle picture arrived in glory, undiminished to this day.

Personal scandals, protests against the immorality of the "vamp" cycle, and, in the 1920's, a slackening of creative power as well as some over-blown investments in real estate, brought the industry to a low point; but stars (including Rin-tin-tin) and the large residual audience that continued to go, no matter what, carried the movies over some rough spots. Sound threatened to destroy the studios but was actually their savior, and a new phase of movie-going began; without sound, the competition of radio, after 1924, would have been fatal. Although the movies went bankrupt in the first years of the depression, movie attendance held at a high level, the public spending a greater share of its income on pictures in 1933 when it had least to spend than it ever did before or after.

It isn't necessary to trace the persistence of the movie habit in further detail. We know now that while it has been, in the past, strong enough to keep the movies going, it has not persisted into maturity and middle age; if the movies lose their foreign markets and stumble over their adjustment to television, the recapture of the adult audience will be an absolute necessity for survival. A few efforts have already been made to discover why movie attendance has slumped; but they are usually based on false assumptions about the motive for going or they accept uncritically whatever catchword is current. During the past three years the catchword has been more intelligent than most: it is "maturity." Mr. Johnston has, indeed, warned his clients that they have not kept pace with the growing intelligence of the public or with the spread of education as represented by the number of high school graduates; he has advised Hollywood to make pictures for adults. The criteria for mature pictures have, however, not been established.

COMING OF AGE IN AMERICA

As Americans pass through the stages of courtship and begin married life, as they go to work, break from the protection and discipline of their parents, and begin to establish families of their own, the need for the particular satisfactions given by the movies becomes less acute. The image of the hero, the throb of passion, the myth of success, *as conceived by the movies*, are no longer needed; and as time goes on they become unacceptable.

A good part of the defection from the movie houses is explained by this gradual maturing of the audience. Neither the friendly encouragement of the dark theater nor the stimulus of unreal passion on the screen is needed when the ritual of courtship is over; the business of getting on in the world and of setting up a new household absorbs both husband and wife; new friends and new ways of being with old friends are developed; there is less free time—until the baby-sitter became a recognized social figure, evenings were particularly taken. But the movies cannot put forward these social and economic changes as a complete explanation. The attraction of the movies grows progressively weaker; there is no return to the theaters after business is going well and money for tickets is to be had and the children are growing up and the total habit of life is firmly grounded. Neither the happily married nor those who bump their way over disappointments and divorce seek consolation from the movies; those for whom the success story of the movies was prophetic stay away, and so do those whom it deluded. The habit broken in the first years of adult life is never resumed.

The changes one undergoes in the years when a life pattern is being set make the movie myth irrelevant; when we see that the myth is actually false, it becomes intolerable. In their twenties young Americans not only marry and set up housekeeping and begin to have children; they become aware of new duties and responsibilities: they have to borrow money and meet their debts; they pay taxes and mortgage their homes; they meet the pressure of law and social opinion; they plant themselves, not as irrevocably as Europeans, but firmly enough, and the pattern their lives will follow begins to form. Under compulsion they begin to see what life is like, not the ultimate philosophical essence of life, but the day-to-day actuality. The atmosphere of American life, since the 1920's at least, tends to delay this coming of age; the movies and radio, the entire advertising business, conspire to prolong adolescence until we are in danger of becoming a nation of teen-agers; but biologic and economic pressures still keep to their appointed paths, and at a point where they converge the cross-mark is made, signifying that a young man or a young woman has become an individual, responsible, fairly integrated, and prepared to continue life in a certain direction. This happens to the ignorant and to the well informed; it has little to do with intellectual capacity; it is a consequence not of education but of experience. To see life steadily and see it whole is given to a minute fraction of humanity; but merely suffering and enjoying the small emotions and the domestic trials of an ordinary life have an effect; and those who go through a few years of adult life cannot change themselves back. That is what the movies, which shrink from changing themselves, are asking the audience to do.

The staple commodity of Hollywood is a small group of myths. Unlike the ancient myths, they are not associated with profound religious experience, but, like those myths, they "embody some popular idea concerning natural or historical phenomena." The rest of the definition (in the Shorter Oxford Dictionary) is also applicable: "a purely fictitious narrative usually involving supernatural persons, actions, or events," and one of the meanings of "mythical" is "having no foundation in fact." The mature mind does not reject a myth that corresponds to actuality, because in its origin any myth is an imaginative explanation of a mystery; but the myth must be incarnated into a story to become fiction as we know it, an imaginative re-creation of reality. The myths we reject are not interpretations but falsifications, and the popular ideas they embody may once have been relevant but are so no longer. Grown men and women, and cynics among them, cherish the legend of Galatea, to which Bernard Shaw gave flesh and blood and fundamental brainwork in *Pygmalion*. They insist that the myth must have its own reality; they are as eager as little children to listen to a story, but the story must be true to life either as they know it or as they want it to be; and it must be a story even if it embodies a myth.

Why Hollywood is committed to mythology and can no longer tell a story will presently become clear. For the moment, we can approach the problem of maturity from another direction, observing the movies that are by common consent called mature and inquiring whether they can actually please an adult but not intellectual audience.

Myths and Movies

ARTHUR L. MAYER

While I was serving in Germany as Chief of the Motion Picture Branch of Military Government, we produced a documentary film one episode of which took place in an amusement park. There were two entrances to the park; one marked, "This Way to Heaven," the other, "This Way to a Lecture on Heaven." The first was deserted but hundreds of ardent Germans were pouring through the second.

Many of my American friends seem to me to have a similar second-hand approach to motion pictures. They read books about them, attend lectures about them, disparage them at cocktail parties. The only thing that they do not do is to attend them, or at least attend those "adult films" about which they talk so earnestly. They pay lip service to the cinema but they don't pay admission. Or else, if they do, they must represent a very small minority, much smaller than you would suppose from the amount of noise they make. . . .

Another prevalent myth among the intelligentsia is that foreign films are far superior to American. Partially this is merely an expression of snobbishness; partially a tribute to the skillful and unremitting research of men like Joseph Burstyn—modesty forbids my mentioning myself. We used to look at hundreds of French and Italian films in an effort to cull out a few that were worthy of importation. Popularity in their domestic market is no assurance of success in the United States. *The Bicycle Thief*, for instance, was a failure in Italy. Theater-goers casually dismissed the plight of the hero which so distressed American audiences. "What a boob," they said. "If his bike was stolen, why didn't he rent another?"

Occasionally, Mr. Burstyn and I would have the Balboa-like thrill of unexpectedly coming upon some superb cinematic treasure but by and large the pictures we looked at were inferior to the American product in story, acting, and technical proficiency. I highly recommend to those who regard Hollywood as a petrified forest of decaying formulas and escapist morasses, a closer acquaintance with the product of Cinecitta and Elstree.

The easy game of taking pot shots at the American penchant for potboilers is also sedulously cultivated in current books for the cultured anent movies and movie making. A myth maker, appropriately named Powdermaker, descends upon the Pacific Coast announcing her intent to investigate the habits of the strange inhabitants of Hollywood, much as she studied the mores of the South Sea Islanders. In the guise of an anthropologist, she collects an anthology of all the ancient and disgruntled gossip which persistently circulates in the film capital as in all other

Arthur L. Mayer, "Myths and Movies," *Harper's*, 202 (June 1951), pp. 71–77.

capitals. This she labels "science" and publishes a book which must be far more embarrassing to anthropologists than to picture people, although practically everyone in the producing end of the industry—directors, writers, actors, alike—is labeled venal or frustrated.

Jack Rosenstein, intriguingly described as "Hedda Hopper's leg-man," is sufficiently candid to make no pretense at scientific research. He announces that nothing is holy in Hollywood, that movies will never produce another great film star, that producers without exception are fat, lazy, and unimaginative, and that the industry has alienated its public by indulging in pictures with social significance. Exactly the opposite attack is leveled by my distinguished friend Gilbert Seldes, who titles the first chapter of his book *The Great Audience,* "The Audience Vanishes," and who is convinced, profit and loss statements to the contrary, that Hollywood is in sore financial straits because it does not produce enough "mature" pictures to appeal to American audiences.

What puzzles me is that these books are greeted with approval in the press although an intensely interesting and informative account of moviemaking procedures, *Case History of a Movie,* written by an expert, Dore Schary, receives comparatively slight attention. Our literary critics seem prepared to applaud anything written about Hollywood as long as it is opprobrious. It is easy to understand that having to read as many books as they do, they should have little time to attend pictures, but with their firsthand awareness of the limited relationship between literary merit and best-seller lists, they should, one would think, accept these easy strictures on the screen scene with a reasonable degree of caution.

Some writers have even gone so far as to prophesy, with obvious relish, that "the cinema theater, as we now know it, is dead as a dodo." Book sales have diminished in the past few years but no one, I think, is under the impression that the publishing business is about to disappear. I am equally confident that the movie theater is an institution, which will, for many years to come, continue to flourish.

Actually, motion-picture attendance has declined only if we regard the amazing business done by the movies in 1946 and 1947 as normal. That is much like saying that because there were fewer marriage licenses in 1949 than in 1946 there is a declining market for sex. Correctly to ascertain the public demand for any available commodity, movies or marriage, you have to study and chart its course over a period of years. . . .

In 1939 American theaters grossed $673 million, and in 1948, the last year for which we have a report from the U.S. Census Bureau, they took in $1,569 million, an increase of 133 per cent. Gone are the lush picture pickings of the years immediately following the war, but the seven major companies last year made a profit of over $50 million, almost three times as great as what they reported in 1940.

This profit was earned in the face of a substantial decline in actual movie attendance due in part to the inroads of television—if I may use so indelicate a word in a magazine designed for home consumption. It hardly seems surprising that the appearance of an amazing new phenomenon in the field of entertainment should exert a profound effect on competitive forms of warding off boredom such as reading books, making love, or going to the movies. It is premature to estimate, however, what the permanent effects of television on motion-picture attendance will prove to be. Investigations conducted in Washington and Detroit seem to indicate that after a period of six to nine months the interest of all except its juvenile devotees wanes and that papa, mama, and the older children revert to previous patterns of passing time.

As far as the movies are concerned, television, like radio, may eventually prove not an antagonist, but an ally. It has already helped to develop talent for the screen. It is serving increasingly as the ideal medium for advertising coming attractions. It will eventually hugely expand the appeal of motion-picture theaters by enabling them to show prize fights, crime investigations, and baseball games while they are taking place, national spokesmen delivering important addresses, and current shows while they are still on Broadway. It may siphon off some of the less critical movie patronage, which might prove to be a blessing in disguise; but the limitations of a comparatively small screen, of an insatiable demand for more talent and material than can reasonably be anticipated, and of advertising budgets which cannot hope to equal potential box-office receipts, will for a long time shackle television as a competitive medium of entertainment. Visualize *King Solomon's Mines* on a nineteen-inch rather than a nineteen-foot screen, William Wyler turning out a picture a week instead of one a year, or *Born Yesterday* with Brod Crawford, after knocking in Judy Holliday's teeth, delivering a few comments concerning the merits of Colgate's Dental Cream, and you have some vision of the problems confronting television.

Most of the industry's highbrow critics, however, are disinterested in the possible inroads of television on movie revenue. When they speak of a "lost audience" they refer to a presumably frustrated group of seekers for "mature films." This substantial segment of the public they affirm is being denied the privilege of seeing the type of pictures they crave by the obstinacy and stupidity of the movie moguls. Many critics at one time or another have leveled all sorts of criticism at Messrs. Skouras and Schenck, Zanuck and Zukor, but never has it been suggested that they were inferior in business acumen and foresight to writers or scientists. The bulk of the pictures they make are rented on the basis of a percentage of exhibitor receipts and the fluctuations of those receipts affords a daily national barometer of what audiences accept and what they reject. If a large portion of the American public really desires pictures with greater intellectual, social, or artistic content it can get them and get them quickly by acting in the only fashion that any business enterprise, whether it makes pictures, pajamas, or pretzels, can understand. It can make them profitable.

In my experience of over thirty years in the motion-picture industry the American people have had plenty of opportunities to support such pictures and almost invariably have failed to do so. Although I have helped to import many of the finest pictures ever brought into this country, I was able to maintain this activity only because I was simultaneously operating the Rialto Theater, which consistently showed the worst. The profits on the bad pictures enabled me to stand the losses on the good ones. Most of the critics of the industry are optimists because they only write and speak about the demand for superior films. I am a pessimist because I have invested my money in them.

My first movie boss was Mr. Sam Goldfish. He was in business with Archie Selwyn and when they separated Archie claimed that Sam not only lost his money but took half of his name. Under any monicker, however, Goldwyn is a lover of the beautiful and a man of fine perceptions. He has frequently been many years ahead of his time and prepared to shelve his unquestioned commercial sagacity for a gesture to posterity. Back in the prehistoric movie days of which I am speaking he proved his courage and endangered his position as president of Goldwyn Pictures by importing the sensational first modern art feature, *The Cabinet of Dr. Caligari.* It was sensationally unsuccessful. I was involved in this disaster and made life-long enemies among exhibitors by inveigling them into buying this futuristic fantasy without first screening it—the only way in which they could ever have been induced to book it.

In the prewar years Warners distinguished themselves with a series of films dealing with the great political and ideological issues of the day— *Juarez, The Magic Bullet, They Won't Forget,* and *Watch on the Rhine.* These fine productions brought out reams of favorable critical comment but a deplorable paucity of patrons. They were discontinued and Warners today would as soon think of producing a picture on a controversial issue as of presenting American motherhood in an unfavorable light.

As far back as 1934 I wrote a piece in *Liberty* entitled "Why Hollywood Loses Money on Good Pictures," which compared in painful detail the box-office receipts of such intelligent productions as *Berkeley Square* and *The Emperor Jones* with the intake of such moronic abortions as *The Half Naked Truth* and *They Had to Get Married.* A short time thereafter I met Cecil B. De Mille and he said: "Mr. Mayer, how can you say good pictures lose money? *My* pictures are invariably profitable." Quick as a flash at this embarrassing moment, I responded, "But yours are the run of De Mille pictures." . . .

Of course there have been exceptions to my thesis. How many depends upon a definition of what maturity in films consists of, a study in semantics left in the limbo of uncertainty by their proponents. *The Lost Weekend, The Best Years of Our Lives, Henry V,* if they qualify, were all unquestioned box-office successes although, I suspect, not entirely for reasons related to their intellectual content. Those who contend that there has been marked progress in recent times in the reception of more serious subjects, are, I think, victims of wishful thinking. Two years ago Humphrey Bogart's *The Treasure of Sierra Madre* was received so unkindly that he had to revert to smacking alluring ladies in alluring places to regain his popularity. Dore Schary, upon becoming head of the Metro studio, made a notable effort to raise the studio's maturity batting average with *Intruder in the Dust,* which Bosley Crowther of the *New York Times* called "one of the great cinematic dramas of our times." It proved one of the great cinematic flops of all times. Mr. Schary has now gone back to the mines—profitable mines, I mean—such as King Solomon's. His recent tribute to liberalism, *The Magnificent Yankee,* is as unworthy of a great judge as it is of a great studio executive. . . .

Two years ago Universal was over $4 million in the red. In 1950 its red corpuscles had been reactivated by a profit of almost a million and a half. This was largely due to the "Ma and Pa Kettles," a series ingeniously tailored for what is insultingly known as the family trade. The pictures cost about $500,000 each to make, and although they play almost exclusively in small towns and neighborhood theaters, gross about $2,500,000. It will require three of them, however, this year to make up for the losses that Universal will suffer from its dalliance with the world of fantasy in a fine screen version of *Harvey.*

Similarly, Paramount redeemed the heavy loss it suffered with Willie Wyler's exquisite *The Heiress* when it produced *Samson and Delilah,* which will gross approximately $11 million, probably the third most successful picture in movie annals. The average film plays to an audience of about thirteen million people but *Samson and Delilah* should triple that figure. It would appear as if what the industry needs is more Victor Matures (not to mention De Milles) rather than more mature pictures. . . .

The indomitable Mr. Seldes, however, is not so easily discouraged. He contends the fault is not with the taste of the public, but with the distribution practices of the major companies. They ought, he says, to play the adult pictures in the little theaters, and I imagine the adultery ones in the big theaters. Prejudiced as I am by a financial stake in several small houses, I heartily agree that pictures are frequently booked into inappropriate theaters. The problem, however, of inadequate public support for what it refers to disparagingly as "message pictures" lies far deeper than any distribution practices. I played King Vidor's stirring pre-New Deal saga, *Our Daily Bread,* at the little Rialto to unprecedentedly low receipts. I sought to enlist the support of every social-minded organization in New York City with a picture about child labor called *Boy Slaves.* I wanted it to be a great success, not only for the personal profit and satisfaction involved but also to encourage RKO to make more pictures of this nature. I advertised it widely in the liberal press. I spoke about it before ladies' clubs and in YMCA halls. I brought it to the attention of editorial writers and columnists. It lasted just six days!

I freely admit that the Rialto, which specialized in pictures of murder, mayhem, and mystery to such an extent that I became known as the Merchant of Menace, was not the correct theater to play a film of this type. It might have done better in one of the so-called art theaters of which there are approximately 250 located in the larger cities and select suburbs. These used to be referred to as "sure-seaters" because of their sadly limited patronage. They are transformed, however, into sure non-seaters when they play pictures whose appeal is sensual rather than sensuous. At present, for instance, *Bitter Rice*, an Italian film, is attracting hold-out audiences in all of the "art" theaters of the United States. It is devoid of cinematic merit, but as Howard Hughes said of *The Outlaw*, there are two good reasons why every man should see it.

There were plenty of good reasons why people of taste and artistic appreciation would want to see *The Titan*, recently crowned by the National Board of Review as the best foreign film of 1950. This magnificent study of the life and works of Michelangelo played in the same group of small theaters but it has not yet recovered the modest cost involved in its American re-editing.

Similarly, my former firm, Mayer-Burstyn, showed *The Quiet One* in these houses. The movie critics rallied to the support of this lovely little picture with the marvelous reviews which it so fully merited. Our final gross was less than that of many Hollywood shorts!

Actually, the only sensational successes scored by Burstyn and myself in the twenty years in which we were engaged in business—incidentally the longest period that anyone has ever survived the hazards of supplying foreign films to American audiences—were with pictures whose artistic and ideological merits were aided and abetted at the box office by their frank sex content. These we were able to exhibit profitably in big theaters as well as small. *Open City* was generally advertised with a misquotation from *Life* adjusted so as to read: "Sexier than Hollywood ever dared to be," together with a still of two young ladies deeply engrossed in a rapt embrace, and another of a man being flogged, designed to tap the sadist trade. The most publicized scene in *Paisan* showed a young lady disrobing herself with an attentive male visitor reclining by her side on what was obviously not a nuptial couch. In the case of *The Bicycle Thief*, which was completely devoid of any erotic embellishments, the exhibitors did their best with an imaginative sketch of a young lady riding a bicycle. The Motion Picture Association rushed in to reinforce their efforts by denying it a seal unless the little boy with an urge to urinate was eliminated. In spite of this inadvertent first aid to the box office, and in spite of the critics' rave reviews, it did far less business than either *Open City* or *Paisan*.

Much has been made of the fact that approximately two-thirds of movie attendance comes from people under thirty-five years of age. I cannot see, however, why this should be a source of surprise to anybody. If I go to a football game, or into a store that sells sheet music or to a night club (I never do, but if I did) I am surrounded almost exclusively by young people. If we can generalize about such matters, youth likes to go out; middle age likes to stay home. Youth is eager for entertainment; middle age prefers ease and comfort. I do not agree, however, for one moment that on youth's shoulders alone rests the responsibility for the popularity of some tawdry, trashy pictures any more than they are responsible for the popularity of some tawdry, trashy books and plays.

Surely it is to the young rather than to the old that we must look for the interest in experimental techniques, the readiness to accept innovations and creative ideas, the willingness to greet new faces on which all progress rests. The vast auditorium where Cinema 16 holds its showings of strange *avant-garde* documentaries is composed 99 per cent of people not under thirty-five but under twenty-five. When I attended Cocteau's *Orpheus* I looked around in loneliness for another gray head beside my own. I thought the picture bordered on the ludicrous but that is exactly how my mother felt thirty years ago about *Caligari*.

If my own experience is a reliable guide, financially the industry would surely be well advised to continue to aim its primary appeal at youth. Recently I imported a charming compilation of movie clips made at the turn of the century whose major box-office value resided in their appeal to a nostalgic older generation. The nostalgic older generation, however, preferred to remain home by the fire or television side. *Paris 1900* bids fair to lose me $19,000. When, however, I acquire a film like *Seven Days to Noon*, which deals realistically with the threat of the atom bomb to men and women of every age, a younger generation which wants to live sweeps the picture to a success.

During the past year, however, Hollywood cannot fairly be accused of catering exclusively to any single age or interest group. It has sought to speak to every segment of the people with diversified products like *All About Eve, Annie Get Your Gun, Asphalt Jungle, Battleground, Born Yesterday, Cheaper by the Dozen, Cyrano de Bergerac, Fourteen Hours, Glass Menagerie, Halls of Montezuma, Harvey, Intruder in the Dust, Jackpot, Mr. 880, No Way Out, Of Men and Music, Panic in the Streets, Red Badge of Courage, Sunset Boulevard, The Brave Bulls, The Men,* and *Twelve O'Clock High*. I do not claim that these are pictures which future ages will cherish, nor do I expect anyone, myself included, to be enthusiastic over every one of them. What I do maintain is that in the face of censorship restrictions, pressure groups, police authorities, and now license commissioners, they represent a wider general appeal and a higher average of merit than that supplied by popular fiction magazines, by the radio, or by television, and fully as high as that of current books or drama.

The results with these films and with all the others released last year, from the incredibly successful *Father of the Bride* to the equally incredible debacle of *The Magnificent Yankee,* are now being carefully appraised in the offices of every major picture producer. These studies are not confined to Hollywood pictures. English and foreign films are given the same meticulous scrutiny. When we imported *Open City* Rossellini was catapulted overnight into world-wide demand, Metro-Goldwyn-Mayer cabled an offer to the Boulting Brothers, producers and directors of *Seven Days to Noon,* almost simultaneously with its successful New York premiere. In the field of distribution and exhibition there may have been collusion and conspiracy among the picture companies, but in their production the fiercest competition exists for talent and for popular means of employing it.

The shape of films to come is daily molded in the curve of yesterday's box-office window. You may deprecate that box office as a standard of merit but in the words of an insignificant writer with whom I find myself constantly in amazing agreement, "It is an unfailing barometer of what we want in our heart of hearts . . . frippery or meaning, shadow or substance. The responsibility," if I may continue to quote from Arthur Mayer in the *Theatre Arts Anthology,* "for making the motion picture a mighty instrument of mankind's hope and salvation lies not with producers, distributors, or exhibitors, not even with authors or directors, but with the audience. That audience is you and me and our relatives and our friends. If we support, not with chatter but with cash, not in the drawing room but in the theater auditorium, those films which give a true account of our honest problems and highest aspirations, we can make our motion pictures a symbol and token of all striving humanity—a living voice speaking among the people."

SUGGESTIONS FOR FURTHER READING

Robert Sklar, *Movie-Made America: A Cultural History of American Movies* (New York: Random House, 1975); Stephen J. Whitfield, *The Culture of the Cold War* (Baltimore: Johns Hopkins University, 1991); Thomas Cripps, *Making Movies Black: The Hollywood Message Movie from World War II to the Civil Rights Era* (New York: Oxford University Press, 1992).

XV

❧

THE SUPREME COURT IN A DEMOCRATIC POLITY: ACTIVISM VERSUS RESTRAINT

During the 1940s and 1950s the U.S. Supreme Court was frequently polarized by the contrasting philosophies of Justice Felix Frankfurter, who believed in judicial restraint, and Justice Hugo L. Black, who embraced a more activist and civil libertarian role for the Court. To complicate matters, Black viewed the First Amendment as "the keystone of our Government," whereas Frankfurter believed that situations could arise when national security interests might take priority over protection of First Amendment rights to freedom of speech. These contested values actually predated the 1940s, and they persist into the present.

In 1940 Congress passed the Smith Act prohibiting the "teaching and advocating" of subversive doctrines. Several hundred American communists were sent to jail as a result. In 1949 the Justice Department prosecuted eleven leaders of the American Communist Party for violation of the Smith Act. Following a long trial, they were convicted and sentenced to prison terms. Those convictions were upheld by the Supreme Court in the case of **Dennis et al. v. United States** (1951). Another 126 party members were then prosecuted, and dozens of others who were aliens were rounded up for deportation. The Communist Party ceased to be a viable entity thereafter. Justice Black believed that portions of the Smith Act, at the least, were unconstitutional.

Frankfurter (1882–1965) taught at the Harvard Law School from 1914 until 1939 when President Roosevelt appointed him to the Court. Frankfurter had been known as a staunch advocate of civil liberties, helped to found the American Civil Liberties Union, and severely criticized the trial of Sacco and Vanzetti, anarchists accused of murder during the 1920s. As a judge, however, Frankfurter believed that his principal obligation was to decide particular cases rather than to reform society. He preferred to leave that role to the people's elected representatives. Activism by unelected judges seemed undemocratic.

Black (1886–1971) served in the U.S. Senate from 1926 until Roosevelt appointed him to the Court in 1937. Initially, Black emerged as part of the "liberal bloc" that sustained *New Deal* legislation. *Subsequently, however, he became best known for his firm defense of the Bill of Rights as a bulwark of personal liberties. Contemporaries often contrasted Black's position with Frankfurter's desire to balance individual rights against the needs of government, and the wishes of a democratic majority and its elected representatives. Black's most important contribution, however, may have been persuading a majority of the Court that the due process clause of the Fourteenth Amendment made the Bill of Rights apply to the states as well as the federal government.*

It should be noted that Chief Justice Fred Vinson wrote the Court's opinion in the Dennis *case and simply assumed that all members of the Communist Party shared violent and subversive intentions. Although Frankfurter voted with the majority, his concurring opinion at least examined the "clear and present danger" test developed during World War I by Justice Oliver Wendell Holmes. How imminent must the danger be? If Eugene Dennis and his associates only wished to* teach *the doctrines of Marxist Leninism, did that alone threaten U.S. national security? It is not clear that Frankfurter believed it did—only that elected officials had the right to legislate against such teaching.*

Although Frankfurter and Black disagreed on many issues of judicial philosophy and came to be known as leaders of contrasting camps, they actually voted together on numerous civil liberties cases during the Cold War era. We are fortunate, however, that enough of their correspondence and memoranda has survived, along with printed opinions, so that we can trace their fascinating contestation of constitutional values over a period spanning more than two decades.

Concurring Opinion in
Dennis et al. v. United States

FELIX FRANKFURTER

Mr. Justice Frankfurter, concurring in affirmance of the judgment.

The defendants were convicted under § 3 of the Smith Act for conspiring to violate § 2 of that Act, which makes it unlawful "to organize or help to organize any society, group, or assembly of persons who teach, advocate, or encourage the overthrow or destruction of any government in the United States by force or violence." . . . The substance of the indictment is that the defendants between April 1, 1945, and July 20, 1948, agreed to bring about the dissolution of a body known as the Communist Political Association and to organize in its place the Communist Party of the United States; that the aim of the new party was "the overthrow and destruction of the Government of the United States by force and violence"; that the defendants were to assume leadership of the Party and to recruit members for it and that the Party was to publish books and conduct classes, teaching the duty and the necessity of forceful overthrow. The jury found all the defendants guilty. With one exception, each was sentenced to imprisonment for five years and to a fine of $10,000. The convictions were affirmed by the Court of Appeals for the Second Circuit. . . . We were asked to review this affirmance on all the grounds considered by the Court of Appeals. These included not only the scope of the freedom of speech guaranteed by the Constitution, but also serious questions regarding the legal composition of the jury and the fair conduct of the trial. We granted certiorari, strictly limited, however, to the contention that §§ 2 and 3 of the Smith Act, inherently and as applied, violated the First and Fifth Amendments. . . .

As thus limited, the controversy in this Court turns essentially on the instructions given to the jury for determining guilt or innocence. . . . The first question is whether—wholly apart from constitutional matters—the judge's charge properly explained to the jury what it is that the Smith Act condemns. The conclusion that he did so requires no labored argument. On the basis of the instructions, the jury found, for the purpose of our review, that the advocacy which the defendants conspired to promote was to be a rule of action, by language reasonably calculated to incite persons to such action, and was intended to cause the overthrow of the Government by force and violence as soon as circumstances permit. This brings us to the ultimate issue. In enacting a statute which makes it a crime

Opinion by Justice Felix Frankfurter in *Dennis et al.* v. *United States* (1951) from *U.S. Reports* 341 U.S. 494, pp. 517–25, 550–52.

for the defendants to conspire to do what they have been found to have conspired to do, did Congress exceed its constitutional power?

Few questions of comparable import have come before this Court in recent years. The appellants maintain that they have a right to advocate a political theory, so long, at least, as their advocacy does not create an immediate danger of obvious magnitude to the very existence of our present scheme of society. On the other hand, the Government asserts the right to safeguard the security of the Nation by such a measure as the Smith Act. Our judgment is thus solicited on a conflict of interests of the utmost concern to the well-being of the country. This conflict of interests cannot be resolved by a dogmatic preference for one or the other, nor by a sonorous formula which is in fact only a euphemistic disguise for an unresolved conflict. If adjudication is to be a rational process, we cannot escape a candid examination of the conflicting claims with full recognition that both are supported by weighty title-deeds.

There come occasions in law, as elsewhere, when the familiar needs to be recalled. Our whole history proves even more decisively than the course of decisions in this Court that the United States has the powers inseparable from a sovereign nation. . . . The right of a government to maintain its existence—self-preservation—is the most pervasive aspect of sovereignty. "Security against foreign danger," wrote Madison, "is one of the primitive objects of civil society." . . . The constitutional power to act upon this basic principle has been recognized by this Court at different periods and under diverse circumstances. . . .

But even the all-embracing power and duty of self-preservation are not absolute. Like the war power, which is indeed an aspect of the power of self-preservation, it is subject to applicable constitutional limitations. . . . Our Constitution has no provision lifting restrictions upon governmental authority during periods of emergency, although the scope of a restriction may depend on the circumstances in which it is invoked.

The First Amendment is such a restriction. It exacts obedience even during periods of war; it is applicable when war clouds are not figments of the imagination no less than when they are. The First Amendment categorically demands that "Congress shall make no law respecting an establishment of religion, or prohibiting the free exercise thereof; or abridging the freedom of speech, or of the press; or the right of the people peaceably to assemble, and to petition the Government for a redress of grievances." The right of a man to think what he pleases, to write what he thinks, and to have his thoughts made available for others to hear or read has an engaging ring of universality. The Smith Act and this conviction under it no doubt restrict the exercise of free speech and assembly. Does that, without more, dispose of the matter?

Just as there are those who regard as invulnerable every measure for which the claim of national survival is invoked, there are those who find in the Constitution a wholly unfettered right of expression. Such literalness treats the words of the Constitution as though they were found on a piece of outworn parchment instead of being words that have called into being a nation with a past to be preserved for the future. The soil in which the Bill of Rights grew was not a soil of arid pedantry. The historic antecedents of the First Amendment preclude the notion that its purpose was to give unqualified immunity to every expression that touched on matters within the range of political interest. . . .

The language of the First Amendment is to be read not as barren words found in a dictionary but as symbols of historic experience illumined by the presuppositions of those who employed them. Not what words did Madison and Hamilton use, but what was it in their minds which they conveyed? Free speech is subject to prohibition of those abuses of expression which a civilized society may forbid. As in the case of every other provision of the Constitution that is not crystallized by the nature of its technical concepts, the fact that the First Amendment is not self-defining and self-enforcing neither impairs its usefulness nor compels its paralysis as a living instrument.

"The law is perfectly well settled," this Court said over fifty years ago, "that the first ten amendments to the Constitution, commonly known as the Bill of Rights, were not intended to lay down any novel principles of government, but simply to embody certain guaranties and immunities which we had inherited from our English ancestors, and which had from time immemorial been subject to certain well-recognized exceptions arising from the necessities of the case. In incorporating these principles into the fundamental law there was no intention of disregarding the exceptions, which continued to be recognized as if they had been formally expressed." *Robertson v. Baldwin,* 165 U.S. 275, 281. That this represents the authentic view of the Bill of Rights and the spirit in which it must be construed has been recognized again and again in cases that have come here within the last fifty years. See, *e.g., Gompers v. United States,* 233 U.S. 604, 610. Absolute rules would inevitably lead to absolute exceptions, and such exceptions would eventually corrode the rules. The demands of free speech in a democratic society as well as the interest in national security are better served by candid and informed weighing of the competing interests, within the confines of the judicial process, than by announcing dogmas too inflexible for the non-Euclidian problems to be solved.

But how are competing interests to be assessed? Since they are not subject to quantitative ascertainment, the issue necessarily resolves itself into asking, who is to make the adjustment?—who is to balance the relevant factors and ascertain which interest is in the circumstances to prevail? Full responsibility for the choice cannot be given to the courts. Courts are not representative bodies. They are not designed to be a good reflex of a democratic society. Their judgment is best informed, and therefore most dependable, within narrow limits. Their essential quality is detachment, founded on independence. History teaches that the independence of the judiciary is jeopardized when courts become embroiled in the passions of the day and assume primary responsibility in choosing between competing political, economic and social pressures.

Primary responsibility for adjusting the interests which compete in the situation before us of necessity belongs to the Congress. The nature of the power to be exercised by this Court has been delineated in decisions not charged with the emotional appeal of situations such as that now before us. We are to set aside the judgment of those whose duty it is to legislate only if there is no reasonable basis for it. . . .

We must not overlook the value of that interchange. Freedom of expression is the well-spring of our civilization—the civilization we seek to maintain and further by recognizing the right of Congress to put some limitation upon expression. Such are the paradoxes of life. For social development of trial and error, the fullest possible opportunity for the free play of the human mind is an indispensable prerequisite. . . .

It is not for us to decide how we would adjust the clash of interests which this case presents were the primary responsibility for reconciling it ours. Congress has determined that the danger created by advocacy of overthrow justifies the ensuing restriction on freedom of speech. The determination was made after due deliberation, and the seriousness of the congressional purpose is attested by the volume of legislation passed to effectuate the same ends.

Can we then say that the judgment Congress exercised was denied it by the Constitution? Can we establish a constitutional doctrine which forbids the elected representatives of the people to make this choice? Can we hold that the First Amendment deprives Congress of what it deemed necessary for the Government's protection?

To make validity of legislation depend on judicial reading of events still in the womb of time—a forecast, that is, of the outcome of forces at best appreciated only with knowledge of the topmost secrets of nations—is to charge the judiciary with duties beyond its equipment. We do not expect courts to pronounce historic verdicts on bygone events. Even historians have conflicting views to this day on the origins and conduct of the French Revolution, or, for that matter, varying interpretations of "the glorious Revolution" of 1688. It is as absurd to be confident that we can measure the present clash of forces and their outcome as to ask us to read history still enveloped in clouds of controversy.

. . . The distinction which the Founders drew between the Court's duty to pass on the power of Congress and its complementary duty not to enter directly the domain of policy is fundamental. But in its actual operation it is rather subtle, certainly to the common understanding. Our duty to abstain from confounding policy with constitutionality demands perceptive humility as well as self-restraint in not declaring unconstitutional what in a judge's private judgment is deemed unwise and even dangerous.

Even when moving strictly within the limits of constitutional adjudication, judges are concerned with issues that may be said to involve vital finalities. The too easy transition from disapproval of what is undesirable to condemnation as unconstitutional, has led some of the wisest judges to question the wisdom of our scheme in lodging such authority in courts. But it is relevant to remind that in sustaining the power of Congress in a case like this nothing irrevocable is done. The democratic process at all events is not impaired or restricted. Power and responsibility remain with the people and immediately with their representatives. All the Court says is that Congress was not forbidden by the Constitution to pass this enactment and that a prosecution under it may be brought against a conspiracy such as the one before us. . . .

Dissenting Opinion in
Dennis et al. v. *United States*

HUGO BLACK

Mr. Justice Black, dissenting.

Here again, . . . my basic disagreement with the Court is not as to how we should explain or reconcile what was said in prior decisions but springs from a fundamental difference in constitutional approach. Consequently, it would serve no useful purpose to state my position at length.

At the outset I want to emphasize what the crime involved in this case is, and what it is not. These petitioners were not charged with an attempt to overthrow the Government. They were not charged with overt acts of any kind designed to overthrow the Government. They were not even charged with saying anything or writing anything designed to overthrow the Government. The charge was that they agreed to assemble and to talk and publish certain ideas at a later date: The indictment is that they conspired to organize the Communist Party and to use speech or newspapers and other publications in the future to teach and advocate the forcible overthrow of the Government. No matter how it is worded, this is a virulent form of prior censorship of speech and press, which I believe the First Amendment forbids. I would hold § 3 of the Smith Act authorizing this prior restraint unconstitutional on its face and as applied.

But let us assume, contrary to all constitutional ideas of fair criminal

Opinion by Justice Hugo L. Black in *Dennis et al.* v. *United States* (1951) from *U.S. Reports* 341 U.S. 494, pp. 579–81.

procedure, that petitioners although not indicted for the crime of actual advocacy, may be punished for it. Even on this radical assumption, the other opinions in this case show that the only way to affirm these convictions is to repudiate directly or indirectly the established "clear and present danger" rule. This the Court does in a way which greatly restricts the protections afforded by the First Amendment. The opinions for affirmance indicate that the chief reason for jettisoning the rule is the expressed fear that advocacy of Communist doctrine endangers the safety of the Republic. Undoubtedly, a governmental policy of unfettered communication of ideas does entail dangers. To the Founders of this Nation, however, the benefits derived from free expression were worth the risk. They embodied the philosophy in the First Amendment's command that "Congress shall make no law . . . abridging the freedom of speech, or of the press. . . ." I have always believed that the First Amendment is the keystone of our Government, that the freedoms it guarantees provide the best insurance against destruction of all freedom. At least as to speech in the realm of public matters, I believe that the "clear and present danger" test does not "mark the furthermost constitutional boundaries of protected expression" but does "no more than recognize a minimum compulsion of the Bill of Rights."

So long as this Court exercises the power of judicial review of legislation, I cannot agree that the First Amendment permits us to sustain laws suppressing freedom of speech and press on the basis of Congress' or our own notions of mere "reasonableness." Such a doctrine waters down the First Amendment so that it amounts to little more than an admonition to Congress. The Amendment as so construed is not likely to protect any but those "safe" or orthodox views which rarely need its protection. I must also express my objection to the holding because, as Mr. Justice Douglas' dissent shows, it sanctions the determination of a crucial issue of fact by the judge rather than by the jury. . . .

SUGGESTIONS FOR FURTHER READING

James F. Simon, *The Antagonists: Hugo Black, Felix Frankfurter and Civil Liberties in Modern America* (New York: Simon and Schuster, 1989); Richard C. Cortner, *The Supreme Court and the Second Bill of Rights: The Fourteenth Amendment and the Nationalization of Civil Liberties* (Madison, Wis.: University of Wisconsin Press, 1981).

XVI

༺◆༻

ENVIRONMENTALISM AND ITS CRITICS

Rachel Carson (1907–64) did graduate work in biology at The Johns Hopkins University during 1929–32 and taught zoology at the University of Maryland from 1931 to 1936. In 1936 she took a job with the federal agency that became the U.S. Fish and Wildlife Service under the Department of Interior in 1940. As an aquatic biologist, Carson became a prolific and influential writer. Her first book, **Under the Sea Wind** *(1941), described ocean life in language that was clear to nonspecialists.* **The Sea Around Us** *(1951) won the National Book Award for nonfiction. In 1952 she resigned her government job to be able to devote more time to writing. The result was* **The Edge of the Sea** *(1955), which described the shoreline of the eastern United States and its interactive chain of life.*

Carson next turned her attention to the rapidly growing use of pesticides. In **Silent Spring** *(1962) she attacked the proliferating use of poisonous chemicals to kill insects. The book generated such lively controversy that President Kennedy established a commission in 1963 to examine the problem. The commission's report basically supported Carson's attack on the escalating use of chemicals and the resulting contamination and destruction throughout the cycle of nature. Her discussion of insects within a framework of Darwinian adaptive evolution indicates the great distance that had been traveled since the Scopes trial in 1925.*

Following Carson's death in 1964, legislation was passed that required stricter regulation of pesticide ingredients. Her final book, **The Sense of Wonder,** *was published in 1965 after her death. Broadly based environmentalism and ecological concern essentially date from the appearance of* **Silent Spring.** *Ironically, Carson was a retiring person who did not like controversy and notoriety. Her "ecological conscience" compelled her to speak out against the destructive uses of pesticides, particularly DDT.*

Many of her critics, such as I. L. Baldwin, were prominent members of the scientific community. Baldwin, a professor of agricultural bacteriology at the University of Wisconsin, also served as chairman of the Committee on Pest Control and Wildlife Relationships of the National Academy of Sciences—National Research Council. The anonymous reviewer for **Time** *magazine acknowledged the power and importance of Carson's book, but declared that scientifically informed people considered her brief to be "unfair, one-sided, and hysterically overemphatic." They felt that she included too many scary and unsound generalizations.*

In the years after Silent Spring, *Carson continued to have severe critics from both the industrial and scientific communities. It is generally recognized, however, that she alerted millions to the perils created by uncontrolled technology and that she is the mother of modern environmentalism.*

Silent Spring

RACHEL CARSON

THE OBLIGATION TO ENDURE

The history of life on earth has been a history of interaction between living things and their surroundings. To a large extent, the physical form and the habits of the earth's vegetation and its animal life have been molded by the environment. Considering the whole span of earthly time, the opposite effect, in which life actually modifies its surroundings, has been relatively slight. Only within the moment of time represented by the present century has one species—man—acquired significant power to alter the nature of his world.

During the past quarter century this power has not only increased to one of disturbing magnitude but it has changed in character. The most alarming of all man's assaults upon the environment is the contamination of air, earth, rivers, and sea with dangerous and even lethal materials. This pollution is for the most part irrecoverable; the chain of evil it initiates not only in the world that must support life but in living tissues is for the most part irreversible. In this now universal contamination of the environment, chemicals are the sinister and little-recognized partners of radiation in changing the very nature of the world—the very nature of its life. Strontium 90, released through nuclear explosions into the air, comes to earth in rain or drifts down as fallout, lodges in soil, enters into the grass or corn or wheat grown there, and in time takes up its abode in the bones of a human being, there to remain until his death. Similarly, chemicals sprayed on croplands or forests or gardens lie long in soil, entering into living organisms, passing from one to another in a chain of poisoning and death. Or they pass mysteriously by underground streams until they emerge and, through the alchemy of air and sunlight, combine into new forms that kill vegetation, sicken cattle, and work unknown harm on those who drink from once pure wells. As Albert Schweitzer has said, "Man can hardly even recognize the devils of his own creation."

It took hundreds of millions of years to produce the life that now inhabits the earth—eons of time in which that developing and evolving and diversifying life reached a state of adjustment and balance with its surroundings. The environment, rigorously shaping and directing the life it supported, contained elements that were hostile as well as supporting.

Rachel Carson, *Silent Spring* (Boston: Houghton Mifflin, 1962), pp. 5–8, 12–13, 246–47, 248–49, 250–51. Copyright © 1962 by Rachel L. Carson. Copyright © renewed 1990 by Roger Christie. Reprinted by permission of Houghton Mifflin Company. All rights reserved.

Certain rocks gave out dangerous radiation; even within the light of the sun, from which all life draws its energy, there were short-wave radiations with power to injure. Given time—time not in years but in millennia—life adjusts, and a balance has been reached. For time is the essential ingredient; but in the modern world there is no time.

The rapidity of change and the speed with which new situations are created follow the impetuous and heedless pace of man rather than the deliberate pace of nature. Radiation is no longer merely the background radiation of rocks, the bombardment of cosmic rays, the ultraviolet of the sun that have existed before there was any life on earth; radiation is now the unnatural creation of man's tampering with the atom. The chemicals to which life is asked to make its adjustment are no longer merely the calcium and silica and copper and all the rest of the minerals washed out of the rocks and carried in rivers to the sea; they are the synthetic creations of man's inventive mind, brewed in his laboratories, and having no counterparts in nature.

To adjust to these chemicals would require time on the scale that is nature's; it would require not merely the years of a man's life but the life of generations. And even this, were it by some miracle possible, would be futile, for the new chemicals come from our laboratories in an endless stream; almost five hundred annually find their way into actual use in the United States alone. The figure is staggering and its implications are not easily grasped—500 new chemicals to which the bodies of men and animals are required somehow to adapt each year, chemicals totally outside the limits of biologic experience.

Among them are many that are used in man's war against nature. Since the mid-1940s over 200 basic chemicals have been created for use in killing insects, weeds, rodents, and other organisms described in the modern vernacular as "pests"; and they are sold under several thousand different brand names.

These sprays, dusts, and aerosols are now applied almost universally to farms, gardens, forests, and homes—nonselective chemicals that have the power to kill every insect, the "good" and the "bad," to still the song of birds and the leaping of fish in the streams, to coat the leaves with a deadly film, and to linger on in soil—all this though the intended target may be only a few weeds or insects. Can anyone believe it is possible to lay down such a barrage of poisons on the surface of the earth without making it unfit for all life? They should not be called "insecticides," but "biocides."

The whole process of spraying seems caught up in an endless spiral. Since DDT was released for civilian use, a process of escalation has been going on in which ever more toxic materials must be found. This has happened because insects, in a triumphant vindication of Darwin's principle of the survival of the fittest, have evolved super races immune to the particular insecticide used, hence a deadlier one has always to be developed—and then a deadlier one than that. It has happened also because, for reasons to be described later, destructive insects often undergo a "flareback," or resurgence, after spraying, in numbers greater than before. Thus the chemical war is never won, and all life is caught in its violent crossfire.

Along with the possibility of the extinction of mankind by nuclear war, the central problem of our age has therefore become the contamination of man's total environment with such substances of incredible potential for harm—substances that accumulate in the tissues of plants and animals and even penetrate the germ cells to shatter or alter the very material of heredity upon which the shape of the future depends. . . . All this is not to say there is no insect problem and no need of control. I am saying, rather, that control must be geared to realities, not to mythical situations, and that the methods employed must be such that they do not destroy us along with the insects. . . .

It is not my contention that chemical insecticides must never be used. I do contend that we have put poisonous and biologically potent chemicals indiscriminately into the hands of persons largely or wholly ignorant of their potentials for harm. We have subjected enormous numbers of people to contact with these poisons, without their consent and often without their knowledge. If the Bill of Rights contains no guarantee that a citizen shall be secure against lethal poisons distributed either by private in-dividuals or by public officials, it is surely only because our forefathers, despite their considerable wisdom and foresight, could conceive of no such problem.

I contend, furthermore, that we have allowed these chemicals to be used with little or no advance investigation of their effect on soil, water, wildlife, and man himself. Future generations are unlikely to condone our lack of prudent concern for the integrity of the natural world that supports all life.

There is still very limited awareness of the nature of the threat. This is an era of specialists, each of whom sees his own problem and is unaware of or intolerant of the larger frame into which it fits. It is also an era dominat-ed by industry, in which the right to make a dollar at whatever cost is seldom challenged. When the public protests, confronted with some obvious evidence of damaging results of pesticide applications, it is fed little tranquilizing pills of half truth. We urgently need an end to these false assurances, to the sugar coating of unpalatable facts. It is the public that is being asked to assume the risks that the insect controllers calculate. The public must decide whether it wishes to continue on the present road, and it can do so only when in full possession of the facts. In the words of Jean Rostand, "The obligation to endure gives us the right to know." . . .

THE BALANCE OF NATURE

From all over the world come reports that make it clear we are in a serious predicament. At the end of a decade or more of intensive chemical control, entomologists were finding that problems they had considered solved a few years earlier had returned to plague them. And new problems had arisen as insects once present only in insignificant numbers had increased to the status of serious pests. By their very nature chemical controls are self-defeating, for they have been devised and applied without taking into account the complex biological systems against which they have been blindly hurled. The chemicals may have been pretested against a few individual species, but not against living communities.

In some quarters nowadays it is fashionable to dismiss the balance of nature as a state of affairs that prevailed in an earlier, simpler world—a state that has now been so thoroughly upset that we might as well forget it. Some find this a convenient assumption, but as a chart for a course of action it is highly dangerous. The balance of nature is not the same today as in Pleistocene times, but it is still there: a complex, precise, and highly integrated system of relationships between living things which cannot safely be ignored any more than the law of gravity can be defied with impunity by a man perched on the edge of a cliff. The balance of nature is not a *status quo*; it is fluid, ever shifting, in a constant state of adjustment. Man, too, is part of this balance. Sometimes the balance is in his favor; sometimes—and all too often through his own activities—it is shifted to his disadvantage.

Two critically important facts have been overlooked in designing the modern insect control programs. The first is that the really effective control of insects is that applied by nature, not by man. Populations are kept in check by something the ecologists call the resistance of the environment, and this has been so since the first life was created. The amount of food available, conditions of weather and climate, the presence of competing or predatory species, all are critically important. "The greatest single factor in preventing insects from overwhelming the rest of the world is the internecine warfare which they carry out among themselves," said the entomologist Robert Metcalf. Yet most of the chemicals now used kill all insects, our friends and enemies alike.

The second neglected fact is the truly explosive power of a species to reproduce once the resistance of the environment has been weakened. The fecundity of many forms of life is almost beyond our power to imagine, though now and then we have suggestive glimpses. I remember from student days the miracle that could be wrought in a jar containing a simple mixture of hay and water merely by adding to it a few drops of material from a mature culture of protozoa. Within a few days the jar would contain a whole galaxy of whirling, darting life—uncountable trillions of the slipper animalcule, *Paramecium*, each small as a dust grain, all multiplying without restraint in their temporary Eden of favorable temperatures, abundant food, absence of enemies. Or I think of shore rocks white with barnacles as far as the eye can see, or of the spectacle of passing through an immense school of jellyfish, mile after mile, with seemingly no end to the pulsing, ghostly forms scarcely more substantial than the water itself.

We see the miracle of nature's control at work when the cod move through winter seas to their spawning grounds, where each female deposits several millions of eggs. The sea does not become a solid mass of cod as it would surely do if all the progeny of all the cod were to survive. The checks that exist in nature are such that out of the millions of young produced by each pair only enough, on the average, survive to adulthood to replace the parent fish. . . .

No one knows how many species of insects inhabit the earth because so many are yet to be identified. But more than 700,000 have already been described. This means that in terms of the number of species, 70 to 80 per cent of the earth's creatures are insects. The vast majority of these insects are held in check by natural forces, without any intervention by man. If this were not so, it is doubtful that any conceivable volume of chemicals— or any other methods—could possibly keep down their populations.

The trouble is that we are seldom aware of the protection afforded by natural enemies until it fails. Most of us walk unseeing through the world, unaware alike of its beauties, its wonders, and the strange and sometimes terrible intensity of the lives that are being lived about us. So it is that the activities of the insect predators and parasites are known to few. Perhaps we may have noticed an oddly shaped insect of ferocious mien on a bush in the garden and been dimly aware that the praying mantis lives at the expense of other insects. But we see with understanding eye only if we have walked in the garden at night and here and there with a flashlight have glimpsed the mantis stealthily creeping upon her prey. Then we sense something of the drama of the hunter and the hunted. Then we begin to feel something of that relentlessly pressing force by which nature controls her own. . . .

Everywhere, in field and hedgerow and garden and forest, the insect predators and parasites are at work. Here, above a pond, the dragonflies dart and the sun strikes fire from their wings. So their ancestors sped through swamps where huge reptiles lived. Now, as in those ancient times, the sharp-eyed dragonflies capture mosquitoes in the air, scooping them in with basket-shaped legs. In the waters below, their young, the dragonfly nymphs, or naiads, prey on the aquatic stages of mosquitoes and other insects.

Or there, almost invisible against a leaf, is the lacewing, with green gauze wings and golden eyes, shy and secretive, descendant of an ancient race that lived in Permian times. The adult lacewing feeds mostly on plant nectars and the honeydew of aphids, and in time she lays her eggs, each on the end of a long stalk which she fastens to a leaf. From these emerge her children—strange, bristled larvae called aphis lions, which live by preying on aphids, scales, or mites, which they capture and suck dry of fluid. Each may consume several hundred aphids before the ceaseless turning of the cycle of its life brings the time when it will spin a white silken cocoon in which to pass the pupal stage.

And there are many wasps, and flies as well, whose very existence depends on the destruction of the eggs or larvae of other insects through parasitism. Some of the egg parasites are exceedingly minute wasps, yet by their numbers and their great activity they hold down the abundance of many crop-destroying species.

All these small creatures are working—working in sun and rain, during the hours of darkness, even when winter's grip has damped down the fires of life to mere embers. Then this vital force is merely smoldering, awaiting the time to flare again into activity when spring awakens the insect world. Meanwhile, under the white blanket of snow, below the frost-hardened soil, in crevices in the bark of trees, and in sheltered caves, the parasites and the predators have found ways to tide themselves over the season of cold.

The eggs of the mantis are secure in little cases of thin parchment attached to the branch of a shrub by the mother who lived her life span with the summer that is gone.

The female *Polistes* wasp, taking shelter in a forgotten corner of some attic, carries in her body the fertilized eggs, the heritage on which the whole future of her colony depends. She, the lone survivor, will start a small paper nest in the spring, lay a few eggs in its cells, and carefully rear a small force of workers. With their help she will then enlarge the nest and develop the colony. Then the workers, foraging ceaselessly through the hot days of summer, will destroy countless caterpillars.

Thus, through the circumstances of their lives, and the nature of our own wants, all these have been our allies in keeping the balance of nature tilted in our favor. Yet we have turned our artillery against our friends. The terrible danger is that we have grossly underestimated their value in keeping at bay a dark tide of enemies that, without their help, can overrun us.

Chemicals and Pests

I. L. BALDWIN

Human society, since the time of recorded history, has encountered many difficulties in adapting itself to changes brought on by the advancement of technology. Although we usually think of the Industrial Revolution as the

I. L. Baldwin, "Chemicals and Pests," *Science,* 137 (September 28, 1962), pp. 1042–43. Copyright © 1962 by the American Association for the Advancement of Science.

starting point of modern technology, the invention of the wheel must have brought about one of the greatest changes in human society the world has seen. In recent years there has been a rapid expansion of scientific endeavors and a consequent rapid increase in the rate of accumulation of knowledge. Technology has quickly translated this new knowledge into materials and procedures for use by society.

The discovery of methods of harnessing nuclear energy, some two decades ago, has so captured public attention that few have given serious attention to the chemical revolution which has occurred during the same period. It is the chemical revolution, however, that has most intimately affected every aspect of our daily life. The development of new fibers, new plastics, new medicinals, and new agricultural chemicals has produced profound changes in our lives. Public health has been improved; the span of life has been greatly extended; our clothes are composed of fibers unknown 20 years ago; our machinery and household utensils are made of new and strange materials; and our rate of productivity in agriculture has been greatly expanded.

Benefits, however, have not been achieved without cost. Many of the new materials have been used without adequate testing, or they have been used under improper conditions. Sometimes lives have been lost or health has been destroyed. At other times our economy has suffered when shoddy materials have been used in clothing, equipment, and structures. Often men have lost their means of livelihood. Rachel Carson's *Silent Spring* (Houghton Mifflin, Boston, 1962. 368 pp., $5) dramatizes in an effective fashion the losses that society has suffered from the use of new pesticides. Her emphasis is upon the danger to human health and the possible irreparable damage to various forms of wildlife.

Silent Spring is superbly written and beautifully illustrated with line drawings. The author has made an exhaustive study of the facts bearing on the problem. It is not, however, a judicial review or a balancing of the gains and losses; rather, it is the prosecuting attorney's impassioned plea for action against the use of these new materials which have received such widespread acceptance, acceptance accorded because of the obvious benefits that their use has conferred. The author has reviewed many of the instances in which unfortunate accidents have occurred. In some cases the accidents were the result of carelessness; in others they were caused by widespread use of materials prior to adequate small-scale testing; in some instances the unfortunate effect on wildlife was a result of the failure of those who used the new pesticide to consider wildlife values.

The author's mode of approach to the use of pesticides will undoubtedly result in wider recognition of the fact that these chemicals are poisons and in a more careful and rigorous control of every step in the pathway that pesticide must travel, from the research laboratory, through the process of obtaining government approval, to use in the field. Perhaps the tremendous improvements in public health and welfare that have resulted from the use of these materials have caused us to become careless in our control and use of them. There are serious hazards involved in the use of pesticides. It has frequently been said: "There are no harmless chemicals, only harmless use of chemicals." The recent case in which the death of several infants in a hospital was caused by the inadvertent use of salt instead of sugar in their food comes to mind.

A MATTER OF PERSPECTIVE

The possible indirect harmful effects of pesticides on humans and wildlife are stressed in *Silent Spring*. It is noted that certain of the pesticides may serve as carcinogens and that some may serve as mutagens. How often all the necessary conditions are met, so that the pesticides do actually serve as carcinogens or mutagens, is unknown. The author feels that such dangers are very great. Most scientists who are familiar with the field, including government workers charged with the responsibility of safeguarding the public health, feel that the danger of damage is slight. The author gives no figures for deaths known to be due to pesticides, but her description of certain cases may leave the impression with the uninformed reader that such cases of death due to the direct effects of pesticides are numerous. Actually human deaths in the United States known to be caused by pesticides are less than 100 annually. To place this in proper perspective, consider that almost twice that many deaths are known to be caused by aspirin and that almost one-half as many deaths are known to be caused by bee stings. Another example, in which the author's choice of language may lead to false impressions, is her reference to the "fall of chemical death rain." Many may be led to believe that, just as rain falls on all of our land, so is all of our land sprayed with pesticides. Actually less than 5 percent of all the area of the United States is annually treated with insecticides.

I can understand that the author felt it necessary to portray as "bad guys" all those who recommend the use of pesticides and as "good guys" all those who oppose the use of such insecticides. I cannot condone, however, the sarcastic and unjustified attack on the ethics and integrity of many scientific workers. The following quotation is only one of such attacks.

> The major chemical companies are pouring money into the universities to support research on insecticides. This creates attractive fellowships for graduate students and attractive staff positions. Biological-control studies, on the other hand, are never so endowed—for the simple reason that they do not promise anyone the fortunes that are to be made in the chemical industry. These are left to state and federal agencies, where the salaries paid are far less.
>
> This situation also explains the otherwise mystifying fact that certain outstanding entomologists are among the leading advocates of chemical control. Inquiry into the background of some of these men reveals that

their entire research program is supported by the chemical industry. Their professional prestige, sometimes their very jobs depend on the perpetuation of chemical methods. Can we then expect them to bite the hand that literally feeds them? But knowing their bias, how much credence can we give to their protests that insecticides are harmless?

The author pleads for a return to the balance of nature as the method of controlling our pests. Greater use of biological control of pests would be desirable, but, if it is to be effective enough to meet human needs, it must result in upsetting the balance of nature. Mankind has been engaged in the process of upsetting the balance of nature since the dawn of civilization. Certain species of plant and animal life that serve the economic or esthetic needs of mankind have been nurtured with great care; other species that have interfered with the health, comfort, or welfare of mankind have been attacked with great vigor; the large majority of the species have been ignored by all but a small portion of the population. Fortunately there is a growing concern, coupled with positive action, for the preservation of all forms of plant and animal life. This effort to preserve our wildlife is too late to save some species and too little to save others, but an encouraging start is being made. Undoubtedly mankind's own self-interests have suffered in the past and are still suffering because of his callous disregard of the damage he does to other species of plant and animal life. But it is equally certain that modern agriculture and modern public health, indeed, modern civilization, could not exist without an unrelenting war against a return of a true balance of nature.

VALUABLE BUT DANGEROUS

Just as it is important for us to be reminded of the dangers inherent in the use of the new pesticides, so must our people also be made aware of the tremendous values to human welfare conferred by the new pesticides. No attempt is made by the author to portray the many positive benefits that society derives from the use of pesticides. No estimates are made of the countless lives that have been saved because of the destruction of insect vectors of disease. No mention is made of the fact that the average length of human life has steadily increased over the last several years. No consideration is given to the important role played by modern pesticides in the production of food and fiber. The author does suggest that, with a surplus of food in the United States, we might well curtail the use of pesticides. Although the United States has a surplus of food, over one half of the people of the world go to bed hungry each night. The greater use of pesticides in most sections of the world would increase food production, alleviate hunger, and improve the health of the people.

Modern agriculture, with its high-quality foods and fibers, could not exist without the use of pesticides. Weeds, disease, and insect pests would take an extremely heavy toll if these chemicals were not used. The yields per acre, the yields per man hour, and the quality of the product would all suffer materially if these chemicals were withdrawn from use. One cannot do more than guess about the changes that would be necessary in American society if pesticides were banned. An immediate back-to-the-farm movement would be necessary, and this would involve many millions of people. It is hoped that someone with Rachel Carson's ability will write a companion volume dramatizing the improvements in human health and welfare derived from the use of pesticides. Such a story would be far more dramatic than the one told by Miss Carson in *Silent Spring*, which deals with the losses society has sustained or may suffer in the future because of the use of these materials.

The problem which Rachel Carson so effectively dramatizes is not a new one. It has long been recognized by workers in government and industrial laboratories and by chemists and biologists wherever they may work. Several years ago the National Academy of Sciences established a committee of outstanding scientists to study the problem of food protection and the influence of pesticides and other chemicals on human health and welfare. Some three years ago a companion committee was established to deal with pesticides and wildlife relationships. These committees and their subcommittees have members from all of the scientific disciplines that might be able to contribute to the problem, including physicians, wildlife specialists, toxicologists, entomologists, agriculturists, biologists, chemists, and economists. Both the Food Protection Committee and the Pesticides and Wildlife Relationships Committee have made a careful and judicial review of all the evidence available, and they have published a series of reports making appropriate recommendations. These reports are not dramatically written, and they were not intended to be best sellers. They are, however, the result of careful study by a wide group of scientists, and they represent balanced judgments in areas in which emotional appeals tend to over-balance sound judgment based on facts.

I suggest that those who read *Silent Spring* include as companion reading the following publications of the National Academy of Sciences (Washington, D.C.). Publications 920-A and 920-B: *Pest Control and Wildlife Relationships*, part 1, *Evaluation of Pesticide-Wildlife Problems;* part 2, *Policy and Procedures for Pest Control* (1962. $1.25 each); Publication 887: *Use of Chemicals in Food Production, Processing, Storage, and Distribution* (1961. $0.50); Publication 470: *Safe Use of Pesticides in Food Production* (1956. $0.50).

The story of *Silent Spring*, so well told by Rachel Carson, even though it presents only one side of a very complex problem, will serve a useful purpose, if research on better methods of pest control is stimulated and if all concerned with the production, control, and use of pesticides are stimulated to exercise greater care in the protection of the public welfare. In the meantime it is my hope that some equally gifted writer will be willing to do the necessary research and to write the even more dramatic story of the values conferred on mankind by the chemical revolution of the last two decades.

Pesticides: The Price for Progress

FROM *TIME*

"There was once a town in the heart of America where all life seemed to be in harmony with its surroundings." It had fertile farms, prosperous farmers, birds in the trees, fish in the streams, and flowers blooming gaily along the roadsides. Then a white powder fell from the sky like snow, and a fearful blight crept over the land. Cattle and sheep sickened; hens could not hatch their eggs. Strange illnesses appeared among the people; children were stricken at play and died within a few hours. The birds sang no more, the fish in the streams died, and the roadsides were lined with browned vegetation as if swept by fire.

Such is the picture drawn of the future in *Silent Spring*, a new book by Rachel Carson, whose *The Sea Around Us* earned her a reputation not only as a competent marine biologist but as a graceful writer. Miss Carson's deadly white powder is not radioactive fallout, as many readers will at first assume. The villains in *Silent Spring* are chemical pesticides, against which Miss Carson has taken up her pen in alarm and anger, putting literary skill second to the task of frightening and arousing her readers. Published this week, the book has already raised a swirl of controversy about the danger to man and wildlife of those modern chemical compounds that have vastly increased agricultural production, banished some diseases, and kept at bay the most bothersome and harmful of insects and rodents.

As Miss Carson sees it, the accomplishments are not worth the price. She explains that no single town has suffered all the misfortunes from spraying and dusting that she describes; "yet every one of these disasters has actually happened somewhere, and many real communities have already suffered a substantial number of them. A grim specter has crept upon us, and this imagined tragedy may easily become a stark reality."

"Pesticides: The Price for Progress," *Time*, September 28, 1962, pp. 45–48. Copyright © 1962 Time Inc. Reprinted by permission.

AS BAD AS THE BORGIAS

The bulk of Miss Carson's book is support for this nightmare curtain raiser. In a chapter titled "Elixirs of Death," she lists the synthetic insecticides, beginning with DDT, that came into use at the end of World War II. All of them are dangerous, she says without reservation. Already they are everywhere: in soil, rivers, ground water, even in the bodies of living animals and humans. "They occur in mother's milk," she says, using emotion-fanning words, "and probably in the tissues of the unborn child." And worse is to come. "This birth-to-death contact," she warns, "contributes to the progressive buildup of chemicals in our bodies and so to cumulative poisoning. We are in little better position than the guests of the Borgias."

There is no doubt about the impact of *Silent Spring;* it is a real shocker. Many unwary readers will be firmly convinced that most of the U.S.—with its animals, plants, soil, water and people—is already laced with poison that will soon start taking a dreadful toll, and that the only hope is to stop using chemical pesticides and let the age-old "balance of nature" take care of obnoxious insects.

Scientists, physicians, and other technically informed people will also be shocked by *Silent Spring*—but for a different reason. They recognize Miss Carson's skill in building her frightening case; but they consider that case unfair, one-sided, and hysterically overemphatic. Many of the scary generalizations—and there are lots of them—are patently unsound. "It is not possible," says Miss Carson, "to add pesticides to water anywhere without threatening the purity of water everywhere." It takes only a moment of reflection to show that this is nonsense. Again she says: "Each insecticide is used for the simple reason that it is a deadly poison. It therefore poisons all life with which it comes in contact." Any housewife who has sprayed flies with a bug bomb and managed to survive without poisoning should spot at least part of the error in that statement.

But Author Carson's oversimplifications and downright errors only serve to highlight a question that has bothered many Americans: Just how dangerous are insecticides? Experts of the Department of Agriculture and the U.S. Public Health Service readily admit that some of them are extremely poisonous to humans as well as to insects and other pests. Parathion, an organic phosphate used against mites and other highly resistant insects, is so deadly that men who spray it must wear respirators and protective clothing.

A few related chemicals are almost as dangerous, but luckily they break down quickly into harmless substances and so leave no poisonous residue on fruits and vegetables or in the soil. Their disadvantage is that they can poison farm workers who handle them carelessly. Miss Carson describes these very rare accidents and gets shock effect out of them, but they are comparable to accidents caused by careless handling of such violent industrial chemicals as sulfuric acid. The highly toxic phosphates are no menace to the general public, which seldom comes in contact with them.

DDT IN EVERY MEAL

The chlorinated hydrocarbons, on the other hand (including the familiar DDT), are used in enormous quantities by almost everyone. Much of Miss Carson's case against spraying depends on her contention that DDT and its near chemical relatives are poisonous to humans, especially since they tend to accumulate in fatty tissues. Experts do not agree. A mere trace of DDT kills insects, but humans and other mammals can absorb large doses without damage. Dr. Wayland J. Hayes, chief of the toxicology section of the U.S. Public Health Service in Atlanta, says that every meal served in the U.S. probably contains a trace of DDT, but that this is nothing to worry about. He and his co-workers fed 200 times the normal amount to 51 convict volunteers. The insecticide accumulated in their bodies for about one year and then was excreted as fast as it arrived. The human guinea pigs felt no ill effects, and doctors pronounced them as healthy as a control group that got the same diet without extra DDT.

EXAGGERATED IMPORTANCE

While many insecticides are roughly as harmless as DDT, others are considerably more poisonous to humans. But in the opinion of respected experts of the U.S. Public Health Service, none have done appreciable damage to the U.S public or are likely to do so. In heavily sprayed cotton-growing areas of the Mississippi Delta, says Assistant Surgeon General Dr. D. E. Price, health is as good as in sparingly sprayed neighboring areas. The same report comes from California, where insecticides are heavily sprayed on orchards and fields. Says Robert Z. Rollins, chief of the division of chemistry of the California department of agriculture: "Pesticides used properly present no threat to people, no matter how widespread their use becomes."

Humans generally protect their domestic animals from any ill effects; wildlife does not fare as well. Wild animals, birds, fish, and friendly insects are among the valued inhabitants of the U.S., and a good part of Miss Carson's book tells about the deadly effect of wholesale spraying on these pleasant and harmless creatures. In vivid language, she tells how DDT spraying to protect elm trees from Dutch elm disease nearly wiped out the bird populations of many Midwestern cities, how fruitless attempts to exterminate the imported fire ant of the South by airplane dusting with dieldrin had dire effects on many kinds of wildlife.

Even scientist defenders of pesticides admit that these things have happened, but they maintain that their importance is exaggerated. According to the Entomological Society of America, only 0.28% of the 640 million acres of U.S. forest land is treated annually, and 613 million acres have never been treated. Insecticides are used mostly on crop lands, which have little wildlife, and on human residential areas to protect shade trees—the use that causes the most conspicuous damage to wildlife.

One result is the wholesale death of robins, which form a large part of suburban bird populations. The robins live on earthworms (that is why they are plentiful in the suburbs, where worm-bearing lawns abound), which concentrate insecticides without being damaged themselves. When the robins eat these insecticide-full worms, they die. The slaughter may continue for several years, until the DDT in the soil has disintegrated.

ELMS VERSUS ROBINS

Death chains of this sort are fortunately not common. A report published by the Wilson Ornithological Society says that most spraying does little damage to most birds, and still less to wild mammals. Fish are more sensitive; when certain insecticides are washed into streams or lakes, they are apt to kill everything that moves on fins. Perhaps the worst effect on birds is the reduction of edible insects, which are important food for many species. But the damage is not complete; not even Miss Carson can point to a single sizable sprayed area where "no birds sing."

To answer insistent complaints, the National Academy of Sciences sponsored a careful study of pesticide damage to wildlife. Its conclusion: the damage, though always regrettable, is not disastrous, and the damaged wildlife population generally recovers in a few years. Sometimes it may be necessary, remarks the Academy, to choose between elms and robins, both of which have their partisans.

INSECT PARADISE

Lovers of wildlife often rhapsodize about the "balance of nature that keeps all living creatures in harmony," but scientists realistically point out that the balance was upset thousands of years ago when man's invention of weapons made him the king of beasts. The balance has never recovered its equilibrium; man is the dominant species on his planet, and as his fields, pastures and cities spread across the land, lesser species are extirpated, pushed into refuge areas, or domesticated.

Some species, most of them insects, benefit increasingly from man's activities. Their attacks on his toothsome crops are as old as recorded history—the Bible often refers to plagues of locusts, canker-worms, lice and flies—but their damage was only sporadically serious when population was small and scattered. Modern, large-scale agriculture offers a paradise for plant-eating insects. Crops are grown year after year in the same or nearby fields, helping insect populations to build up. Many of the worst pests are insect invaders from foreign countries that have left their natural enemies behind and so are as free as man himself from the check of nature's balance.

Agricultural scientists try hard to find ways to check insect pests by tricks of cultivation. They import the ancient enemies of invading foreign insects and foster the resident enemies of native pests. They are developing bacterial diseases to spread pestilence among insect populations. Because these tactics alone are seldom enough to protect the tender plants of modern, high-yield farms, the use of insecticides is economically necessary. Tests run by the Department of Agriculture show that failure to use pesticides would cost a major part of many crops; a 20-year study proved that cotton yields would be cut by 40%. Production of many kinds of fruit and vegetables would be impossible; unsprayed apple trees, for instance, no longer yield fruit that is sound enough to be marketed.[1] Potato fields swept by the Colorado beetle or late blight (the fungus that caused the great Irish potato famine of 1846) yield hardly any crop.

A QUANDARY OF SURPLUSES

Chemical insecticides are now a necessary part of modern U.S. agriculture, whose near-miraculous efficiency has turned the ancient tragedy of recurrent famine into the biologically happy problem of what to do with food surpluses. Says entomologist George C. Decker of the Illinois Agricultural Experiment Station: "If we in North America were to adopt a policy of 'Let nature take its course,' as some individuals thoughtlessly advocate, it is possible that these would-be experts would find disposing of the 200 million surplus human beings even more perplexing than the disposition of America's current corn, cotton and wheat surpluses."

Many scientists sympathize with Miss Carson's love of wildlife, and even with her mystical attachment to the balance of nature. But they fear that her emotional and inaccurate outburst in *Silent Spring* may do harm by alarming the nontechnical public, while doing no good for the things that she loves.

SUGGESTIONS FOR FURTHER READING

Paul Brooks, *The House of Life: Rachel Carson at Work* (Boston: Houghton, Mifflin, 1972); Frank Graham, Jr., *Since Silent Spring* (Boston: Houghton, Mifflin, 1970); for a hostile response to Carson's impassioned plea, see John Maddox, *The Doomsday Syndrome* (New York: McGraw Hill, 1972); for context, see Victor B. Scheffer, *The Shaping of Environmentalism in America* (Seattle, Wash.: University of Washington Press, 1991).

---

[1]In the smaller orchards of prespraying days, fruit had a better chance to escape heavy insect damage, and since quality standards were lower, moderately damaged fruit often went to market.

XVII

༺⚭༻

BLACKS IN AMERICA: INTEGRATION OR SEPARATISM? NONVIOLENCE OR MILITANCE?

There is a tendency to look back to the civil rights movement of the 1960s as a singular struggle in which all African Americans were in agreement on matters of strategy, never mind such ultimate objectives as racial integration or separatism. Here is a revealing extract from the autobiography of popular musician and entertainer Nina Simone, who came of age as an activist in the early 1960s.

> It was a great debate that was going on all around me, and after listening to various opinions I realized the first thing I had to sort out personally was whether I believed in integration or separatism. I loved Dr. King for his goodness and compassion and—like everyone else—marvelled at his speech during the March on Washington. But those words, in August 1963, came just eighteen days before the four young girls were blown to pieces in their church in Birmingham. Much as I liked the idea of the world being as one and wanted it to be true, the more I looked around, the more I learned, and the less I thought it would ever happen. It was the black Moslems, led by Malcolm X, whose talk of self-reliance and self-defense seemed to echo the distrust of white America that I was feeling.[1]

Martin Luther King, Jr. (1929–68), the son of a Baptist minister, was born in Atlanta and earned advanced degrees in theology from Crozer Seminary and Boston University. In 1954 he became pastor of a Baptist church in Montgomery, Alabama. During 1955–56 he led an important economic boycott to protest racial segregation. In 1957 the Southern Christian Leadership Conference was formed to coordinate civil rights efforts, and King was chosen president. In 1963 he organized a major campaign against segregation in Birmingham, Alabama, where he encoun-

---

[1]*The Autobiography of Nina Simone: I Put a Spell on You* (New York: Pantheon, 1991), pp. 98–99.

tered strong resistance from police as well as white and black moderates. Arrested and placed in jail for eight days, King wrote a public letter to white moderates in which he defended nonviolent protest and civil disobedience. In 1964 he became the youngest recipient of the Nobel Peace Prize. Four years later he was assassinated in Memphis, Tennessee, by a white man.

Malcolm X (1925–65), born Malcolm Little, was also the son of a Baptist minister. As a hustler he profited from drugs, prostitution, and robbery. When he got out of prison in 1952, he joined the Nation of Islam and helped to establish Black Muslim temples in major American cities. After his split with leader Elijah Muhammad late in 1963, Malcolm formed his own militant organization and urged blacks to arm themselves. In 1964 his public criticism of the Nation of Islam deepened, and in February 1965 he was assassinated, presumably by followers of Elijah Muhammad.

Malcolm attacked racial integration and intermarriage. He ridiculed leaders of the mainstream civil rights movement and Martin Luther King in particular. King's "letter" and other statements expressed concern about "two opposing forces in the Negro community," and worried particularly about the force committed to "bitterness and hatred" that "comes perilously close to advocating violence."

A serious debate continues over the effectiveness of Gandhian nonviolence and the value of integration in a society that is not yet purged of racism. In each of the two selections presented here it is clear that King and Malcolm X listened to one another with wary attentiveness and concern. Each one represented an understandable position in the struggle for social justice.

Letter from Birmingham Jail

MARTIN LUTHER KING, JR.

April 16, 1963

My Dear Fellow Clergymen:

While confined here in the Birmingham city jail, I came across your recent statement calling my present activities "unwise and untimely." Seldom do I pause to answer criticism of my work and ideas. If I sought to answer all the criticisms that cross my desk, my secretaries would have little time for anything other than such correspondence in the course of the day, and I would have no time for constructive work. But since I feel that you are men of genuine good will and that your criticisms are sincerely set forth, I want to try to answer your statement in what I hope will be patient and reasonable terms.

I think I should indicate why I am here in Birmingham, since you have been influenced by the view which argues against "outsiders coming in." I have the honor of serving as president of the Southern Christian Leadership Conference, an organization operating in every southern state, with headquarters in Atlanta, Georgia. We have some eighty-five affiliated organizations across the South, and one of them is the Alabama Christian Movement for Human Rights. Frequently we share staff, educational and financial resources with our affiliates. Several months ago the affiliate here in Birmingham asked us to be on call to engage in a nonviolent direct-action program if such were deemed necessary. We readily consented, and when the hour came we lived up to our promise. So I, along with several members of my staff, am here because I was invited here. I am here because I have organizational ties here.

But more basically, I am in Birmingham because injustice is here. Just as the prophets of the eighth century B.C. left their villages and carried their "thus saith the Lord" far beyond the boundaries of their home towns, and just as the Apostle Paul left his village of Tarsus and carried the gospel of Jesus Christ to the far corners of the Greco-Roman world, so am I compelled to carry the gospel of freedom beyond my own home town. Like Paul, I must constantly respond to the Macedonian call for aid.

Moreover, I am cognizant of the interrelatedness of all communities and states. I cannot sit idly by in Atlanta and not be concerned about what happens in Birmingham. Injustice anywhere is a threat to justice everywhere. We are caught in an inescapable network of mutuality, tied in a single garment of destiny. Whatever affects one directly, affects all in-

Martin Luther King, Jr., "Letter from Birmingham Jail," in *Why We Can't Wait* (New York: Harper & Row, 1964), pp. 77–100. Copyright © 1963, 1964 by Martin Luther King, Jr. Reprinted by permission of HarperCollins Publishers.

directly. Never again can we afford to live with the narrow, provincial "outside agitator" idea. Anyone who lives inside the United States can never be considered an outsider anywhere within its bounds.

You deplore the demonstrations taking place in Birmingham. But your statement, I am sorry to say, fails to express a similar concern for the conditions that brought about the demonstrations. I am sure that none of you would want to rest content with the superficial kind of social analysis that deals merely with effects and does not grapple with underlying causes. It is unfortunate that demonstrations are taking place in Birmingham, but it is even more unfortunate that the city's white power structure left the Negro community with no alternative.

In any nonviolent campaign there are four basic steps: collection of the facts to determine whether injustices exist; negotiation; self-purification; and direct action. We have gone through all these steps in Birmingham. There can be no gainsaying the fact that racial injustice engulfs this community. Birmingham is probably the most thoroughly segregated city in the United States. Its ugly record of brutality is widely known. Negroes have experienced grossly unjust treatment in the courts. There have been more unsolved bombings of Negro homes and churches in Birmingham than in any other city in the nation. These are the hard, brutal facts of the case. On the basis of these conditions, Negro leaders sought to negotiate with the city fathers. But the latter consistently refused to engage in good-faith negotiation.

Then, last September, came the opportunity to talk with leaders of Birmingham's economic community. In the course of the negotiations, certain promises were made by the merchants—for example, to remove the stores' humiliating racial signs. On the basis of these promises, the Reverend Fred Shuttlesworth and the leaders of the Alabama Christian Movement for Human Rights agreed to a moratorium on all demonstrations. As the weeks and months went by, we realized that we were the victims of a broken promise. A few signs, briefly removed, returned; the others remained.

As in so many past experiences, our hopes had been blasted, and the shadow of deep disappointment settled upon us. We had no alternative except to prepare for direct action, whereby we would present our very bodies as a means of laying our case before the conscience of the local and the national community. Mindful of the difficulties involved, we decided to undertake a process of self-purification. We began a series of workshops on nonviolence, and we repeatedly asked ourselves: "Are you able to accept blows without retaliating?" "Are you able to endure the ordeal of jail?" We decided to schedule our direct-action program for the Easter season, realizing that except for Christmas, this is the main shopping period of the year. Knowing that a strong economic-withdrawal program would be the by-product of direct action, we felt that this would be the best time to bring pressure to bear on the merchants for the needed change.

Then it occurred to us that Birmingham's mayoral election was coming up in March, and we speedily decided to postpone action until after election day. When we discovered that the Commissioner of Public Safety, Eugene "Bull" Connor, had piled up enough votes to be in the run-off, we decided again to postpone action until the day after the run-off so that the demonstrations could not be used to cloud the issues. Like many others, we waited to see Mr. Connor defeated, and to this end we endured postponement after postponement. Having aided in this community need, we felt that our direct-action program could be delayed no longer.

You may well ask: "Why direct action? Why sit-ins, marches and so forth? Isn't negotiation a better path?" You are quite right in calling for negotiation. Indeed, this is the very purpose of direct action. Nonviolent direct action seeks to create such a crisis and foster such a tension that a community which has constantly refused to negotiate is forced to confront the issue. It seeks so to dramatize the issue that it can no longer be ignored. My citing the creation of tension as part of the work of the nonviolent-resister may sound rather shocking. But I must confess that I am not afraid of the word "tension." I have earnestly opposed violent tension, but there is a type of constructive, nonviolent tension which is necessary for growth. Just as Socrates felt that it was necessary to create a tension in the mind so that individuals could rise from the bondage of myths and half-truths to the unfettered realm of creative analysis and objective appraisal, so must we see the need for nonviolent gadflies to create the kind of tension in society that will help men rise from the dark depths of prejudice and racism to the majestic heights of understanding and brotherhood. . . .

. . . My friends, I must say to you that we have not made a single gain in civil rights without determined legal and nonviolent pressure. Lamentably, it is an historical fact that privileged groups seldom give up their privileges voluntarily. Individuals may see the moral light and voluntarily give up their unjust posture; but, as Reinhold Niebuhr has reminded us, groups tend to be more immoral than individuals.

We know through painful experience that freedom is never voluntarily given by the oppressor; it must be demanded by the oppressed. Frankly, I have yet to engage in a direct-action campaign that was "well timed" in the view of those who have not suffered unduly from the disease of segregation. For years now I have heard the word "Wait!" It rings in the ear of every Negro with piercing familiarity. This "Wait" has almost always meant "Never." We must come to see, with one of our distinguished jurists, that "justice too long delayed is justice denied."

We have waited for more than 340 years for our constitutional and God-given rights. The nations of Asia and Africa are moving with jetlike speed toward gaining political independence, but we still creep at horse-and-buggy pace toward gaining a cup of coffee at a lunch counter. Perhaps it is easy for those who have never felt the stinging darts of segregation to say, "Wait." But when you have seen vicious mobs lynch your mothers and fathers at will and drown your sisters and brothers at whim; when you have seen hate-filled policemen curse, kick and even kill your black brothers and sisters; when you see the vast majority of your twenty million Negro brothers smothering in an airtight cage of poverty in the midst of an affluent society; when you suddenly find your tongue twisted and your speech stammering as you seek to explain to your six-year-old daughter why she can't go to the public amusement park that has just been advertised on television, and see tears welling up in her eyes when she is told that Funtown is closed to colored children, and see ominous clouds of inferiority beginning to form in her little mental sky, and see her beginning to distort her personality by developing an unconscious bitterness toward white people; when you have to concoct an answer for a five-year-old son who is asking: "Daddy, why do white people treat colored people so mean?"; when you take a cross-country drive and find it necessary to sleep night after night in the uncomfortable corners of your automobile because no motel will accept you; when you are humiliated day in and day out by nagging signs reading "white" and "colored"; when your first name becomes "nigger," your middle name becomes "boy" (however old you are) and your last name becomes "John," and your wife and mother are never given the respected title "Mrs."; when you are harried by day and haunted by night by the fact that you are a Negro, living constantly at tiptoe stance, never quite knowing what to expect next, and are plagued with inner fears and outer resentments; when you are forever fighting a degenerating sense of "nobodiness"—then you will understand why we find it difficult to wait. There comes a time when the cup of endurance runs over, and men are no longer willing to be plunged into the abyss of despair. I hope, sirs, you can understand our legitimate and unavoidable impatience.

You express a great deal of anxiety over our willingness to break laws. This is certainly a legitimate concern. Since we so diligently urge people to obey the Supreme Court's decision of 1954 outlawing segregation in the public schools, at first glance it may seem rather paradoxical for us consciously to break laws. One may well ask: "How can you advocate breaking some laws and obeying others?" The answer lies in the fact that there are two types of laws: just and unjust. I would be the first to advocate obeying just laws. One has not only a legal but a moral responsibility to obey just laws. Conversely, one has a moral responsibility to disobey unjust laws. I would agree with St. Augustine that "an unjust law is no law at all."

Now, what is the difference between the two? How does one determine whether a law is just or unjust? A just law is a man-made code that squares with the moral law or the law of God. An unjust law is a code that is out of harmony with the moral law. To put it in the terms of St. Thomas Aquinas: An unjust law is a human law that is not rooted in eternal law and natural law. Any law that uplifts human personality is just. Any law that degrades human personality is unjust. All segregation statutes are unjust because segregation distorts the soul and damages the personality.

It gives the segregator a false sense of superiority and the segregated a false sense of inferiority. . . .

Let me give another explanation. A law is unjust if it is inflicted on a minority that, as a result of being denied the right to vote, had no part in enacting or devising the law. Who can say that the legislature of Alabama which set up that state's segregation laws was democratically elected? Throughout Alabama all sorts of devious methods are used to prevent Negroes from becoming registered voters, and there are some counties in which, even though Negroes constitute a majority of the population, not a single Negro is registered. Can any law enacted under such circumstances be considered democratically structured?

Sometimes a law is just on its face and unjust in its application. For instance, I have been arrested on a charge of parading without a permit. Now, there is nothing wrong in having an ordinance which requires a permit for a parade. But such an ordinance becomes unjust when it is used to maintain segregation and to deny citizens the First-Amendment privilege of peaceful assembly and protest.

I hope you are able to see the distinction I am trying to point out. In no sense do I advocate evading or defying the law, as would the rabid segregationist. That would lead to anarchy. One who breaks an unjust law must do so openly, lovingly, and with a willingness to accept the penalty. I submit that an individual who breaks a law that conscience tells him is unjust, and who willingly accepts the penalty of imprisonment in order to arouse the conscience of the community over its injustice, is in reality expressing the highest respect for law. . . .

I must make two honest confessions to you, my Christian and Jewish brothers. First, I must confess that over the past few years I have been gravely disappointed with the white moderate. I have almost reached the regrettable conclusion that the Negro's great stumbling block in his stride toward freedom is not the White Citizen's Counciler or the Ku Klux Klanner, but the white moderate, who is more devoted to "order" than to justice; who prefers a negative peace which is the absence of tension to a positive peace which is the presence of justice; who constantly says: "I agree with you in the goal you seek, but I cannot agree with your methods of direct action"; who paternalistically believes he can set the timetable for another man's freedom; who lives by a mythical concept of time and who constantly advises the Negro to wait for a "more convenient season." Shallow understanding from people of good will is more frustrating than absolute misunderstanding from people of ill will. Lukewarm acceptance is much more bewildering than outright rejection.

I had hoped that the white moderate would understand that law and order exist for the purpose of establishing justice and that when they fail in this purpose they become the dangerously structured dams that block the flow of social progress. I had hoped that the white moderate would understand that the present tension in the South is a necessary phase of the transition from an obnoxious negative peace, in which the Negro passively accepted his unjust plight, to a substantive and positive peace, in which all men will respect the dignity and worth of human personality. Actually, we who engage in nonviolent direct action are not the creators of tension. We merely bring to the surface the hidden tension that is already alive. We bring it out in the open, where it can be seen and dealt with. Like a boil that can never be cured so long as it is covered up but must be opened with all its ugliness to the natural medicines of air and light, injustice must be exposed, with all the tension its exposure creates, to the light of human conscience and the air of national opinion before it can be cured. . . .

You speak of our activity in Birmingham as extreme. At first I was rather disappointed that fellow clergymen would see my nonviolent efforts as those of an extremist. I began thinking about the fact that I stand in the middle of two opposing forces in the Negro community. One is a force of complacency, made up in part of Negroes who, as a result of long years of oppression, are so drained of self-respect and a sense of "somebodiness" that they have adjusted to segregation; and in part of a few middle-class Negroes who, because of a degree of academic and economic security and because in some ways they profit by segregation, have become insensitive to the problems of the masses. The other force is one of bitterness and hatred, and it comes perilously close to advocating violence. It is expressed in the various black nationalist groups that are springing up across the nation, the largest and best-known being Elijah Muhammad's Muslim movement. Nourished by the Negro's frustration over the continued existence of racial discrimination, this movement is made up of people who have lost faith in America, who have absolutely repudiated Christianity, and who have concluded that the white man is an incorrigible "devil."

I have tried to stand between these two forces, saying that we need emulate neither the "do-nothingism" of the complacent nor the hatred and despair of the black nationalist. For there is the more excellent way of love and nonviolent protest. I am grateful to God that, through the influence of the Negro church, the way of nonviolence became an integral part of our struggle.

If this philosophy had not emerged, by now many streets of the South would, I am convinced, be flowing with blood. And I am further convinced that if our white brothers dismiss as "rabble-rousers" and "outside agitators" those of us who employ nonviolent direct action, and if they refuse to support our nonviolent efforts, millions of Negroes will, out of frustration and despair, seek solace and security in black-nationalist ideologies—a development that would inevitably lead to a frightening racial nightmare. . . .

I had hoped that the white moderate would see this need. Perhaps I was too optimistic; perhaps I expected too much. I suppose I should have realized that few members of the oppressor race can understand the deep groans and passionate yearnings of the oppressed race, and still fewer have the vision to see that injustice must be rooted out by strong, persistent and determined action. . . .

When I was suddenly catapulted into the leadership of the bus protest in Montgomery, Alabama, a few years ago, I felt we would be supported by the white church. I felt that the white ministers, priests and rabbis of the South would be among our strongest allies. Instead, some have been outright opponents, refusing to understand the freedom movement and misrepresenting its leaders; all too many others have been more cautious than courageous and have remained silent behind the anesthetizing security of stained-glass windows.

In spite of my shattered dreams, I came to Birmingham with the hope that the white religious leadership of this community would see the justice of our cause and, with deep moral concern, would serve as the channel through which our just grievances could reach the power structure. I had hoped that each of you would understand. But again I have been disappointed.

I have heard numerous southern religious leaders admonish their worshipers to comply with a desegregation decision because it is the law, but I have longed to hear white ministers declare: "Follow this decree because integration is morally right and because the Negro is your brother." In the midst of blatant injustices inflicted upon the Negro, I have watched white churchmen stand on the sideline and mouth pious irrelevancies and sanctimonious trivialities. In the midst of a mighty struggle to rid our nation of racial and economic injustice, I have heard many ministers say: "Those are social issues, with which the gospel has no real concern." And I have watched many churches commit themselves to a completely otherworldly religion which makes a strange, un-Biblical distinction between body and soul, between the sacred and the secular. . . .

Perhaps I have once again been too optimistic. Is organized religion too inextricably bound to the status quo to save our nation and the world? Perhaps I must turn my faith to the inner spiritual church, the church within the church, as the true *ekklesia* and the hope of the world. But again I am thankful to God that some noble souls from the ranks of organized religion have broken loose from the paralyzing chains of conformity and joined us as active partners in the struggle for freedom. They have left their secure congregations and walked the streets of Albany, Georgia, with us. They have gone down the highways of the South on tortuous rides for freedom. Yes, they have gone to jail with us. Some have been dismissed from their churches, have lost the support of their bishops and fellow ministers. But they have acted in the faith that right defeated is stronger than evil triumphant. Their witness has been the spiritual salt that has preserved the true meaning of the gospel in these troubled times. They have carved a tunnel of hope through the dark mountain of disappointment.

I hope the church as a whole will meet the challenge of this decisive hour. But even if the church does not come to the aid of justice, I have no despair about the future. I have no fear about the outcome of our struggle in Birmingham, even if our motives are at present misunderstood. We will reach the goal of freedom in Birmingham and all over the nation, because the goal of America is freedom. Abused and scorned though we may be, our destiny is tied up with America's destiny. Before the pilgrims landed at Plymouth, we were here. Before the pen of Jefferson etched the majestic words of the Declaration of Independence across the pages of history, we were here. For more than two centuries our forebears labored in this country without wages; they made cotton king; they built the homes of their masters while suffering gross injustice and shameful humiliation— and yet out of a bottomless vitality they continued to thrive and develop. If the inexpressible cruelties of slavery could not stop us, the opposition we now face will surely fail. We will win our freedom because the sacred heritage of our nation and the eternal will of God are embodied in our echoing demands.

Before closing I feel impelled to mention one other point in your statement that has troubled me profoundly. You warmly commended the Birmingham police force for keeping "order" and "preventing violence." I doubt that you would have so warmly commended the police force if you had seen its dogs sinking their teeth into unarmed, nonviolent Negroes. I doubt that you would so quickly commend the policemen if you were to observe their ugly and inhumane treatment of Negroes here in the city jail; if you were to watch them push and curse old Negro women and young Negro girls; if you were to see them slap and kick old Negro men and young boys; if you were to observe them, as they did on two occasions, refuse to give us food because we wanted to sing our grace together. I cannot join you in your praise of the Birmingham police department. . . .

I wish you had commended the Negro sit-inners and demonstrators of Birmingham for their sublime courage, their willingness to suffer and their amazing discipline in the midst of great provocation. One day the South will recognize its real heroes. They will be the James Merediths, with the noble sense of purpose that enables them to face jeering and hostile mobs, and with the agonizing loneliness that characterizes the life of the pioneer. They will be old, oppressed, battered Negro women, symbolized in a seventy-two-year-old woman in Montgomery, Alabama, who rose up with a sense of dignity and with her people decided not to ride segregated buses, and who responded with ungrammatical profundity to one who inquired about her weariness: "My feets is tired, but my soul is at rest." They will be the young high school and college students, the young ministers of the gospel and a host of their elders, courageously and non-

violently sitting in at lunch counters and willingly going to jail for conscience' sake. One day the South will know that when these disinherited
children of God sat down at lunch counters, they were in reality standing
up for what is best in the American dream and for the most sacred values
in our Judaeo-Christian heritage, thereby bringing our nation back to those
great wells of democracy which were dug deep by the founding fathers
in their formulation of the Constitution and the Declaration of Independence. . . .

> Yours for the cause of Peace and Brotherhood,
> Martin Luther King, Jr.

On March 26, 1964, the Reverend Martin Luther King, Jr., and Malcolm X met at the Capitol in Washington, D.C., to plan a protest if southern senators filibustered against the Civil Rights bill. *AP/Wide World Photos*

The Autobiography of Malcolm X

MALCOLM X

I must be honest. Negroes—Afro-Americans—showed no inclination to rush to the United Nations and demand justice for themselves here in America. I really had known in advance that they wouldn't. The American white man has so thoroughly brainwashed the black man to see himself as only a domestic "civil rights" problem that it will probably take longer than I live before the Negro sees that the struggle of the American black man is international.

And I had known, too, that Negroes would not rush to follow me into the orthodox Islam which had given me the insight and perspective to see that the black men and white men truly could be brothers. America's Negroes—especially older Negroes—are too indelibly soaked in Christianity's double standard of oppression.

So, in the "public invited" meetings which I began holding each Sunday afternoon or evening in Harlem's well-known Audubon Ballroom, as I addressed predominantly non-Muslim Negro audiences, I did not immediately attempt to press the Islamic religion, but instead to embrace all who sat before me: "—not Muslim, nor Christian, Catholic, nor Protestant . . . Baptist nor Methodist, Democrat nor Republican, Mason nor Elk! I mean the black people of America—and the black people all over this earth! Because it is as this collective mass of black people that we have been deprived not only of our civil rights, but even of our human rights, the right to human dignity. . . ."

On the streets, after my speeches, in the faces and the voices of the people I met—even those who would pump my hands and want my autograph—I would feel the wait-and-see attitude. I would feel—and I understood—their uncertainty about where I stood. Since the Civil War's "freedom," the black man has gone down so many fruitless paths. His leaders, very largely, had failed him. The religion of Christianity had failed him. The black man was scarred, he was cautious, he was apprehensive. . . .

In Mecca, too, I had played back for myself the twelve years I had spent with Elijah Muhammad as if it were a motion picture. I guess it would be impossible for anyone ever to realize fully how complete was my belief in Elijah Muhammad. I believed in him not only as a leader in the ordinary *human* sense, but also I believed in him as a *divine* leader. I believed he had no human weaknesses or faults, and that, therefore, he

Malcolm X, *The Autobiography of Malcolm X* with Alex Haley (New York: Grove Press, 1964), pp. 364–379. Copyright © by Alex Haley and Malcolm X. Copyright © 1965 by Alex Haley and Betty Shabazz. Reprinted by permission of Random House, Inc.

could make no mistakes and that he could do no wrong. There on a Holy World hilltop, I realized how very dangerous it is for people to hold any human being in such esteem, especially to consider anyone some sort of "divinely guided" and "protected" person. . . .

Largely, the American white man's press refused to convey that I was now attempting to teach Negroes a new direction. With the 1964 "long, hot summer" steadily producing new incidents, I was constantly accused of "stirring up Negroes." Every time I had another radio or television microphone at my mouth, when I was asked about "stirring up Negroes" or "inciting violence," I'd get hot. . . .

They called me "the angriest Negro in America." I wouldn't deny that charge. I spoke exactly as I felt. "I *believe* in anger. The Bible says there is a *time* for anger." They called me "a teacher, a fomentor of violence." I would say point blank, "That is a lie. I'm not for wanton violence, I'm for justice. I feel that if white people were attacked by Negroes—if the forces of law prove unable, or inadequate, or reluctant to protect those whites from those Negroes—then those white people should protect and defend themselves from those Negroes, using arms if necessary. And I feel that when the law fails to protect Negroes from whites' attack, then those Negroes should use arms, if necessary, to defend themselves."

"Malcolm X Advocates Armed Negroes!"

What was wrong with that? I'll tell you what was wrong. I was a black man talking about physical defense against the white man. The white man can lynch and burn and bomb and beat Negroes—that's all right: "Have patience" . . . "The customs are entrenched" . . . "Things are getting better."

Well, I believe it's a crime for anyone who is being brutalized to continue to accept that brutality without doing something to defend himself. If that's how "Christian" philosophy is interpreted, if that's what Gandhian philosophy teaches, well, then, I will call them criminal philosophies.

I tried in every speech I made to clarify my new position regarding white people—"I don't speak against the sincere, well-meaning, good white people. I have learned that there *are* some. I have learned that not all white people are racists. I am speaking against and my fight is against the white *racists*. I firmly believe that Negroes have the right to fight against these racists, by any means that are necessary."

But the white reporters kept wanting me linked with that word "violence." I doubt if I had one interview without having to deal with that accusation.

"I *am* for violence if non-violence means we continue postponing a solution to the American black man's problem—just to *avoid* violence. I don't go for non-violence if it also means a delayed solution. To me a delayed solution is a non-solution. Or I'll say it another way. If it must take violence to get the black man his human rights in this country, I'm *for* violence exactly as you know the Irish, the Poles, or Jews would be if they were flagrantly discriminated against. I am just as they would be in that case, and they would be for violence—no matter what the consequences, no matter who was hurt by the violence."

White society *hates* to hear anybody, especially a black man, talk about the crime the white man has perpetrated on the black man. I have always understood that's why I have been so frequently called "a revolutionist." It sounds as if I have done some crime! Well, it may be the American black man does need to become involved in a *real* revolution. . . . So how does anybody sound talking about the Negro in America waging some "revolution"? Yes, he is condemning a system—but he's not trying to overturn the system, or to destroy it. The Negro's so-called "revolt" is merely an asking to be *accepted* into the existing system! A *true* Negro revolt might entail, for instance, fighting for separate black states within this country—which several groups and individuals have advocated, long before Elijah Muhammad came along.

When the white man came into this country, he certainly wasn't demonstrating any "non-violence." In fact, the very man whose name symbolizes non-violence here today has stated:

"Our nation was born in genocide when it embraced the doctrine that the original American, the Indian, was an inferior race. Even before there were large numbers of Negroes on our shores, the scar of racial hatred had already disfigured colonial society. From the sixteenth century forward, blood flowed in battles over racial supremacy. We are perhaps the only nation which tried as a matter of national policy to wipe out its indigenous population. Moreover, we elevated that tragic experience into a noble crusade. Indeed, even today we have not permitted ourselves to reject or to feel remorse for this shameful episode. Our literature, our films, our drama, our folklore all exalt it. Our children are still taught to respect the violence which reduced a red-skinned people of an earlier culture into a few fragmented groups herded into impoverished reservations." . . .

I am in agreement one hundred per cent with those racists who say that no government laws ever can *force* brotherhood. The only true world solution today is governments guided by true religion—of the spirit. Here in race-torn America, I am convinced that the Islam religion is desperately needed, particularly by the American black man. The black man needs to reflect that he has been America's most fervent Christian—and where has it gotten him? In fact, in the white man's hands, in the white man's interpretation . . . where has Christianity brought this *world*? . . .

Well, if *this* is so—if the so-called "Christianity" now being practiced in America displays the best that world Christianity has left to offer—no one in his right mind should need any much greater proof that very close at hand is the *end* of Christianity. . . .

Is white America really sorry for her crimes against the black people?

Does white America have the capacity to repent—and to atone? Does the capacity to repent, to atone, exist in a majority, in one-half, in even one-third of American white society?

Many black men, the victims—in fact most black men—would like to be able to forgive, to forget, the crimes.

But most American white people seem not to have it in them to make any serious atonement—to do justice to the black man.

Indeed, how *can* white society atone for enslaving, for raping, for unmanning, for otherwise brutalizing *millions* of human beings, for centuries? What atonement would the God of Justice demand for the robbery of the black people's labor, their lives, their true identities, their culture, their history—and even their human dignity?

A desegregated cup of coffee, a theater, public toilets—the whole range of hypocritical "integration"—these are not atonement. . . .

I kept having all kinds of troubles trying to develop the kind of Black Nationalist organization I wanted to build for the American Negro. Why Black Nationalism? Well, in the competitive American society, how can there ever be any white-black solidarity before there is first some black solidarity? If you will remember, in my childhood I had been exposed to the Black Nationalist teachings of Marcus Garvey—which, in fact, I had been told had led to my father's murder. Even when I was a follower of Elijah Muhammad, I had been strongly aware of how the Black Nationalist political, economic and social philosophies had the ability to instill within black men the racial dignity, the incentive, and the confidence that the black race needs today to get up off its knees, and to get on its feet, and get rid of its scars, and to take a stand for itself.

One of the major troubles that I was having in building the organization that I wanted—an all-black organization whose ultimate objective was to help create a society in which there could exist honest white-black brotherhood—was that my earlier public image, my old so-called "Black Muslim" image, kept blocking me. I was trying to gradually reshape that image. I was trying to turn a corner, into a new regard by the public, especially Negroes; I was no less angry than I had been, but at the same time the true brotherhood I had seen in the Holy World had influenced me to recognize that anger can blind human vision.

Every free moment I could find, I did a lot of talking to key people whom I knew around Harlem, and I made a lot of speeches, saying: "True Islam taught me that it takes *all* of the religious, political, economic, psychological, and racial ingredients, or characteristics, to make the Human Family and the Human Society complete.

"Since I learned the *truth* in Mecca, my dearest friends have come to include *all* kinds—some Christians, Jews, Buddhists, Hindus, agnostics, and even atheists! I have friends who are called capitalists, Socialists, and Communists! Some of my friends are moderates, conservatives, extremists—some are even Uncle Toms! My friends today are black, brown, red, yellow, and *white!*"

I said to Harlem street audiences that only when mankind would submit to the One God who created all—only then would mankind even approach the "peace" of which so much *talk* could be heard . . . but toward which so little *action* was seen.

I said that on the American racial level, we had to approach the black man's struggle against the white man's racism as a human problem, that we had to forget hypocritical politics and propaganda. I said that both races, as human beings, had the obligation, the responsibility, of helping to correct America's human problem. The well-meaning white people, I said, had to combat, actively and directly, the racism in other white people. And the black people had to build within themselves much greater awareness that along with equal rights there had to be the bearing of equal responsibilities. . . .

. . . I mean nothing against any sincere whites when I say that as members of black organizations, generally whites' very presence subtly renders the black organization automatically less effective. Even the best white members will slow down the Negroes' discovery of what they need to do, and particularly of what they can do—for themselves, working by themselves, among their own kind, in their own communities.

I sure don't want to hurt anybody's feelings, but in fact I'll even go so far as to say that I never really trust the kind of white people who are always so anxious to hang around Negroes, or to hang around in Negro communities. I don't trust the kind of whites who love having Negroes always hanging around them. I don't know—this feeling may be a throwback to the years when I was hustling in Harlem and all of those red-faced, drunk whites in the afterhours clubs were always grabbing hold of some Negroes and talking about "I just want you to know you're just as good as I am—" And then they got back in their taxicabs and black limousines and went back downtown to the places where they lived and worked, where no blacks except servants had better get caught. But, anyway, I know that every time that whites join a black organization, you watch, pretty soon the blacks will be leaning on the whites to support it, and before you know it a black may be up front with a title, but the whites, because of their money, are the real controllers.

I tell sincere white people, "Work in conjunction with us—each of us working among our own kind." Let sincere white individuals find all other white people they can who feel as they do—and let them form their own all-white groups, to work trying to convert other white people who are thinking and acting so racist. Let sincere whites go and teach non-violence to white people!

We will completely respect our white co-workers. They will deserve every credit. We will give them every credit. We will meanwhile be working among our own kind, in our own black communities—showing and teaching black men in ways that only other black men can—that the black man has got to help himself. Working separately, the sincere white people and sincere black people actually will be working together.

In our mutual sincerity we might be able to show a road to the salvation of America's very soul. It can only be salvaged if human rights and dignity, in full, are extended to black men. Only such real, meaningful actions as those which are sincerely motivated from a deep sense of humanism and moral responsibility can get at the basic causes that pro-duce the racial explosions in America today. Otherwise, the racial ex-plosions are only going to grow worse. Certainly nothing is ever going to be solved by throwing upon me and other so-called black "extremists" and "demagogues" the blame for the racism that is in America.

Sometimes, I have dared to dream to myself that one day, history may even say that my voice—which disturbed the white man's smugness, and his arrogance, and his complacency—that my voice helped to save America from a grave, possibly even a fatal catastrophe.

The goal has always been the same, with the approaches to it as different as mine and Dr. Martin Luther King's non-violent marching, that dramatizes the brutality and the evil of the white man against defenseless blacks. And in the racial climate of this country today, it is anybody's guess which of the "extremes" in approach to the black man's problems might *personally* meet a fatal catastrophe first—"non-violent" Dr. King, or so-called "violent" me. . . .

To speculate about dying doesn't distrub me as it might some people. I never have felt that I would live to become an old man. Even before I was a Muslim—when I was a hustler in the ghetto jungle, and then a criminal in prison, it always stayed on my mind that I would die a violent death. In fact, it runs in my family. My father and most of his brothers died by violence—my father because of what he believed in. To come right down to it, if I take the kind of things in which I believe, then add to that the kind of temperament that I have, plus the one hundred per cent dedication I have to whatever I believe in—these are ingredients which make it just about impossible for me to die of old age. . . .

In this year, 1965, I am certain that more—and worse—riots are going to erupt, in yet more cities, in spite of the conscience-salving Civil Rights Bill. The reason is that the *cause* of these riots, the racist malignancy in America, has been too long unattended.

I believe that it would be almost impossible to find anywhere in America a black man who has lived further down in the mud of human society than I have; or a black man who has been any more ignorant than I have been; or a black man who has suffered more anguish during his life than I have. But it is only after the deepest darkness that the greatest joy can come; it is only after slavery and prison that the sweetest appreciation of freedom can come.

For the freedom of my 22 million black brothers and sisters here in America, I do believe that I have fought the best that I knew how, and the best that I could, with the shortcomings that I have had. I know that my shortcomings are many. . . .

SUGGESTIONS FOR FURTHER READING

Harold Cruse, *The Crisis of the Negro Intellectual* (New York: Morrow, 1967), especially pp. 402–19; Taylor Branch, *Parting the Waters: America in the King Years, 1954–63* (New York: Simon and Schuster, 1988); Peter J. Paris, *Black Religious Leaders: Conflict in Unity* (Louisville, Ky.: Westminster/John Knox Press, 1991).

XVIII

⟪✧⟫

THE ROLE OF
JOURNALISTS
IN VIETNAM

What is the proper role of a free press in a democratic society? That is not a simple question under ordinary circumstances, and it becomes even more difficult during an unpopular war whose morality and political wisdom are contested. How should the press balance the imperatives of national obligation against the public's right to know and possibly dissent? How often does it happen that in the interest of their personal careers journalists sensationalize war coverage in ways that do not best serve the interests of the government or the public? That happened in the case of Richard Harding Davis during the Spanish-American War and John Reed when the United States intervened in Mexico during Woodrow Wilson's first administration. There appears to be a consensus, however, that Edward R. Murrow did an excellent job for both CBS and the United States when he covered the Anglo-German crisis in London during 1940. Here was the right person in the right place at the right time.

Government officials seem to feel the least ambivalence; national security and the safety of troops are their top priorities. Reporters ought to be mature and experienced; if they cannot be objective about the events they are covering, they should be replaced. Moral scruples and ideological commitments are an impediment to dispassionate journalism.

The press corps acknowledges that war correspondents work under special psychological circumstances. They are committed to freedom of information and to the pursuit of truth. They speculate whether there may be events so complex that conventional journalism simply cannot present or explain them. They acknowledge that an apparently unjust or unwise war places unusual strains on conscience as well as objectivity.

Although the debate over the role of journalists in Vietnam began long before the United States withdrew in 1973 and continued to rage for more than a decade afterward, many observers believe that the situation in Vietnam was not unique. It is certainly true that a lot of the same issues arose in 1991 when the press felt deeply constrained in trying to cover the Gulf War in Iraq and Kuwait.

Phillip Knightley is a British journalist who served as a feature writer for the Sunday Times *of London starting in 1963. He is coauthor of* The Philby

Conspiracy *(1968) and author of* The First Casualty *(1975), which won the* Overseas Press Club Award.

Major General Winant Sidle *(U.S. Army, retired) served as chief of information for General William Westmoreland in Saigon (1967–69), then as the U.S. Army's chief of information (1969–73), and as deputy assistant secretary of defense—public affairs (1974–75).*

David Halberstam *was in Vietnam as a reporter for the* New York Times *(1962–63) and received the Pulitzer Prize for international reporting in 1964. He is the author of* The Making of a Quagmire *(1965),* The Best and the Brightest *(1972),* The Powers That Be *(1979), and* The Breaks of the Game *(1982).*

A Feature Writer's Perspective

PHILLIP KNIGHTLEY

As more and more Americans arrived in Vietnam and the United States involvement became more open, the reporting changed. Increasing numbers of reporters thought that the war was unjust, and they sought out stories to support this view. I see nothing ethically wrong with this sort of subjective journalism, providing the correspondent does not resort to lies and invention to make his case and does not attempt to disguise his stance. And, to balance those correspondents who wrote what the war was doing to innocent civilians, there were others who wrote stirring stories about American heroism and the praiseworthiness of American war aims.[1]

The significant point about the flush of stories in this period, attacking U.S. involvement, is not that they were written—that was inevitable—but that the United States provided the access and the freedom that enabled them to be written. Other democracies would have been much less tolerant. Look how Britain managed the news during the Falklands campaign.[2] Or, perhaps more to the point, consider an encounter that correspondent Murray Sayle had with an Israeli press officer when, in 1967, he switched from reporting Vietnam to the Six-Day War. "Just a word of warning," the Israeli press officer said. "You're not in Vietnam now. You can't do or write anything you like here. Here you do what we say. Okay?"[3]

True, a lot of Vietnam stories and photographs ran into problems in the United States because they were considered "too tough for American readers" (Martha Gellhorn's series of articles on hospitals and orphanages), or "too harrowing for the American market" (Philip Jones-Griffith's pictures). But you cannot suppress a good story indefinitely, and all the good Vietnam stories *were* published somewhere, sooner or later.

Nevertheless, half of all Americans, according to Gallup, had no idea what the war in Vietnam was all about. The reporting of Tet, with its emphasis on the ability of the enemy—fourteen years after the first American commitment to South Vietnam—to penetrate the grounds of the United States Embassy, suggested that whatever it was about it was a war the United States appeared to be losing. Yet, most correspondents got Tet

Phillip Knightley, "A Feature Writer's Perspective," in Harrison Salisbury, ed. *Vietnam Reconsidered: Lessons from a War* (New York: HarperCollins, 1984), pp. 106–09. Copyright © 1984 by Harrison E. Salisbury. Reprinted by permission of HarperCollins Publishers.
[1]See, for example, Jim Lucas, *Dateline Vietnam* (New York, Award Books, 1967); and Frank Harvey, *Air War Vietnam* (New York, Bantam, 1967).
[2]See Phillip Knightley, "The Falklands: How Britannia Ruled the News," *Columbia Journalism Review* (September–October, 1982).
[3]Robert Elegant, "How to Lose a War: Reflections of a Foreign Correspondent," *Encounter* (August, 1981), p. 83.

wrong. As a whole it was such a military disaster for the Vietcong that they never really recovered. How could this misreporting have happened?

A war correspondent is in a different psychological position from any other reporter because he cannot avoid sharing some of the risk taken by the people he is writing about. A reporter covering the proceedings in a police court runs no danger of the judge suddenly saying, "The press is also convicted and is hereby sentenced to eighteen months in the state penitentiary." The war correspondent's involvement makes it difficult for a genuinely concerned correspondent to take a lofty *j'accuse* position. He knows that both sides die in wars; both are brave and cowardly; both are kind, both cruel, both equally capable of atrocities. (The overall proportions no doubt vary, but how do you discover what the proportions are while the war is still on?)

So the honest correspondent sticks to what he himself has seen, and is careful not to edit his material to make one side do all the nasty things and the other do all the good. But in a war with no easily identifiable enemy, no simply explained cause, no clearly designated villain, no front line—in a war with complicated political issues and in which the correspondent had regularly to try to make sense out of a whirl of experience and ghastly sights—this did not work. No one correspondent could hope to get a broad, general experience of it; all that most correspondents succeeded in doing was obtaining a limited, spotty experience.

It was a complex war, equally difficult to understand and convey in all its ramifications. One indication of this was the proliferation of symbols or images of the war offered by correspondents as substitutes for explanation, and grasped by the readers and viewers as substitutes for understanding. The Marines raising the flag on Iwo Jima remains the lasting image of World War II. In Vietnam, we have the soldier with the Zippo lighter, General Loan shooting the man in the checked shirt, the Vietcong with black tape across his eyes, the Vietnamese woman swimming a river with a child on her back, the Vietnamese child with napalm burns running down a road, the children dying at My Lai, and the famous quotation, "We had to destroy this village in order to save it." The lesson must be: Beware of too many symbols; they represent the easy way out.

Now, if it was impossible to convey all the ramifications of Vietnam to the public, then what we are facing is not a failure on the part of the correspondents but a flaw in the very nature of journalism. We have had the arrogance to believe that there was nothing in the tide of human affairs that journalism could not select, encompass, analyze, and explain; no event, no matter its magnitude or complexity, that could not successfully be subjected to the journalistic process. We now have to consider the possibility that we were wrong; that there are happenings of such dimensions—and I submit that Vietnam was one—that journalism alone is unable to present or explain adequately.

That is the bad news. The good news is that in any assessment of the

quality of story that the correspondents *were* able to tell, the basic constitutional guarantees of the United States worked. There were hiccups.
Some stories did not get the emphasis they deserved; others were over-
played; there was pressure and government lying. But to pretend that this
was unique to Vietnam is to ignore reality. In the end, the story as the
correspondents saw it came out, warts and all. Do not forget that the first
step that led to the uncovering of My Lai was, as in so many stories, that
most elementary act in the democractic process: an ordinary citizen writing
to his congressman.

As to the effects of these stories, I find myself undecided. You can
accept one of two versions. The first is that the reporting toppled a president, destroyed a major American policy, lost the war, tilted the global
balance of power, and is directly responsible for the sad state of Southeast
Asia today. If that is true, then so be it. Either one believes in a free press or
one does not. If you tinker with the concept, if you try to achieve a
three-quarter-free press, or a half-free press, you risk destroying it. Because governments will always find reasons why, on just this one occasion, the press should surrender some of its freedom in the national
interest.

The other version is that the first view is an exaggeration, and that the
reporting from Vietnam, mainly because of the flaw in journalism discussed above, did not have the influence attributed to it; that journalists
failed to convey the war's significance to the public. But—and this cannot
be emphasized too strongly—this was not because the correspondents did
not try, or because of any conspiracy of distortion. It was because Vietnam
was such a complex tragedy that the reporters, like everyone else, were
overwhelmed by it.

An Army General's Perspective

MAJOR GENERAL WINANT SIDLE

In a study of Vietnam news reporting done by the American Society of
Newspaper Editors (ASNE), the quality of the press corps in Vietnam—
and hence the reporting—was characterized as not sufficiently professional
as a whole. The reasons cited included: too many inexpert free-lancers and

Winant Sidle, "An Army General's Perspective," in Harrison Salisbury, ed. *Vietnam Reconsidered: Lessons from a War* (New York: HarperCollins, 1984), pp. 110–112. Copyright © 1984 by
Harrison E. Salisbury. Reprinted by permission of HarperCollins Publishers.

stringers; too many short tours; too many reporters trying to make a name for themselves.

These are valid conclusions, and I would add the following based on my experience there: there were too many reporters. We had 649 accredited in-country at the end of March 1968. That's far too many, especially when most of them stayed in Saigon. Only approximately seventy-five to eighty regularly went into the field.

There were too many inexperienced reporters. This ties in with ASNE's "too short tour" criticism. I was surprised that so many of the media sent over young reporters with no appropriate background. One newcomer, representing a major U.S. newspaper, asked me at the end of his initial briefing, "What's a battalion?" He proved to be so ignorant about military and political matters that he was fired at the end of a year. But during that year, think of what his many thousands of readers "learned" about Vietnam! Some of the young reporters who stayed a year or longer eventually became quite good, but the American people suffered while these gentlemen did their on-the-job training.

There were too many reporters unwilling to check stories before filing. Some were lazy; some believed we wouldn't give them facts; some felt it was unnecessary to check. We all know that not checking out stories invariably leads to mistakes and low-quality reporting.

There was too much stateside editing of stories sent in from the field. There were many examples of fair stories edited by ignorant, biased editors into slanted inaccuracy. I remember one story in a major news magazine which reported three rather poorly conducted ARVN operations. It was converted into a vitriolic, inaccurate downgrading of the entire South Vietnam military. When I asked the reporter about it and he showed me the copy of what he had sent in, I found little relationship between what he had written and what was printed. His comment was, "There is a bunch of kids back there who don't know the score." When I came back to the States in late 1969, I arranged a meeting with the group of four news magazine editors who normally handled Vietnam copy. The oldest was twenty-eight; the others were under twenty-five. None had any military background, none had spent more than a few days in Vietnam. All, however, were firmly convinced they knew everything about everything going on in Vietnam. This does *not* lead to quality coverage.

My last point is, perhaps, the most important. The quality of reporting from Vietnam suffered from advocacy journalism. Too many reporters, especially the younger ones, arrived firmly convinced that the war was unjust, immoral, or whatever, and that the U.S. should not be there. This trend became more noticeable after Tet. These advocacy journalists seemed to think that Americans are incapable of reaching sound, reasoned opinions based on plain old factual, complete, and objective reporting. So the reporter tried to convince his audience via his *news* coverage that his opinions should be their opinions.

I must add that, while I thought the overall reporting in Vietnam left much to be desired from a quality standpoint, there was a lot of good reporting done by the true professionals. They tried to tell the story as it was really happening. Unfortunately, they were considerably out-numbered by the non-pros.

Perhaps Dan Henkin, assistant secretary of defense for public affairs during part of my tour in Vietnam, had the answer. He liked to point out that the Baseball Writers Association had more stringent rules for the assignment of reporters than did the U.S. media. To be the official scorer of a baseball game, a writer had to have five years' experience in covering baseball. To be eligible to vote for membership in the Baseball Hall of Fame required ten years' experience. Had our media used similar rules for the assignment of reporters to Vietnam, I believe reporting of the war would have been much more objective. And this might well have changed the entire outcome.

A Reporter's Perspective

DAVID HALBERSTAM

Hearing General Sidle last night left me with a melancholy feeling that the debate over Vietnam reporting, even ten years later, had not progressed. His critique was woefully incomplete. He said there had been too many short-term reporters there, but the Department of Defense was constantly flying in reporters from hometown papers because they were more malle-able than the resident correspondents like Peter Arnett; he said that *Newsweek* and *Time* wrote softer in Saigon and had it made tough in New York, a canard of the first order; and above all he challenged reporters for failing to verify stories when the most constant use of misinformation and lack of verification went on day after day in the "five o'clock follies" [press brief-ings sponsored by Military Assistance Command, Vietnam (MACV)]. There, reports from Vietnamese officers, never substantiated or witnessed by American officers, would be passed on, and would thereupon come out as "American sources said." Each day, then, there would be a positive story coming out of the briefing. Even though some reporter might have sat there and torn the flesh off an American briefing officer, he or the

David Halberstam, "A Reporter's Perspective," in Harrison Salisbury, ed. *Vietnam Reconsi-dered: Lessons from a War* (New York: HarperCollins, 1984), pp. 113–16. Copyright © 1984 by Harrison E. Salisbury. Reprinted by permission of HarperCollins Publishers.

others could still go back and write the story they were programmed to write about how we had once again defeated the Vietcong and the NVA, thus negating or effectively neutralizing the story that Peter Arnett or Horst Faas would be doing that day.

We need a far larger context to see what journalists did in Vietnam and why it caused so much contention and pain. The war was an extension, finally, of a policy conceived in lies and fear—the fear not that Vietnam would be lost to Communism but the fear that if that happened the Democrats would lose Washington to the Republicans—a misconception of the other side, and an unwillingness to understand what the French Indochina war had done to nationalism. Reporters faced a situation in which our highest political officers, for example our secretary of state, still believed that there was no split between the Chinese and the Russians, a president systematically upping the ante without admitting that he was—saying it was a small war while going on to a big war—and the highest levels of military officers and the secretary of defense lying. No wonder, then, that we who were the reporters in Vietnam came under such criticism and found ourselves, again and again, challenging the alleged norms being set by Washington. There was no comparable tough-minded reporting coming from our colleagues in Washington. In fact, the government quite skillfully used the meat-grinder journalistic style of *Time* and *Newsweek* to offset the reporting coming out of the field. So there we were, in an odd way, the single group trying to sort out the projected aims from the realities.

Since the people who started that war and made the combat commitment completely and absolutely misassessed the strength, vitality, resilience, and historical dynamism of the other side, since they largely misassessed the comparable strengths of their ally, since they did not understand the dynamic of the French Indochina war and what that had done, there was from day one a flaw in American policy. The basic hope, that American technology could do it through bombing, was quickly shown to be unrealistic. The policy of a small war, won by technology, on the cheap, was proven, in fact, false from day one. The other side came into the country very quickly; the bombing failed to interdict them; and those of us who were the reporters there caught the shit for the failure of reality to match American hopes. And that made us different from war reporters in the past. And there is to this day, in this room, bitter division among us, none of it pleasant, old enmities not yet settled. In terms of our assumptions of our duties, it is not so much an ideological as a generational divide between those who go back to the loyalties engendered by World War II and Korea, and who had a simpler and more traditional view of what a reporter does and what his loyalty is to the flag, right or wrong; and the generation to which I, and Peter Arnett, and Morley Safer belong, who found that duty more conflicted and who found that the ideals of democracy made it harder to automatically salute the flag each night. That made us controversial. Were we going to be loyal first and foremost to the ideals of American democracy, or were we going to be loyal to—in the immortal words of so many American officials—"the team"? It was not fun; it was often very painful. During the fall of 1963, I was twenty-eight years old, and I went to the Mekong Delta with a man named Richard Tregaskis; he had been a classic war correspondent of World War II, a hero of mine, who had written a book, *Guadalcanal Diary*, that I had greatly admired as a boy. We had spent what I thought were an entirely pleasant two days in the Mekong Delta. I had introduced him to treasured sources of mine. On the way back to Saigon, he turned to me and in a very soft voice said to me, "If I were doing what you are doing, I would be ashamed of myself." We traveled the rest of the way in stony silence; my face, I am sure, was ashen. The attacks which were to come from higher officials, even from the president of the United States, never shook me and upset me so much as that harsh condemnation from a man whom I had once thought I so admired.

I am enormously proud of the military reporting we did. I am not nearly so proud of my political reporting. I don't think it was nearly so profound. I think I have always been criticized for the wrong thing: I have always been criticized for being too pessimistic. In truth, I was not pessimistic enough. Our military sources were very good, and a good reporter can always find good sources. Our political sources—the people in the embassy—were not nearly so good. The McCarthy era had wiped out a generation of state department people, just ravaged it. It wiped out not only the old Asia hands, but the next generation coming after them who might have served in Vietnam, who might have phrased some of these things in a historical way, given us younger reporters a sense of their expertise. They were gone; there was a vacuum there; and thus we as reporters and we as a nation were weaker for it.

It was relatively easy, in 1962, to ascertain that the war was not going well and the reasons why. Slowly, and only by late 1963, did we begin to understand that the failings of Diem were not so much causes as symptoms of a leadership that had stayed on the sidelines during the French Indochina war. The painful lesson, one we had to learn ourselves, was that there was a great deal of replay of the postwar China situation—of a feudal society coming apart and being challenged by a more modern, nationalistic one.

SUGGESTIONS FOR FURTHER READING

William M. Hammond, *Public Affairs: The Military and the Media, 1962–1968* (Washington, D.C.: Center for Military History, 1988); Kathleen J. Turner, *Lyndon Johnson's Dual War: Vietnam and the Press* (Chicago: University of Chicago Press, 1985); Edwin Emery and Michael Emery, *The Press and America: An Interpretive History of the Mass Media*, 5th ed. (Englewood Cliffs, N.J.: Prentice-Hall, 1984).

XIX

❦

WOMEN AND WORK: DIFFERENCES OF CLASS AND RACE

This final set of readings is fascinating but may require just a bit of explanation. It would appear, at first glance, that in 1971 Professor Mary E. Mebane prepared a response to two essays that Gloria Steinem did not write until 1979. Needless to say, by 1971 the basic views of Steinem, an outspoken defender of women's causes since the 1960s, were widely known, especially among feminists. As the reader will see, the two writers certainly engage one another.

A second question may also arise. Is it unfair, or asymmetrical, to juxtapose two earnest statements by Steinem against a brief one that appears to be written with tongue in cheek by Mebane? There is some risk that readers may enjoy Mebane's wry humor but fail to take her seriously; but that would be a mistake. Historical perspective can be helpful.

At the close of the 1960s, African-American women voiced profound and passionate concerns about their relationship to the feminist movement, black men, and their domestic relations. Two extracts from essays published in 1970 indicate the essential seriousness of Mary Mebane's open letter to Gloria Steinem. The first extract was written by Kay Lindsey.

As the movement toward the liberation of women grows, the Black woman will find herself, if she is at all sensitive to the issues of feminism, in a serious dilemma. For the Black movement is primarily concerned with the liberation of Blacks as a class and does not promote women's liberation as a priority. Indeed, the movement is for the most part spearheaded by males. The feminist movement, on the other hand, is concerned with the oppression of women as a class, but is almost totally composed of white females. Thus the Black woman finds herself on the outside of both political entities, in spite of the fact that she is the object of both forms of oppression.[1]

The second extract was written by Gail Stokes. She pleads with the black man to hear her anguish.

---

[1]Kay Lindsey, "The Black Woman as a Woman," *The Black Woman: An Anthology*, Toni Cade, ed. (New York: New American Library, 1970), p. 85.

What is it? Isn't the food good? I carefully prepared it and let it simmer gently all the time you were gone. Perhaps, I have added just a little too much sugar and the sweetness of it grows sickening or maybe it contains too much of my soul. In my mind, I look back and stare and wonder at my preparations; are they to be in vain? My quivering senses detect your apathy. It frightens me and I become very angry! . . .

Where are you, Black man? Spread forth your arms. Lead me. For it is very dark. I need your comfort. I need reassurance that what I am struggling so violently for is real, and that which is not now yours nor mine will be ours soon, in the not too distant future.[2]

Mary Mebane's open letter was written at a particular moment in time, an historical moment when the campaigns for women's liberation and black liberation intersected with a deepening concern about personal relations within the African-American community.

Mary Elizabeth Mebane (1933–   ) grew up in North Carolina and received her Ph.D. at the University of North Carolina at Chapel Hill in 1973. She taught English and music in public schools (1955–60); taught English at several colleges (1960–74); and became a professor of English and composition at the University of South Carolina (1974–77) and at the University of Wisconsin thereafter. She is the author of numerous essays, a play, and Mary, Wayfarer, *an autobiographical book (1983).*

Gloria Steinem (1934–   ) was educated at Smith College and has been a free-lance writer, editor, and lecturer for more than thirty years. She is a cofounder and editor of Ms. *magazine (1971–   ), and has been active in numerous civil rights, peace, and political campaigns. She has been a leader of the National Women's Political Caucus since 1971 and the Coalition of Labor Union Women since 1974. Her books include* The Beach Book *(1963),* Marilyn: Norma Jean *(1986), and* Revolution from Within: A Book of Self-Esteem *(1992).*

---

[2]Gail Stokes, "Black Man, My Man Listen!" *The Black Woman: An Anthology,* Toni Cade, ed. (New York: New American Library, 1970) pp. 111–12.

The Importance of Work

GLORIA STEINEM

Toward the end of the 1970s, *The Wall Street Journal* devoted an eight-part, front-page series to "the working woman"—that is, the influx of women into the paid-labor force—as the greatest change in American life since the Industrial Revolution.

Many women readers greeted both the news and the definition with cynicism. After all, women have always worked. If all the productive work of human maintenance that women do in the home were valued at its replacement cost, the gross national product of the United States would go up by 26 percent. It's just that we are now more likely than ever before to leave our poorly rewarded, low-security, high-risk job of homemaking (though we're still trying to explain that it's a perfectly good one and that the problem is male society's refusal both to do it and to give it an economic value) for more secure, independent, and better-paid jobs outside the home.

Obviously, the real work revolution won't come until all productive work is rewarded—including child rearing and other jobs done in the home—and men are integrated into so-called women's work as well as vice versa. But the radical change being touted by the *Journal* and other media is one part of that long integration process: the unprecedented flood of women into salaried jobs, that is, into the labor force as it has been male-defined and previously occupied by men. We are already more than 41 percent of it—the highest proportion in history. Given the fact that women also make up a whopping 69 percent of the "discouraged labor force" (that is, people who need jobs but don't get counted in the unemployment statistics because they've given up looking), plus an official female unemployment rate that is substantially higher than men's, it's clear that we could expand to become fully half of the national work force by 1990.

Faced with this determination of women to find a little independence and to be paid and honored for our work, experts have rushed to ask: "Why?" It's a question rarely directed at male workers. Their basic motivations of survival and personal satisfaction are taken for granted. Indeed, men are regarded as "odd" and therefore subjects for sociological study and journalistic reports only when they *don't* have work, even if they are rich and don't need jobs or are poor and can't find them. Nonetheless,

Gloria Steinem, "The Importance of Work," in *Outrageous Acts and Everyday Rebellions* (New York: Holt, Rinehart, & Winston, 1983), pp. 167–72, 282–86. Copyright © 1983 by Gloria Steinem. Copyright © by E. Toledo Productions, Inc. Reprinted by permission of Henry Holt and Company, Inc.

pollsters and sociologists have gone to great expense to prove that women work outside the home because of dire financial need, or if we persist despite the presence of a wage-earning male, out of some desire to buy "little extras" for our families, or even out of good old-fashioned penis envy.

Job interviewers and even our own families may still ask salaried women the big "Why?" If we have small children at home or are in some job regarded as "men's work," the incidence of such questions increases. Condescending or accusatory versions of "What's a nice girl like you doing in a place like this?" have not disappeared from the workplace.

How do we answer these assumptions that we are "working" out of some pressing or peculiar need? Do we feel okay about arguing that it's as natural for us to have salaried jobs as for our husbands—whether or not we have young children at home? Can we enjoy strong career ambitions without worrying about being thought "unfeminine"? When we confront men's growing resentment of women competing in the work force (often in the form of such guilt-producing accusations as "You're taking men's jobs away" or "You're damaging your children"), do we simply state that a decent job is a basic human right for everybody?

I'm afraid the answer is often no. As individuals and as a movement, we tend to retreat into some version of a tactically questionable defense: "Womenworkbecausewehaveto." The phrase has become one word, one key on the typewriter—an economic form of the socially "feminine" stance of passivity and self-sacrifice. Under attack, we still tend to present ourselves as creatures of economic necessity and familial devotion. "Womenworkbecausewehaveto" has become the easiest thing to say.

Like most truisms, this one is easy to prove with statistics. Economic need *is* the most consistent work motive—for women as well as men. In 1976, for instance, 43 percent of all women in the paid-labor force were single, widowed, separated, or divorced, and working to support themselves and their dependents. An additional 21 percent were married to men who had earned less than ten thousand dollars in the previous year, the minimum then required to support a family of four. In fact, if you take men's pensions, stocks, real estate, and various forms of accumulated wealth into account, a good statistical case can be made that there are more women who "have" to work (that is, who have neither the accumulated wealth, nor husbands whose work or wealth can support them for the rest of their lives) than there are men with the same need. If we were going to ask one group "Do you really need this job?", we should ask men.

But the first weakness of the whole "have to work" defense is its deceptiveness. Anyone who has ever experienced dehumanized life on welfare or any other confidence-shaking dependency knows that a paid job may be preferable to the dole, even when the handout is coming from a family member. Yet the will and self-confidence to work on one's own can diminish as dependency and fear increase. That may explain why—

contrary to the "have to" rationale—wives of men who earn less than three thousand dollars a year are actually *less* likely to be employed than wives whose husbands make ten thousand dollars a year or more.

Furthermore, the greatest proportion of employed wives is found among families with a total household income of twenty-five to fifty thousand dollars a year. This is the statistical underpinning used by some sociologists to prove that women's work is mainly important for boosting families into the middle or upper middle class. Thus, women's incomes are largely used for buying "luxuries" and "little extras": a neat double-whammy that renders us secondary within our families, and makes our jobs expendable in hard times. We may even go along with this interpretation (at least, up to the point of getting fired so a male can have our job). It preserves a husbandly ego-need to be seen as the primary breadwinner, and still allows us a safe "feminine" excuse for working.

But there are often rewards that we're not confessing. As noted in *The Two-Career Couple*, by Francine and Douglas Hall: "Women who hold jobs by choice, even blue-collar routine jobs, are more satisfied with their lives than are the full-time housewives."

In addition to personal satisfaction, there is also society's need for all its members' talents. Suppose that jobs were given out on only a "have to work" basis to both women and men—one job per household. It would be unthinkable to lose the unique abilities of, for instance, Eleanor Holmes Norton, the distinguished chair of the Equal Employment Opportunity Commission. But would we then be forced to question the important work of her husband, Edward Norton, who is also a distinguished lawyer? Since men earn more than twice as much as women on the average, the wife in most households would be more likely to give up her job. Does that mean the nation could do as well without millions of its nurses, teachers, and secretaries? Or that the rare man who earns less than his wife should give up his job?

It was this kind of waste of human talents on a society-wide scale that traumatized millions of unemployed or underemployed Americans during the Depression. Then, a one-job-per-household rule seemed somewhat justified, yet the concept was used to displace women workers only, create intolerable dependencies, and waste female talent that the country needed. That Depression experience, plus the energy and example of women who were finally allowed to work during the manpower shortage created by World War II, led Congress to reinterpret the meaning of the country's full-employment goal in its Economic Act of 1946. Full employment was officially defined as "the employment of those who want to work, without regard to whether their employment is, by some definition, necessary. This goal applies equally to men and to women." Since bad economic times are again creating a resentment of employed women—as well as creating more need for women to be employed—we need such a goal more than ever. Women are again being caught in a tragic double bind: We are required to be strong and then punished for our strength.

Clearly, anything less than government and popular commitment to this 1946 definition of full employment will leave the less powerful groups, whoever they may be, in danger. Almost as important as the financial penalty paid by the powerless is the suffering that comes from being shut out of paid and recognized work. Without it, we lose much of our self-respect and our ability to prove that we are alive by making some difference in the world. That's just as true for the suburban woman as it is for the unemployed steel worker.

But it won't be easy to give up the passive defense of "weworkbecausewehaveto."

When a woman who is struggling to support her children and grand-children on welfare sees her neighbor working as a waitress, even though that neighbor's husband has a job, she may feel resentful; and the waitress (of course, not the waitress's husband) may feel guilty. Yet unless we establish the obligation to provide a job for everyone who is willing and able to work, that welfare woman may herself be penalized by policies that give out only one public-service job per household. She and her daughter will have to make a painful and divisive decision about which of them gets that precious job, and the whole household will have to survive on only one salary.

A job as a human right is a principle that applies to men as well as women. But women have more cause to fight for it. The phenomenon of the "working woman" has been held responsible for everything from an increase in male impotence (which turned out, incidently, to be attribut-able to medication for high blood pressure) to the rising cost of steak (which was due to high energy costs and beef import restrictions, not women's refusal to prepare the cheaper, slower-cooking cuts). Unless we see a job as part of every citizen's right to autonomy and personal fulfill-ment, we will continue to be vulnerable to someone else's idea of what "need" is, and whose "need" counts the most.

In many ways, women who do not have to work for simple survival, but who choose to do so nonetheless, are on the frontier of asserting this right for all women. Those with well-to-do husbands are dangerously easy for us to resent and put down. It's easier still to resent women from families of inherited wealth, even though men generally control and bene-fit from that wealth. (There is no Rockefeller Sisters Fund, no J. P. Morgan & Daughters, and sons-in-law may be the ones who really sleep their way to power.) But to prevent a woman whose husband or father is wealthy from earning her own living, and from gaining the self-confidence that comes with that ability, is to keep her needful of that unearned power and less willing to disperse it. Moreover, it is to lose forever her unique talents.

Perhaps modern feminists have been guilty of a kind of reverse snob-bism that keeps us from reaching out to the wives and daughters of wealthy men; yet it was exactly such women who refused the restrictions of class and financed the first wave of feminist revolution.

For most of us, however, "womenworkbecausewehaveto" is just true enough to be seductive as a personal defense.

If we use it without also staking out the larger human right to a job, however, we will never achieve that right. And we will always be subject to the false argument that independence for women is a luxury affordable only in good economic times. Alternatives to layoffs will not be explored, acceptable unemployment will always be used to frighten those with jobs into accepting low wages, and we will never remedy the real cost, both to families and to the country, of dependent women and a massive loss of talent.

Worst of all, we may never learn to find productive, honored work as a natural part of ourselves and as one of life's basic pleasures.

An Introductory Statement

GLORIA STEINEM

As a student learning American history from the textbooks of the 1950s, I read that white and black women had been "given" the vote in 1920, an unexplained fifty years after black men had been "given" the vote as a result of a civil war fought on their behalf. I learned little about the many black people who had risen up in revolt and fought for their own freedom, and nothing about the more than one hundred years of struggle by nation-wide networks of white and black women who organized and lectured around the country for both Negro and women's suffrage at a time when they were not even supposed to speak in public. They lobbied their all-male legislatures, demonstrated in the streets, went on hunger strikes and went to jail, and opposed this country's right to "fight for democracy" in World War I when half of American citizens had no political rights at all. In short, I did not learn that several generations of our foremothers had nearly brought the country to a halt in order to win a legal identity as human beings for women of all races.

At least the right to vote was cited in history books, however, as one

Gloria Steinem, "An Introductory Statement," *Outrageous Acts and Everyday Rebellions* (New York: Holt, Rinehart, & Winston, 1983), pp. 167–72, 282–86. Copyright © 1983 by Gloria Steinem. Copyright © by E. Toledo Productions, Inc. Reprinted by permission of Henry Holt and Company, Inc.

that American women had not always enjoyed. Other parts of that legal identity—the goal of this country's long, first wave of feminism—were not mentioned. How many of us learned what it meant, for instance, for females to be the human property of husbands and fathers, and to die a "civil death" under the marriage laws? It was a condition of chattel so clear that the first seventeenth-century American slaveholders simply adopted it, as Gunnar Myrdal has pointed out, as the "nearest and most natural analogy" for the legal status of slaves.[1] As young students, how many of us understood that the right of an adult American female to own property, to sue in court, or to sign a will; to keep a salary she earned instead of turning it over to a husband or father who "owned" her; to go to school, to have legal custody of her own children, to leave her husband's home without danger of being forcibly and legally returned; to escape a husband's right to physically discipline her; to challenge the social prison of being a lifelong minor if she remained unmarried or a legal nonperson if she did marry— how many of us were instructed that all of these rights had been won through generations of effort by an independent women's movement?

When we studied American progress toward religious freedom, did we read about the many nineteenth-century feminists who challenged the patriarchal structure of the church, who dared question such scriptural rhetoric as the injunction of the Apostle Paul to "Wives, submit yourselves unto your husbands as unto the Lord"? Were we given a book called *The Woman's Bible,* a scholarly and very courageous revision of the scriptures undertaken by Elizabeth Cady Stanton?

If we read about religious and political persecution in America, did we learn that the frenzy of the New England witch trials, tortures, and burnings were usually the persecutions of independent or knowledgeable women, of midwives who performed abortions and taught contraception, of women who challenged the masculine power structure in many ways?

When we heard about courageous people who harbored runaway slaves, did they include women like Susan B. Anthony, who scandalized and alienated abolitionist allies by helping not only black slaves, but runaway wives and children who were escaping the brutality of white husbands and fathers who "owned" them?

Of course, to record the fact that both blacks and women were legal chattel, or that their parallel myths of "natural" inferiority were (and sometimes still are) used to turn both into a source of cheap labor, is not to be confused with equating these two groups. Black women and men often suffered more awful restrictions on their freedom, a more overt cruelty and violence, and their lives were put at greater risk. To teach a white girl child to read might be condemned as dangerous and even sinful, but it was not against the law, as it was for blacks in many slave states of the South. White women were far less likely than black slaves to risk their lives or be

---

[1] Gunnar Myrdal, *An American Dilemma* (New York: Harper and Brothers, 1944), 1073.

separated from their children, and particularly less so than black women who were forced to be breeders of more slaves as well as slaves themselves. Angelina Grimke, one of the courageous white southern feminists who worked against both race and sex slavery, always pointed out that "We have not felt the slaveholder's lash . . . we have not had our hands manacled."[2]

Nonetheless, white women were sometimes tortured or killed in "justified" domestic beatings or sold as indentured workers as a punishment for poverty, or for a liaison with a black man, or for breaking a law of obedience. Hard work combined with the years of coerced childbearing designed to populate this new land may have made white women's life expectancy as low as half that of white men. Early American graveyards full of young women who died in childbirth testify to the desperation with which many women must have sought out midwives for contraception or abortion. The most typical white female punishment was humiliation, the loss of freedom and identity, or to have her health and spirit broken. As Angelina Grimke explained, "I rejoice exceedingly that our resolution should combine us with the Negro. I feel that we have been with him; that the iron has entered into our souls . . . our *hearts* have been crushed."[3]

But why did so many of my history books assume that white women and blacks could have no issues in common, so much so that they failed to report on the real coalitions of the past? Historians seem to pay little attention to movements among the powerless. Perhaps the intimate, majority challenge presented by women of all races and men of color was (and still is) too threatening to the power of a white male minority.

Certainly, the lessons of history were not ignored because they were invisible at the time. Much of the long struggle for black and female personhood had been spent as a functioning, conscious coalition. ("*Resolved.* There never can be a true peace in this Republic until the civil and political rights of all citizens of African descent and all women are practically established."[4] That statement was made by Elizabeth Cady Stanton and passed at a New York convention in 1863.) Like most early feminists, Stanton believed that sex and race prejudice had to be fought together; that both were "produced by the same cause, and manifested very much in the same way. The Negro's skin and the woman's sex are both [used as] *prima facie* evidence that they were intended to be in subjection to the white Saxon man."[5] Frederick Douglass, the fugitive slave who became an important national leader of the movement to abolish slavery and to establish the personhood of all females, vowed in his autobiography that, "When the true history of the antislavery cause shall be written, women will occupy a

---

[2]Angelina Grimke, in Elizabeth Cady Stanton et al., *The History of Woman Suffrage*, Vol. II. (Rochester: Charles Mann, 1899).
[3]Ibid.
[4]Ibid.
[5]Ibid.

large space in its pages, for the cause of the slave has been peculiarly women's cause."[6] When Douglass died, newspapers reported a national mourning for him as a "friend of women" as well as an abolitionist pioneer. And there were many more such conscious statements and obvious lessons.

If more of us had learned the parallels and origins of the abolitionist and suffragist movements, there might have been less surprise when a new movement called "women's liberation" grew from the politicization of white and black women in the civil rights movement of the 1960s. Certainly a familiarity with the words of Frederick Douglass might have prevented some of the white and black men in both the civil rights and peace movements from feeling that their dignity depended on women's second-classness, or from seeing that they themselves were sometimes waging a sexual war against women, in Vietnam villages and at home. If women had been taught that feelings of emotional connection to other powerless groups were logical—that women also lacked power as a caste, and that we might feel understandably supportive when peace or civil rights sit-ins rejected violence as proofs of manhood—certainly I and many other women of my generation would have wasted less time being mystified by our odd and frequent sense of identification with all the "wrong" groups: the black movement, migrant workers, or with male contemporaries who were defying the "masculine" role by refusing to fight in Vietnam.

As it was, however, suffragists were often portrayed as boring, ludicrous bluestockings when they were in history books at all: certainly no heroines you would need in modern America where we were, as male authorities kept telling us resentfully, "the most privileged women in the world." Some of us were further discouraged from exploring our real human strengths by accusations of Freudian penis envy, the dominating-mother syndrome, careerism, a black matriarchy that was (according to some white sociologists) more dangerous to black men than white racism, plus other punishable offenses. Men often emerged from World War II, Freudian analysis, and locker rooms with vague threats that they would replace any uppity women with more subservient ones—an Asian or European war bride instead of a "spoiled" American, a "feminine" white woman to replace a black "matriarch," or just some worshipful young "other woman."

There were many painful years of reinventing the wheel before we relearned the lessons that our foremothers could have taught us: that a false mythology of inferiority based on sex and race was being used to turn both groups into a support system. Limited intellectual ability, childlike natures, special job skills (always the poorly paid ones), greater emotionalism and closeness to nature, an inability to get along with our own group, chronic lateness and irresponsibility, happiness with our "natural" place—

---

[6]*The Life and Times of Frederick Douglass* (New York: Collier, 1962), p. 469.

all these similar arguments were used against women of every race and men of color. . . .

An Open Letter to Gloria Steinem

MARY E. MEBANE (LIZA)

Dear Miss Steinem:

How are you? I am asking your help. You see, I am in something of a dilemma. I have learned that it is your view that we blacks have a great deal in common with women's liberationists and, you see, Miss Steinem, I am both black and a woman, excuse me, female, and I am having trouble identifying, uh, relating to your group.

I mean, Miss Steinem, there are some difficulties there. Now you take food, Miss Steinem; that presents a difficult problem. It seems that women libbers don't want to cook it. But, Miss Steinem, I'm a good cook (I come from a race, oops, ethnic group, of good cooks, a heretical position, I know) and our problem is to find someone to buy the food. You know, feed us. We black women gripe, Miss Steinem, because we have to buy it ourselves. We have a saying, Miss Steinem. We say that if he buys the bacon, we'll cook it. We mean that, too, Miss S. We'll get up at two o'clock in the morning and cook it if he's hungry and we won't ask him where he's been. Of course, we'd appreciate it if he said he had a flat tire or, better still, was by the bedside of a sick friend, but *c'est la vie* Miss Steinem, you can't have everything. About such matters, we are philosophical. As one of our earthy philosophers observed, "He didn't take away anything that he didn't bring back."

We are for equal pay for equal work, Miss Steinem, especially for spinsters, but we think it would be so much nicer if the man made enough money to support us.

I even see a few misguided soul sisters in the Women's Liberation Movement. Come now, ladies. We've been more than equal for nearly four hundred years, ever since we stood in some Southern sun and chopped cotton from morning till night. Now you are complaining because some

Mary E. Mebane, "An Open Letter to Gloria Steinem," *New York Times,* October 29, 1971, p. 41. Reprinted by permission of the author's Estate and the agents for the Estate, Scott Meredith Literary Agency, Inc., 845 Third Avenue, New York, New York 10022-6687.

man believes that your place is in the home where you can stay all day and watch the stories and look after the children, rather than work over somebody's steaming stove and farm the children out to their grandmother or a neighbor and then come home and do your work. And you don't want to do that. You've got to be kidding.

As for the dramatic charge of sexual exploitation, Miss Steinem, if the man has reached puberty plus ten years, such a charge is charitable; if he has been around long enough to acquire position or possessions or a steady job, such a charge is sheer fantasy, Miss Steinem, sheer fantasy.

Would you believe that there are women meeting the clock every day in factories, offices, stores, lunch rooms and school rooms who don't think that the life of a housewife is so bad? Think it over, Miss Steinem.

What We Should Be Doing, Sister

MARGARET SLOAN

CHICAGO, ILL.

Dear Liza,

After reading your open letter to Gloria Steinem (Mary Mebane [Liza], Oct. 29, 1971) I felt I had to reply for a couple of reasons—because I am a black woman and because I am a personal friend of Gloria's.

Not believing that I am one of the "few misguided soul sisters in the women's liberation movement" but someone who feels a dual oppression as a black woman, I thought maybe we could establish some rapport. Your letter indicates you have an interpretation of the women's movement as something other than it is, i.e., "that women-libbers don't want to cook," or that they want to get us all out of the house, and into poorly paid factory jobs.

As a black woman who has been actively involved and still is in the black movement, part of my frustration has been that—after risking my life in sit-ins, pickets, marches; you name it—I was allowed to make coffee, not decisions. And so from there came the realization that I was going to help the brothers realize that as black women we cannot allow black men to do to us what white men have been doing to their women all these years. I

Margaret Sloan, "What We Should Be Doing, Sister," a letter to the *New York Times*, December 8, 1971, p. 37. Copyright © 1971 by The New York Times Company. Reprinted by permission.

decided to point out, as Bobby Seale said in "Seize the Time," that real manhood doesn't depend on the subjugation of anyone; to remind him that the racist Patrick Moynihan lied when he said that the problem with black men is black women.

Because we know that the problem with black men is white racism and no amount of going back to the kitchen is going to give a black man a job. It is an insult to black men to say that black women must be behind them pushing them into their manhood. Sister, I want to make sure that, come the revolution, I will be able to use all my talents and creativity and energies, which has nothing to do with cooking grits for the revolutionaries.

Black women do work. In fact, most women in this country work, and yet a black female with a bachelor's degree earns slightly less than a high-school educated black male. It is incorrect to assume that all black women are living at home with a man and depending on a man's income. The reality is that a large percentage of the black work force is women. We are often heads of households, and supporting children as well. That's why black women are concerned about equal pay for equal work, and decent day care for their children.

As many women die each year from botched, illegal abortions as American men die in Vietnam—and a disproportionate number of these are black and brown women. That is why we want repeal of all abortion laws. It is a fact that black women are having abortions, and if the brothers are concerned about genocide, then they will fight with us to establish community-controlled health clinics. We know that once the black warrior has planted his revolutionary seed in our black (or white) womb, we're the ones who often face the reality of raising, clothing, feeding that child by ourselves, while he is sowing oats in other fields. If we can't get equal pay for equal work, how can we survive? How can the children survive? To assume that black women are not concerned about themselves as women is really a putdown. Because we do get raped, we do get sterilized against our will, we do get left with unwanted pregnancies, we do get worse treatment in jails, the courts, the schools, in fact in every institution in this country, than men. We are on the welfare rolls in infinitely greater numbers than men, for sexist reasons. We do, in fact, suffer from a dual stigma in this racist and sexist society.

Gloria Steinem happens to be one woman involved in the Women's Movement and the broader struggle for the liberation of all people. She fights her oppression where she feels it, not as a white—liberally saving black people, but working for all women. She talks about sexism and racism whenever she speaks. She almost always speaks with Dorothy Pittman Hughes, Flo Kennedy or myself because we are black women who have lived that dual oppression all our lives, and the parallel that is "the deepest truth in American life."

Sister, what we should be doing is coming down on the white male press together instead of writing letters against each other for the delectation of white male editors. You might not agree with the things I have said, but I have only attempted to offer you a different viewpoint, which is not as much in the minority as you might think.

SUGGESTIONS FOR FURTHER READING

Alice Kessler-Harris, *Women Have Always Worked: A Historical Overview* (Old Westbury, N.Y.: Feminist Press, 1981); Toni Cade, ed., *The Black Woman: An Anthology* (New York: New American Library, 1970); Nancie Caraway, *Segregated Sisterhood: Racism and the Politics of American Feminism* (Knoxville, Tenn.: University of Tennessee Press, 1991).

A Note about the Author

Michael Kammen is the Newton C. Farr Professor of American History and Culture at Cornell University. He was the Times-Mirror Foundation Research Professor of American Studies in 1993–1994 at the Huntington Library in San Marino, California, and the first holder of the chair in American History at the École des Hautes Études en Sciences Sociales, Paris, in the years 1980–1981. He has also been a Senior Fellow and a Constitutional Fellow of the National Endowment for the Humanities, a Fellow at the Center for Advanced Study in the Behavioral Sciences at Stanford, a John Simon Guggenheim Fellow, and a Regents Fellow of the Smithsonian Institution. Professor Kammen is President-elect of the Organization of American Historians for the 1995–96 term.

He is the author of many books, among them *A Rope of Sand* (1968), *Empire & Interest* (1970), *People of Paradox* (1972)—awarded the Pulitzer Prize for History in 1973—*Spheres of Liberty* (1986), *Sovereignty and Liberty* (1988), *Mystic Chords of Memory* (1991), *Meadows of Memory* (1992), and, most recently, *A Machine That Would Go of Itself: The Constitution in American Culture* (1994), which received both the Francis Parkman Prize and the Henry Adams Prize.